Encyclopedia of the

CAR

Encyclopedia of the
CAR

CHARTWELL BOOKS, INC.

Edited by Chris Horton
Foreword by Karl Ludvigsen

Pages 2–3 1997 BMW M3 Evolution Convertible

Pages 4–5 Jaguar 'E' type Roadster

Pages12–13 1932 Delage D8 Coupé de Ville

Published in 1998 by
Chartwell Books, Inc.
A Division of Book Sales, Inc.
Raritan Center
114 Northfield Avenue
Edison, NJ 08818
USA

ISBN 0-7858-1015-3

Printed in Italy

Acknowledgements

The publishers would like to thank Neill Bruce, Nick Baldwin, Teddy Herridge and the motor manufacturers and agents for their help in the illustration of this book.

Photographs were supplied by:
Neill Bruce
Neil Bruce/Peter Roberts Collection
Nick Baldwin
Brian Crichton
Andy Willsheer

Alfa Romeo (Great Britian) Limited; Aston Martin Lagonda Limited; Automobili Lamborghini SpA.; BMW (GB) Limited; BMW AG; Bristol Cars; Buick Motor Division, GMC; Cadillac Motor Car Division, GMC; Chevrolet Motor Division, GMC; Chrysler Corporation; Citroên UK Ltd., The Colt Car Company Limited; De Tomaso Modena SpA., Fiat Auto (UK) Limited; Ford Motor Company; Ford Motor Company Limited; General Motors Overseas Distribution Corporation; Honda Motor Co. Ltd.; Honda UK Ltd.; Jaguar Cars Limited; Jensen Car Company Ltd.; Lancia Lancar Ltd.; Land Rover; Lincoln-Mercury Division, Ford; Lotus; Marcos Sales Limited; Mazda Cars (UK) Limited; Mercedez-Benz (United Kingdom Ltd.); Morgan Motor Co. Ltd.; Nissan (UK) Limited; Officine Alfieri Maserati SpA.; Oldsmobile Division, GMC; Peugeot Talbot Motor Co. Ltd.; Pontiac Motor Division, GMC; Porsche Cars Great Britain Limited; Reliant Motors plc; Renault UK Ltd.; Rolls-Royce Motor Cars Ltd.; Rover Cars; Saab Great Britain Ltd.; SEAT Concessionaires (UK) Ltd.; Skoda (Great Britain) Ltd.; Toyota; TVR Engineering Ltd.; V.A.G. (United Kingdom) Limited; Vauxhall Motors Ltd.; Volvo Concessionaires Ltd.

Contents

Above: 1935 8 cylinder Hudson Custom Convertible

Foreword

I think of the car as the 'seven-league boots' of the legend that first gave man the ability to cover huge distances with ease. Even the most basic motor vehicle offers tremendous powers of liberation. This creates a demand and a desire for cars that is, dare I say it, frankly gratifying to those of us who both love cars and eke out a living from their creation and use.

This powerful man/machine symbiosis no doubt accounts for the many cars that are named after their creators. Leafing **Encyclopedia of the Car**, you will find these in by far the majority.

No decree exists stating that cars should be named for the men that brought them into being (and with no exception that I can recall they have indeed been men rather than women). Benz and Daimler, however, started the fashion early. That many others followed suit can be attributed as much to ego as to rationality.

To be sure, many of the creators gave their cars names that in retrospect are wonderful. Consider Chrysler, Cord and Duesenberg, for example, Ferrari too is resonant of ripping exhausts – even though the name is Italian for Smith.

As a joint effort, no car name surpasses the marriage of C.S. Rolls with Henry Royce. I remind myself that Rolls-Royce is hyphenated

by the saying that Claude Johnson, the firm's indefatigable secretary, was the hyphen between Rolls and Royce.

Naming cars after their creators has continued to the present day. Among the more recent, DeLorean and Honda had an advantage, in my opinion, in tonal resonance over Tucker and Bricklin.

The more prolific car creators created problems with their second-generation efforts that for the most part they neatly solved. Ran-

som E. Olds went on to build the REO after leaving the Oldsmobile behind at General Motors. Having given up the brand bearing his surname, Harry C. Stutz was less successful with the HCs.

August Horch tried a second time with Audi, the Latin word for his German surname: 'listen'. Only after leaving the company he founded, General Motors, was William C. Durant able to build a car in his own name. Some of the creators showed striking modesty.

Either Cadillac or Lincoln could have been named after the Leland brothers that brought both marques to life. Although we are quite happy with Cisitalia, would Dusio not have been even more evocative?

Rarest, perhaps, have been the cars that bear first or given names. They range from the sublime (Mercedes) to the ridiculous (Henry J). Not to be forgotten is the Edsel, an inapt tribute to the member of the Ford family with the finest eye for design, or the Doretti, whose name was a variation upon Dorothy – an inspirer rather than a creator. Emil Jellinek was the entrepreneur who named the Daimler-build product after his daughter Mercedes. Herr Jellinek was less successful with his next such effort. The Austrian-built Maja was a fine car but not a survivor.

I am not among those who easily use Mercedes alone to describe the cars built by Daimler-Benz after the fusion of the two companies in 1926. My researches into the racing cars they built convinced me that the talents of the Benz men contributed as much or more to their successes than did those of the Daimler (Mercedes) engineers. I can only refer to the post-1926 marque as Mercedes-Benz.

Cars have also been given geographical place names, although the relevance of some is obscure. William Gunn, for example, is said to have found Lagonda on a map of Ohio, but I have not yet had the chance to confirm that in a gazetteer of that Midwestern American state.

The Hispano-Suiza marque honoured the conjoint Spanish and Swiss origins of those great cars and aero engines. Tatra and Steyr were named for Czech and Austrian regions respectively. Auburn is an Indiana city and Mercer a New Jersey county. And when the *Mayflower* landed at Plymouth Rock, another car marque was created (as well as a model name for Triumph).

As hood ornaments or mascots Plymouths once carried replicas of the *Mayflower* in full sail. Pontiacs flaunted the profile of the American Indian chief for whom the marque's town of manufacture was named. In the early 1950s, Pontiacs were among the most boring cars in America. Encumbered by their 'silver streaks' and Indian heads, they were relentlessly

1965 Shelby Mustang GT 350

dull if worthy cars. This so frustrated the car stylists as G.M. that they argued that the Pontiac should be renamed. Instead, 'Bunkie' Knudsen changed the car – which went on to tremendous success.

Peculiarly European (with some exceptions mentioned earlier) has been the naming of cars with acronyms. Some are pronounced letter by letter, like Britain's AC, TVR, G.N., M.G. and H.R.G. and Germany's BMW, N.S.U. and D.K.W. Others are pronounced as words, like Daf, Fiat, SEAT, Saab and the Alfa that is paired with the surname of Nicola Romeo.

In a world awash with acronyms, especially in Europe, their use for car marques should hold great promise. Future framers of acronyms for cars may be interested in a suggestion: make them work as a mirror image so they will read properly when they are seen in the rear-view mirror of the car ahead. An example: MAXXAM. I am just full of bright ideas for car names. When I worked for Fiat we were seeking a better name for the Ritmo for the American market. I dared to suggest we call it the Fiat Berry. We could then say it was Berry economical, Berry lively and Berry pratical. Blueberry and blackberry were just a few of the colours. As a secretary at Fiat aptly observed, a used car would be known as an Elderberry. I still think it's a berry good idea.

Other names that are in regular use must surely be leading candidates for use as car marques. I refer to names that on 16 weekends each year receive worldwide television exposure of incalculable value. Among them are Williams, Lola, Arrows, March and Brabham – the racing cars which have no road counterparts. Only McLaren, whose Gordon Murray has designed an exotic, high-tech supercar has seized the opportunity, although Renault launched the successful and sought after Clio Williams hot hatchback.

Incredibly, companies that have had access to evocative car marques have not hesitated to give them up. Rover Group, formerly Austin-Rover and now owned by BMW, let Morris and Austin wither on the car marque vine. First they neglected their nurturing. Next they expressed surprise that the names no longer had positive associations, a fact they discovered in their effort to relaunch M.G. as a separate marque. Throughout the 1980s the only sign of the M.G. octagon was on the sporty versions of Metros, Maestros and Montegos. Almost all association with proper sports cars had gone. Thankfully, the large amount of MGBs still running around meant that the public were forced to remember and the marque's relaunch was a success, but only following the launch of its second car, the MCF.

Such cavalier treatment of car marques will not serve in the future. Rather, car manufacturers need to take even more care in defining, positoning and communicating the characters and attributes of their brands. Many have started to do so, by strengthening the corporate image of their cars by reintroducing features for which their marques were famous. Rover Group, for example, reintroduced the traditional Rover grille in the early 1990s.

This need has arisen for several reasons. The 'commonization' of cars under the skin to save production costs will accelerate, under Ford 2000, for example, which aims to reduce the number of Ford car platforms by the year 2000, placing a greater burden on image communication.

Competition is intensifying in markets that are increasingly cluttered with 'manufactured' brands like Geo, Saturn, Acura, Lexus and Infiniti. Starting now, to meet the competition of the next century, the successful car makers will foster and, if needed, create marques that have the power to achieve fully global scope and impact.

A recent survey was made on the awareness and esteem accorded to 300 product brands, in Japan, the U.S.A. and Europe. Among the top 20 best known brands in those three markets, seven were automotive, eight if you count a tyre manufacturer.

The survey sharply contrasted attitudes to car marques in the U.S.A. and those in Europe. In the U.S.A. not one car marque, foreign or domestic, was among the 20 most powerful brands. In Europe, nine of the top twenty brands were automotive, with seven of them ranked in the top ten. One, Mercedes-Benz, was considered to be Europe's most potent brand name.

The strength in their images at home will serve the European auto makers well as they improve their efficiency and consolidate their powers to meet increasing competition from the rest of the world. 'What's in a name?' To William Shakespeare's question there is a ready answer from the motor industry: quite a lot.

1966 Ferrari 275 GTB2 'Longnose'

Abarth

Italy
1941-1971

Born in Yugoslavia of Italian parents, Carlo Abarth moved to Italy at the end of World War II, where he worked as an engineering consultant and later became Porsche's Italian representative.

The link with Porsche soon saw him involved with Cisitalia. When Cisitalia failed, Abarth took over the racing side and started his own company in 1949. He soon started building his own racing cars and later branched out into producing aftermarket tuning equipment, mainly for Fiat.

Abarth's first production car was the 204 Berlinetta, launched in 1950. It used a tuned 1100cc Fiat engine and Porsche-type torsion

Above: Abarth 750s at Le Mans in 1960   *Below: Abarth 750 Zagato 'Double Bubble'*

bar suspension. Despite its small engine it could top 110mph and even took Tazio Nuvolari to his last win.

In 1956 Abarth signed an agreement with Fiat which led to many of his cars being Fiat-based. The first was a tuned version of Fiat's tiny 600 saloon. Over the years he developed it into a highly specialized twin-cam Group 2 competition car. Meanwhile, the tuning parts side of the business was booming and provided Abarth with a stable financial base to build even more of his exotic automotive creations.

A range of beautiful coupés soon followed, many of them becoming very successful competition cars, with incredible power outputs being squeezed from their tiny Fiat-based engines. The company continued to modify Fiat saloons and later also built a Simca-based sports car in 1966.

The end came in 1971. Abarth's enthusiasm for racing cars had led him to neglect other areas of his business, putting him in deep financial trouble. Fiat came to the rescue and took over the tuning side of the business with Carlo Abarth as a technical consultant. The Abarth name did not die however, and went on to adorn many high-performance versions of Fiat models. Today, Abarth extras are limited to sporty steering wheels and wide alloy road wheels but the Abarth Scorpion logo can even be seen on Fiat's tiny Cinquecento.

Top: Abarth-Simca 1300, 1962
Left: 1959 Abarth 850 Allemano
Below: Abarth Spider by Zagato, 1959

AC

Great Britain 1904 to date

The origins of AC date back to 1904 when engineer John Weller and partner John Portwine, who owned a chain of butchers' shops, formed Autocars and Accessories Ltd.

This company, based in West Norwood, London, made cheap three-wheeled trade carriers from 1907 for businesses who could not afford a four-wheeled van. Customers included Selfridges and the Great Western Railway.

A passenger version called the AC Sociable was launched in 1908 and remained in production until 1914.

The company was renamed Auto Carriers in 1907 and moved to new premises at Thames Ditton, Surrey, four years later.

Bottom: AC Sociable, built around 1910

Production was halted by World War I, by which time the company had made a four-wheeled light car with 10hp French-built Fivet engine in limited numbers. S.F. Edge, from Napier, joined the board of AC in 1921 and was left in charge when Weller and Portwine resigned in 1922.

The company changed its name to AC Cars in 1922 and then AC (Acedes) in 1927. This company went into liquidation in 1929 and only the service department continued.

Above: 1923 AC Empire

Above: 1929 Acedes Magna

William and Charles Hurlock bought the factory in 1930 and William Hurlock was so pleased with a car assembled for him by the service manager that production began again.

Production was limited, however, and stopped during World War II.

The first post-war cars left the factory in 1947 and by 1951, with sales of AC's stylish but old-fashioned two-litre saloon falling, the company diversified into

Above: The AC Cobra was launched in 1962 with a 4.7-litre V8 engine and a top speed of 220km/h (138mph). American tuner Carroll Shelby first produced the 427 cubic inch (7-litre) version in 1965. The Cobra is now reproduced as the AC Mk 4.

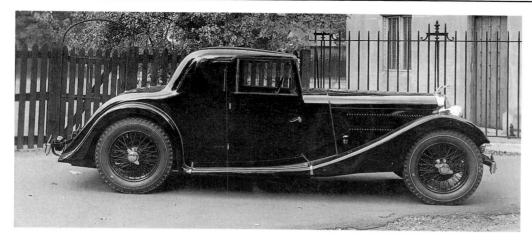

Above: Two-seater AC built around 1934

Below: 1955 Ace (left) and 1956 Aceca

different fields, including three-wheeled invalid carriages.

The first of the sporting roadsters was the Ace – derived from a two-litre Bristol-engined competition car built by John Tojeiro. It was followed by the Aceca coupé in 1954 and the four-seater Greyhound in 1959.

American racing driver Caroll Shelby was interested in the Ace's competition successes and this led to the Ford V8-engined AC Cobra of which 1,070 were made between 1962 and 1969. The fastest of these, the 427-cubic inch (seven-litre) version introduced in 1965, developed 400bhp, which allowed 0-60mph acceleration in 4.2 seconds and a top speed exceeding 265km/h (165mph).

Under the guidance of Derek Hurlock, son of William, AC built the ME3000 (with a Ford three-litre V6 engine) which went into production in January 1979.

Fewer than 100 were made and, following company losses, news came in 1984 that a Scottish businessman had bought the company and formed AC (Scotland) Ltd. This company went out of business in 1985, having made just 30 Ford-engined cars at the Glasgow factory, but the AC name was kept alive by Surrey-based engineer Brian Angliss, whose Autokraft company assembles AC Cobras under licence from Ford.

In late 1986 Angliss revealed a new targa-top two-seater, the AC Ace, which employed a Ford engine and running gear and had been styled by members of Ford's European design group. One year later Ford acquired a controlling interest in AC, retaining Angliss as its managing director, and decided to substantially alter the Ace prior to its delayed launch in 1990.

Above: AC 428 Convertible launched 1966

Right: 1984 AC Mk IV

Adler

Germany
1900–1939

The Adler company was well known as a manufacturer of bicycles and typewriters before it began building cars in Frankfurt am Main in 1900, initially with De Dion engines. From 1902, the company made its own engines and the arrival of Edmund

Right: The 1913 Morgan-Adler Carette seated driver and passenger in tandem

Above: Four-cylinder 12hp Adler
Right: 1910 two-seater with 12hp engine

Rumpler in 1903 led to much-improved designs. By 1905, most models had four-cylinder engines, although there were still singles and vee-twins. Success was such that, by 1914, one car in every five in Germany was an Adler.

A selection of the more popular pre-war models reappeared in 1919. The first six-cylinder Adler arrived in 1925, later being joined by a straight-eight model in 1928. But the mainstay of the 1920s range was the 1½-litre Favorit, a four-cylinder model introduced in 1925.

The company introduced the 1½-litre Trumpf in 1932, with a front-wheel-drive layout designed by Hans Gustav Röhr, and the success of this model encouraged Adler to launch a smaller one-litre version in 1934, the Trumpf Junior. The engine size of the Trumpf was twice increased (to 1.7 then 1.9-litres), and although performance would always be modest, excellent handling helped competition versions to do well. Adlers also took 22 international long-distance records.

Rear-wheel drive was not abandoned, however. The 1½-litre engine was also offered with a conventional drivetrain layout from 1932, and the larger Adlers, including an aerodynamically styled 2½-litre six-cylinder model in 1937, would always have this configuration.

Adler production stopped with the advent of war in 1939 and, although a post-war prototype was shown in 1948, no more cars were made. The company continued to make motor-cycles until 1957.

Left: 1912 Adler 7/15hp had dual ignition and a three-speed gearbox
Right: 1936 Adler Trumpf cabriolet

Alfa Romeo

Italy
1909 to date

The Alfa Romeo story starts in France. Car manufacturer Alexandre Darracq set up a factory at Portello on the outskirts of Milan and supplied parts from Paris for single-and twin-cylinder cars.

It was not the success he had hoped for, however, and in 1909 he sold his ailing Italian outpost to the Italian group Anonina Lombardo Fabbrica Automobil – A.L.F.A for short.

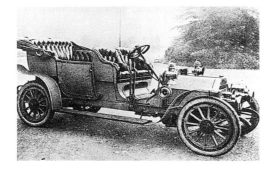

Above: 1910 Alfa Romeo with 24hp engine
Below: 1912 15/20 in racing trim

In 1915 the Romeo connection was made when Nicola Romeo took over the reins. A racing enthusiast and a great engineer, he turned the make into a world-beater.

The factory's early sidevalve and overhead-valve four-cylinder engines gave way to six- and eight-cylinder designs from designers Merosi and Jano. Later followed supercharged double-overhead-camshaft models including the three-litre eight-

Above: This 20/30hp Berlina was built in 1921

Below: The 1921 P1 racer designed by Merosi, with Sivocci at the wheel

cylinder Tipo B, the Bimotore which featured two eight-cylinder engines, and a 4.5-litre V12.

Opera singer Guiseppe Campari gave Alfa its first race victory in 1920. He also won the 1924 French Grand Prix behind the wheel of Alfa's first Grand Prix car to be used in anger, the P2 designed by Vittorio Jano.

Alfa's P3 was the first *monoposto* (single-seat) G.P. racing car. It was introduced in 1932 when regulations

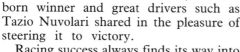

Above: 1924 supercharged P2 racer
Below: Six-cylinder RL, 1923 to 1928

Above: 1928 6C Sport Zagato 1500
Below: Finely proportioned 1932 Monza

Above: The highly successful 1932 P3

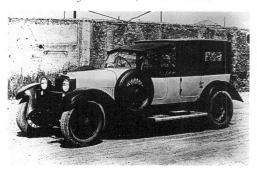

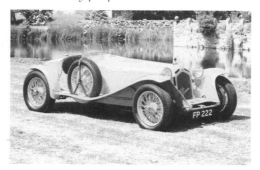

2300cc two-seat Spyder of 1932 was a direct result of racing pedigree.

We have Alfa Romeo to thank for the term GT which many would argue has been overused and abused during recent decades. The term *'gran turismo'* was applied to the supercharged six-cylinder 1750cc long-chassis sports car.

Financial complications led to the company being taken over by the Italian government in 1933. Racing was encouraged by Mussolini and at that time care of the racing team was entrusted to Enzo Ferrari.

requiring two-seater bodies were dropped. A beautiful machine of its time, it was a born winner and great drivers such as Tazio Nuvolari shared in the pleasure of steering it to victory.

Racing success always finds its way into road cars, and the exquisite straight-eight

The 1911 12hp Alfa, inspired by the earlier 24hp car, was introduced with a 2414cc engine and three-speed gearbox. There was also a sports version for racing. By 1915 around 330 cars had been sold.

Above: The 6C 1750 Gran Sport of 1930 was inspired by the P2 racing car. The 1752cc six-cylinder engine featured two gear-driven overhead-camshafts and, with a Roots-type supercharger, it developed 84bhp at 4,500rpm. The body was by coachbuilder Zagato.

Below: 1936 8C 2900A

Right: 1939 6C 2500 Coloniale

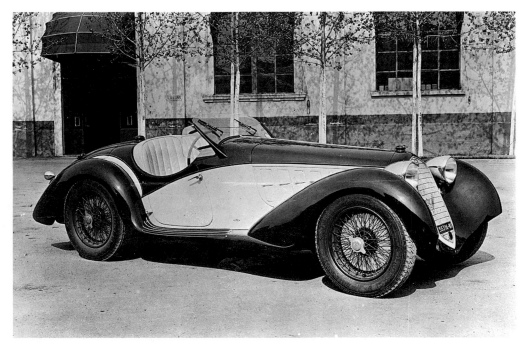

The early 1930s was a glorious time for Alfa. It was building up victories which led to a total of 11 Mille Miglia and four Le Mans wins.

Many regard Alfa's greatest pre-war glory as the 1935 German Grand Prix when Nuvolari, in a 3.8-litre P3, beat the might of the Mercedes and Auto Union teams on their home territory.

Engineering genius Gioacchino Colombo worked with Ferrari in creating the Type 158 'Alfetta' which was soon back in action after World War II had ended. It dominated the 1948 Grand Prix season and, in rejuvenated form, won the first-ever world drivers' championship in 1950 driven by Giuseppe Farina.

The only other race winner that year was Juan-Manuel Fangio who also drove a Type 158 1½-litre straight-eight car with twin Roots superchargers. At the time the car was described as 'obsolete but unbeatable'.

Below: The eight-cylinder 2905cc 8C 2900 was introduced in 1937. Exquisitely styled, it was probably the fastest road car of its day; 30 were built during its two-year lifespan.

Fangio retained the F1 title for Alfa the following year. But by this time a new era had dawned. Fabulous and thrilling though the racing cars and pre-war single- and twin-cam Jano designs were with their Touring and Zagato bodywork, the world was clamoring for cheap personal transportation.

With the factory three parts destroyed during the war, Alfa Romeo had a massive task ahead. To satisfy the road market the company was back in production by 1947 when it introduced the 2.5-litre *Freccia d'Oro* (Golden Arrow) with column gear change.

In 1950 came Alfa Romeo's first four-cylinder car for 25 years, a 1900cc saloon with integral chassis-body construction. Super and Sprint versions were subsequently added followed by the *Disco Volante* (Flying Saucer) in 1952. This radical body shape by Touring of Milan

was built for publicity purposes and never went into production, though a racing version minus the startling bodywork and with a six-cylinder engine finished second in the 1953 Mille Miglia and won the Grand Prix at Merano.

Above: 8C 35 and 12C 36 in 1937
Right: 1952 1900cc doc Berlina
Below: 1952 Disco Volante or Flying Saucer

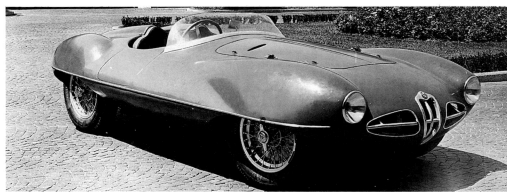

Then in 1954 Alfa Romeo introduced a car with immediate appeal for the buying public – the Giulietta. With a twin-cam four-cylinder engine of 1300cc it was a winning combination of performance and economy. It was produced in two-door coupé and four-door berlina versions followed by Pininfarina, Zagato and Bertone variants with even higher performance.

The project was overseen by former Porsche engineer Rudolf Hruschka, one of the co-ordinators on the Volkswagen Beetle. The Giulietta saloon had fallen behind schedule and when the new cars were not available to be presented as prizes for a shareholders' draw, something had to be done.

With managing director Ing. Quarino, Hruschka commissioned Bertone to prepare bodies in time for the 1954 Turin

show. The fastback styling of Bertone's two-door coupé proved to be a real winner. Hruschka's insistence that the car be sporting throughout had been the right recipe. The lucky shareholders found their wait worthwhile after all.

Italy experienced a tremendous growth rate in car production from 1950 to 1955 and the Giulietta was part of that success.

Top left: 1953-5 1900 saloon
Centre left: 1954 six-cylinder cabriolet
Left: 1954 four-cylinder Giulietta Sprint by Bertone

Above: 1300cc Giulietta Spider built around 1960

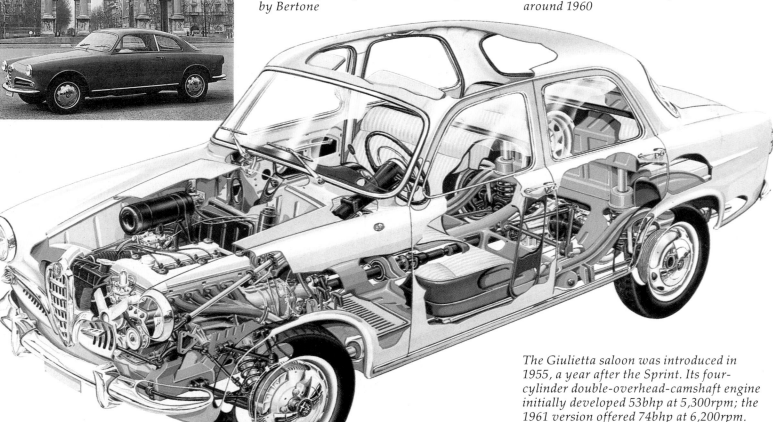

The Giulietta saloon was introduced in 1955, a year after the Sprint. Its four-cylinder double-overhead-camshaft engine initially developed 53bhp at 5,300rpm; the 1961 version offered 74bhp at 6,200rpm. Over 178,000 Giuliettas were built between 1954 and 1965.

This car and its variants became Alfa Romeo's backbone for eight years. In 1962 a 'grown up' option was offered, the larger Giulia with optional 1570cc twin-cam engine, five-speed gearbox and disc brakes.

The 1900 Super continued. Its capacity was increased to 2000cc in 1962 and a six-cylinder twin-cam 2.6-litre car introduced. All were available with a wide choice of body styles and performance specifications and they were loved for their performance and handling.

The following year construction of a new factory to replace the limited Portello works was started at Arese, also on the outskirts of Milan. From the new factory came the V8 two-litre twin-cam Tipo 33 mid-engined race car. Enlarged to three litres it won the Targa Florio, Brands Hatch 1000km race and Watkins Glen six-hour event in 1971, but the car was never without its problems, though it was instrumental in the production of a great road car in the old Alfa tradition.

This was the Bertone-styled Montreal (conceived as an exhibit for the 1967 Montreal World Fair) which used a 2.6-litre version of the twin-cam V8. A two-plus-two with fuel injection and five-speed gearbox, here was a fast road car with a pure racing engine. Top speed was quoted at 222km/h (138mph). With disc brakes all round it was based on the 1600 Giulia coupé floorpan and featured a live rear axle. While this was not regarded as

Above left: 1958-1961 2000 saloon
Above: 1971 1750 GTV
Below left: 1971 1300 Giulia Super
Below: 1971 1750 Berlina
Bottom: 1973 front-wheel-drive Alfasud

much of a plus point the car gained a glamorous reputation and was the pride of the factory, 3,925 examples being built from 1970 to 1975.

In 1968 a new Giulia with a 1779cc engine had been introduced and to boost jobs in the south of Italy the government that year persuaded Alfa Romeo to set up a manufacturing plant near Naples. It opened in 1971 with production of the 1186cc flat-four Alfasud (Alfa South). A completely new car, it featured front-wheel-drive and MacPherson-strut front suspension, belt-drive single-overhead camshafts and a four-speed transaxle.

The Hruschka design was acclaimed for its roadholding thanks to wide track and dead axle with leading and trailing arms and Panhard rod. With disc brakes all round the 63bhp car encouraged enthusiastic driving, but many found the Giugiaro styling boring.

From a marketing point of view it was a leader, however, and higher-performance versions saw that it never strayed far from pole position in the hot small-car sales war.

Also in 1971 Alfa's 1750cc road engine was bored to 1962cc and the following year the Alfetta name was revived with 1779cc four-cylinder twin-cam power and a De Dion rear axle incorporating a five-speed gearbox as used in the 1951 race car.

The 1972 Alfetta was the first production car to employ this system of front engine and rear-mounted clutch, gearbox and differential, giving excellent weight distribution.

A more economical 1.6-litre Giulia-powered version was later introduced, plus GT 1.6, 1.8 and two-litre variants.

The Alfasud became a hatchback model in 1981 and lasted until 1984 when the 33 model took over with 1350cc, 1490cc and 1712cc engines.

Top left: Bertone-styled V8-engined Montreal
Centre left: 1600 Spider with Pininfarina body
Bottom left: 1976 twin-cam Alfetta GT
Below: 1984 Alfetta Gold Cloverleaf
Opposite top: Giulietta 1.6 was introduced in 1978
Opposite centre left: 1985-specification 33 1.3 saloon
Opposite centre: High-performance GTV available with in-line four or V6 engine
Opposite centre right: The Sprint was a successful Alfasud variant
Opposite bottom: 1986 4wd 33 estate

Left: 1990-specification 75 Twin-Spark
Above: Stunning three-litre V6 164 Lusso
Below: Alfa 90 in Gold Cloverleaf trim

The Giulietta name lasted over 20 years. It was finally ousted by the 1986 '75' – so called because it was introduced to celebrate the company's 75th birthday. (This is called Milano in the United States.) Retaining the same floorpan and De Dion rear suspension the model ranges from 1779cc four-cylinder cars to 2959cc 188bhp models, all with rear-wheel-drive.

For 1988 Alfa introduced the 164 powered by a 192bhp 2959cc V6 with a 220km/h (137mph) top speed, sumptuous interior, front-wheel-drive, all-independent suspension and anti-lock braking as an option. It looks set to carry the company's national pride well into the 1990s.

Below: The Pininfarina-styled Spider was still in production in 1990, well over 20 years after its introduction in its original boat-tailed form.

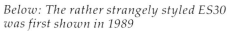

Above: The 75's saloon body was also available with a three-litre V6 engine

Below: The rather strangely styled ES30 was first shown in 1989

Top: Alfa Romeo 33 1.7 Veloce
Above: 33-bodied 1.7 Sportswagon

The introduction of the 164 heralded a new start for Alfa Romeo. Whereas the eighties had seen little more than rebodied seventies cars, by the nineties Alfa was starting to be a little more adventurous with its styling and developing new, more competitive models.

The 164 was still in production in 1997 and remained almost unchanged in its 10-year production span but gained a quad cam 24-valve V6 engine in 1992.

The ES30 show car, first shown at the Geneva show in 1989, became a production model in 1990, badged as the SZ (Sport Zagato). This hard-top sports coupé with its 3-litre V6 and brutally-styled glassfibre body-work, was an instant classic. A convertible version, the RZ, became available in 1992. Unfortunately, sales were not good and the model was soon dropped from the range.

Previous page: Alfa Romeo Nuvola concept car
Top: The 145 hatchback was launched in 1994 with the old four-cylinder boxer engine but received the new twin-cam four in 1996
Right: The new Spider was launched in 1994

The first car in the range to be replaced was the quirkily-styled but outmoded 75 or Milano, in 1992. The replacement model was the 155, launched initially with 2.0-litre Twin Spark and 2.5-litre V6 engines. Alfa's new corporate identity was beginning to form with the new car carrying a similar Alfa Romeo grille that was more integrated into the front end, as first seen on the 164. The range was expanded with the addition of a 1.8-litre twin spark engine and a rapid 2.0-litre four-wheel-drive version.

The 145, launched in 1994 to replace the ageing 33 saw even more innovative design. This stylish little three-door hatchback had a distinctive step in the door window-frames and an unusual tailgate treatment with a notch in the lower edge of the rear wind-shield. A notchback, five-door version, the 146, followed a year later. The four-cylinder boxer engine, developed originally for the Alfasud, remained determinedly under the hood until 1996, when it was replaced by the new Fiat-based twin-cam twin-spark engine

in 1.4-, 1.6-, 1.8- and 2.0-litre forms. Unusually for a marque with such a sporting history, the 145/146 range is also available with a 1.9-litre turbodiesel engine on some markets.

Alfa's greatest move in recent years was its replacement of the original Spider in 1993. By this stage, no amount of plastic add-ons or spoilers could keep the car looking up to date. The replacement Spider, not launched until 1996, is one of the most striking pro-duction cars on the road today, together with the hardtop version the GTV, both products of a collaboration between Pininfarina and the Alfa Romeo/Fiat design studio. These new cars carried a completely new engine for Alfa. Yes, it was still a twin-cam 2.0-litre design, but the new power unit, part of Fiat's new family of modular engines, used a Fiat block with an exclusive twin-cam, twin-spark cylinder head. An output of 150bhp gave reasonable performance, but the excellent suspension was capable of dealing with a whole lot more, despite the limitations of its front-wheel-drive layout. The solution was the addition of the 3.0-litre, quad-cam V6, giving the car the performance that its stunning looks deserved. A turbocharged 2.0-litre V6-engined GTV was also available on certain markets.

Top: The GTV, like the Spider, was styled in conjunction with Pininfarina and gained the 3.0-litre V6 engine in 1996

Above: The 146 was a small Alfa for those who found the styling of the mechanically similar 145 too quirky for their tastes

Left: Alfa's design studio came up with the beautiful 156 for 1997

Allard

Great Britain
1937–1960

Sydney Allard was born in 1910 and started business in 1930 as Adlards Motors Ltd. in small premises at Putney, South London.

The name came from building firm Roberts Adlard which Sydney's father had acquired.

Allard was successful in trials with a Ford V8 fitted with a Bugatti tail. The first version was built for sale in 1937.

A total of 12 Allards were built between 1937 and September 1939, ranging from trials cars to four-seater tourers.

The Allard Motor Company Ltd. was formed in February 1945, although Adlards Motors Ltd. remained in business until 1976, and new premises were acquired in nearby Clapham.

Above: 1953-4 M2X 4-seater convertible

The new range of cars used mostly Ford components and bodies by Whittingham and Mitchel and Paramount Sheet Metal. The first production cars were ready by 1946, six leaving the factory that year.

Above: The spacious Safari estate

Models included the V8-engined K two-seaters and L four-seaters. The P-Type saloon was added to the range in time for the 1948 London Motor Show.

All Ford dealerships were listed as

The Allard J2 was introduced in 1949. With a 3197cc Mercury engine producing 140bhp, it could reach 177km/h (110mph). A limited number of J2 replicas have been built recently in Ontario, Canada.

official Allard agents and the company was represented in several countries.

Allards continued to be competitive in sporting events, using engines such as Cadillacs, Chryslers and Dodges.

Production of the larger cars fell during the late 1950s and the last three had 3.4-litre Jaguar engines. This was ironic because it was Jaguar's success with the XK120 which had been partly responsible for Allard's falling sales.

The company won a contract with the London Ambulance Service in 1959 to convert B.M.C. and Bedford chassis to De Dion axles, and other work included tuning Ford Anglias, sold as Allardettes.

Allard also became world distributors and manufacturers of Shorrock superchargers.

Sydney Allard died in April 1966 but the business was carried on by Reg Canham, who controlled the Ford dealership of Adlards, and Sydney's son Alan, who put his efforts into superchargers, tuning and sunroofs. Allards closed in 1976 and Alan Allard ran a factory at Daventry until 1975, moving to Ross-on-Wye and founding Allard Turbochargers.

Replica Allard J2s have been made in Ontario, Canada, but production has been extremely limited.

Below: 1952 Allard J2X

Alpine

France
1955 to date

Based at Dieppe in northern France, Automobiles Alpine produces a single-model range of rear-engined grand-touring cars with a decidedly sporting bias. The Alpine factory has always relied on an association with Renault for its components.

The first Alpine appeared in 1955, making its debut in the Mille Miglia race in the hands of its sponsor Jean Redélé whose father was the Renault agent in Dieppe during the early 1950s. Redélé rallied a modified 750cc Renault 4CV, winning a Coupe des Alpes in 1954 and the 750cc class in the Mille Miglia.

Having obtained an engineering degree, the 33-year-old Redélé gave up the car-repair side of the family business and set up in limited production using the name Société Automobiles Alpine. The first car was called the Mille Miles to celebrate his racing successes in the Mille Miglia. This vehicle was a glassfibre-bodied coupé styled by Michelotti and built in Paris by Chappe Frères, with Renault 4CV running gear which could include Redélé's own five-speed gearbox. The A106 as it was termed was a class-winner in the 1956 Mille Miglia, and although production was fairly limited, by 1957 customers could order cabriolet styling and more-powerful 845cc or bored-out 904cc and 948cc Dauphine engines.

Above: Alpine 1600 Coupé with A110 body
Below right: Le Mans, 1966, with Alpine Renault leading the pack at Tertre Rouge

Right: Delageneste and Chinisse co-drove 1.3-litre car at Le Mans in 1967
Below right: 3-litre A220 at Le Mans, 1968

Alpine evolution kept pace with the development of Renault production models, and included the steel-bodied A107 prototype and, in 1961, a 2+2 coupé and Tour de France Berlinette. The factory was producing around 100 units a year by now, and in 1963 came the classic rear-engined rear-wheel-drive A110, which remained in production for 15 years, during which time engine capacity rose in stages from 1108cc to 1800cc.

The A110 was highly successful in

Below left: One-litre Alpine Renault at Le Mans, 1963
Below: Le Mans, 1964, Delageneste and Morrogh

Far left: 1.3-litre A210 of Nicholas and Andruet
Left: Specially prepared 1966 Le Mans car

competitions, finishing first, second and third in the 1971 Monte Carlo Rally. Alpine was by now responsible for the Renault Competitions Department, and also heavily sponsored by Elf, the French state-owned petrol company, and the A110 took the World Rally Championship in 1973.

Alongside development of the road cars, Alpines were also campaigned in the World Sportscar Championship, where cars based on the A210 regularly carried off the Index of Performance trophy at Le Mans. Real glory came in 1978 – four years after Automobiles Alpine was taken over by Renault – when the Renault-Alpine A442 drive by Jean-Pierre Jaussaud and Didier Pironi won Le Mans outright.

Forays into single-seater racing were less successful but, by 1969, the company had moved into new premises, and the new A310 was launched in 1971. Initially powered by a tuned Renault 16 engine producing 140bhp, then the 2664cc V6 engine from the Renault 30 saloon, this was sold in all Renault dealerships and covered by Renault guarantee. It was manufactured in a number of countries including Spain, Brazil and Mexico, and achieved a peak production of around 2,000 units a year.

Ten years later, its replacement, the 151mph Renault Alpine GTA V6 was introduced, and was available in normally aspirated or turbocharged form. In some quarters it is seen as a stylish and modern alternative to the Porsche 911.

Below: Launched in 1963 with an 1108cc Renault Gordini engine, the A110 took first, second and third place in the 1971 Monte Carlo Rally with a 1600cc unit.

Alvis

Great Britain
1920–1967

The Alvis 12/50 is one of the most famous of all vintage cars. Produced from 1923 until 1932, it had a 1½-litre overhead-valve four-cylinder engine, although the cubic capacity varied from model to model.

Alvis was founded in Coventry by T.G. John in 1919, and he led the company for its first quarter-century. The first car was a bought-out design, the sidevalve 10/30, but this soon evolved into a 12/40 and then into the overhead-valve 12/50, with which Alvis established itself as the builder of high-quality sporting machinery.

Finances were precarious, however, and a receiver was appointed in 1924. Yet Alvis survived to experiment with front-wheel-drive, both in supercharged 1½-litre eight-cylinder competition models, and in four-cylinder road cars which were too expensive to sell well. Rear-wheel-drive returned for the 1930s, when Alvis produced a range of well-engineered and rakishly styled six-cylinder models with evocative names like Silver Eagle, Crested Eagle, Speed Twenty, and so on. The 4.3-litre model of the late 1930s was one of only a handful of British cars which could attain 100mph (160km/h).

During World War II, Alvis concentrated on the aero-engines which it had begun to build in 1935 and on military vehicles. After 1945, these would keep the

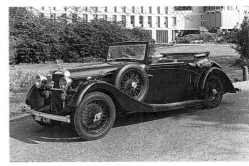

Above: 1934 Speed 20 Tourer by Cross and Ellis
Below: 1936 Silver Eagle drophead coupé

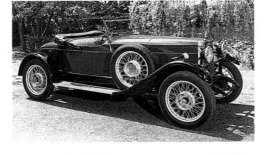

Centre: 1927 12/50 'Beetleback'
Right: 1928 front-wheel-drive 12/75

company afloat, while the cars became a secondary activity. The first post-war car was the TA14, which picked up pre-war themes, but in 1950 a new independent front suspension chassis and three-litre engine arrived in the TA21. The majority of both models had saloon or drophead bodies, although a few sports tourers were built and designated TB14 or TB21. The basic chassis design remained unchanged for the TC21/100 'Grey Lady' 160km/h (100mph) sports saloon of 1955 and the range of TD21, TE21 and TF21 models fitted with the Graber-styled two-door body after 1958. Alvis merged with Rover in 1965, but plans for new models were never realized. The last car was built in August 1967 and the company concentrated thereafter solely on military vehicles.

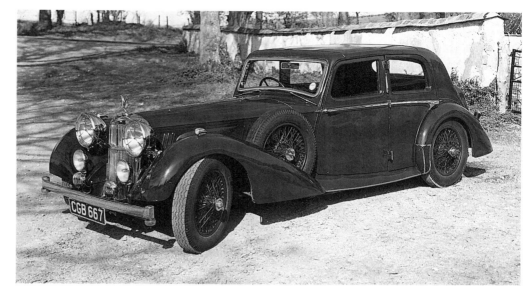

Above: 1938 Speed 25 saloon by Charlesworth
Left: 1939 short-chassis 4.3-litre by Vanden Plas
Centre left: 1946 TA14 shooting brake
Bottom left: 1953 TC21/100 Grey Lady
Right: 1955 TD21 Grey Lady
Below: The last Alvis, the TF21, was built in 1967

A.M.C.
U.S.A.
1968-1988

In 1954 Nash and Hudson merged and under the presidency of George Romney became known as American Motors Corporation. Romney concentrated company efforts on the 1950-introduced Nash Rambler, which by 1957 had expanded to a 20-model range. Around 1959 A.M.C. reintroduced the Ambassador with a 5359cc V8 engine as its top-of-the-range model, while at the same time reviving the six-cylinder Rambler as the American. The cars were well received, with production continuing until 1970, when the Rambler was dropped and A.M.C. acquired Kaiser-Jeep Corp. In 1974 production of the Ambassador ceased.

One of the most exciting cars produced by A.M.C. was the sporty and very successful four-seater Javelin introduced in 1968 with a choice of either a 'small' 3.8-litre V6 or a 3.7-, 5.6- or 6.4-litre V8 engine. Front disc brakes were optional on the V8 cars, at a time when big drum brakes were the norm.

The ANX two-seater and the hatchback Gremlin were introduced in quick succession, while in 1974 A.M.C. adopted a new approach when it announced the sporting Pacer series.

Top: 1956 Rambler station wagon
Above: The Javelin SST, introduced in 1968

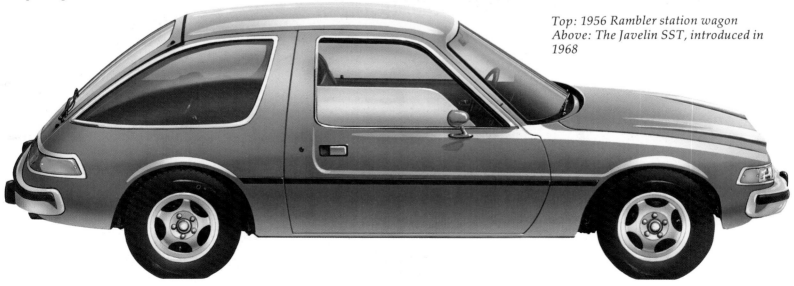

In 1975 an agreement with Renault allowed A.M.C. to build and sell the Renault R18, while in the same year the Spirit was introduced to replace the Gremlin, available as a hatchback or saloon.

In the late 1980s A.M.C. was building both the Renault Encore (1397cc engine) and the Renault Alliance (1397cc or 1721cc) in addition to its own Eagle Series saloons and station wagons with either a 105bhp 2460cc engine or the 112bhp 4228cc six-cylinder unit.

In 1980 Renault purchased a 41.6 per cent holding in A.M.C., and finally Chrysler bought A.M.C. in 1987 for its Jeep line and assembly facilities, but not its name.

Top: 1964 Rambler Ambassador
Above: 1974 Pacer hatchback
Right: A.M.C.'s 1984 Jeep CJ-7 Laredo

Left: The 1974 Pacer placed great emphasis on passenger space and visibility. It was short but wide, and was claimed to have windows covering a third of its exterior. Straight-six engines of 3802 and 4228cc were offered, with manual or automatic transmission.

Amilcar

France
1921–1939

The famous French firm of Amilcar was established in 1921, producing sports models which could be enjoyed to the full in that country at the time. The firm's founders were Messieurs Lamy and Akar, whose names were blended to form the company title.

The company's first cars – the CC, CS and 4C Types, designed by Edmond Moyet – were sporting two-seaters which used one-litre, sidevalve four-cylinder power units. In 1924 the nine-horsepower, overhead-valve CGS was introduced with a top speed approaching 128km/h (80mph) and braking on the front wheels as well as the rears. The lower CGSS model (which was more powerful still) became available two years later. This car – the Surbaissé model, with its 1100cc power unit and abbreviated motorcycle-type mudguards – is very much sought after today. The models to date featured simple chassis design and narrow, streamlined body-work.

Amilcar built cars with specifications and performance which sound creditable today, let alone in the 1920s. The C6 Course, for example, also introduced in 1926, featured a twin-overhead-camshaft six-cylinder engine which propelled the car to 193km/h (120mph). This car was very successful in racing.

Another Amilcar which gained recognition for its handling and performance was the overhead-camshaft straight-eight C8 of

Above: 1925 Amilcar CGS Grand Sport

1928, which gave 128km/h (80mph) from 1800cc.

The company's advanced, sporting products provided exhilarating motoring and in the firm's heyday during the late 1920s cars were being built at the rate of some 12,000 per year.

For the 1930s Amilcar offered a two-litre version of the C8; an M-Type (initially with 1250cc, later 1700cc); a five-horsepower Type C (from 1933); a 12-horsepower N7 (powered by Delahaye) and a 14-horsepower G36 model.

Just prior to World War II Hotchkiss produced some fascinating 1200cc Amilcar saloons with lightweight unitary-construction bodywork, all-round independent suspension and front-wheel-drive.

Sadly, there were to be no post-war Amilcars.

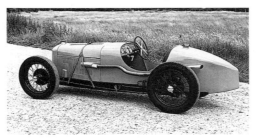

Above: Early Amilcars were CC, CS and 4C models
Right: 1926 C6 production racer
Below: The CGSS Surbaissé was a further developed version of the CGS, and was both lower and faster than its predecessor. Later models featured a differential.

Below: 1927 CGSS Surbaissé model
Bottom: 1928 ohc straight-eight C8

Armstrong–Siddeley

Great Britain
1919–1960

The Coventry-based Siddeley-Deasy company merged with the car-making side of Armstrong-Whitworth to form Armstrong-Siddeley in 1919, and the first fruit of the merger was that year's 30hp model, a large and solidly built six-cylinder machine which lasted until 1932. This was joined in 1921 by a scaled-down 18hp model, which gained an enlarged engine in 1925 and was redesignated a 20hp two years later.

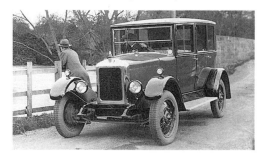

Above: 1926 14hp with a 1825cc engine

The six-cylinder models were joined by a four-cylinder 14hp in 1925, but this lasted only until 1929, when the company reverted to its all-six-cylinder policy. In that year, too, appeared the first models with a Wilson preselector gearbox, which was standardized across the range in 1933. The most popular pre-war model was the 12hp, however, introduced in 1928 and offered with a wide variety of body styles. Its sidevalve engine was the smallest six-cylinder unit available on the British market but, after 1936, all models had six-cylinder engines.

Above: 1934 12hp tourer, a popular model
Below: 1930 30hp six-cylinder landaulette

The 1991cc overhead-valve engine first seen in 1938 also powered the 1946 16hp model, available in saloon and drophead styles with names evocative of the warplanes built by the related aircraft company. The range was revised in 1948 and centred on an 18hp engine, but new and distinctive styling arrived in 1953 on the Sapphire 346 luxury saloon. From 1958, the more powerful Star Sapphire was offered, but even a proper automatic transmission and disc front brakes could not disguise the fact that the separate-chassis design of these cars was behind the times. Sales of the smaller Sapphire 234 and 236 saloons, introduced

Above: The rather formal 1936 20/25
Left: 1928 30hp six-cylinder London

Above: 1935 20hp four-light saloon
Below: 1936 20/25 touring saloon

in 1955 with bodies partly panelled in Hiduminium aircraft alloy, proved disappointing and these were withdrawn in 1958. Production ceased in 1960 when the parent Hawker-Siddeley concern merged with the Bristol aircraft company.

Above: 1953 Sapphire four-light saloon
Below: 1956 Sapphire 346 automatic

Arrol-Johnston/ Arrol-Aster

Scotland 1895–1929

It was not until the mid-1880s that the first reliable petrol-driven cars appeared, developed independently in Germany by Gottlieb Daimler and Karl Benz. Meanwhile in Scotland, locomotive engineer George Johnston, disenchanted with his experimental steam tram, turned his hand to the internal-combustion engine, developing a four-piston, opposed-twin engine with combustion occurring between two pistons moving in opposite directions, but connected by rocking beams to the same single crank-shaft.

This engine was mounted in a heavy dog-cart and launched in 1895 by the company then managed by engineer Sir William Arrol, of Forth Bridge fame, with production continuing until 1906.

In 1905 a 3023cc 12/15hp car using the same opposed-piston engine was unveiled, while in the same year a 3795cc opposed-twin Arrol-Johnston beat the Rolls-Royce of Percy Northey to win the very first Isle of Man Tourist Trophy Race. More orthodox engines were then developed in the form of the 1906 24/30hp vertical four of 4654cc and the 1907 8832cc unit, with the old horizontal-twin 12/15 model being phased out in 1909.

In the same year T.C. Pullinger, previously of Darracq and Humber, joined the company and produced a new range of cars with a 15.9hp 2835cc engine, a dashboard radiator and four-wheel braking, making Arrol-Johnston and Crossley the first British manufacturers to introduce this controversial braking system. With the foot pedal operating the front wheels and the hand-brake the rear ones, an inexperienced driver could quite easily lose control and spin the car.

Model followed model until in 1913 production moved from Paisley to Dumfries, where some 50 electric cars were built for Edison, while some six years laer, the 'unsellable and unreliable' 2651cc

Above: Arrol-Johnston c. 1901

Below: Charlesworth-bodied 15.9hp model

Victory model was announced. Around 1925 a 3290cc Empire model was built for the Colonies and in 1927 Arrol-Johnston merged with Aster – makers of the sleeve-valve engine. The company's final model, the straight-eight sleeve-valve 70hp 3292cc Arrol-Aster, was unsuccessful, and the company closed down in 1929.

Below: 1927 six-cylinder model

Aston Martin

Great Britain
1922 to date

Aston Martin was registered as a company in 1913. It was formed by engineer Robert Bamford and wealthy car enthusiast Lionel Martin, and based at Kensington, London.

The company's first car was a one-off competition machine using a 1400cc four-cylinder Coventry-Simplex engine grafted into a 1908 Grand Prix des Voiturettes Isotta-Fraschini chassis.

The name of the car – Aston Martin – was evolved from Martin's successful outings at the Aston Clinton hill-climb in Buckinghamshire in his 10hp Singer.

World War I cut short the company's car development and Bamford resigned in 1920 with Martin's wife taking over his share. Several racing cars were built – such as a double-overhead-camshaft car ordered by Count Louis Zborowski – but it was to be three years before the first road-going cars were offered to the public.

But despite racing successes, the company reaped no profits and went into receivership in November 1924.

The firm was bought by Birmingham-based consulting engineers Renwick and Bertelli.

The new Aston Martin announced for the 1927 Olympia Show used the four-cylinder overhead-cam 10hp engine Bertelli had designed for the Enfield Allday (one car was built before the acquisition of Aston Martin).

Production moved to a new factory at Feltham, Middlesex, but Renwick withdrew support. Bertelli managed to gain the backing of various people including P. C. Kidner of Vauxhall.

Production of the first series of cars totalled just 19, with a mixture of saloons, tourers and two competition two-seaters. The racers, built by Bertelli's brother, won the Rudge Whitworth Cup in the 1928 Le Mans race.

By 1931 the company was in trouble yet again, mainly because of the high costs of

Above: 1927 T-type tourer
Below: 1933 2/4 Le Mans

The first Aston Martin, made available to the public in 1923. It had a 1.5-litre Coventry Simplex engine with a Rubery Owen chassis and, unusual for those days, front-wheel brakes.

the racing programme. It changed hands twice, ending up in the hands of London motor distributor Lance Prideaux-Brune and R. Gordon Sutherland, son of a wealthy ship-owner.

Bertelli's skills and Sutherland's money combined to produce a flourishing company, and the 1930s saw many racing successes, including the Le Mans Tourist Trophy.

Only the 1½-litre engine designed by Bertelli in 1926 was offered. It was replaced by a two-litre overhead-cam unit in 1936, designed by Bertelli and Claude Hill, and about 140 saloons and two-seaters were made up to the start of World War II.

The last pre-war model was the Atom which had independent front suspension and – in the end – a new pushrod engine.

Above: The DB3 sports racer

Above: DB3, developed into 1955 DB3S

Above: Two-litre, built from 1936 to 1939

Control of Aston Martin was taken over by tractor manufacturer David Brown in February 1947, and the DB1 went into production the following year, using the pushrod engine developed just before the outbreak of war.

David Brown then bought Lagonda and used that company's 2½-litre double-overhead-camshaft in-line six, designed by W. O. Bentley, for the DB2. That went into production in May 1950, followed by the DB3. All production was transferred to Newport Pagnell, Buckinghamshire, in 1955.

Below: 1950 DB2 with 2.6-litre engine

The 1959 DB4 was the start of a new breed because it did not use the old Atom's chassis and Lagonda engine. It was a two-door fastback coupé or convertible, with the Lagonda Rapide offered to customers who wanted a four-door body.

The 3.7-litre DB4 gave way to the four-litre DB5, DB6 and DBS. The DBS gained a 5.3-litre V8 in September 1969.

The losses involved in this development, however, were so great that Aston Martin was sold to Company Developments Ltd. in February 1972. The workforce was cut and all six-cylinder cars dropped.

But by December 1974, the company was insolvent. Much of its money had been spent adapting the V8 for the American market. Canadian Rolls-Royce distributor George Minden and American Peter Sprague formed a new company – Aston Martin Lagonda (1975) Ltd. Additional cash came from sources including Sheffield Steel.

The company had changed hands again by 1981, being bought by the chairman of Pace Petroleum, Victor Gauntlett, and Tim Healey, chairman of CH Industrials.

Above: 1960 DB4 GT capable of 244km/h (152mph)
Below: 1964 DB5 was a fast tourer
Bottom: Early DBS with straight-six engine

Above: Six-cylinder DBS

Above: 1968 Aston Martin DB6

Above: 1968 DB6 Volante convertible

Aston Martin Tickford was established, producing luxury versions of production cars from other manufacturers.

Production in the early 1980s concentrated on the Aston Martin Vantage saloon and Volante convertible and the William Towns-designed Lagonda saloon. Production was running at four cars a week by the autumn of 1985 by which time Gauntlett owned 25 per cent of the marque and the Greek Livanos shipping family the remainder.

Ford acquired control of the company in September 1987 and the new Aston Martin Virage was announced at the end of 1988, replacing the familiar V8 cars. An open-top version of the Virage, called Volante, followed a year later.

Below: 1987 Aston Martin Vantage Zagato, built in extremely limited numbers

Above: V8-powered Volante convertible

Above: Aston Martin Lagonda

Above: V8-powered Virage, announced at the 1988 Motor Show

Below: The dramatically angular Aston Martin Lagonda was a triumph of engineering and technical innovation, but has often been criticized for its looks. The 5.3-litre V8 engine gives it a top speed of 225km/h (140mph).

The Aston Martin range, consisting only of Virage and Volante, continued unchanged until 1992 when the new Vantage model was launched at the Birmingham Motor Show. This extremely high performance version of the Virage sported flared wheel arches, deeper chin spoiler and had an altogether more aggressive look. Under the hood lay one of the most powerful production car engines of the time. By fitting twin Roots-type Eaton superchargers, Aston Martin engineers managed to raise the power output of the hand-built alloy V8 to over 550bhp. A six-speed gearbox was also added to make better use of the extra power. Speeds of nearly 180mph (290km/h) were attainable in this luxury heavyweight and the mighty engine could take its super-rich owners to 60mph (100km/h)in a shade over 4.5 seconds.

In 1996 the standard Virage was updated with prettier, softer lines and an increase in power from 330 to 350bhp.

The biggest news at Aston Martin during the 1990s was the new DB7, launched in 1993. Available in fixed-head coupé or open-top Volante forms (from 1996), the handsome DB7 was a very welcome new model to the range. With a straight six engine, designed by TWR, the supercharged DB7 was the real spiritual successor to the long-dead DB6.

Above: The Virage was renamed the V8 in 1996

Above: 1997 DB7 Volante

Above: 1997 V8 Volante

Above: The fearsome 550bhp V8 Vantage

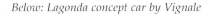

Above: The DB7 coupé was the 'cheap' Aston   *Below: Lagonda concept car by Vignale*

Asia Motors

Asia Motors, owned by Korean manufacturer Kia, is one of the many companies worldwide building a vehicle that is very obviously influenced by the original wartime Jeep. In fact it was used by the Korean Army, in more basic trim, long before the western world was offered it as a recreational fun vehicle. The Asia Rocsta, launched in 1994, was available with a 1.8-litre gasoline or 2.2-litre diesel engine. There were two body styles, a hardtop and a convertible. The Jeep styling was modernized with the use of plenty of black plastic, some graphics, and a set of alloy wheels. As is typical of this kind of vehicle, the performance figures could be measured with an hour-glass rather than a stop-watch, especially for the diesel model.

Above: The Rocsta's low price and rugged build meant it made a good heavy-duty working vehicle for farmers

Left: Asia Motors really tried to push the Rocsta as a lifestyle vehicle, but it didn't have the fashionable image of the Japanese four-wheel-drive recreational vehicles

Below: The car's soft top was a crude affair, as on most Jeep-type vehicles, but it was more popular than the hard-top model

Auburn

U.S.A.
1900–1937

The first Auburn was built in 1900 by Frank and Morris Eckhardt, who sold small numbers of their early models in and around Auburn, Indiana, and named their company after that town. Their first proper production model was a single-cylinder runabout with chain drive, introduced in 1903, but further models were gradually added to the range, and the twin-cylinder engines introduced in 1905 continued until a four-cylinder model with a bought-in engine arrived in 1910. A six-cylinder engine was added to the range in 1912.

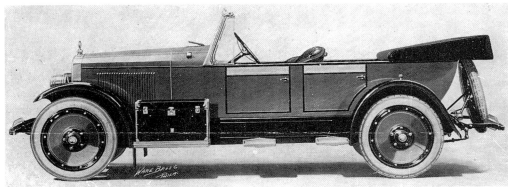

Above: 1904 Auburn runabout

Four- and six-cylinder models were offered through to 1919, and it was possible to order right-hand or left-hand steering after 1914. Engines were still bought in, from Continental, Rutenber, and Teetor. The Eckhardts sold out to a group of Chicago businessmen in 1919, and that year's Beauty Six model betrayed more conscious styling. It evolved two years later into the 6-51 sports model, but production figures remained modest. The 1923 Auburns had either Continental or Weidely six-cylinder engines, but that year was a bad one for the U.S. motor industry and by 1924 Auburn was in trouble.

That year, however, the company was bought out by Errett Lobban Cord. Cord appointed James Crawford as Chief

Engineer and had the entire range redesigned for 1925. The engineering of the new models was so advanced that almost no changes were made before 1930. All were attractively styled and well constructed, and the Auburn name in the late 1920s came to stand for cars with handsome bodies and good performance. Four-, six- and eight-cylinder models were offered; but the four-cylinder model was dropped in 1927, as the company moved upmarket.

Although a radically-styled Cabin Speedster on the eight-cylinder 115 chassis fell victim to the Depression and was withdrawn, Auburn was remarkably unaffected by the sales slump. The year 1931 was a record one for sales, aided by new and sleek styling on the 8-98 model. Later, the company followed the trend towards multi-cylinder engines with the introduction of a 6.4-litre V12 engine in 1932, which made the Auburn the first twelve-cylinder car to sell for under $1000. But this was a bad time to be breaking into

Top: Beauty Six was announced in 1919
Above: 1925 Auburn 8-88 Sedan
Below: 1935 6-120 Sedan
Bottom: 80-8 with straight-eight engine

the luxury car market, and the V12 had to be dropped in 1934.

The 1931 designs were replaced in 1934, and a six-cylinder engine was added to the range. But it was 1935 which represented Auburn's classic year, with the addition to the 653 six-cylinder and 851 eight-cylinder ranges of a supercharged 851 model and a strikingly attractive boat-tailed Speedster body, developed by Gordon Buehrig from an earlier design by Count Alexis de Saknoffsky. The addition of a Schwitzer-Cummins supercharger to the 279-cubic inch Lycoming straight-eight engine gave 150bhp, and all the supercharged Auburns were guaranteed to have been test-driven at more than 100mph (160km/h). Sadly, the company lost money on every one of these fine cars, and the range continued for only two more years; although new models were planned for 1937, none was produced and the company went into liquidation that year.

The classic speedsters have inspired several replica vehicles in more recent years, all using modern power units and chassis engineering under the 1930s-styled bodies.

Above: 1935 851 available with or without supercharger

The glamorous 851 Speedster was guaranteed capable of 161km/h (100mph). The boat-tailed speedster body was adapted from an earlier design by Count Alexis de Saknoffsky.

Audi

Germany
1910–1939,
1965 to date

Above: The Type E 22/50PS

Above: Dr Horch with his 14/38PS

Above: The 1929-32 Zwickau had a Rickenbacker-designed engine
Far left: Eight-cylinder Type R also known as Imperator
Bottom: The Type K, powered by a 3.5-litre overhead-valve engine producing 50bhp, finally succeeded the Type C

When August Horch left the company bearing his name to start up on his own for a second time, he was prevented from using his own name again, so he chose instead to identify the new company by the Latin word for the literal meaning in German of his own name, *horchen*; 'to listen'. The first car to be produced by Horch as an Audi, the Type B, appeared in 1910 and brought immediate success.

Reviving his connections with motor sport, Horch entered the 1911 Austrian Alpine Trials in a Type B, leading a team of drivers which included two of his engineers, Lange and Graumuller. Horch completed the event without a penalty point, entering in the same type of car the following year, then again in 1913 in a

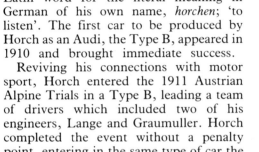

Type C. The Type C won that year and the year after, to become known as the *Alpensieger* – 'Alpine Victor'.

Other pre-war models were the Types D and E, although these were made in limited numbers. With the outbreak of hostility in 1914 Audi began producing two-ton trucks on reinforced Type C chassis, as well as military vehicles. The Types C, D and E were continued after World War I, alongside the new Type G, although Horch's own personal interest in the company had waned with the inevitable creative stagnation during the war and he left Audi in 1920.

By 1922 the long-running Type C was superseded by the Type G, and two years later Audi began building its range of six- and eight-cylinder cars. The unsuccessful Type R Imperator of 1928 is considered to be the last of the true Audis, since after

that time the company became increasingly involved in assembling other manufacturers' components.

It was also in 1928 that J. S. Rasmussen of D.K.W. took the major shareholding in

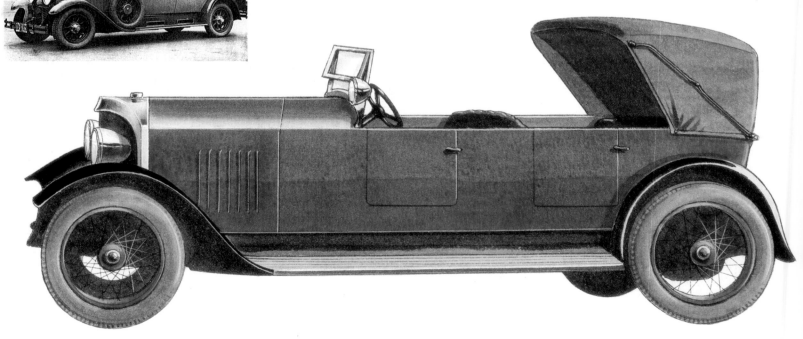

Below: The Type 225 in roadster form

Below: Audi Front sport cabriolet

Above: 1934 fwd Type 225 Front

the company. He brought with him the design and manufacturing rights to the Rickenbacker engine from the U.S.A. German-built engines of this type were used in subsequent Audi models.

In 1931 a smaller Audi with a D.K.W. chassis and an 1100cc Peugeot engine was produced, and the year after that Audi, along with D.K.W., Wanderer, and Horch, became part of Auto-Union. Two Wanderer-powered front-wheel-drive models followed, and sold well in the years leading up to World War II, although the last pre-war model was the rear-driven Type 920.

Far left: 3.2-litre saloon built in 1938
Left: 1939-40 Audi A6

After the war Audi was nationalized, together with the other Auto-Union companies, as part of Industrie-Vereinigung Volkseigner Fahrzeugwerke, and the Audi factory at Zwickau was used to build D.K.W.-based cars. This only lasted until 1949 when Auto-Union re-established itself with a Mercedes-Benz majority shareholding.

The Audi name was allowed to lapse until after 1965, when Volkswagen gained a majority shareholding and a new front-wheel-drive saloon was introduced. By the end of 1968 sales had picked up and the Audi range had been considerably extended.

In 1969 Audi merged with N.S.U. to form Audi N.S.U. Auto-Union AG, although N.S.U. production ceased eight years later. Under V.W. control, however, Audi continued to improve and develop its range, with May 1973 seeing the one millionth Audi car sold.

Among the company's technological milestones have been the five-cylinder engine, first launched in the 100 Series during the late 1970s, turbocharging and four-wheel drive, the latter with the Quattro introduced in 1980/81.

Above: Auto Union Monza Coupé
Below: Auto Union 1700 saloon

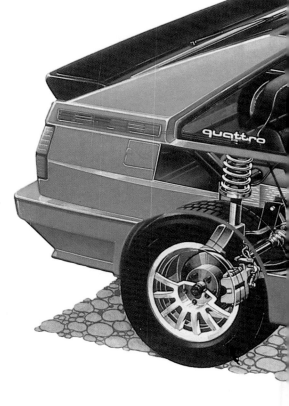

Above: The short-wheelbase Quattro Sport was announced at the 1983 Frankfurt Motor Show with a five-cylinder double-overhead-camshaft engine and an innovative four-wheel-drive transmission. Quattros took first and second places in the 1983 R.A.C. rally.

Above left: The 1972 four-cylinder Audi 80
Above: The 1977 100 saloon, the first Audi with a five-cylinder engine

The Audi Quattro and short-wheelbase Quattro Sport, both combining high performance with supercar standards of roadholding, won practically every major competition for which they were entered, leading both Audi and its Volkswagen parent to introduce four-wheel-drive on an increasing number of their road-going models. The four rings of the Audi badge, incidentally, represent the four companies originally absorbed into the Auto-Union.

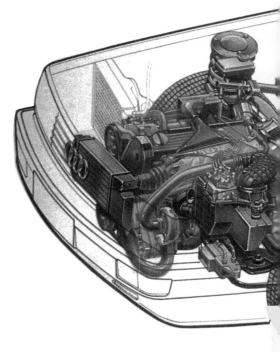

Above: 20-valve Quattro Coupé provides 220bhp

Above: Five-cylinder 100 Avant 2.3E

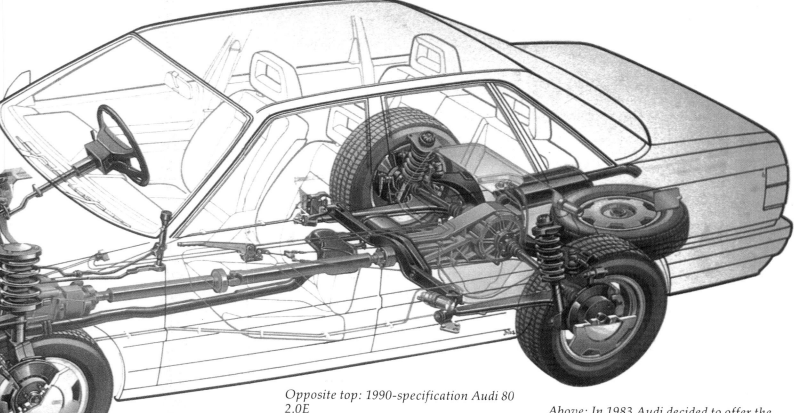

Opposite top: 1990-specification Audi 80 2.0E
Opposite centre: The turbocharged five-cylinder 100 saloon
Opposite bottom: 170bhp Coupé Quattro 20V

Above: In 1983 Audi decided to offer the Audi 200 with a four-wheel-drive system derived from the company's Quattro rally cars. In this form the 200 enjoys excellent traction and very good handling.

Audi's rapid improvement during the 1980s continued with a vengeance into the next decade. The 80 and 90 range of 1986 continued unchanged until 1991 when they received a face-lift. The 90 tag, previously used to denote the use of a five-cylinder engine, was dropped and all cars were badged as 80s with models being indicated simply by their engine size. Four- and five-cylinder models remained largely unchanged but the new updated car was available with a 2.8-litre V6 giving 174bhp. The four-wheel-drive Quattro models were continued and were available with both the V6 and the 137bhp 2.0-litre 16-valve engine.

The replacement of the famous turbo-charged Quattro and its lesser (non-turbocharged) brother, the Coupé, was

Left: The Audi A6, launched in 1997, was good enough to frighten BMW. It competed directly with the BMW 5-series, which had also been updated in the same year

Right: Top of Audi's range was the A8. It used a 4.2-litre V8 in an all-aluminium bodyshell

Middle right: Audi's estate cars were always well regarded. This is a 1997 A4 estate

Bottom right: The A3 gave Audi a new entry-level car to attract a new breed of younger potential Audi buyers

Below: The 1997 Audi Cabriolet range. There was a 2.0-litre four and two V6s, one at 2.6 litres, the other at 2.8 litres

launched in 1988. The handsome new Coupé was based on 80/90 running gear and used the same four- and five-cylinder engines. The most potent model was the 230bhp S2 Quattro, but it lacked its predecessor's brutal appeal. The Coupé was dropped in 1995.

The revolutionary Audi 100 of 1983, famous for its low Cd of 0.30, was also updated in 1991. It gained the V6 engine and more aggressive styling. The similarly-bodied 200 was dropped in favour of a new model, the V8, sharing the 100's new bodyshell. A blatant attempt to rival the range-topping models of BMW and Lexus, the Audi lacked the sporting character of the former and the refinement of the latter.

The company's next attempt at a large executive express was a great deal more successful. Launched in early 1994, the new alloy-bodied car was initially available in front-wheel-drive 2.8 V6 or 4.2-litre engine Quattro forms. A 3.7-litre V8 arrived in 1995 and a new 30-valve 2.8-litre V6 the following year. Top of the range in 1997 was the 340bhp S8 with standard four-wheel-drive. The high-tech A8 had the presence and ability to rival the world's finest prestige vehicles.

Audi launched its first cabriolet in 1991. Also based on the 80/90 range, the Cabriolet was available with four- or six-cylinder engines. Appeal and sales were enhanced by the fact that Princess Diana drove one.

Audi's range underwent another great change late in 1994 with the launch of the

Above: The Audi Cabriolet, launched at the 1991 Geneva Motor Show, rose to fame as the car chosen by Princess Diana in preference to a Mercedes convertible. It was launched only with the four-cylinder engine

Right and top right: The sharply-styled A4, launched in 1994, was the successor to the old 80. It was a best-seller for Audi in the mid-1990s and was widely praised by the motoring press

Below: The A3 was a fashionable hatchback and used the next-generation Volkswagen Golf platform. The 1.8-litre four-cylinder engine had five valves per cylinder and gave 125bhp. The turbodiesel gave a healthy 90bhp

A4 and A6, to replace the 80 and 100 models. These sharply-styled new cars offered top-notch levels of ride and refinement, first-rate build quality, and were a huge improvement on their predecessors.

To complete the range, Audi added the hatchback A3, based on the floorpan of the fourth generation VW Golf and with styling that closely related it to the rest of the range.

The A6 was updated in 1997 with new sharper styling, improved ride and roadholding and better performance. This was a car to worry even Mercedes and BMW.

By the late 1990s, Audi's image was right up with BMW and the company's cars were considered as stylish alternatives to the other German luxury brands.

Austin

Great Britain 1905-1989

As a young man Herbert Austin (later Lord Austin) emigrated to Australia, where he met Frederick Wolseley, and joined the Wolseley Sheep Shearing Company. On returning to the U.K. he built his first car – a three-wheeler – for Wolseley. He also built other Wolseleys but the first Austin emerged in 1905, from Longbridge, Birmingham, home of Austins thereafter. It was a chain-driven,

four-speed 25/30hp vehicle, with a four-cylinder engine featuring detachable valve covers to allow easy access to the valves.

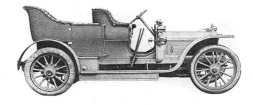

Above: 1905 25/30hp Endcliffe Phaeton

This very first car proved itself in reliability events, including the 1906 Scottish Trial.

Austin produced single-, four- and

six-cylinder cars in the early years, the biggest of which was a 9.7-litre 60hp model. The most popular of these Austins was the Twenty, with a Ten being introduced in 1910. Austin also built Gladiators for the home market, and a 1600cc ten-horsepower model, initially for export only.

By 1914, the largest 30hp Austin featured an electrically operated starter and electric lights.

Above: 1914 Vitesse Phaeton
Below: 1920 four-cylinder 20hp tourer

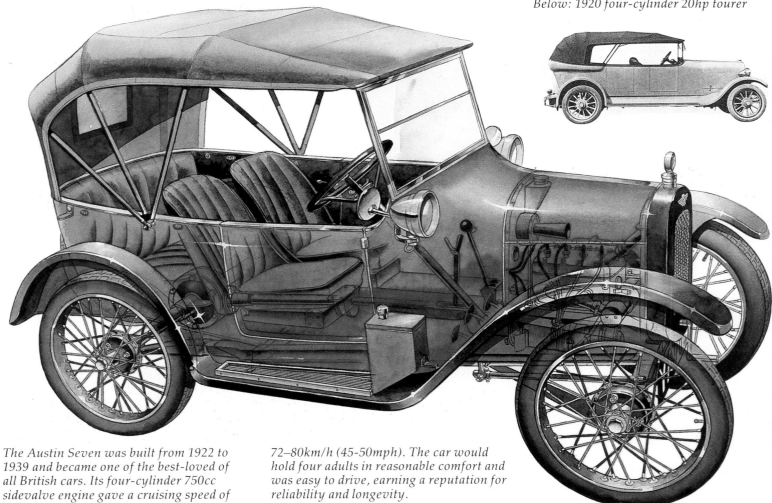

The Austin Seven was built from 1922 to 1939 and became one of the best-loved of all British cars. Its four-cylinder 750cc sidevalve engine gave a cruising speed of *72–80km/h (45-50mph). The car would hold four adults in reasonable comfort and was easy to drive, earning a reputation for reliability and longevity.*

After World War I, Austin built just the four-cylinder Twenty, with a 3.6-litre sidevalve engine. This model was produced until 1929. Another long-lived model, the 1.7-litre Twelve, joined the Twenty in 1921, and was built until 1936, although with an enlarged (1.9-litre) engine from 1927.

A six-cylinder, 3.4-litre Twenty model was introduced in 1927, and a smaller, 2.3-litre Sixteen in 1928.

The most famous pre-World War II car of all, the Austin Seven, was introduced in 1922, with all but the earliest examples having a 747cc sidevalve four-cylinder engine developing 13bhp.

Above: The prototype Austin Seven
Below: Austin 20 tourer, c. 1927

The tough and reliable Seven was built in many versions, including tourers and saloons, and was built under licence in other countries, including France, Germany, the U.S.A. and Japan. The last 750cc Austin Seven was the Ruby, first introduced in 1934, and built until 1938, by which time Austin had introduced a larger Seven – the longer-wheelbase 900cc 'Big Seven'. However, the Ruby's engine was built under licence by Reliant until 1962.

Another Austin to find favour among many families was the famous Ten. First introduced in 1932, the model was steadily developed throughout the 1930s. The 1937 model was known as the Cambridge, and by 1939 the Ten had bodywork of semi-integral construction, as had the smaller (900cc) Eight. Power for the Ten was from an 1125cc engine developing 32bhp (later models), and giving a top speed of around 65mph (104km/h).

Austin built similarly-styled Twelves, Fourteens, Sixteens, Eighteens and Twenty-Eights until the late 1930s.

Below: Popular 14hp Ascot cabriolet, 1938

Above: Austin 10 saloon, launched in 1932
Below: 10hp Sherbourne Saloon, 1936

After World War II, Austin re-introduced the Eight, Ten and Twelve, as well as a similar-looking Sixteen, which used 1940 Austin Twelve chassis/bodywork, but which featured an overhead-valve 2.2-litre engine. The engine remained in use until the late 1960s in the four-wheel-drive Austin Gipsy, and also in Austin Taxis.

In 1947 a new luxury mode, the four-litre A125 Sheerline, was introduced, the first Austin with independent front suspension. A larger derivative was the A135 Princess, with triple carburettors.

Above: A90 Atlantic c. 1947
Above right: 1951 A40 Devon

The first all-new post-war family Austin was the 1200cc A40 Devon/Dorset (two or four doors respectively) introduced in late 1947. The A40 helped Britain's export drive of the late 1940s. The car was followed a year later by the A70 Hampshire, powered by the Austin Sixteen's engine. All the new Austins of this era were to be designated by their approximate brake horsepower output, rather than by the previously used R.A.C. rating method.

In 1949 the 2.6-litre, four-cylinder A90 Atlantic coupé was introduced, aimed at the American market. In 1951 the A70 was rebodied and named the Hereford, and a Jensen-built aluminium-bodied sports version of the A40 was introduced. The next year, the A40 Somerset, with similar styling to the Hereford, replaced the Devon and Dorset.

The 1952 model year saw the creation of the British Motor Corporation, following the merger of Austin and Morris, and the introduction of an important new Austin Seven – the A30. It had unitary-construction bodywork, with styling similar to that of the larger Austins, and a scaled-down (800cc) version of the A40's

1200cc engine. Unusual for so small a car, it was initially available only in four-door form.

In 1954 a new A40 (Cambridge) was announced, together with a larger-engined, 1489cc A50, which used identical bodywork. The A90 was a larger version, powered by a 2.6-litre six-cylinder engine.

Developments of these models were the A55 and A95/A105 saloons, from 1956 on. In that year the A35 was announced with a stronger 948cc engine and a more precise remote gearchange among other improvements.

The Metropolitan, originally produced for the American market in 1.2-litre form, was sold in the U.K. with the A50's engine and a three-speed gearbox, from 1957.

In 1958 the rubber-suspension Gipsy was introduced, along with the Farina-styled A40, which used A35 running gear. A 'hatchback' Countryman (estate-car) version was also available.

The A55, in Mark II form, was also styled by Farina from 1959, as was the A99 Westminster, now with a three-litre engine.

The most notable introduction of 1959 was, of course, the revoluntary Mini. Designed by Alec Issigonis (later Sir Alec), it provided four seats and reasonable comfort yet also had a miserly thirst for fuel.

Available under both Austin (Seven)

Above: The well-appointed A125 Sheerline
Below: A110 Westminster superseded A99

and Morris (Mini Minor) designations, the Mini featured a transversely mounted engine, sitting on top of the gearbox/differential unit, and driving tiny (ten-inch) front wheels. Underneath the box-like body the suspension was by rubber cones and the distinctive 'wheel-at-each-corner' design afforded excellent roadholding.

For use in the Mini, B.M.C.'s A Series

Above: 1964 Mini-Cooper 1275S

Above: 1300cc version of AD016

Above: 1982 Austin Mini Metro City

engine was derated to 848cc and 34bhp, although the car's light weight meant it was still capable of around 116km/h (72mph), and would reach 60mph from standstill in just over 20 seconds.

In 1960, the Mini van was introduced, as were the estate-car versions – the Traveller (Morris) and Countryman (Austin), which initially featured wooden exterior bodywork trims.

Vanden Plas Princess versions of Austins were always built to a high specification, and the three-litre model of 1960 was no exception. From 1964 a four-litre Rolls-Royce-engined Princess was available.

For 1961, the handy pickup version of the Mini was introduced, as was the first Mini-Cooper. In 997cc form, it produced 55bhp and was capable of 145km/h (90mph). Coopers later used engines of 998cc, 1071cc (making 68bhp in the Cooper S), and 1275cc (making 76bhp in the 1275S). The latter had a top speed of 160km/h (100mph), and would accelerate from rest to 96km/h (60mph) in just over 11 seconds.

Extremely successful in competition, the 1275S gained famous victories in the Monte Carlo Rallies of 1964, 1965, and 1966. And a short-stroke version of this car, the 64bhp 970S, was used with success in the under-1000cc classes of motor sport.

The Wolseley Hornet and Riley Elf were announced for the 1962 model year, these being badge-engineered luxury versions of the Mini. Also for 1962, the A55 was developed into the 1622cc A60, and the

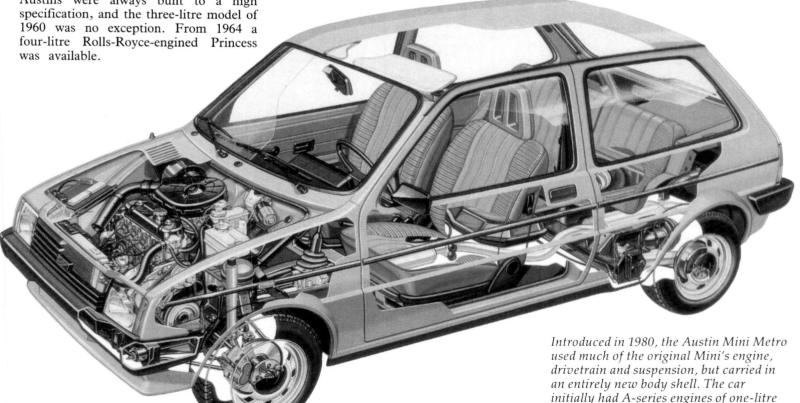

Introduced in 1980, the Austin Mini Metro used much of the original Mini's engine, drivetrain and suspension, but carried in an entirely new body shell. The car initially had A-series engines of one-litre or 1.3-litre capacity, but by 1990 the 16-valve K-series unit was available.

A110 Westminster was introduced. Late in 1962 the A40 received the 48bhp 1098cc version of the A-Series engine.

In 1964 the Austin version of BMC's front-wheel-drive 1100 saloon was introduced, and subsequent developments of it followed those of the similar Morris models. Another front-wheel-drive Austin – the large and comfortable 1800 – arrived for 1965.

The Austin 3-litre was announced in October 1967. It was a luxurious car with body styling similar to that of the 1800, but with a 2.9-litre six-cylinder engine driving the rear wheels.

The A60 was discontinued in early 1969, and a new front-wheel-drive model arrived in April 1969 – the versatile five-door Maxi hatchback, powered by a new B-Series overhead-camshaft four-cylinder engine of 1485cc, driving through a five-speed gearbox. A 1750cc engine was available from September 1970.

In September 1969 an uprated 1800 model was introduced – the twin carburettor 'S'.

The Mini 1275S gave way to the less aggressive 1275 GT in 1969, two years after the entire Mini range had been updated with Mark II models. These were essentially similar to the earlier cars, but had a larger glass area, and the option of the 998cc engine as already used in the Riley Elf and Wolseley Hornet (which were discontinued in 1969).

Also in 1969, the Mini Clubman was introduced with the 998cc power unit and a slightly different body shell which featured an extended bonnet line and front wings and concealed door hinges.

For 1970 the Mini was given individual-make status. The Clubman gained the 48bhp 1098cc A Series engine for 1975, and the Mini's 848cc unit finally disappeared in 1980, to be universally replaced by the 998cc engine.

The early 1970s saw the introduction of a new front-wheel-drive saloon – the 1973

three-door (and, later, five-door) Metro hatchback, developed from Mini design but featuring gas suspension. Power was from A-Plus Series engines of 998cc or 1275cc capacity.

Despite competition from the Metro and many other modern small cars, the Mini continued to sell well during the 1980s, special-edition models and its anachronistic styling broadening its appeal.

The Princess was developed into the hatchback Ambassador range from March 1982, the top-of-the-range model being the Vanden Plas.

A new five-door hatchback, the Maestro, appeared in March 1983, with a choice of 1275cc A-Plus, or overhead-camshaft 1598cc R-Series engines.

In April 1984 a new Austin saloon – the Montego – was introduced, with 1275cc (A-Plus) 1598cc (overhead-camshaft S-Series) or 1993cc (O-Series) engines. The S-Series engine was fitted to Maestros from July 1984.

Above: Metro GTi, 16V launched in May 1990
Right: 1990 diesel-engined Maestro

Below: The Mini, still being built over 30 years after its launch
Below right: Montego saloon, popular with the fleet market

Allegro, to replace the 1100/1300 range. The Allegro was available with a choice of 1.1- or 1.3-litre (A Series) or 1.5- or 1.7-litre (E-Series) engines.

In 1975 the wedge-shaped Princess saloons were introduced. The initial choice of engine was between the 1798cc B-Series or 2227cc E-Series units. From July 1978 the overhead-camshaft O-Series engines were fitted, in 1695cc or 1993cc forms.

The next all-new Austin was the

Austin-Healey

Great Britain 1953–1971

Cornishman Donald Healey was interested in motoring and motor sport from an early age. After being invalided out of the Royal Flying Corps in 1917, he set up his own garage, before building a successful career in the motor industry. He started work with Riley in 1931.

In the meantime he had already achieved a number of successes in trials and rallying, and his participation in major events continued throughout the 1930s.

Healey hatched his ideas of producing his own car during World War II, and a prototype Healey was produced in 1945, at the Benford factory in Warwick. The 2.4-litre Riley-powered car had coil-spring/trailing-arm suspension, torque-tube transmission and, in production form, a choice of saloon or open two-seater bodywork. The saloon version was, in fact, the fastest production saloon in the world at the time, having a top speed of nearly 105mph (168km/h).

The model was developed from its original A-type, through B-, C-, D-, E- and F-types, until 1951.

As a result of co-operation between Healey and the American Nash-Kelvinator company, a new model – the Nash-Healey – was introduced in 1950, using a 3.8–litre six-cylinder Nash power unit. A restyled version with a 4.1-litre engine was also produced.

In 1951, a G-type convertible was produced, fitted with a three-litre Alvis engine.

By the end of the same year Donald Healey and his son Geoffrey had decided to produce a new sports car, and they approached Austin, who duly provided the engine and running gear – all from the A90 Atlantic, powered by a four-cylinder 2.7-litre overhead-valve unit. The Gerry

Right: Known originally simply as the Healey 100, the Austin-Healey 100 was introduced at the 1952 Earls Court Motor Show. The car took its four-cylinder overhead-valve engine and running gear from the Austin A90 Atlantic saloon.

Above: 100 BN2, unveiled in 1952

Below: First 'Frogeye' Sprite

Above: Last of the big Healeys was the 1959 3000

Coker-styled car – the Healey 100 – had two-seater bodywork, and this fast, sleek model made its debut at the 1952 Earls Court Motor Show.

B.M.C. – under Leonard Lord – adopted the design, and the production car became the Austin-Healey 100 from 1953. Changes were later made to the transmission, including the fitting of a

four-speed gearbox. The aluminium-bodied, disc-braked 100S model arrived in 1955, as did the 100M, with a Le Mans specification engine.

The 100 Six model was introduced in 1956, fitted with B.M.C.'s six-cylinder

C-Type engine of 2.6 litres and producing 102bhp. The car was developed into the 2.9-litre Austin-Healey 3000 of 1959, this model giving 124bhp and a top speed of nearly 120mph (193km/h). A triple-carburettor 132bhp Mark II version was introduced in 1961, and this continued in production, with minor modifications, until 1967, when the last so-called 'Big Healey' was built.

In the meantime, Austin-Healey had produced its small two-seater sports car, the Sprite, launched in May 1958. The car, designed by Geoffrey Healey and Gerry Coker, cleverly used many of the running gear components of the then-current Austin A35, including the front suspension, engine and transmission. Morris Minor-type rack-and-pinion steering was employed.

The engine was uprated by the use of twin carburettors to develop 43bhp (34bhp in the A35), giving a top speed of 85mph (136km/h). The distinctive styling of the original Sprite included headlamps mounted on top of the bonnet, giving rise to the universally adopted nickname of 'Frogeye'.

The Sprite was updated in 1961, the Mark II versions sharing restyled, flatter bodywork with the new M.G. Midget. The 948cc engine was retained, a higher compression ratio allowing it to produce another 6bhp. B.M.C.'s 1098cc A-Series engine, developing 56bhp, was fitted in 1963, and disc brakes were now employed at the front.

The specification was again revised in early 1964; the Mark III cars featured wind-up side windows, a new dashboard and semi-elliptic rear springs instead of the previous quarter-elliptics.

The last Austin-Healey Sprite was the Mark IV. Introduced for 1967, the new model was powered by a 65bhp version of the 1275cc A-Series engine, giving a top speed of well over 90mph (145km/h). The last Austin-Healey Sprite was built in 1971, although the similar M.G. Midgets continued in production.

Above: 1958 100/6 with C-type engine

Below: 1958 Sprite with 948cc engine

Above: 1963 ex-works 3000 Mk III

Below: 1967 ex-works Sprite in racing trim

Austro-Daimler

Austria
1899–1936

In 1899 the Vienna company, Bierenz-Fischer & Co., agreed to build 100 Daimler cars a year under licence from the German manufacturer in Cannstatt. Production from this new company, Österreichische Daimler Motoren AG, was poor, however, resulting in Daimler's son Paul being sent to organize matters in 1902.

Above: 1909 Austro-Daimler charabanc

Following this the Austrian company separated from its parent (although full financial independence was not achieved until 1906) and in 1903 Ferdinand Porsche took over as director. Porsche was full of new ideas but these took time to put into operation, and the company agreed to build the unexciting Maja cars for Emile Jellinek, consul-general of the Austro-Hungarian Empire in Nice. This

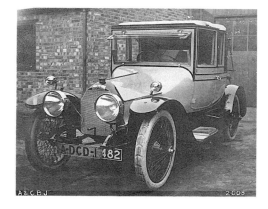

Above: 25/30hp Austro-Daimler tourer

continued until 1914.

In the meantime, Porsche introduced a couple of well-made standard designs until his 1910 Prince Henry Tour winner, of the same name, gave the company an international reputation. All links with the German firm were then dropped and the cars officially took on the name Austro-Daimler in 1911. It was that same year that a Porsche-designed car won the Austrian Alpine Tour, and by the outbreak of World War I the Vienna firm was Austria's biggest car manufacturer.

During the war Austro-Daimler made military vehicles, some of which were

Below: The first new post-war Austro-Daimler fast tourer, the 1921 AD 617, was powered by a six-cylinder 4.4-litre single-overhead-cam engine.

Above: c. 1919 Sascha racing voiturette

interchangeable between road and railway, and afterwards a number of the earlier cars were assembled in Liège from pre-war parts as Alfa-Legias. As well as reworking some of the pre-war designs, Austro-Daimler introduced some exciting fast tourers which were also successful in motor sport.

Unhappy, Porsche returned to Daimler in 1923, being replaced by Karl Rabe. In 1925 Austro-Daimler became connected with Austro-Fiat, also of Vienna, then three years later it merged with Puch-Werke to become Austro-Daimler-Puchwerke.

By 1935 that company's six-year association with Steyr-Werke, and the similarity between the two products, lead their joint bankers to force an amalgamation as Steyr-Daimler-Puch. By the following year the Austro-Daimler name had disappeared.

Above: 1931 4.6-litre ADR8

Ballot

France
1919–1933

Ernest Ballot gained his engineering experience with the merchant marine, founding Ballot et Cie in Paris in 1906 to build marine engines. By the outbreak of war in 1914 he had expanded into cars, producing commercial and competition engines for Delage, Mass and La Licorne, having formed the Etablissements Ballot in 1910. Ballot was administration director of this company, with financial backing coming from people such as Adolphe Clément, Fernand Charron and Pierre Forgeot, the last-named a future government minister.

Above: 1922 two-litre Grand Prix car
Left: 1924 overhead-camshaft 2LT tourer

The first of Ballot's own racing cars, equipped with an eight-cylinder engine of 4.9-litres capacity, appeared at the end of World War I for the 1919 Indianapolis 500 race. It was designed by Ernest Henry, famous for his pre-war competition Peugeots. In 1921 Henry designed a three-litre car for Ballot especially for the French Grand Prix, and Ballot also developed a two-litre four-cylinder racer. A limited number of purely road-going vehicles, based on that car and with extraordinary performance, soon followed. The same year a more practical fast tourer was also produced, almost unique in France at that time.

Three years later a tuned tourer was offered, this designed by Henry's successor, Fernand Vadier, who had left Panhard to join Ballot's marine-diesel department just after the war. Vadier himself left Ballot in 1926 to sell Dewandre servo-operated brakes to the car manufacturing industry.

A six-cylinder car appeared in 1927, with a 2.6-litre straight-eight being launched at that year's Paris Salon, Ballot's first of that design since his Grand Prix cars of 1921. This was further developed into a three-litre car in 1930, but unfortunately by then the Depression had

Above: 1926 2LT saloon

Above: 1928 2LTS

Below: 2.6-litre straight-eight RH saloon

reduced the demand for such vehicles. Sales slumped, Ballot was fired by Forgeot and the company was taken over by Hispano-Suiza in 1930. A Ballot chassis was used with a Hispano-Suiza engine for the Junior, which was produced in the old Ballot works until their closure in 1933.

Below: The 2LS, Ballot's first road-going car, was developed from a straight-eight racer, built for the French Grand Prix in 1921. It was fitted with brakes on all wheels.

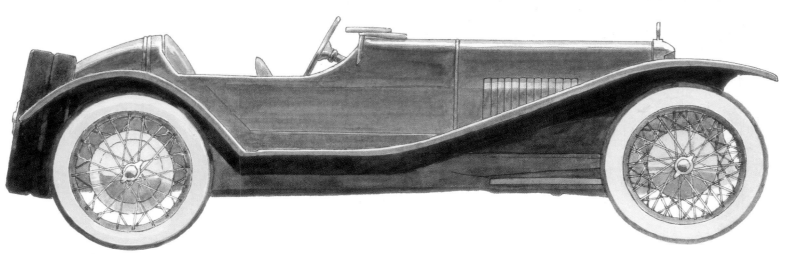

Bentley

Great Britain
1921 to date

Walter Owen Bentley started out as a railway apprentice, but progressed to racing motorcycles and then to distributing the French D.F.P. car in London. Successful modifications he designed for the D.F.P. persuaded him to design his own car in 1919, and the four-cylinder three-litre Bentley entered production in 1921.

Over the next ten years, the Bentley name signified expensive and powerful cars; the four-cylinder 4½-litre and its limited-production supercharged derivative in 1927 continued the line of sporting models, while the 1925 six-cylinder 6½-litre and its eight-litre successor of 1930 were designed for the carriage trade.

Below: The Bentley Super Sports, a variant of the legendary 3-litre model, had a distinctive tapering radiator. Its four-cylinder engine could take it up to 160km/h (100mph), but its handling was uncertain and only a few were built.

Bentley sales hard, however. In 1931, the company slid into receivership and was bought by Rolls-Royce.

The first new Bentley, built at the Rolls-Royce factory in Derby rather than Bentley's earlier Cricklewood, London, home, was the the 1933 3½-litre. This 'Silent Sports Car' was very different from the huge and muscular Bentleys which had gone before, having a tuned version of the contemporary Rolls-Royce 20/25 engine in a new chassis frame. When the 20/25 became a 25/30 in 1936, the Bentley followed suit and took the larger engine to become a 4¼-litre. When World War II put an end to production, Bentley had just introduced a new model called the Mark V, but only a handful were built.

Above left: 1925 Bentley three-litre tourer

Only the curiously undistinguished four-litre model of 1930 failed to enhance the marque's reputation.

Bentleys scored numerous racing and record-breaking successes, most notably five wins at Le Mans. But the cars were built in only small numbers and the cost of the racing programme was high. Massive losses in 1924 were followed by liquidation and reorganization of the company in 1925, and only the intervention of the millionaire sportsman and Bentley racing driver Woolf Barnato put the company back on its feet. The Depression which followed the Wall Street Crash in 1929 hit

Above: 1927 4½-litre
Right: Eight-litre in-line six saloon
Below: Gurney Nutting-bodied 3½-litre
Bottom: 1938 model with 4½-litre chassis

Below: 1928 Bentley, 1961 Glidden Tour

Like Rolls-Royce, Bentley had only ever offered chassis before 1946, leaving bodywork to the customer's choice of coachbuilder. Careful rationalization for the post-war range, however, saw the Mark VI introduced with a 'standard-steel' saloon body made by Pressed Steel. Now built at Crewe, the post-war Bentleys were largely badge-engineered Rolls-Royce models (and their characteristics will be found under the entry for Rolls-Royce). All were made in far smaller numbers than their Rolls-Royce equivalents.

Nevertheless, there were always some differences between the ranges. Thus, Bentley never offered a large limousine model, and there was never a Rolls-Royce equivalent of the fabulous R-type

Below: The 1946 standard-bodied Mark VI

Above: The stunning 1951 S1 Continental
Below: 1953 R-type Continental

Below: One of the last cars to be built before the company's collapse and takeover by Rolls-Royce was a four-cylinder sports car, the 4½-litre.

Continental introduced in 1952. Continental versions of the S-type introduced in 1955 had better performance than the standard models, but there was none of the Bentley sporting heritage evident in them.

After 1982, Bentley was revitalized as a separate marque through new models for which there was no direct Rolls-Royce equivalent: the Eight and the Mulsanne Turbo, for example, both derived from the Roll-Royce Silver Spirit first seen in 1980. The revised Turbo R model for 1985 indicated the way Bentley would go in the future, blending the sumptuous luxury of Crewe's best with very high performance and superb handling; a return, in fact, to the Bentley characteristics of the 1920s and 1930s.

Above: The T-series, the first monocoque
Below: The turbo 1989 Bentley Eight

Bentley went further to separate its range from that of Rolls-Royce with the introduction of the Continental R in 1991. This two-door coupé version of the Turbo R helped to rebuild the company's image as a manufacturer of high-quality sporting vehicles. The name, too, conjured up memories of one of the greatest post-war grand touring Bentleys, the Continental R of 1952. Rolls-Royce offered no two-door car in their own range.

The car's sporting appeal was further enhanced with a smaller version of the Continental, named the Continental T, launched in 1996.

In early June 1998, Volkswagen bought the parent company Rolls-Royce (see Rolls-Royce entry). The new Arnage model was by then touring the world's roads with a BMW V-8 engine, plus much other technology. The inclusion of Cosworth Engineering in the deal was relied upon for an extra £120m by VW to solve the engine problem which was scheduled to arise a year later, when BMW pulled the plug.

Top right: The 1997 Bentley Turbo R

Middle Right: The two-door Continental T

Below: 1997 Bentley Brooklands R

Above: The Azure was Bentley's only convertible during the 1990s

Below: The Continental T had the most powerful engine in the range at 405bhp

Benz

Germany
1885–1926

Karl Benz had worked as a young man for a Stuttgart carriage builder, but the burgeoning gas-engine industry tempted him to design his own two-stroke stationary engine and to join a modest but established stationary-engine enterprise. His next step was to secure financial backing and to set up on his own in the stationary-engine business in Mannheim.

Benz soon became interested in combining his knowledge of the carriage trade with his expertise in stationary engines to build a self-propelled vehicle. Using petrol instead of gas as fuel, he built his first car – generally considered to have been the first in the world – in 1885.

The engine for the 1885 Tricycle was a single-cylinder four-stroke of one horsepower, producing a maximum speed of 16km/h (10mph).

Benz continued experimenting and refining this invention for the next five years, and began limited car production in 1890. He was joined in that year by two partners who relieved him of the responsibility for sales and administration, leaving him free to deal with technical innovation. This permitted rapid progress

Above: Model 3 vis-à-vis *car*
Below: 1892 Benz Viktoria

Below: 1901 single-cylinder sports

from the original three-wheeled designs to a four-wheeler called the Viktoria in 1891, and four years later Benz developed a van and bus from the basic design. Meanwhile, the technical advances of the expensive Viktoria had been adapted to a much cheaper model known as the Velo and introduced in 1894. This was the world's first series-production car.

The company continued to introduce new models and by the end of the decade it had built 2,000 cars and had a production capacity of 600 cars a year. In addition, it had sales agencies in several far-flung countries. All this was sufficient to make the Benz company the world's leading motor manufacturer at the turn of the century. Yet Benz himself was a man of conservative disposition, and his designs rapidly became outmoded as motor-car development progressed by leaps and bounds. In an attempt to halt the resulting sales decline, Benz's sales director engaged another designer to build a new model which went on sale in 1902. This provoked a rift: Benz left his own company a year later, was persuaded to rejoin briefly in 1905, but then left for good in 1906.

Above: 1894 rear-engined Velo
Below: 1895 Benz omnibus

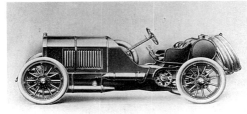

Above: 1908 four-cylinder Grand Prix car
Left: 1903 twin-cylinder Sport-Phaeton
Below left: 1905-7 four-cylinder tourer

This left the ailing company under the guidance of its chief engineer, Hans Nibel, who believed that motor racing would both lead to technical improvements and gather the publicity which would restore the Benz fortunes. A comeback began in 1907, and by 1909 sufficient technical progress had been made for the company to build the 200bhp Blitzen-Benz, which broke the World Land Speed Record that year and held it until 1922.

Under Nibel, the Benz company introduced a wide range of road cars, which sold to an increasingly broad market, and in 1914 it introduced its first six-cylinder model. Wartime saw the inevitable concentration on trucks and

Right: 1918 6/18 had a four-cylinder ohc engine
Below: The 1909 Blitzen-Benz was powered by a 21,495cc four-cylinder Benz airship engine developing 200bhp at 1300rpm.

aero-engines, but when peace returned in 1918 the Benz company faced problems. Germany's economy had been shattered, and the car market was slow to recover. Although there were brave attempts at publicity through racing – notably with the rear-engined Tropfenwagen of 1923 – the road cars were mainly conventional vehicles derived from a 1914 design.

Germany was gripped by serious inflation after 1923, and it rapidly became apparent that either the Benz company or its rivals at Daimler would go under. In 1924, the two companies reached a co-operative agreement, and in 1926 they merged as the Daimler-Benz Aktiengesellschaft (*see Mercedes-Benz*).

Left: 1909-13 four-cylinder 14/30   *Above: 1923 Tropfenwagen Grand Prix*

Berliet

France 1895–1939

The firm of Berliet, based in Lyon, France, began producing cars as early as 1895. Small numbers were produced in the early years, but the cars were advanced for their time, with wheel-controlled steering and four-speed gearboxes. Power came from a rear-mounted engine.

Right: 1901 Type B with chain drive
Far right: 1908 Double Phaeton

Below: A post World War One four-cylinder sidevalve-engined car producing 16hp.

In 1901 the firm of Audibert-Lavirotte came under Berliet's wing, and the range of cars was enlarged – two- and four-cylinder models were now available.

Berliet concentrated on large cars for several years from 1902, producing, for example, 40hp (6.3-litre), 60hp (8.6-litre) and 80hp (11-litre) models. Berliets of this period were built on pressed-steel chassis and many featured overhead inlet valves. Indeed, they were similar in concept and layout to the grand Mercedes of the period.

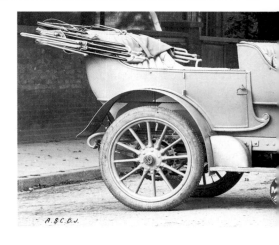

Shaft-drive chassis were available from 1907, and Berliet offered a wide range of models until the outbreak of World War I, with engines ranging from small twin-cylinder units to very large sixes.

After the war the company built sidevalve-engined four-cylinder cars,

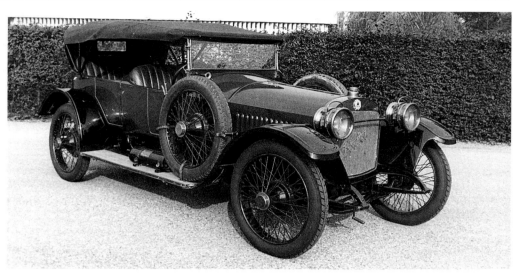

Above: 1906 22hp car
Below: 1919 overhead-valve Berliet VB

Peugeot 402 bodywork.

No Berliet cars were produced after the war, although the company was already – and continues to be – a highly successful commercial vehicle manufacturer.

Above: 1911 four-cylinder 22hp car
Below left: 1923 Model VI
Below: 1936 2-litre Dauphine
Bottom: The last Berliet car was a 1937 2-litre Dauphine

although by the mid-1920s innovative features such as four-speed gearboxes, front-wheel brakes and overhead valves were appearing in the specifications of some Berliets, notably the 1200cc 10/20 and the four-litre 23/70 models.

The late 1920s saw a mixture of sidevalve- and overhead-valve engines being used, in capacities ranging from 1.5 litres (four cylinders) to 4.1 litres (six cylinders).

In 1933 came the introduction of the 1600cc 9CV (or, optionally, two-litre 11CV) Type 944, with American-influenced styling. Deluxe models had independent front suspension, while overhead- or sidevalve-engine options were available initially.

The last Berliet saloon was the Dauphine, built from 1936. Chassis design was advanced, with rack-and-pinion steering, independent front suspension and a synchromesh gearbox. As World War II approached, Berliet bought bodies from Peugeot, so the last Dauphines had

Bignan

France
1919–1931

Although Jacques Bignan first collaborated with Lucien Picker in 1911 to set up an engine firm at Courbevoie, Paris, their first completed car under the Bignan name did not appear until 1919. This was the 17CV, a big 3½-litre tourer which was actually produced in the Grégoire factory at Poissy, on a de la Fournaise chassis frame.

The 17CV's sidevalve engine was designed by Nemorin Causan, who had worked on early Delage competition engines and for Corre La Licorne. Causan also assisted development of engines for Bignan's own racing entries. In Bignan's first event, the Grand Prix de Voiturettes in 1920, however, he raced in a 1400cc T-head four-cylinder car which he had designed himself in 1914. The two cars finished second and third.

The 17CV's engine was enlarged to three litres in 1921. This car was marketed in England as the Grégoire-Campbell, but ceased production in 1923.

The 2-litre 11CV appeared in 1922, and

this was to provide the basis for the future Bignan range. In that year the company also introduced its famous desmodromic-valve racer. This system, where the valves were both opened *and* closed positively by means of cams, was never as successful as the company anticipated, and was dropped in favour of a more orthodox arrangement, winning the Spanish Touring Car Grands Prix two years running.

Together, Bignan and Causan successfully extracted higher performances from sidevalve engines designed before World War I. Their reputation was for producing vehicles with the evocative Bignan grille but with relatively cheap mechanical components. Their cars of the early 1920s often used proprietary Ballot, S.C.A.P. and C.I.M.E. engines, but the sporting image was kept up.

In 1924 a Bignan two-litre tourer won the Monte Carlo Rally, and competition entry remained strong until 1927, when a lower placing in the Spanish Touring Car event was to mark the company's last attempt; although Bignan himself continued racing, winning the 1928 Monte Carlo Rally in a Fiat.

By 1926 Bignan's financial situation was dire but the company was kept going by a trust until 1931, producing a rebadged E.H.P. as the Bignan-M.O.P.

Below: 1922 2-litre racer

BMW

Germany
1928 to date

The Bayerische Motoren Werke AG began life in Munich as a manufacturer of aircraft engines, and turned to motor-cycle production in 1923. That year's shaft-drive R-32 model became hugely successful, and motor cycles remain a BMW strength today.

Above: 1898-1900 Decauville-Wartburg

In 1928 the company diversified into car manufacture by taking over Dixi, who were already building the British Austin Seven under licence at Einsenach. This model was rapidly developed, initially as the BMW 3/15, and by 1933 the company was confident enough to introduce a six-cylinder model with a stretched wheelbase which betrayed none of its Austin Seven ancestry. Within a year, the six-cylinder engine had reached a capacity of 1.5 litres and the mundane saloons and tourers had been complemented by a sporting model called the 315.

Above: 1922 Dixi with 1.5-litre engine

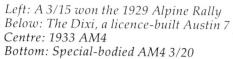

Left: A 3/15 won the 1929 Alpine Rally
Below: The Dixi, a licence-built Austin 7
Centre: 1933 AM4
Bottom: Special-bodied AM4 3/20

Above: 1933 303 with two doors
Below: The 1936 BMW 326 was powered by a 1971cc 50hp engine, and was in direct competition with the small Mercedes of the period.

The engine size was increased to two litres in 1935, and this powered the 1936 326, which was the decade's most significant model. This had a new chassis and flowing styling, and was to sire all the BMWs of the late 1930s. These included the 328 two-seater sports car of 1937, which quickly became a significant force in European road-racing, and the attractively styled 327 coupés and convertibles. The last pre-war development was the 3½-litre 334 of 1939, but only a few were built. These BMWs of the late 1930s were sold in Britain as Frazer-Nash BMWs.

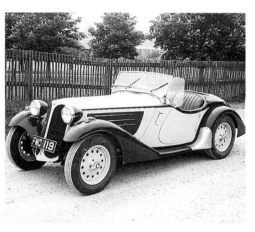

Top: 315 with 1490cc six-cylinder engine
Above: 1934 1.5-litre BMW Type 315

Above: The pre-war 315 roadster was capable of 100km/h (62mph)

BMW introduced the 328 in 1936. It set new standards in precision, roadholding and cornering, and took first place at the Nürburgring in June that year.

Left: 1939-41 335 saloon
Top: 1938 328, a much-admired sports car
Below: The 328 won the 1940 Mille Miglia

BMW hit serious difficulties after World War II, with its Munich factories bombed out and its Eisenach plant lost to East Germany. But motor-cycle production resumed in 1948, and booming sales financed the introduction of a new car in 1952: the 501 saloon. Its basic shape continued until 1964, gaining larger six-cylinder engines and a pair of V8s; and the drivetrains appeared after 1955 in sleek coupé models called 503s. Yet sales of all these expensive models, and of the excellent V8-engined 507 sports model of 1957 were slow. The money came from smaller BMWs, the Isetta bubble-car built under licence after 1955, and the rear-engined 700 after 1959.

Below: Four-door state car on 501 chassis

Above: 1952 six-cylinder 501

Below: 1956 V-8 507 roadster

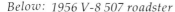

Above: The V8-engined 502 arrived in 1955

Below: Produced from 1955 the BMW 507 was a truly beautiful car which could reach a top speed of 200km/h (124mph). It had a five-speed gear box and an optional self-locking differential.

It was the medium-sized 1500 saloon of 1961 which saved BMW from bankruptcy. This initiated a series of high-quality four-cylinder models over the next decade, with engines ranging from 80bhp in the 1500 to 170bhp in the limited-production Turbo 2002, while there were two-door, four-door, cabriolet, and (after 1971) hatchback 'Touring' bodies.

Top left: 700 Cabriolet boasted 40bhp
Left: 1960 BMW Isetta derived from Italian Iso

Top: 1962 1500cc four-door saloon
Above: Bertone-styled 1962 3200CS
Below: 2002 Turbo offered 170bhp

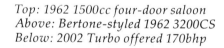

The success of this range made the acquisition of extra production capacity necessary and, in 1967, BMW bought the Glas company, into whose factory it expanded after a year or so of making modified Glas coupés as BMW 1600GTs. Meanwhile, the big coupé line was continued after 1965 by Bertone-styled models, and a six-cylinder engine arrived in 1968 to power a new range of larger saloons and a face-lifted coupé. By 1971, this engine had been stretched to three litres for both ranges, and to 3.2 litres for the saloons.

Above: 1971 2002 ti1 offered luxury with performance

For the 1970s and 1980s, BMW rationalized its model ranges. The '3' series would be medium-sized saloons, the '5' series executive saloons, the '7' series luxury saloons, and the '6' series big sporting coupés. Engines from 1.6 litres to 3.5 litres allowed a large choice of models.

Top: 1974 225km/h (140mph) 3.0 CSi
Above: 1971 2500 luxury saloon

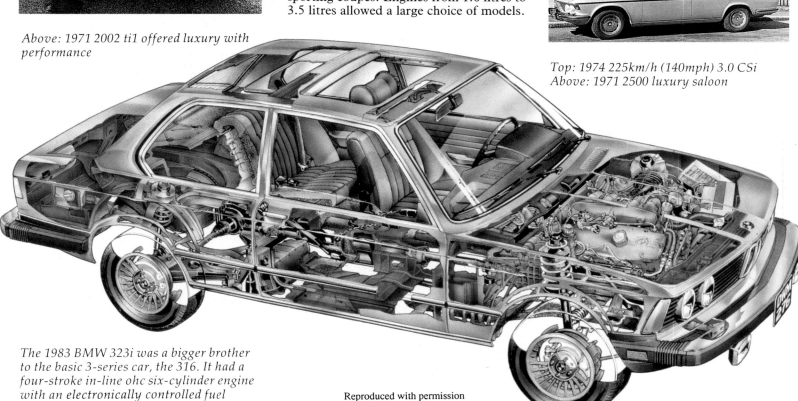

The 1983 BMW 323i was a bigger brother to the basic 3-series car, the 316. It had a four-stroke in-line ohc six-cylinder engine with an electronically controlled fuel injection system.

High-performance versions marketed under the Alpina banner after 1978, plus the 260km/h (162mph) mid-engined M1 coupé of 1979, promoted a sporting image. So too did the success of BMW's 1.5-litre turbocharged Formula One engine, which propelled Nelson Piquet's Brabham to the world driver's crown in 1981 and 1983, and the marketing of 'M' cars (M3, M5, M535i, M635 Csi) which were built by BMW's Motorsport department.

Right and below: Two views of this fast mid-engine sports car, the BMW M1
Bottom: The 528i executive express

Above: 1983 two-door 323i
Left: 628 CSi coupé
Below: 732i four-door saloon

An internal rival to this department, the BMW Technik think-tank division, designed and produced the Z1 two-seat sports car which went on sale in 1989. Meant to continue the tradition of low-volume high-technology roadsters established by the 328 and 507, it employs the 170bhp 2.5-litre straight-six engine of the 325i.

Above: 1990 8-series coupé

BMW's most significant move as it prepared for the 1990s was the introduction of all-new '5', '7' and '8' series cars (the latter replacing the '6'). The '5' was instantly acclaimed for its well-sorted chassis and refinement; the top-line '7', the 750iL with its 300bhp 5.0-litre V12, presented a convincing challenge to German market leader Mercedes-Benz; and the similarly powered 850i 2+2-seater sports coupé, artificially limited to 250km/h (155mph) but capable of 274km/h (170mph) emphasized BMW's determination to achieve technical supremacy over Mercedes.

Based around the company's outstanding 170bhp six-cylinder engine from the 325i, the sleek Z1 has scintillating performance and superb handling.

A new 3-series arrived for 1990. Initially available only in four-door saloon form, the new car had smoother, more contemporary lines and featured the Z-axle rear suspension developed on the Z1 roadster. Engines remained the same, with a choice of four- and six-cylinder units from 1.6 to 2.5 litres. BMW followed the saloon with a two-door coupé in 1992, and in the same year brought out a new sporting M3 with a 286bhp 3.0-litre engine and later a 321bhp 3.2-litre version, making it one of the fastest production BMWs ever built. The range was further expanded with cabriolet and touring (estate) models, as well as a new hatchback version called the Compact.

The old 2.5-litre in-line six engine was replaced in 1995 for a new more efficient and lighter alloy 2.8-litre version. The 2.8 possessed plenty of low-down torque making the 3 series a very relaxed and swift car.

The often-forgotten but highly competent 5-series range was expanded with the introduction of the four-wheel-drive 525ix Touring – a useful go-anywhere load carrier

Above: The M3 was a true status symbol of the 1990s and gave 321bhp

Below: The 3-series Compact provided a cheap entry-level car for younger buyers

Above: The M3 Evolution was also available in four-door form from 1995

with fine road manners. New V8 engines became available in 1992, in 3- and 4-litre forms. These new power units displaced the larger capacity straight-six motors. The 5-series was completely revamped for the end of 1995 to much acclaim from the motoring press. Some magazines even described it as the greatest car in the world. It was certainly the finest car available in its class.

The luxurious 7-series received its face-lift in 1994 and gained the new 3.5- and 4.5-litre V8 engines in 1996. Despite its advanced technical specification, high performance and fine chassis, the 8 -series was never a big seller. A smaller V8-engined derivative helped sales a little, due to a lower price and similar performance to the V12-

Above: The 5-series estate was available from 1991. This is a 1997 model

Right: The 3-series Touring didn't offer as much space as many rivals but still sold well

engined version.

A high price had also adversely affected the Z1 sports car, forcing BMW to bring production to an end in the early 1990s. But the company had not given up on the sports car yet. In 1995 the Z3 was launched. It was based on the 3-series compact, meaning it didn't even carry the Z-axle its name suggested and was initially available with either a 1.8- or 1.9-litre engine. Cries for more power soon led to the introduction of a 2.8-litre model and later a fire-breathing M3-engined version.

The Z3 was the first car to be built in BMW's new American factory, based at Spartanburg, South Carolina.

Top: The 5-series was updated in 1997 and set new standards of refinement

Right: The V12-engined 850 was joined by the cheaper V8 840 in 1993

Above: The new 3-series convertible proved to be just as popular as it predecessor

Left: The Z3 was initially only available with four-cylinder engine

In 1994 BMW bought the British company, Rover, and the valuable Land-Rover subsidiary, from owners British Aerospace. The company also announced that it would lend its expertise to Rolls-Royce to help develop two new engines.

Right: BMW's top-end saloon, the 7-series, was available with a 5.4-litre V12 engine

Below: After the launch of the Z3, BMW announced there was a coupé version on the drawing board

Léon Bollée

France
1895–1933

Léon Bollée's interest in motor cars began with his father, Amédée Sr., who pioneered steam-powered road-going vehicles, and also his brother, Amédée Jr., who joined his father's firm.

Léon set up on his own, producing his first small petrol-driven car in 1895. It was he who named this machine a *voiturette*, literally 'little car', which soon became the accepted term for vehicles of this type. It was manufactured by various firms for the next four years, when Bollée followed it with a less-successful larger vehicle, causing the marque to disappear from the market between 1901 and 1903.

Bollée then returned with two more powerful, expensive cars financially

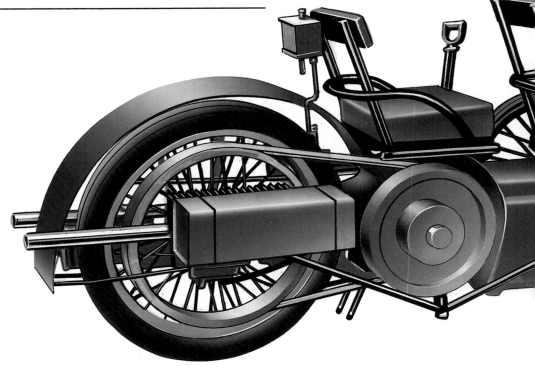

Below: Bollée steam carriage, c. 1880

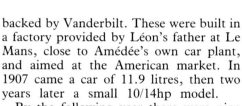

Left: Léon Bollée named his small two-seater car of 1895 'voiturette'. The 650cc, 3hp three-wheeler featured hot tube ignition, three-speed transmission, and belt drive. It was a fast machine for its time, and was capable of more than 48km/h (30mph).

Mans factory was sold to Sir William Morris in 1924. Automobiles Léon Bollée became Morris Motors Ltd., Usines Léon Bollée, and began producing more elegant Van Vestrant and Hans Landstad-designed versions of the current Morris range. Harry Smith was brought in from Morris's engine branch to become the new works' manager.

By the end of the 1920s, however, the Morris-run operation was making six-figure losses and sales had plummeted. With the onset of the Depression the company pulled out in 1931, selling the factory to Société Nouvelle Léon Bollée, a syndicate containing Harry Smith and A. Dunlop Mackenzie, and in which one of the main component suppliers had an interest.

This was not a success, with just a few cars and commercials being produced, and lasted for only two years, folding in 1933.

Below: c. 1910 Léon Bollée chassis
Bottom: The four-seater, four-door Léon Bollée Type M of 1926

backed by Vanderbilt. These were built in a factory provided by Léon's father at Le Mans, close to Amédée's own car plant, and aimed at the American market. In 1907 came a car of 11.9 litres, then two years later a small 10/14hp model.

By the following year there were nine cars in the range and between 150 and 350 were being produced per year. In 1913 Léon Bollée met an early death, with control of car manufacturing falling to his widow.

After World War I the marque became increasingly old-fashioned, and the Le

Brasier

France
1897–1930

Georges Richard's firm, based in Paris, initially produced electrical meters and photographic and optical equipment, and had already been established for over 45 years when it produced its first car. This was in 1897, and it took the form of a simple, Benz-inspired vehicle.

By 1900, however, Société Anonyme Georges Richard, run by Georges and his brother Max, was producing Vivinus cars under licence from Belgium, although they were badged under the Richard name.

New investment in the Richard firm from the Franco-Swiss Indusmine company enabled it to build a factory near the Panhard et Levassor works at Ivry-Port and employ 300 men. In 1901 a new vehicle appeared – Richard's first shaft-driven model – following the style of Renault and Darracq.

Also in 1901, designer Henri Brasier joined the company from Mors, producing a 14hp car with an Arbel steel frame for the

following year. Brasier introduced little that was new and although four new cars were introduced in 1902, badged as Richard-Brasiers, they were nothing startling and very much resembled other makes of the period.

In 1904 and 1905 two Brasier-designed

vehicles won the Gordon Bennett Trophy for France races, but 1905 saw the withdrawal of Georges Richard from the company, leaving Brasier in charge. The firm became first *Trèfle a Quatre Feuilles* ('Four Leaf Clover') after its badge, then Brasier, then Automobiles Brasier, and

Above: 1903 Richard-Brasier 24hp Wagonette

Below: The 14hp Richard-Brasier tourer of 1905 was a chain-driven, four-seater
Right: 1914 Brasier 24hp six-cylinder

Above: 1911 Brasier 12-18hp Cabriolet

Above: This 1908 Brasier VL is typical of the conventionally designed vehicles built by the firm prior to World War I. After 1905, when Georges Richard departed to build the Unic, the 'Richard' prefix was dropped from the firm's name.

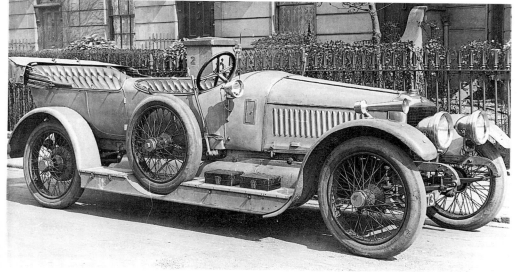

cars were even made under licence in Italy as Fides.

Until World War I, Brasier cars were unexcitingly conventional, with the exception of a modern light car introduced in 1912. During the hostilities commercial vehicles were continued and the company also built Hispano-Suiza aero-engines.

After the war Brasier continued to produce expensive four-cylinder cars, but demand was failing. Reorganization in 1926 led to the company becoming Chaigneau-Brasier and two years later it introduced a car which was of too unusual a design and far too costly for the period to sell well. Georges Irat's son Michel then took over, producing cars under that name until the factory closed in 1930 and was eventually bought by Delahaye.

Bristol

Great Britain
1947 to date

The Bristol has always been an individualistic and expensive high-performance car. After World War II, the Bristol Aeroplane Company found itself with surplus engineering capacity and skill; under Sir George White, it turned these to the small-scale manufacture of aircraft-quality motor cars. Bristol's association with BMW's U.K. importers, AFN Ltd., ensured that the first model – the 1947 400 – had an engine and some styling features derived from the pre-war Type 328 BMW.

The 401 was introduced in 1948, with a more aerodynamic body built under Superleggera Touring patents, and a drop-head 402 version followed. In 1953 came the 403 and 404, the former a more powerful version of the 401 and the latter a handsome, short-wheelbase, fixed-head two-plus-two coupé which quickly became known as the Businessman's Express. The 406 of 1954 offered the 404's styling but with four doors on the longer-wheelbase chassis.

With minor but effective face-lifts, the styling introduced for the 1957 406 saloon served until the demise of the 1969 411 in 1978. The old BMW-derived engine had reached the limit of its development long before this, however, and the 1961 407 was the first Bristol to use a modified Canadian Chrysler V8 engine with automatic transmission. Meanwhile, car manufacture had been separated from that of aircraft, and Bristol Cars Ltd. was set up in 1961 under Sir George White and former racing driver Tony Crook. Crook took sole control in 1973.

New styling arrived with the 1978 603 saloon, and Italian Gianni Zagato styled the 412 Targa-top model, which became the turbocharged Beaufighter in 1980. Still with anachronistic separate-chassis construction and distinctive styling derived from the 603, the range continued after 1982 with the Britannia saloon, the turbocharged Brigand and the export-only Beaufort.

Above: 1949 drophead Bristol 402

Above: 1950 Bristol 400

Above: 1958 Bristol 404

Above: Bristol Type 411, introduced 1969

Above: 1978 Bristol 603 V8

B.S.A.

Great Britain
1907–1940

Better known in the world of motor cycling, B.S.A. (British Small Arms) had a reputation before World War I for cars of simplicity and low cost, some of them boasting front-wheel drive.

The company originated in 1861 in Small Heath, Birmingham, making guns. Its well-known 'piled arms' trademark was adopted in 1880 when applied to the Otto Dicycle which was, in fact, a tricycle. Its first car, a copy of the 40hp Italia, was introduced in 1908.

In 1910 the company made the first wholly B.S.A. motor-cycle and acquired Daimler, Britain's first car manufacturer. From 1911 B.S.A. effectively made scaled-down Daimlers with sleeve-valve engines.

After World War I the company introduced the vee-twin Ten which was built until 1924, being outlived by the sleeve-valve car which lasted until 1926.

The vee-twin returned in 1929 to power a front-wheel-drive three-wheeler which acquired a fourth wheel in 1932. The vehicle became more of a 'proper' car the following year when a four-cylinder engine was fitted.

After a year-long break in production manufacture recommenced in 1935 when the car was christened the B.S.A. Scout. It remained in production until 1940 when B.S.A. reverted to munitions and military vehicles to help the war effort led by chief executive James Leek.

During the war the Scout light reconnaissance car and the heavier Daimler Mark I armoured car – B.S.A. had anticipated the war – excelled in their military duties, and the factory was able to claim that not a single major modification was necessary to cope with all theatres of war.

When the war ended in 1945, the Daimler division of B.S.A. resumed production while B.S.A. decided to concentrate on two-wheelers, soon becoming world leaders in this field.

B.S.A.'s war-time Scout featured four-wheel drive from a central differential, fluid-flywheel transmission and a 2.5-litre Daimler engine. It was designed to reach 60mph (96km/h) in forward gear and 55mph (88km/h) in reverse, with steering at both ends and independent suspension. The vehicle was conceived in 1938 at the request of the War Office and B.S.A. staff worked with the Wheeled Vehicles Experimental Department at Farnborough on the project. Only 152cm (60in) high, the armoured vehicle excelled in the desert, where Rommel even made his escape in a captured Scout.

Top: 1910 18/23hp Single Landaulette

Below left: 1914 13.9hp B.S.A.

Below: 1924 B.S.A. 'Ten'

Above: 1933 B.S.A. four-cylinder 'trike'

Above: 1935 B.S.A. Sports Coupé
Below: 1938 front-wheel-drive B.S.A. Scout

Bugatti

Germany 1909–1918 France 1918–1956

Ettore Bugatti showed a remarkable affinity for cars at a comparatively young age. Born in Milan, Italy, in 1881, he was successfully racing a twin-engined tricycle at the age of 18, and two years later he designed and built a four-cylinder car.

He worked as a designer for several companies, including Deutz at Cologne. While there, he is reputed to have designed and built in the cellar of his home a small car with a 1208cc eight-valve four-cylinder engine with shaft drive. This was to form the basis of the cars he

Below: The Bugatti Brescia (Type 22) was made until 1926 and had a 1386cc 16-valve engine. The name came from its success in the 1921 Brescia Grand Prix in northern Italy.

Left: 1327cc Type 13, built around 1913
Right: A British-owned 1925 Brescia model

manufactured in 1910 after leaving the company.

Five 1327cc-engined Bugattis were made that year at his premises in Molsheim, Alsace, but the number rose to 75 the following year. Bugatti built a smaller 855cc-engined car in 1911 and Peugeot took it up and called it the Bébé Peugeot, making no less than 3,095 examples.

Bugatti's partner Ernst Friderich began racing Bugattis and won his class in the 1911 Grand Prix de France.

Bugatti built a five-litre car in 1913 – which had three valves per cylinder – two inlet and one exhaust. Only seven were made but they paved the way for the three-valve Type 30 and Type 37 engines which were to come in the 1920s. The smaller Type 13, as it was known, continued to be produced until World War I.

Alsace was a province of Germany until 1918 and Bugatti's premises were turned over to the war effort. Bugatti himself spent the war years in Paris where he was responsible for the design of aero-engines, including the 16-cylinder double-bank 500bhp engine made by the Duesenberg Motors Corporation of Elizabeth, New Jersey.

Molsheim became French territory at the end of World War I and Bugatti returned and resumed production of the Type 13. Its successor was a 16-valve model which was later called the Brescia after Friderich's win in the 1921 Grand Prix de Voiturettes at Brescia in northern Italy.

The car was an immediate success and about 2000 were made until 1926, many built under licence in other countries.

Bugatti entered the more exclusive end of the market with the Type 30 in 1922. It had a two-litre straight-eight engine. The later Type 35 had the rare distinction of being capable of winning Grands Prix and also being available for sale to amateurs. Between the wars it was the most

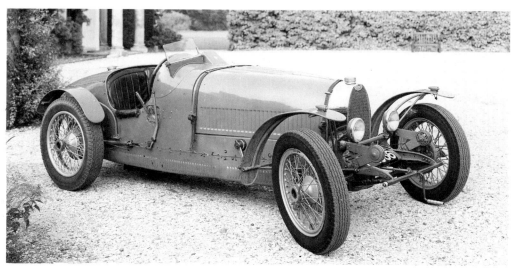

Above right: Type 35B, a very successful racer
Right: 1925 1.5-litre Type 37

successful racing car available, winning 12 major Grands Prix in 1926.

The 1½-litre Type 37 was available for those not wealthy enough to buy a Type 35, and the Type 40 was affectionately dubbed Ettore's Morris Cowley because of its relatively modest performance and reasonable price.

Bugatti had dreamed of making the ultimate car to beat the world as far back as 1913. His dream came true with the Type 41 Royale in 1926. With a 15-litre engine and a claimed 300bhp it was a sensational car in its day, but only six were made and just three were sold. The rest remained with Bugatti's family.

Bugatti later concentrated on building

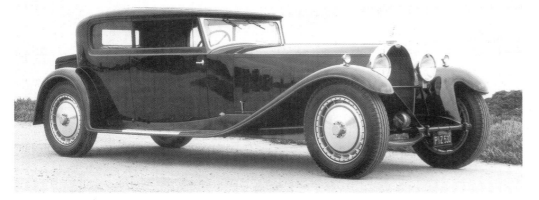

Above: 1927 2.3-litre Type 43
Left: Kellner-bodied Type 41 "Royale"

property speculations seriously hit Bugatti's finances and he moved to Paris to design aircraft and boats, leaving his son Jean in charge at Molsheim.

Jean was principally responsible for the last serious production Bugatti – the 3.3-litre double-overhead-camshaft straight-eight Type 57 which was introduced in 1934. By 1939, a total of 683 had been made. Jean was killed test-driving a racing car near Molsheim in August 1939, just

high-speed rail-cars, with the first going into production in 1933.

The Depression, the price of his straight-eight cars and a number of bad

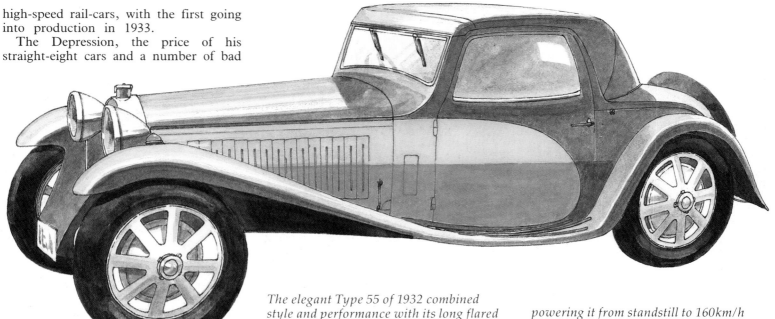

The elegant Type 55 of 1932 combined style and performance with its long flared wings and cutaway sides. Its eight-cylinder, 2.3-litre engine was capable of powering it from standstill to 160km/h (100mph) in 43 seconds and on to a top speed of 185km/h (115mph).

before the outbreak of World War II.
Molsheim once again had to contribute to the war effort. Bugatti moved to Bordeaux and worked on a number of projects. With the help of his younger son Roland he produced the 1½-litre Type 73, although few had been made by the time of his death in August 1947.

Above: Eight-cylinder, 200bhp Type 50T

Below left: 1952 supercharged Type 101C

An updated Type 57 went into production at Molsheim in 1951 under the direction of Pierre Marco, but only about 20 left the factory.

Further attempts to keep the company alive failed and it was bought by Hispano-Suiza in 1963, later being absorbed by S.N.E.C.M.A., the nationalized French aerospace conglomerate. Production at Molsheim was switched to the manufacture of aircraft parts.

Fearing that it might eventually be devalued as a 'designer' label, in 1987 a group of European businessmen acquired rights to the Bugatti name. Only afterwards, they claim, did they have the idea of reviving the marque. From a brand-new factory in Campogalliano, Italy, Bugatti Automobili SpA. intends to introduce a 322km/h (200mph) supercar, all-wheel-driven by a 550bhp 3.5-litre quad-turbo V12, in the early 1990s.

Bugatti Automobili

Italy
1987-1994

The rebirth of Bugatti was much welcomed when Bugatti Automobili SpA was founded in Modena in 1987. New owner, Romano Artioli, soon set about building a factory and quickly revealed that the first of the new Bugattis would have four-wheel-drive and a brand-new V12 engine. The new car, the EB110 GT was not launched until three years later, in 1991, the first car being delivered to its buyer the following year.

It was a car that went straight to the top of the supercar league, and was much praised by the motoring press. Everything seemed to be going well and the factory was soon promising to deliver a further 150 cars in 1993, although by the end of the year it was announced that only 98 had been built. However, in the same year, a stunning new model, the EB112 saloon, designed by and to be built by ItalDesign, was revealed at the 1993 Geneva show. Also in 1993 Bugatti bought Lotus for a rumoured £30 million, building Elans from the leftover components.

But by 1994 the rot had set in and Bugatti began to descend down the slippery slope towards bankruptcy: Artioli's promised production levels had once again not been reached, and ItalDesign stopped work on the EB112, citing lack of payment. Finally, after months of rumoured buyouts, several failed rescue attempts, and many court hearings, the end came. Bugatti Automobili SpA was declared bankrupt.: the company never disclosed any production or sales figures. The actual number built will probably never be known, such was the secrecy behind this fantastic supercar. Thankfully, Lotus was not brought down with Bugatti and was rescued by the Malaysian company, Proton.

Below: Bugatti boss, Romano Artioli's sense of tradition was tremendously strong and the standard EB110 was painted in unmistakable Bugatti blue. This was traditional but the construction was not. The EB110 used a carbonfibre monocoque designed by the French company, Aérospatiale

Right: This silver car, shown outside the Bugatti factory is an EB110S, the sports-racing version of the EB110. It was stripped for lightness, had an extra 40bhp and a fixed rear wing, unlike the standard car whose rear wing rose automatically at speed

Buick

U.S.A.
1903 to date

David Dunbar Buick formed the Buick Motor Company in 1903, but the company had a hesitant start and production proper did not get under way until 1904. Buick was poorly financed and had little in the way of future plans until William C. Durant bought it that year as his first car venture. Durant reorganized Buick for greater production and bought it a new factory. The 1905 Model 'C' became a great success and, by 1907, Buick was second only to Ford in U.S. sales. Nearly 14,000 cars had been built by the time Durant made the marque the cornerstone of his General Motors empire in 1908.

Buick's success weathered G.M.'s financial problems of 1910, and that year's sales figures outstripped those of every other manufacturer worldwide. There-

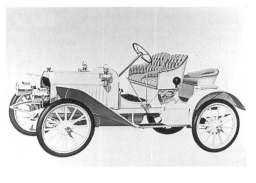

Above: 1905 Model C with 20bhp flat-twin
Below: 1908 Model 10 runabout

Above: Rakish lines of 1908 runabout
Below: A typical 1912 Buick tourer

Below: Buick's first six-cylinder car arrived in 1914, but the 1924 models, such as this Six, were distinguished by a Packard-like radiator and the company's first four-wheel brakes.

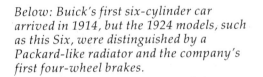

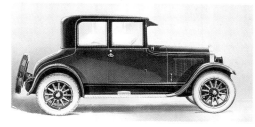

Above: Four-cylinder 1912 model Buick
Below: 1927 six-cylinder Buick

Above: 1914 B-55, the first six-cylinder
Below: 1932 Series 80 four-door sedan

Above: 1925 Standard Six
Below centre: 1937 convertible model 80C

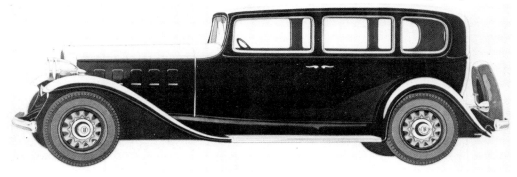

after, Buick would always figure among the best-sellers. Delco electric lighting and starting were standard by 1914, when Buick marketed its first six-cylinder model, and it would be the six-cylinder range which would be the marque's sales strength throughout the 1920s, although there were four-cylinder models on offer as well.

An overhead-valve straight-eight was introduced in 1931 for all models, but Buick's evolution in the 1930s was dictated largely by General Motors policy. Thus, synchromesh gearboxes became standard in 1932, a cruciform-braced frame and no-draught ventilation arrived in 1933, 'knee-action' independent front suspension came in 1934, and turret-top styling, downdraught carburation and hydraulic brakes in 1936. Top of the range were the Roadmaster and Limited models, though the Century range of 1935–1942 put the biggest engine into a lighter and smaller package to give sparkling performance.

After World War II, straight-eight production was resumed, but 1948 saw changes with the arrival of two-speed Dynaflow automatic transmission and G.M.'s first 'hard-top' body in the shape of the Roadmaster Riviera. After 1953, the straight-eight remained for only a year

longer in the cheaper Special range, while the Super and Roadmaster models had the marque's first V8, a 188bhp overhead-valve design which was standardized

across the range in 1954. Between then and 1957, the high-performance Buicks were the Century range, which featured ever more powerful variants of that V8 engine.

Below: 1949 Model 71 Roadmaster

Below: 1948 Series 50 Eight Super

The Buicks of 1957 were heavier and slower, and sales dropped in 1958. In common with other G.M. marques, the 1961 models were down-sized to include a new all-aluminium 215-cubic inch V8 of 155bhp in the compact Special. But the demand for 'muscle cars' ensured the survival of the big V8s in models like the 1963 Riviera sports coupé. By 1966, Buick

Above: 1963 Buick Electra
Below: 1963 325bhp Riviera hardtop

Above: 'Compact' 1963 Special Wagon
Below: 1968 Wildcat custom hardtop coupé

had an altogether more sporting image, with V6 or small-block V8 engines in its smaller cars, while large V8s continued in the bigger models. Engine capacities continued to rise until the end of the decade, but the Buicks of the 1970s and 1980s began to lose their individuality as G.M. marques began to share more and more components.

The accent was now on fuel economy, not performance. Catalytic converters were standardized across the range in 1975 to meet the new U.S. exhaust emissions

Below: This 1934 model convertible Buick had an overhead-valve straight-eight engine of 278 cubic inches, giving 100bhp. Front suspension was General Motors' new 'knee-action' type, designed by Maurice Olley.

Above: 1973 Century Luxus coupé

Above: 1975 Electra Park Avenue (left) and V6 Skyhawk sub-compact (right)

Above: 1978 V6 Century Limited saloon

laws, and engines became smaller: a V6 became available again, though big V8s remained available until 1981. The first diesel-powered Buick arrived in 1980, and even four-cylinder engines were available in the cheapest Skylark, which was little more than a badge-engineered Chevrolet. As the cars became smaller, so did Buick's sales figures – between 1984 and 1988, those almost halved. Managers of the marque finally realized Buicks should seek to regain their traditional, opulent character, quite distinct from Oldsmobiles and Chevrolets.

Below: 1980 turbocharged Regal Sport
Bottom: 1980 Skyhawk with V6 engine

Above: 1980 Le Sabre sedan
Below: 1990 Reatta convertible

Left: The stunning Buick Riviera coupé was available with a supercharged V6

Above: The 1998 Buick Park Avenue Ultra had a large amount of standard luxury features

Below: The Buick Skylark was face-lifted in 1991 and used four- and six-cylinder engines. The Skylark name dates back to 1953

By the late 1990s Buick was starting to regain its luxury image, but was still struggling to keep pace with the competition, especially the new luxury Japanese imports. Staying with the traditional Buick model names, the company set about modernizing its range. By 1997, all Buick models had front-wheel-drive and the large displacement V8s seemed to be gone for good.

The new range used transversely-mounted pushrod V6s, with capacities ranging from 3.1 to 3.8 litres. Performance models relied on supercharging rather than cubic inches for the extra power.

Perhaps the best-looking nineties Buick was the Riviera, which was restyled in 1993. It had ultra-modern coupé styling and its V6 engine was available in 208bhp or 243bhp supercharged forms. It was a long way from the 1963 original but was just as desirable and really helped place Buick near the top of the General Motors family tree. The Regal and Park Avenue were also available with the supercharged engine.

The 1997 Park Avenue Ultra was Buick's flagship. It was all-new and a bigger car than its predecessor. Buick's best seller in the nineties though, was the LeSabre. The company built on the car's success by sticking with a winning formula and only minor cosmetic changes were made.

Right: 1998 Buick Century Custom. By 1998 it was a long way removed from its 1981 ancestor, with modern styling and mechanicals

Above: Buick Regal LS

Below: Buick Le Sabre LTD

Cadillac
U.S.A.
1902 to date

Cadillac began life in 1899 as the Detroit Automobile Company, became the Henry Ford Company briefly in 1901, and was renamed Cadillac after the founder of Detroit in 1902 when it was taken over by Henry Leland, owner of an established machinery and foundry plant supplying the car industry.

Above: 1909 four-cylinder model

Above: 1911 enclosed-body Model 30
Below: 1912 model two-seater runabout

Above: 1902 Model A runabout

Above: 1911 four-door touring model

The first Cadillacs were modest single-cylinder runabouts, but four-cylinder models arrived in 1905, and the 1907 Thirty was a notable success. Meanwhile, Leland had introduced his precision manufacturing methods which allowed parts to be swapped from one car to another. These won Cadillac the R.A.C.'s Dewar Trophy in 1908, and the company won this trophy again in 1913 for its pioneering use of electric lighting, starting and ignition.

Cadillac's success had attracted William C. Durant of General Motors, who added

the marque to his empire in 1908 to cover the top end of the market. Leland left to found Lincoln in 1917, but advanced engineering remained a Cadillac hallmark. In 1915, the Type 51 introduced the world's first commercially viable V8 engine, as smooth and powerful as the sixes favoured elsewhere but more compact; and 1923 models had an inherently balanced V8 and four-wheel brakes.

1927 was also the year in which Cadillac

Below: 1911 Model 30

Above: 1913 40/50hp roadster
Below: 1914 Model 30 roadster

Above: 1908 Model S runabout

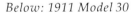

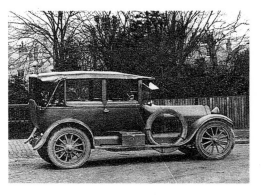

Above: 1916 Model 53 with V8 engine
Right: 1918 Type 57 V8 limousine

was joined by a companion make, the La Salle. Studies made by G.M. had shown that there was a gap in the market for a car in the upper-medium-price range, between Buick and Cadillac, and that the Cadillac division was the better placed to build it. Thus, just as Oakland was joined by Pontiac, Oldsmobile by Viking, and Buick by Marquetta, so La Salle became Cadillac's second make.

It was a La Salle which became the first G.M. car to have styling by Harley Earl, although Cadillac followed close behind. The first La Salle models were essentially lighter and smaller Cadillacs even though the two marques retained their

Left: 1929 Model 341B with Fisher body

Below: By the time this 1926 Model 314 seven-passenger car was built, the V8 engine was an inherently-balanced type and all Cadillacs had four-wheel brakes.

Above: Harley Earl styled the 1929 models

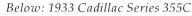

independence of one another; but by 1931 the La Salle was almost identical with the contemporary smaller Cadillac, and shared both its engine and its chassis.

The Depression hit La Salle hard and

Above: 1932 La Salle Type 345B sedan   *Below: 1933 Cadillac Series 355C*

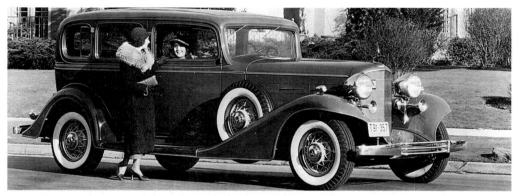

Above: 1931 V-16 Phaeton
Below: 1932 V-12 convertible coupé

multi-cylinder supercar, and Cadillac was among the pioneers in this field with its fabulous 425-cubic-inch V16 engine, introduced in 1930. This was followed

Left: 1935 La Salle 350 straight-eight
Below: 1937 Series 85 V-12 town car

G.M. planned to drop the marque after 1933, but Harley Earl's attractive proposal for the 1934 models swayed the balance and the La Salle continued. Sales were never enormous, however, and in the late 1930s La Salle and Cadillac grew too close to one another once again. The last La Salle models were built in 1940, after which date the market gap was plugged by the top Buicks and by a revived 'cheap' Cadillac, the Series 61.

The 1930s saw the advent of the

later the same year by a 368-cubic-inch V12, actually conceived at the same time and designed to use a number of common parts. Although the V16 would always be a loss-leader after 1933 (and was replaced by a cheaper version in 1948), the V12 competed effectively with similar engines from other U.S. manufacturers throughout the 1930s. A wide range of bodies was

available on both chassis, and the styling and appointments of the fashionable Fleetwood bodies did much to enhance Cadillac's reputation as a producer of top-quality cars. Meanwhile, the mainstream models retained V8 engines, and styling remained in the hands of the Harley Earl studios.

Cadillac was kept afloat during the Depression by the sales of cheaper G.M. marques, but Alfred P. Sloan, who had been the Corporation's President and Chief Executive since 1923, recognized that the division could not afford to rest on its laurels indefinitely. There were major changes in 1934 under Cadillac's new General Manager, Nicholas Dreystadt, with new styling and an independent front

Left: 1937 Series 75 'turret-top' sedan
Below: 1949 Series 62 Touring Sedan

suspension shared with the other G.M. marques. This policy of sharing components with other G.M. models helped to reverse the Cadillac sales decline. 'Turret-top' all-steel bodies arrived in 1936 along with a vee-windscreen, all-hydraulic brakes and a new monobloc L-head V8 engine with hydraulic valve lifters which would remain in production until 1948. The decade's greatest success, however, was the 1938 60 Special, with influential styling by William Mitchell of the Harley Earl studio.

The next decade saw Cadillac triumph over its rival Lincoln and the traditional market leader, Packard, to become the top American car status symbol. The 1941 models introduced rear wheel spats, while 1942 saw fastback styling on the few cars built before Cadillac turned over to war work. The 1946–47 cars were face-lifted 1942 models, but these were followed by significant advances for 1948 and 1949, and it was these which established Cadillac as an industry leader.

For 1948, a long-standing criticism that Cadillac models looked too much like lesser G.M. marques was countered by the introduction of the two-door Sedanet model of kicked-up trailing edges to the rear wings, inspired by the twin tailplane of the Lockheed P-38 fighter aircraft. These began a trend which culminated in the tail fins seen throughout the industry

Below: Like other GM marques, Cadillac contributed to the Motoramas of the 1950s, which showcased prototypes and 'dream cars' such as this 1954 convertible styled by Pininfarina.

in the later 1950s. Then, for 1949, came a new overhead-valve V8 to replace the ageing L-head design. This was a remarkable engine in many ways: light, compact, robust and powerful, it gave all Cadillacs class-leading 100mph (160km/h) performance, and for the next six years the luxury marque was also a leader in the performance field. There were notable successes at Le Mans in 1950 (by Briggs Cunningham) and at the Daytona Beach Speed Trials in 1954.

However, styling was the real Cadillac watchword between 1949 and 1961, and a series of fabulous 'dream cars' displayed at the G.M. Motorama exhibitions previewed production styling features. Concentrating now on the very top of the market, Cadillac dropped its cheaper models in 1951, standardized automatic transmission in 1952, and introduced the expensive, low-volume Eldorado range in 1953.

Above: 1950 Series 62 with overhead-valve V8
Top right: 1956 Eldorado Biarritz Convertible
Centre: 1957 Eldorado Brougham
Right: 1952 Series 62 two-door Sedanet
Far right: Custom-built 1959 Series 62
Below: Destined never to go into production, this 1957 Eldorado Brougham was a Motorama Show Car.

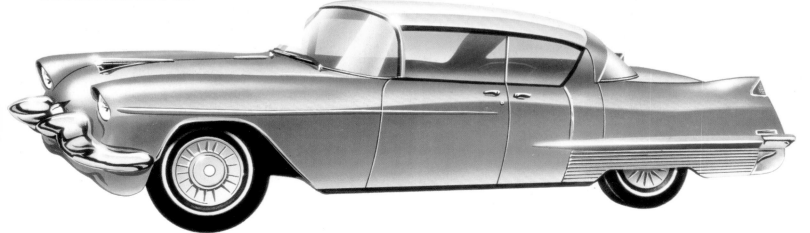

Top: 1959 Fleetwood Sixty Special sedan
Above: 1959 two-door Coupe de Ville
Right: 1959 Series 75 limousine

Long, low, and wide styling now prevailed, and all models sprouted tail fins for 1956, following their introduction on 1955's Eldorado. These grew yearly larger, reaching their zenith in 1959.

Meanwhile, a new chassis design in 1957

had permitted even lower and sleeker lines, and the twin headlamps first seen on that year's top-of-the-range Eldorado Brougham became standard for 1958. Air suspension was also tried on the Eldorado

Brougham models between 1956 and 1960. Central locking and cruise control became available for 1960, in which season the flamboyant styling was toned down.

A new V8 engine, shorter and narrower

Above left: 1960 Eldorado Seville
Above: 1960 Sedan de Ville

than the existing design, made its appearance in 1963, and for 1965 there was a new perimeter-frame chassis which permitted a lower floor level and allowed the engine to be further forward without upsetting the weight distribution, thus giving more length in the passenger cabin. But it was styling and appointments rather than engineering which attracted attention to the Cadillacs of the early 1960s.

The 1964 models, for example,

Above: 1962 Series 62 four-window sedan

Above: 1964 Series 62 Coupé

Below: 1965 Calais hardtop coupé

Below: 1963 Coupe de Ville

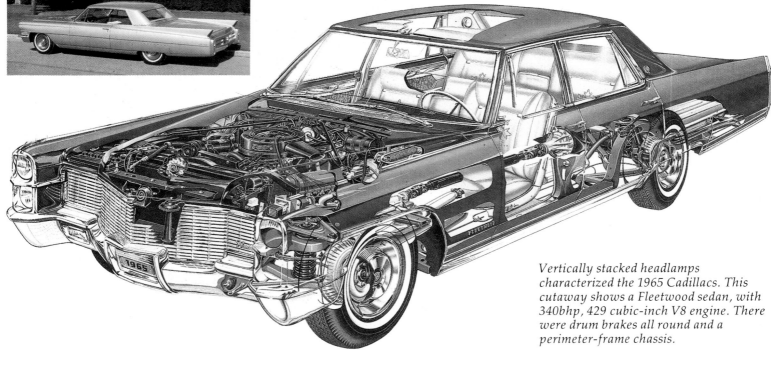

Vertically stacked headlamps characterized the 1965 Cadillacs. This cutaway shows a Fleetwood sedan, with 340bhp, 429 cubic-inch V8 engine. There were drum brakes all round and a perimeter-frame chassis.

Above: 1967 Fleetwood Eldorado

Top: 1965 Fleetwood Eldorado
Above: 1962 Fleetwood Sixty Special

Below: 1974 Fleetwood Eldorado
Bottom: 1974 Coupe de Ville

introduced the option of a padded vinyl roof covering (which was later enthusiastically adopted right across the industry), together with automatic air conditioning, a courtesy-light delay, and the so-called 'Twilight Sentinel', which automatically switched the headlamps on and off to suit the light conditions. The 1965 models also had cornering lights designed to light the way around corners in the dark.

Some of these items were little more than gimmicks; but as Cadillac styling became less flamboyant – tail fins disappeared altogether for 1965 – so advanced engineering resumed its importance as the marque's foremost characteristic. Thus, the 1967 Eldorado had a front-wheel-drive layout derived from the Oldsmobile Toronado, even though other models retained rear-wheel-drive. Engineering was thrust to the fore once again as new safety and exhaust-emission regulations affected the models of the late 1960s.

The crisply sculpted styling of the 1960s

became more rounded for the 1970s, but the biggest changes were caused by the need to meet ever more stringent U.S. Government fuel economy regulations. Cadillacs became smaller, and in the process lost a great deal of their character as large luxury cars; the 1975 Seville was a compact, European-sized saloon which was more than two feet (61cm) shorter than the contemporary De Ville, a traditional-sized Cadillac. Even the top-model Eldorado had been scaled down by 1979. The big V8s meanwhile grew smaller, and in 1978 were joined by a diesel variant, borrowed from Oldsmobile.

The engines of the 1980s continued this economy trend, with a V6 in 1981, petrol V8s which could run on four, six or eight cylinders, and even a 1.8-litre four-cylinder engine in the smallest Cimarron. Although the big limousines continued to dominate their traditional market, it was clear by the mid-1980s that the smaller Cadillacs, based on other G.M. mass-market saloons, were failing to satisfy public perceptions of the marque.

Even the unusually ambitious Allanté model – the two-seat luxury convertible whose body shell is built by Pininfarina in Italy and freighted across the Atlantic in specially-chartered Jumbo Jets – failed to

Below: 1984 1.8-litre Cimarron   *Top: 1978 Seville sedan*   *Above: 1980 Coupe de Ville*

Above: 1989 Brougham

bring the sales or prestige Cadillac had hoped for. But this cumbersome and costly manufacturing arrangement did spotlight Cadillac's keenness to equal the appeal of European imports, especially BMW, Jaguar and Mercedes-Benz.

Above: 1989 Coupe de Ville

Below: Pininfarina styled the 1988 Allanté, a two-door 'personal car' aimed at Mercedes-Benz SL buyers and powered by a 170bhp V8 engine. It was a new type of car for Cadillac.

Top: 1989 Allanté luxury sports model
Centre: 1989 Fleetwood Sixty Special
Above: 1989 Sedan de Ville

As the 1990s approached, Cadillac was faced with a new threat. In addition to the European imports, there were now fine Japanese luxury cars being shipped into the country. Lexus, Honda and Infiniti all offered large luxury cars that competed directly with Cadillac. They were all technologically advanced and highlighted how dated Cadillac's designs really were.

To combat this threat, the company had to buck up its ideas and re-think its designs. By the mid-1990s the Cadillac range was all-new and so were the engines. It was the Northstar V8 that really showed the world that Cadillac could compete technically with the Japanese. It was an all-alloy V8 with two camshafts per cylinder bank and four valves per cylinder. The engine was built to last and was designed to travel 100,000 miles before the first scheduled tune-up. It could even run without its coolant. Should a coolant leak occur, the engine could continue to run safely in limp-home mode by cycling air through deactivated cylinders to cool the engine. Power outputs were impressive too. The top specification Northstar V8

produced 300bhp.

Other technical wizardry appeared in the form of computer-controlled variable-rate dampers, anti-lock braking, traction control, variable-assist power steering and

Above: The 1998 Cadillac DeVille, the saloon version of the Eldorado

Below: The Cadillac DeVille D'Elegance featured more chrome than the standard car

StabiliTrak, Cadillac's unique stability control system.

A new departure for Cadillac was the Catera, a luxury version of the Opel Omega V6. Launched in 1996, the car was the entry-level Cadillac, designed to attract younger buyers, competing with the top import competitors like the Lexus ES300, Mercedes-Benz C-class, and BMW 3-series. It was an important market sector, with the entry-luxury segment making up 40 per cent of the luxury car market.

The Eldorado two-door, and DeVille, its four-door sister, were classic Cadillacs, available with the Northstar V8 and an alarming level of luxury. The Seville, a muscular-looking saloon, was the performance model capable of 150mph.

Cadillac's plans, as the new millenium approached, included expanding abroad with new distribution channels, as well as a new global car. It was estimated that 20 per cent of sales of the new Seville for 1998 would be outside the United States. There were even plans to make a right-hand-drive model. Relatively compact dimensions also increased appeal to foreign markets.

Top left: Cadillac DeVille Concours

Above: 1998 Eldorado

Left: 1997 Cadillac Catera

Below: Eldorado Touring Coupé

Chadwick
U.S.A.
1904–1916

Lee Sherman Chadwick was an engineer who built his first experimental cars while working for a ball-bearing manufacturer in order to demonstrate the company's wares. He then became a designer for the

The following year the Chadwick Engineering Works was formed in Pottstown, Pennsylvania, conveniently close to a major supplier, the Light Foundry Co. By 1908 a larger factory had been opened and Chadwick was employing 90 men. His cars were finished to a very high standard, trimmed with hand-stitched leather and hickory. Chadwicks were also very fast, with an early lightweight version being timed at over 100mph (160km/h). They are widely

financial trouble. When the Light Foundry Co. refused to supply him he considered setting up his own foundry, but this proved to be a totally uneconomic proposition. The following year this innovative perfectionist left not only his company, but the motor industry as well, for employment with the Perfection Stove Co. Production of his cars went on for another four years, however, and finally ceased in 1916, with a total of only approximately 265 cars ever built.

Searchmont Motor Co., where he was backed in plans for a four-cylinder car. When the backers withdrew and Searchmont went bankrupt in 1903, Chadwick bought the necessary parts and set up to build the cars himself.

The following year he founded the Fairmont Engineering Works to build Chadwicks and repair other makes. By 1906 he had produced around 40 cars and introduced an enormous 11.2-litre-engined vehicle.

considered to be the first high-performance U.S.-manufactured car.

Another first for Chadwick was scored by his competition vehicles, which began hill-climbing in 1908 and later went on to racing. In the Vanderbilt Cup and the Savannah Grand Prize of that year, Chadwicks were fitted with the earliest-recorded superchargers on a petrol engine, although this device was never offered on the company's road-going vehicles.

By 1910, however, Chadwick was in

Above: The enormous 11.2-litre Great Chadwick Six. The six-cylinder engine, called the Type 19, featured an overhead valve arrangement and in a stripped-out car was capable of speeds in excess of 160km/h (100mph).

Chenard-Walcker

France
1901–1946

Ernest Chenard started making bicycles at Asnières, Seine, in 1883, before going into partnership with Henri Walcker in 1898 to make tricycles. Their first venture into car manufacture was an 1160cc T-head twin-cylinder machine which featured coil ignition and a double-back-axle arrangement. Progress was rapid, and by 1906 they were making over 400 cars a year, had become involved with marine engines, and were in a position to go public. This tied in with a move to larger premises at Gennevilliers, Seine, where the company remained until its demise.

Although Chenard-Walcker ventured into light trucks and taxis, the company concentrated mainly on medium-sized, reasonably priced passenger cars. These ranged from a 942cc single-cylinder voiturette introduced in 1910, through a mid-range three-litre model to 6.3-litre straight-fours of 1911. Walcker died in 1910, by which time production had risen to 1,200 cars a year. By the outbreak of World War I annual production stood at 1,500 cars, and included a 4.5-litre six-cylinder model.

After the war, the three-litre model was revived, and some commercials were made using the same engine. These took the form of road tractors, which came to be made under licence by Beardmore in Britain and Minerva in Belgium. By 1931 these vehicles had grown to 250bhp monsters powered by two 7.5-litre Panhard engines.

Chenard himself died in 1922, and his son Lucien carried on the business, supported by the Donnay family and his brother-in-law Georges Stein. A new car designed by Henri Toutée appeared that year, a three-litre single-overhead camshaft straight-four with Hallot servo brakes which acted on the front wheels and the transmission. One such won the very first Le Mans 24-Hour race, and the works entered a four-litre straight-eight. The company also made quite successful

1.5-litre cars with all-enveloping 'tank' bodies.

These were the halcyon days for Chenard-Walcker, who had by now become the fourth-largest manufacturer in France, producing 100 cars a day. It had acquired the firm of Sénéchal, and continued to produce this company's small sports cars. It also made AEM electric vans, and in 1927 entered into a consortium with Delahaye.

In 1933 came the front-wheel-drive models designed by Jean Grégoire. The 2.4-litre model featured independent front suspension and a Cotal gearbox, and some 1,300 cars of two and 2.4 litres were sold.

Above: 1923 three-litre Le Mans
Below: Chenard-Walcker Aigle-8, c. 1936

A 3.5-litre V8 was tried but, by 1936, this diversification was proving a strain and the company was in financial problems.

Coachbuilders Chausson, who had been supplying saloon bodies to Chenard-Walcker and Matford, gained financial control in 1936. Engines now came from Citroën and Matford in the shape of a 1911cc straight-four and a 3622cc V8. The Chenard-Walcker Aigle-8 convertibles had the very attractive Labourdette *Vutotal* ('see everything') pillarless windscreens, and although car production more or less ceased in 1939 with the outbreak of World War II, a few were assembled in 1946.

Chenard-Walcker continued to build light forward-control vans between 1947 and 1951, when it was finally taken over by Peugeot; the van itself survived as a Peugeot until 1965.

Chevrolet

U.S.A.
1911 to date

Louis Chevrolet, from whom the marque name was taken, was a successful racing driver of Swiss descent. He was born in La Chaux de Fonds in 1878, soon moving to Beaune, France, with his family. From there he spent time in Paris, working for Mors, before deciding to head for Canada with his brothers Arthur and Gaston. New York offered new opportunities for Louis, where he worked for car and later truck manufacturer William Walter, and also for the importers of De Dion-Bouton cars.

He then spent varying amounts of time with different manufacturers, becoming well known in competition, and building himself a racer based on a Buick. It was this which brought him to the notice of William Durant, founder of General Motors and former Flint buggy manufacturer. Arthur Chevrolet became chauffeur to Durant, who had, by this time, lost his control over General Motors.

Louis Chevrolet and Durant then got together on the design of a new French-style car, called the Chevrolet in order to cash in on both Louis's and Arthur's racing fame. By 1911 the Classic Six went into production in premises at 3939 Grand River Avenue, Detroit. On 3 November that year the Chevrolet Motor Co. was incorporated, leasing better workshops at 1145 West Grand Boulevard. By 1912 production of the Classic Six had reached 2,999 units.

Chevrolet production moved to Durant's Little Motor Co. in Flint, while the Mason Motor Co., also under Durant's control, supplied engines. The firms merged into Chevrolet in 1913, moving to the Flint Wagon Works and building the Little Runabout as the Little Four. In 1913 Chevrolet launched the four-cylinder Baby Grand Tourer, together with its single-seat version, the Royal Mail. The Baby Grand was the first car to carry the distinctive blue-and-white Chevrolet badge, said to have come from a wallpaper design Durant once saw in a French hotel.

Above: 1914 Baby Grand

In 1913 Louis Chevrolet left to go into partnership with V. R. Hefler and J. Boyer, starting such firms as the Chevrolet Brothers Manufacturing Co. and the Chevrolet Aircraft Corporation. His endeavours failed in the Depression, however, and he died in obscurity in 1941, having worked briefly for Chevrolet during the 1930s.

By 1914 the company bearing his name had purchased the Maxwell Motor Co. plant in Tarrytown, New York, for assembly, and some 5,005 cars were built.

Above: 1917 Type 490

The following year the 490 model was launched, so called because of its $490 price, with Chevrolet going for the economy market. By 1916 production had reach 70,701 and the year after that the first closed-body cars were offered. Commercial vehicles began in 1918, with the Light Delivery and the Ton Truck.

In 1919 Chevrolet became a Division of Durant's old company, General Motors, production by this time running at 149,904, but the post-war economic depression caused losses of U.S. $5 million in 1921 and the company only narrowly escaped closure. G.M. president, Pierre S. du Pont, called in industrial engineers to

Above: 1919 FB-50 touring car

Above: 1912 Classic Six

Above: 1914 tourer

Above: 1922 Type 490 four-door sedan

assess Chevrolet, who told him that the firm could not hope to compete in the field which it was aiming for. Du Pont's assistant, Alfred P. Sloan, took the statement as a challenge and set out to prove them wrong. In 1922 William S. Knudsen was appointed head of the Chevrolet Division, taking over from Karl W. Zimmershield. Five years later Chevrolet was the largest car manufacturer in the world.

Above: 1923 Superior Series B sedan

Right: 1923 roadster

Below: The 1923 'Copper-cooled' Superior model cost $525 and had an air-cooled engine on a standard chassis. It gave so many problems that all except one car were recalled to the factory.

It was not all easy. In 1923 a successor for the 490, the air-cooled Superior, was such a disaster that it was recalled to the factory. The previous year, however, production had run at 243,479 and Chevrolet had expanded with new plants in Janesville, Buffalo and Norwood, and a pressed-metal plant in Flint was started.

By 1927 Chevrolet had introduced the closed-cab utility vehicle, made 1,001,880

Above: 1928 coupé

Above: 1924 Superior Series F coach
Below: 1925 Superior Series K coach

Above: 1926 Superior Series V Landau sedan
Below: 1928 National Series AB cabriolet

vehicles and gained first place in the industry. By the following year it had begun laying plans to adopt a new six-cylinder engine – 'Six for the price of Four' – having survived until then on the four-cylinder overhead-valve unit. It was launched in 1929 and production peaked at 1,328,605. The Depression was weathered without too many problems, with Chevrolet staying the most popular car in America into the 1930s.

Below: 1930 Universal Series AD coach

Below: 1930 Universal sport roadster

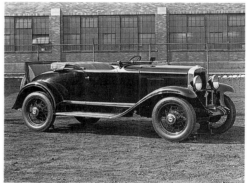

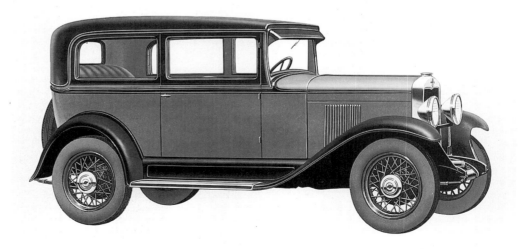

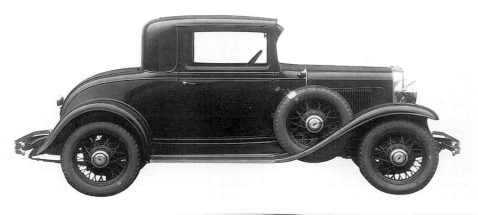

Left: 1931 Independence coupé
Above: 1934 Master two-door Town Sedan
Below: 1935 Master De Luxe coach

Above left: 1932 Confederate roadster
Above: 1936 Master De Luxe sedan
Below: 1937 Master De Luxe coach

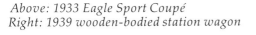

Above: 1933 Eagle Sport Coupé
Right: 1939 wooden-bodied station wagon

By 1933 Knudsen had become G.M. executive vice-president and M. E. Coyle became General Manager of Chevrolet. Synchromesh transmission, all-steel bodywork (known as the 'turret top') and independent front suspension had all been adopted by 1935, with hydraulic brakes arriving a year later. The ten millionth car was produced in 1935, and the 15 millionth four years after that, when the station wagon joined the Chevrolet range.

Above: 1941 Special De Luxe Series AH

A phenomenal 1.4 million sales were recorded in 1941, before the company's factories were turned over to war work. That year Juan Manuel Fangio had his first big win in an Argentinian endurance race, driving a Chevrolet coupé.

Above: 1942 Fleetline Aero Sedan

In 1946 Nicholas Dreystadt, formerly of Cadillac, took over briefly from Coyle, but died two years later to be replaced by W. F. Armstrong, a vice-president of

Below: 1947 Fleetmaster station wagon

G.M., and General Managership passed to T.H. Keating. Keating succeeded Armstrong in 1949. The Chevrolets of that year were given completely new styling, and the Bel Air hard-top was introduced in 1950, when Powerglide fully automatic transmission became available even on the cheaper models. Three years later the extraordinary Corvette was launched.

Below: 1954 Corvette sports roadster

Above: 1949 Styleline De Luxe sedan

Above: 1952 Styleline De Luxe convertible

Above: 1955 Bel Air four-door sedan

Above: 1956 Bel Air convertible

Although often credited as the work of Russian engineer Zora Arkus Duntov, the Corvette, designed by Harley J. Earl, was already being constructed when Duntov joined G.M. The car was underpowered to begin with and not noted for stable handling, but Duntov worked to improve the suspension, and the use of a V8 power unit and manual gearbox saw the car take off as a rival for the Thunderbird introduced by Ford in 1955.

Right: 1957 'Two Ten' Sport Sedan
Below: 1958 Delray Utility Sedan
Below right: 1957 Impala Sport Coupé

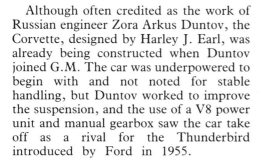

Below: The Corvair was built between 1960 and 1969, and had a unitary-construction body, all-independent suspension, and a rear-mounted air-cooled flat-six engine. After the Corvair was publicly condemned as unsafe, its sales slumped.

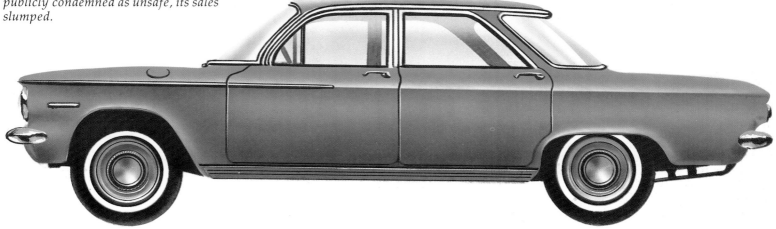

Above: 1959 Impala Sport sedan hardtop
Right: 1961 Nomad station wagon

The compact Corvair went on sale in 1959, as did the first of the Impala range, but the former was too unusual for a conservative market to sell well, although it was not dropped until 1969. In 1962

Right: 1961 Corvette

Above: 1961 Corvair 700 coupé

Above: 1962 Impala hardtop sedan

The 1964 Corvette Sting Ray lost the previous year's split rear window but was otherwise little changed. With fuel injection, the Corvette's 5.7-litre V8 engine developed 395bhp.

The Camaro Z-28 was a four-seater sports coupé with a 4948cc V8 engine giving 290bhp. It featured unitary construction, coil-spring-and-wishbone independent front suspension, and semi-elliptic leaf-spring rear suspension.

Above: 1963 Chevy II compact sedan
Below: Some of the 1964 Chevrolet range

Above: 1963 Impala Sport Sedan

came the Chevy II, to bridge the gap between the Corvair and the larger Impala, Biscayne, and Bel Air models. The slightly bigger Chevelle model followed in 1964, together with the Corvette Sting Ray, and the model range was then priced from U.S. $2,028 for the simple 90bhp four-cylinder Chevy II, to U.S. $3,347 for the Caprice Custom station wagon.

The Camaro sports coupé was introduced in 1967, tapping into the booming muscle-car market. It was a late challenge to the Ford Mustang, but more than two decades later the Camaro name – and the classic front-engine, rear-wheel-drive concept – was still exciting driving enthusiasts. Memorably, the Camaro IROC-Z of 1989 adopted the 350-cubic inch (5.7-litre) V-8 of the L98-engined Corvette, its outputs of 240bhp and 345lb-ft of torque allowing a top speed close to 240km/h (150mph).

By the 1970s Chevrolet engines were being used by a variety of other manufacturers in their products. The largest eight-cylinder Opels were Chevrolet-powered, as were the smaller six-cylinder Oldsmobiles. The new version of the 8/10 Cord also used a Chevrolet engine, as did the limited-production Gordon-Keeble and the US–Italian Iso and Bizzarini, as well as Canadian-built products such as Pontiac, Acadian, and the last of the Studebakers.

In the early 1970s Chevrolet bought into the Japanese Isuzu company, beginning to integrate some of that company's models into its own range. The fuel crisis caused it hastily to scale down the size of its cars and sales were down, too. The sub-compact Vega was offered in 1971, and two years later the range included the Chevy II, Nova, Monte Carlo, Bel Air, Camaro, Corvette, Caprice luxury model and the Blazer and Suburban station wagon/utility vehicles. Chevrolet brought out what it described as a 'world car' in 1976 in the form of the compact Chevette.

By 1980 the front-wheel-drive Citation was launched, with a transverse engine, and Oldsmobile diesel units were in use in larger V8-engined models. Four years later the introduction of the Cavalier brought great success to the company. In the mid-1980s the company began using its Japanese contacts, offering Isuzu and Suzuki models under different names, and collaborating with Toyota on the 1984 Nova model.

Chevrolet's production of cars and utility vehicles is still among the largest in the world, although it lost pole position in 1980. The company's most interesting current offering is the amazing six-speed Corvette ZR-1.

Above: 1972 Camaro Z-28
Below: 1974 Vega hatchback coupé

Below: 1974 Monte Carlo Landau coupé
Bottom: 1987 Camaro Z-28

Top: 1987 Camaro LT
Above: 1989 Caprice Classic sedan
Below: 1989 Beretta GT coupé

Above: 1989 Corsica hatchback

Below: 1989 Camaro IROC-Z

Left: 1989 Celebrity Eurosport sedan

Below: the 1989 Corvette ZR-1 had a 380bhp V8 engine developed in conjunction with Lotus. There was a six-speed gearbox and limited-slip differential. Zero to 96km/h (0-60mph) was claimed to take just over 4 seconds.

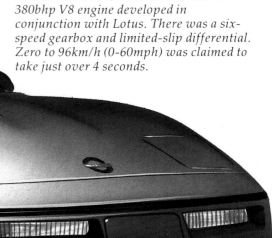

By the early 1990s G.M.'s market share had fallen from its peak of 46 per cent in the late seventies to 35 per cent, despite a large increase in the number of staff.

Whereas other companies had more successfully changed with the times, Chevrolet, G.M.'s largest division was starting to look a little old and inefficient. The firm took around a third more man hours to build a car than its Big 3 rivals and losses within G.M. of around $800 million a month were enough to curb spending on new models.

In 1992 Chevrolet had 38 different cars and 80 different truck models. The way ahead was clear; Chevy would have to cut the number of models, so that's just what it did. Management planned to cut 20 per cent by the turn of the century and to reduce the number of different vehicle platforms from 21 to just seven in order to spread out engineering costs and increase the number of common components. This helped to stem the huge losses that the company was experiencing and started to turn the tide of Chevrolet's fortune.

In 1995, G.M. finally abandoned production of its ageing 'land yachts', the full-sized, rear-drive leviathans like Chevrolet's bulbous Caprice. The Caprice plant was switched to truck production, to cash in on the truck's rise in popularity by the mid-1990s. At the same time, the company was undergoing radical changes to its working practices, with Japanese-style

Above: 1998 Chevrolet Blazer four-door LT

management structures, in an attempt to increase efficiency.

By 1997, G.M. had launched more new models than it had done in years and was showing signs of returning to the form of the great company that it had been. One new model that was particularly welcome was the sixth generation Corvette, a high-tech marvel that was easily capable of taking on some of the world's greatest sports cars. Unlike previous Corvettes, it was rumoured that this model would also go to Europe.

Below: Chevrolet Monte Carlo Z34 coupé

Below: Cavalier LS convertible

Above: 1997 Chevrolet Geo Prizm

Above: Camaro Z28 Brickyard 400 pace car

Above: The 1997 Chevrolet Corvette coupé is shown with its ancestors, the previous four styles of Corvette sports cars

Above: Chevrolet S-series pick-up

Above: Corvette convertible

Above: The Tracker was rebadged Suzuki Vitara

Above: Chevrolet Geo Metro LSI

Above: 1997 Lumina Sedan

Above: Regular wheelbase Venture

Chrysler

U.S.A.
1923 to date

In November 1921 Walter P. Chrysler took control of the Maxwell Motor Corporation, outbidding Willys, White, Studebaker and Durant to do so. He became president of the firm and continued producing Maxwell-badged cars for the next four years.

In 1923, however, Chrysler recruited three former Studebaker designers, Owen Skelton, Fred Zeder and Carl Breer to work on a model to be launched under his own name. This appeared the following year as the Chrysler 70, and was produced in Detroit, at the former Chalmers factory. There were 4,000 dealer outlets for the new car, which achieved sales of over 30,000 in that first year. Also in 1925 the Maxwell name disappeared.

Below: The 1926 B-series was offered with a variety of bodies; this is a five-passenger brougham. All the B-series cars had L-head six-cylinder engines and four-wheel hydraulic brakes.

The Chrysler Corporation was formed in June of that year, with capital of U.S. $400 million and seven plants in three different states and Canada.

There were four models offered in the 1926 range, including the sophisticated Chrysler 60, and the first Imperial,

destined to become a separate marque from 1954, which used bodies by various coachbuilders, including Fisher and LeBaron.

In 1927 responsibility for manufacturing was taken over by former General Motors man, K. T. Keller, who went on to become president in 1935. The following year the De Soto line was offered to compete with Pontiac, Oldsmobile and the less-expensive Nashes. To rival the cheap

Left: 1925 Series B-70 tourer

Above: 1926 Imperial E-80

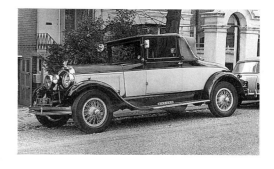

Above: 1928 72 cabriolet
Below: 1927 Chrysler 62

Above: 1926 Chrysler 60

Above: 1929 Roadster

Below: 1930 Model 70 Sportsman's Coupé

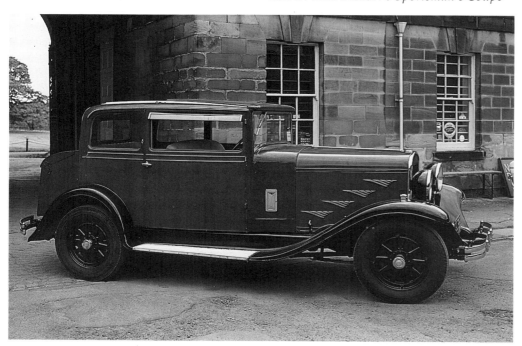

Ford and Chevrolet cars the Plymouth marque appeared the same year. The acquisition of Dodge for U.S. $175 million in 1928 filled the slot just above De Soto's price range, also providing Chrysler with a truck manufacturer, and moved the firm up to third place in the American sales league. Factory space increased five-fold.

Fred L. Rockelman took control of the company from 1930 and the first straight-eight-engined cars were launched the year after. The company survived the Depression only showing a loss in 1932. Chrysler was noted for experimentation and technical development, introducing power brakes, automatic clutches and a free spare wheel in 1932. A new method of rubber mounting engines, called Floating Power, was brought in during this time, and was soon adopted by Citroën. The following year saw the arrival of synchromesh transmission.

In 1928 Chrysler had begun development of a revolutionary new car of streamlined unitary construction which

Above: 1935 Airflow C-1

was finally launched in 1934, with the company's new automatic overdrive. The Airflow proved too futuristic for the motoring public and was a commercial disaster, although it was continued for appearances' sake until 1937. Chrysler hurriedly rushed out the less-extravagant Airstream in 1935 to try and salvage sales. This failure caused the company's styling policy to become over-cautious until Virgil Exner's Flite Sweep bodywork of the mid-1950s. Further technical improvements appeared in 1937 – hypoid rear axles and independent front suspension – and in 1939 came a steering-column gear change and optional fluid drive or torque converter.

In 1940 Walter Chrysler died and Keller took over as Chief Executive. Two years later the company went over to war production, making a variety of military equipment, including aircraft fuselages and tanks. Chrysler is still a major tank manufacturer.

Civilian production resumed in 1946 when Town and Country wooden exterior trim appeared on Chrysler models. A new

Below: The 1949 New Yorker had an eight-cylinder engine of 135bhp and could be ordered with Prestomatic semi-automatic transmission. The 1949 models were very conservative in appearance, but had distinctive tail lights.

feature in 1949 was ignition-key starting and two years later came the innovative overhead-valve V8, designed by Chief Engineer Rob Roger, James Zeder, and Owen Skelton, which was followed by Power Flight automatic transmission in 1953. The new engine finally completely replaced the old six-cylinder sidevalve unit in 1955, and was used by a variety of other manufacturers, including Allard, Cunningham, and Jensen in England.

In the mid-1950s Chrysler began experimenting with gas-turbine-powered cars, which boosted its image. Earlier, Exner had helped increase Chrysler's prestige with his range of dream-car designs, actually built by Ghia under the Dual-Ghia name. In 1955 came the new styling, which brought the appearance of the cars up to their interior and build quality.

By 1958 De Soto's sales had slumped so badly that the marque was discontinued two years later. That year Plymouth launched the Valiant compact range, sold under the Chrysler name abroad. In 1965 Virgil Boyd took over as president and Elwood P. Engel was in charge of styling. The V8 Barracuda, a successful model based on the Valiant, was offered that year.

Meanwhile Chrysler had been expanding its interests overseas, taking control of Simca in 1963, and partly purchasing the British Rootes group to form Chrysler United Kingdom Ltd. by 1970. That year the company also gained a 15 per cent holding in Mitsubishi (since reduced to release cash), its later compacts showing

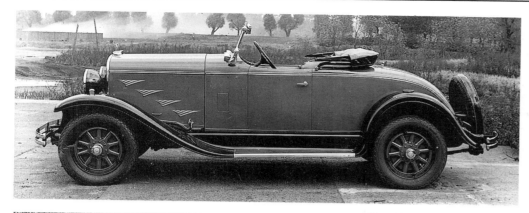

Left: 1930 Series 70 roadster

Above: 1931 CD Eight convertible coupé

Above: 1946 C-38W Windsor Traveler
sedan
Right: 1955 C300 coupé

Above: 1975 Chrysler (UK) Alpine S

Left: 1974 New Yorker four-door hardtop

Above: 1976 Chrysler (UK) Avenger
Super
Left: 1975 Chrysler (UK) Hunter De Luxe

both French and Japanese influences. The company also had interests in the Barreiros truck company in Spain.

These acquisitions were rationalized during the oil crisis of the early 1970s, and the Rootes-based group only narrowly escaped collapse. South African and South American interests were also affected. E. A. Cafiero became president in the mid-1970s, followed by former Ford chairman Lee A. Iacocca. Chrysler's fortunes wavered between small profits and hefty losses, and at one time it had U.S. $1,000 million debts with 115 different banks. The Imperial line was axed in 1975 and towards the end of that decade four-cylinder cars began to gain importance.

Above: 1977 Chrysler (UK) Sunbeam S

Below: The 1970 Chrysler 180 was actually a Rootes design, but was built in France at the Simca factory which Chrysler owned. Its 100bhp four-cylinder engine of 1812cc drove through a four-speed gearbox.

Top left: 1990 Eagle Talon sports coupé
Above left: Le Baron Turbo GTC
Top: 1990 TC sports coupé
Above: 1990 New Yorker luxury sedan

Above: 1990 Eagle Premier ES sedan
Right: 1990 Le Baron sedan

Below: 1990 Eagle Premier ES Limited

Left: 1990 Eagle Premier LX sedan
Below: 1990 Eagle Summit ES sedan
Bottom: 1990 Eagle Summit LX sports sedan

Mitsubishi engines were increasingly used in the early 1980s, when the respected LeBaron name was revived. By 1982 the company was back in profit, retaining interests in Japan and Peugeot in France. In 1986 came the Chrysler-Maserati collaboration on an image-building convertible the 'T.C. by Maserati', but this relationship was always fraught. In the late 1980s Chrysler acquired American Motors, including Jeep, and also bought Lamborghini, which led to a V12 Formula One engine, and to Chrysler partially severing its ties with Maserati. After the AMC takeover in 1987, Chrysler launched the Eagle marque in December of that year.

Top: 1980 Jeep Cherokee Chief
Centre left: 1990 Jeep Wrangler Laredo
Centre right: 1980 Jeep CJ-7 Laredo

Left: 1990 Jeep Wrangler S
Above: 1990 Jeep Wrangler Islander

Top: 1990 Jeep Wagoneer Limited
Above: 1990 Jeep Grand Wagoneer
Top right: 1989 Conquest TS1
Right: 1990 Chrysler TC by Maserati

Below: The 1986 Chrysler-Maserati convertible was the result of Chrysler's collaboration with the famous Italian maker, but the relationship was not wholly successful. The Chrysler 2.2-litre engine was tuned by Maserati.

By the late 1980s, Chrysler was lagging behind the other members of America's Big Three and looked set to continue on a downward slide. However, clever management and design rationalization soon saw the company on the route to recovery.

While many of Chrysler's cars had been Mitsubishi-based during the 1980s, the 1990s saw the company starting to push its own products. The biggest step forward was the development of the L/H range of cars, which some wags in the industry suggested stood for 'Last Hope'. To cigar-smoking Chrysler President Bob Lutz, they meant 'Latest Hit', and he was right.

The new car's cab forward design soon proved popular with buyers, improving the company's sales and image in the process.

The L/H cars weren't just good-looking though; much thought had gone into their design and construction. By economizing without sacrificing quality, Chrysler were able to make more profit per car sold than

either Ford or General Motors.

The success of the L/H cars led to the Neon compact car. The Big Three had by this time largely abandoned building their own small cars, so it was unusual for Chrysler to consider re-entering the market. Building on the management techniques that had brought the company the L/H cars, Chrysler managed to take the Neon from concept car to production vehicle in only 31 months and the project required only half the amount of engineers usually assigned to

Top: The Jeep Cherokee was updated under the skin in 1996 but was outwardly almost exactly the same

Left: 1997 Chrysler Neon

Below: The Chrysler World HQ and technology centre in Detroit

Cherokee, launched in 1992, soon attracted the same kind of following.

In May 1998 Chrysler, whose marques include Plymouth, Dodge and Jeep, entered into a £24 billion merger with Daimler-Benz. The split was 57% to Daimler-Benz, who will concentrate mostly on passenger cars, and 43% to Chrysler, who are expected to develop the sport utility and pickup market, sharing platforms and development costs.

Above: Chrysler Sebring Convertible

Right: 1998 Jeep Grand Cherokee

such a project. The cost, too, of $1.3 billion, was a fraction of what is normally spent. Ford's Mondeo project, for example, cost around $6 billion.

While Chrysler's factories didn't even rate in the top 10 most efficient car plants in North America, it was still able to make more profit per car.

The Jeep Wrangler and Cherokee 4x4s continued to sell well in an atmosphere where truck sales were growing rapidly, and had gathered a cult following. The Grand

Above: Chrysler Town and Country

Right: 1998 Sebring Coupé

Below right: Chrysler Concorde

Below:: 1996 Jeep Wrangler

Cisitalia

Italy
1946–1965

Piero Dusio, founder of Cisitalia, was a professional footballer forced to retire early because of injury. He went successfully into sales for a large textile firm, affording not only to buy his own competition cars, but also to set up Scuderia Torino, sponsoring others to race. By the end of the 1930s he was a wealthy industrialist whose interests included manufacturing sporting goods. His organization was called Consorzio Industriale Sportivo Italia, from which the name Cisitalia is derived.

After World War II Dusio realized his idea of building competition cars, utilizing the considerable talents of ex-Fiat engineer Dante Giacosa to design the new car. This was to be a spartan racer easy to mass-produce and based, with that company's consent, on Fiat components.

Giacosa designed his own chassis for a Fiat engine and in mid-1945 Dusio took on Dr. Giovanni Savonuzzi, also previously with Fiat, to organize production. This car, the D46, had immediate racing success, considerably boosting Cisitalia's sporting reputation.

Various other prototype bodies were produced around this time, by Farina,

Vignale and Pininfarina. High placings in the 1947 Mille Miglia brought increased orders that Cisitalia had trouble meeting, but Dusio had dreams of entering the Grand Prix arena. Through Carlo Abarth in Turin, Dusio contacted Dr. Ferdinand Porsche who designed a suitable supercharged car for him. Working alongside Porsche were competition engineers Dr. Eberan von Eberhorst and Ing. Karl Rabe.

Unfortunately, the project soon exceeded its budget, and when Savonuzzi's fears that the final costs would be five times the initial estimate were ignored, he resigned. Dusio replaced him with Rudolf Hrushka and continued at the expense of all else. By 1949 he was bankrupt.

Dusio then sold the remains of his company to Automotores Argentinos – Autoar – in the hope of reviving the marque with government backing, but only Cisitalia-badged Willys-type vehicles were built. In 1952 Dusio tried again in Italy, with his son Carlo, producing an unsuccessful series of rebodied Fiats. The last Cisitalias, built between 1961 and 1965, were the generally unremarkable small-engined Coupé Tourism Specials.

Below: The bodywork on this 1947 Cisitalia 202 coupé was by Pininfarina. The engine was a 1090cc Fiat four-cylinder, tuned to produce 60bhp. Few were made before financial troubles overtook the company.

Citroën

France
1919 to date

André Citroën was a graduate of the élite *Ecole Polytechnique* in Paris who was taken on as Chief Engineer by the Mors concern in 1908 after spending time in the French Army as an engineering officer. His genius lay in production methods, and he demonstrated this by streamlining the Mors assembly lines.

Above: 1922 Type A 5CV two-seater

Above: 1922 Type B2 'Caddy' roadster

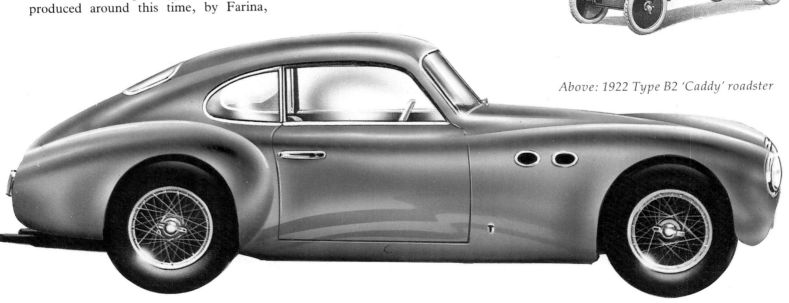

But Citroën was anxious to set up on his own and, in 1913, he started his own company to manufacture gearwheels, in particular of the double-helical design which would later be reflected in the chevrons adopted as the Citroën car company's emblem. During World War I, the French Government helped him to buy a large factory in Paris where he applied his manufacturing flair to the mass-production of shells for the French Army.

After the war, Citroën devoted this factory and its modern American machine-tools to car production. He started in 1919 with the type A, designed in association with Jules Salomon (who had already worked for Le Zebre and

Above: Citroën London taxi, mid-1920s

Above right: 1925 B12 all-steel Torpedo
Right: 1926 B14 Coupé de Ville taxi

would later move on to Rosengart). The type A was intended to be a car for Everyman, and Citroën mass-produced it in far larger numbers than his rivals could achieve. This lasted until 1921, when it was replaced with the type B2, an improved version with a larger engine.

As before, a variety of bodies could be had, running costs were cheap and the volume-production enabled Citroën to keep the purchase price low. In 1921 Citroën also launched the small type C, broadly similar to the B2 in design and intended to appeal to women drivers. This was another huge success, but was withdrawn in 1926 when Citroën recognized that there was more profit to be made from his larger cars.

The 5CV Type C model was introduced in 1921. Its 856cc engine had coil ignition and a detachable head. The car soon earned itself the punning nickname of 'Petit Citron' ('little lemon') after its most popular colour.

By this stage, Citroën had already branched out far beyond car manufacture. In 1923, he had set up his own taxi company, using exclusively his own B2 taxis. A thriving commercial-vehicle range was also in production, having grown gradually out of the B2 cars, and from 1932 the *Société des Transports André Citroën* ran a vast network of bus and coach services all over France – using, of course, single-deck buses built by Citroën.

Such services, besides bringing additional revenue to the Citroën empire, also functioned as a form of advertising, which was a sphere in which André Citroën excelled. Going far further than his contemporaries, he advertised his products not only in the usual specialist publications but also in the national press; he arranged for the company name to be written in the sky over Paris by an aeroplane in 1922; and he displayed it in lights on all four sides of the Eiffel Tower at night. Throughout the 1920s and early 1930s, he even sent convoys of Citroën vehicles – mostly the half-track *Kégresse* models – across the most impenetrable deserts in order to demonstrate their ruggedness and durability.

Seeking still-more efficient production methods, Citroën signed an agreement with the American Budd Company to produce all-steel bodies under licence. The first such bodies appeared on B10 models in 1924, and the B range was progressively improved until its demise in 1928. The inherent design flexibility of the later models allowed Citroën to produce a large number of variants of the same basic model relatively cheaply.

The B range was replaced by the C4 (four-cylinder) and C6 (six-cylinder) models, which showed strong American design influence. These lasted until 1932 when a new 'Rosalie' range arrived, with simpler and stronger bodies based on a common new design. Citroën was able to juggle trim and specification levels and, approving the offerings of outside coachbuilders, catalogued no fewer than 83 different models.

Up to this point, Citroën models had been largely conventional in their design, but an individualistic streak came to the fore in 1934, when the Rosalies were replaced by the revolutionary *Traction Avant* (literally, 'front-wheel-drive').

Above: 1925 Type C
Left: 1932 C6 coach

Left: 1928 C4 four-door saloon
Above: 1928 Rosalie 15CV saloon

The 1934 Traction Avant featured an all-steel monocoque with the engine and transmission mounted on a detachable subframe, front-wheel-drive, and all-independent suspension by torsion bars.

Again offering a wide range of variants based on a common design, this was the first mass-produced car in Europe to feature chassisless monocoque construction, independent suspension on all four wheels, and front-wheel-drive. Its overhead-valve wet-liner engine was also new. This outstandingly successful vehicle remained available until 1957, but the cost of getting it into production drove Citroën to bankruptcy and the company was bought at the end of 1934 by its principal creditors, the Michelin tyre firm. André Citroën himself died a year later.

A new small Citroën was introduced in 1948. This was the 2CV, with an air-cooled flat-twin engine driving the front wheels and an interconnected suspension system. It offered ingenious solutions to the problems of cheap motoring, and soon became a cult car, continuing in production for the next four decades. Even after French production ceased in 1988, 2CV manufacture continued in some of Citroën's overseas plants. It had been joined in 1961 by the larger Ami and in 1967 by the more sophisticated Dyane, both of which were based on the same design. Both, however, ceased production in the 1970s.

Meanwhile, the introduction in 1955 of the new large Citroën had again demonstrated the company's commitment to advanced technology. The futuristically styled S saloon had high pressure hydraulic circuits for its self-levelling suspension, brakes, steering and gearchange, and broke new ground with its revolutionary 'base-unit' construction, consisting of a steel inner skeleton to which unstressed outer panels were bolted. The D was also the first production car in the world to have front-wheel disc brakes as standard; in 1967 it pioneered auxiliary headlights which turned with the steering to light the road on bends; and, in 1969, the DS21 version became the first French production car to have electronic fuel-injection.

Citroën experimented with rotary engines in the late 1960s and early 1970s, sharing development with the German NSU company, but the production cars of the 1970s retained their conventional piston engines. The GS of 1971 fitted between the D range and the small 2CV/Ami/Dyane models, offering a

Above: 1933 Rosalie 8CV Faux-Cabriolet   *Above right: 1934 Traction Avant 11CV saloon*

Reproduced with permission
© Haynes Publishing Group, 1981

Above: 1955 DS19 saloon
Below: 1948 375cc 2CV
Bottom: 1959 DS Safari estate

Above: 1961 British-built Bijou
Below: 1961 Ami-6 saloon

Left: The 2CV was designed as a car for French rural communities and put ease of maintenance, practicality and frugality above all other qualities. The 1948 original was still readily recognizable in this 1970s 602cc version.

light-alloy, air-cooled, overhead-valve flat-four engine, disc brakes and the hydropneumatic suspension among its many refinements, while the low-volume SM grand tourer of 1970 added a high-performance Maserati engine gained through a short-lived link with the Italian manufacturer to the characteristic Citroën technology.

The SM previewed some of the features which would be seen in the CX saloons, introduced in 1974 to replace the D models. This included a controversial steering system with power-assisted self-centring. In appearance, the CX was less idiosyncratic than recent Citroëns had been, although this was perhaps more a result of other manufacturers catching up than of Citroën regressing. On its introduction, the CX won Europe's Car of the Year award, plus a safety award and a further award for body design, thus becoming the first car ever to claim all three awards at once. A wide range of variants followed, including the first diesel-powered Citroën in 1975; and the range remained in production until 1989, when it was replaced by the distinctive, Bertone-styled XM. Notable for its

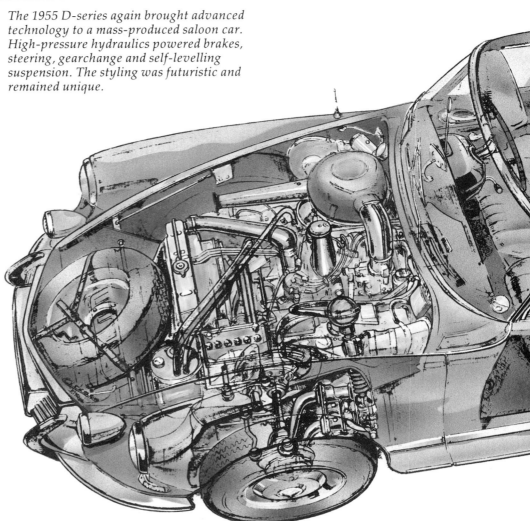

The 1955 D-series again brought advanced technology to a mass-produced saloon car. High-pressure hydraulics powered brakes, steering, gearchange and self-levelling suspension. The styling was futuristic and remained unique.

Above: 1971 GS saloon

Above: 1972 Dyane 6

Below: 1974 SM coupé

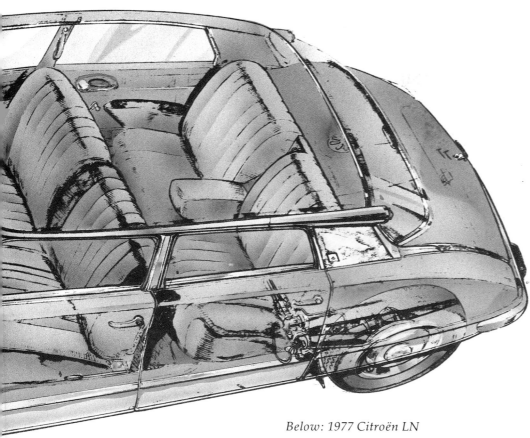

'hydractive' suspension system – which automatically adjusts spring and damper settings to allow an absorbent ride over poor surfaces but sharply composed handling through corners – this was also acclaimed Car of the Year, in 1990.

Citroën was bought by former rival Peugeot in 1975, and the marque began to lose some of its individuality. The small LN and later LNA models simply fitted Citroën's air-cooled twin-cylinder engine into a Peugeot body shell; and the Visa initially added the air-cooled flat-twin and a new body to a Peugeot floorpan, later taking on a four-cylinder Peugeot engine option as well.

In the 1980s, however, this cross-fertilization between the two companies was no longer so apparent. The first new model was the BX of 1983, which replaced the GS range. Although the engines were conventional designs from the Peugeot stable, the BX had Citroën's characteristic self-levelling hydropneumatic suspension and disc brakes all round. Styling – by Lamborghini, Miura and Countach designer Marcello Cardini while he was at Bertone – was distinctive if somewhat less outrageous than Citroën designs of recent years had tended to be. And, most importantly, the BX sold extremely well.

Below: 1977 Citroën LN

Production of the 2CV for Citroën's main markets finally ceased in 1988, but the model which was to replace it had arrived the previous year. Once again, Peugeot engines were used, and the car fitted into the existing 'supermini' bracket rather than creating its own market niche as the 2CV had done 40 years earlier. Nevertheless, the AX offered an attractive combination of style, practicality and cheap running costs. Light commercials based on the Visa car range were also available into the late 1980s, and Citroën continued to manufacture or assemble cars in several foreign countries, while some Citroën-based designs were being built under licence in eastern European countries.

Above: 1979 Visa Super

Above: 1979 CX2400 Pallas

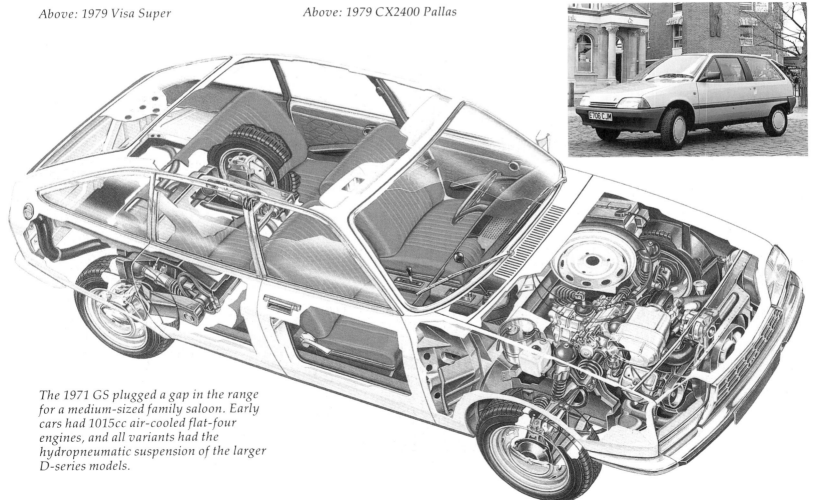

The 1971 GS plugged a gap in the range for a medium-sized family saloon. Early cars had 1015cc air-cooled flat-four engines, and all variants had the hydropneumatic suspension of the larger D-series models.

Left: 1987 AX 11TRE hatchback   *Above: 1979 GS Club Break (estate car)*   *Below: 1989 XM saloon*

As well as producing more conventional models, Citroën also persisted with developing hydropneumatic suspension. In the Xantia (the BX replacement, launched in 1992), Citroën engineers fitted an active suspension that cancelled out body roll completely. This system, known as Activa by Citroën, was usually fitted to the larger 2.0- or 3.0-litre engine models.

For those who were frightened by all the traditional Citroën plumbing, there were more conventional models, such as the ZX, also launched in 1992 with normal, coil-sprung suspension. A sales success, the ZX was also available as an estate.

The little AX continued well into the 1990s and was still sold following the launch of its replacement, the Saxo, in 1995. The Saxo was little more than a Peugeot 106 with a new nose and tail. The engine range was the same as the Peugeot's and included a hot 118bhp 1.6-litre unit for the very sporting Saxo VTS.

The quirky XM remained relatively unchanged as Citroën's slow-selling, top-of-the range model.

A new departure for the company was the launch of the Synergie, or Evasion, as it was known on some markets. This people carrier, Citroën's first, was the result of a collaboration between Peugeot/Citroën and Fiat/Lancia, who all had their own versions of the same car.

Right: By Citroën standards, the ZX was a very conventional car. It was also the company's best-selling car. In 1991, the Rally Raid version won the Paris-Dakar Rally with a comfortable lead

Above: The XM was a traditonal Citroën with strange looks and even stranger mechanics. Unfortunately, it wasn't a big seller

Left: The Berlingo was Citroën's answer to Renault's successful Mégane Scenic in the new mini MPV class

Above: The Citroën Xantia was the first production car to have active suspension

Above: The Saxo replaced the AX in 1996. This is the top-of-the-range model, the VTS

Above: The Synergie, or Evasion, was built in conjunction with Peugeot, Fiat and Lancia

Clyno

Great Britain
1922–1929

The Wolverhampton firm of Clyno – originally motorcycle manufacturers – began assembling cars in 1922. The 10.8hp Clyno used the dependable 1.4-litre Coventry-Climax engine. This drove the rear wheels via a torque tube, a cone-type clutch and the company's own three-speed gearbox.

Clyno earned a justifiable reputation for reliability, and by 1926 up to 350 10.8s were being produced each week. By this time, the car had gained a differential, plain (instead of roller-type) engine bearings, four-wheel braking, and semi-elliptic leaf-spring suspension. The 10.8 ('Eleven') was built in several versions, including a high-specification Royal model.

Clyno's Frank Smith aimed his company's vehicles at the market dominated by the huge rival firm of Morris and, indeed, the 10.8hp Clyno challenged the Cowley of the same era for sales, with virtually identical pricing and improved equipment. The saloon version of the Clyno had four doors and four-wheel brakes, for example, compared with two of each on the equivalent Morris Cowley.

In an attempt to repeat this success against the larger Morris Oxford, a Clyno 12/28 model was introduced, based on the short-lived 1924 11.9hp, and the company's premises were expanded.

Unfortunately, by the late 1920s Clynos were beginning to look a little dated, and sales started to decline.

Problems multiplied because Frank Smith tried to build cars down to a price – specifically as close as possible to the magical £100 figure. In Clyno's attempt to achieve this, the fabric-bodied Nine, introduced in 1928, was made available in a very basic form as the Century but it was not a success. This did not help an already under-capitalized firm, nor did the withdrawal by the distributors, Rootes.

Although Clyno built larger models, notably the 12/35, and had even

Above: The popular Clyno 10.8hp (1926)   Below: 1926 Clyno Royale

experimented with a 22hp, straight-eight-cylinder prototype, the writing was on the wall. The company did not survive beyond 1929, having by this time built some 36,000 cars.

Above: One of the larger Clynos, the 12/35hp, like this 1927 example, performed well but did not sell in large numbers
Below: 1927 Clyno 10.8hp

Continental
U.S.A.
1955–1960

The Continental marque was produced by a separate division of the Ford Motor Co., which was created in 1955 with the aim of producing luxury, up-market cars to compete with Cadillac.

Since production of the original Lincoln Continental ceased in 1948, Ford had been under pressure to produce a successor and, in 1956, the Continental Mark II was introduced.

The Special Products Division, as it was known, was headed by William Clay Ford, younger brother of Henry Ford II who commissioned several outside consultants to produce design proposals for the new car. The management committee finally selected the design from the Special Products Division, and Harley F. Copp, chief engineer, designed a unique chassis for the new model that was low enough between the axles to give a high seating position but without a high roof line.

Designed primarily as an 'image' car rather than a profit maker, the Mark II was flawlessly hand-built, had graceful lines and was priced at U.S. $10,000. The car was powered by a specially assembled Lincoln V8 engine and three-speed automatic transmission.

Although there was initial enthusiasm for the Mark II, it did not sell very well, and G.M. was still the leader in the luxury-car market. A lower-priced 'new' Continental model, dubbed the Mark III, was available from 1959 to 1960, based on the standard Lincoln model, but even at U.S. $6,000 this did not sell very well either. In view of the disappointing sales, the four-door Berline and convertible models were never produced.

In 1959, in line with an upper management decision, the 'Continental' marque was dropped and the car became a Lincoln as it had been before, and Continental as a separate division was gone by late 1960, merged with Lincoln and Mercury.

Cord

U.S.A.
1929–1937

Cord entered the car scene at the end of the 1920s. This rakish American marque was launched in 1929 by Erret Lobban Cord, who gave the U.S.A. its first front-wheel-drive car in reasonable numbers.

As a teenager Cord had made and lost considerable sums of money buying and selling used Model T Fords in and around Los Angeles, California. Legend has it that he was down on his luck with only 20 dollars in his pocket and he decided to try for better fortune in Chicago. There he got himself a job as a salesman for a Moon dealership, selling the Victory model which became extremely popular.

His talents as a salesman in his early twenties saw him earn terrific commission, and his wages were reported to be 15 times those of a skilled worker.

When sales of the Victory model began to decline Cord showed an interest in the Auburn Automobile Company which, in 1924, was in the hands of a receiver.

He was given the chance to reorganize the company and within a year he had restored its fortunes and expanded the manufacturing plant at Auburn, Indiana.

Cord then decided he wanted to build a car bearing his name, and the Cord L-29 was introduced into Auburn showrooms in October 1929. This front-wheel-drive car, with a straight-eight-cylinder 125bhp Lycoming FDA engine of 4.9 litres, created tremendous interest. Resembling the J-series Duesenberg, the exclusive Cord was long and sleek. It was available in four styles – Brougham, Sedan, Convertible Cabriolet and Convertible Phaeton.

The car remained in production until 1932 (the worst sales year in the U.S.A. since the end of World War I), some 4,429 having been built during that time. Magnificent though it was, however, it had an Achilles' heel of universal-joint failure because of the front-wheel-drive.

The Depression of the early 1930s did not help matters and production of Cord

Above: 1929 Cord L29

cars was not taken up again until 1936 when Cord brought out an all-new 810 model designed by Gordon Buehrig.

Originally conceived as a 'small' Duesenberg, the new machine continued the front-wheel-drive crusade and was powered by a 4.7-litre Lycoming V8 engine giving 125bhp at 3,500rpm.

A supercharged version, the 812 giving 195bhp, was introduced in 1937, but these stunning but expensive new models were not sales successes. Perhaps one of the reasons was that they were too modern for their day, for in later years they gained great appreciation and esteem, the design

being cited for its beauty by the Museum of Modern Art in New York.

Also some small companies made replicas starting with Glenn Pray of Oklahoma who used a flat-six Chevrolet Corvair engine to power his glassfibre homage to the 810/812 series which came to a halt in 1937 after only 2,320 had been built. Pray's replica, made from 1964–72, stayed faithful to the front-wheel-drive concept.

The passing of the Cord signified the passing of a flamboyant time in American

The Cord L-29 was introduced in 1929. The front-wheel-drive system came from engineering genius Harry Miller who had designed a fwd racing car in 1925. The engine was a 4894cc Lycoming straight eight.

automotive history. The victim of high prices and a lengthy depression, the Cord was part of an Auburn-Cord-Duesenberg triumvirate which produced some of the most magnificent machines in the history of motoring.

Former racing driver Cord, who earned a reputation for buying companies 'on the cheap', had acquired Duesenberg in 1928 plus the Lycoming engine factory. Auburn production ceased in 1936, and Duesenberg joined the Cord marque when it disappeared in 1937.

In that year Cord himself is reported to have gone bankrupt, but the dynamic entrepreneur held on to his Lycoming engine factory and supplied aero-engines during World War II. The man who made and lost fortunes and shaped some of the world's most stylish cars died in 1974.

Top: 1936 Cord 810 Sportsman   Above: 1937 Cord 812 Phaeton   Below: 1937 Cord 812 Sedan

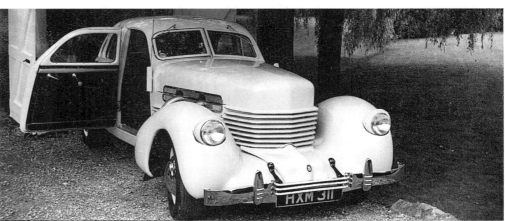

Crossley

Great Britain
1904–1937

Crossley made stationary engines before building vehicles, but the first Crossley car – a 22hp four-cylinder machine with Mercedes-like design and chain-drive – appeared in 1904. This car and its successors, the 20/28 and 40hp models, were designed by J. S. Critchley (from Daimler) and W. M. MacFarland.

The Manchester-based company turned from chain- to shaft-drive in 1906, and had used four-wheel brakes by 1910. For this year two new models were introduced – the 12/14 and the four-litre 20hp, both designed by G. Hubert Woods and A. W. Reeves. These cars developed into 15hp and 20/25hp models, which were produced by a new subsidiary company – Crossley Motors Ltd. – set up for manufacturing vehicles.

In 1913 a 15hp 'Shelsley' model was introduced, with a monobloc L-head engine.

Many Crossley 20/25s were used by the War Department during World War I. After the war, the 20/25 was developed

Top: Ex. World War I 4½-litre Crossley 25/30
Left: The reliable Crossley 20/25

Below: 1925/6 Crossley 12/14

into the larger, 4½-litre 25/30.

A new Crossley for 1921 was the 19.6hp model. Designed by T. D. Wishart, the car featured a detachable cylinder head, as did the sports version, the 20/70hp, a heavy car, but guaranteed by the manufacturers to achieve 75mph (120 km/h).

In 1923, Crossley offered a 12/14hp model, but by 1926 the company had turned from sidevalve fours to overhead-valve sixes, and the 2.6-litre 18/50 emerged. Two years later the engine was enlarged to 3.2 litres (now rated at 20.9hp), this version being made for some nine years.

In 1928, Crossley introduced a two-litre 15.7hp saloon, with a sports ('Shelsley') version available from1929. The 15.7 was built into the 1930s, the engine also being used by Lagonda for its 16/80.

In 1932 the Crossley Ten was announced. It had an 1100cc Coventry-Climax engine and a preselector gearbox. Another fascinating car was the independently sprung, rear-engined Crossley-Burney of 1934, powered by the six-cylinder, two-litre 15.7hp engine. Sadly, only two dozen were built.

In 1935 the attractive Regis – in four-cylinder, 1100cc 'Ten', or six-cylinder, 1500cc form – was introduced. However, even these were discontinued after 1937.

Above: The Crossley 19.6hp, 1921 on
Left: An early Crossley 22hp

Left: 1907 Crossley 30/40hp
Below: 1933 Crossley Torquay Ten

Cunningham

U.S.A. 1907–1937; 1951–1955

There were two quite unrelated Cunningham marques. One specialized in building high-class carriages and cars while the other built competition sports cars. James Cunningham, Son and Co. of Rochester, New York, had been carriage builders since 1842, but it was not until 1907 that their first car, electrically powered, was unveiled. This was quickly succeeded by petrol-driven cars using Continental as well as their own four-cylinder engines, and by 1915 the Cunningham cars had become larger, more powerful (thanks to their new V8 engine) and much more expensive.

The cars were highly rated and well able to compete with the prestigious American Rolls-Royce and the best of the Packards and McFarlans, and over the next decade the luxurious Cunninghams occupied a small but profitable niche in the American market. The company also manufactured high-quality funeral vehicles and ambulances. However, during the Depression sales began to decline with the last cars being built in 1931, although the company continued to make special bodies for other peoples' chassis until 1937 when the company finally closed down.

Briggs Swift Cunningham, born in 1907, was a wealthy sportsman with interests in ocean sailing and motor racing and most of his sports cars were built with competition in mind, particularly the Le Mans 24-Hour race.

The 1951 prototype C-1 sports car, with its V8 Cadillac engine, was quickly followed by open- and closed-body C-2Rs powered by 300bhp Chrysler engines. Although three of these cars failed to finish in the 1951 Le Mans, the following year saw a C-4R driven by Cunningham himself take fourth place, while in 1953 Cunninghams came third, seventh and tenth. These competition cars had stubby, purposeful bodies designed by Robert Blake (later of Jaguar) and were strong and powerful, as were the production cars, such as the fine-looking 1952 GT with its 200bhp Chrysler engine.

One of Cunningham's greatest achievements was an outright win in the 1953 Sebring 12-hour race in Florida, but this was not to be repeated at Le Mans and in 1955 Cunningham decided to call it a day and the manufacture of his cars ceased. However, Briggs Cunningham did continue racing other marques including Lister, Jaguar, Maserati and Chevrolet, with a GT category win in a Corvette in the 1960 Le Mans. In later years he was famous for his extensive collection of cars.

Above: 1912 Model 'J' Cunningham Limousine

Below: For the 1952 Le Mans 24-Hour race, Cunningham entered three new vehicles: two C4R open cars and a special C4RK coupé. The cars were big and strong, with 325bhp available from the Chrysler V8 engine.

Daewoo

South Korea
1980 to date

A new entrant to the world car market during the 1990s was Daewoo. The Korean company, which began in textiles, had been building cars for the home market since 1980 but only started selling cars elsewhere in the mid-1990s. By the time the cars came to Europe, Daewoo was already building more vehicles per year than the largest British manufacturer. It was the 33rd biggest company in the world (bigger than Coca-Cola), building everything from oil tankers to aircraft and diggers.

At first, Daewoo set its sights on Europe, hoping to establish itself there. The cars were nothing special, simply repackaged Vauxhalls and Opels, but the way in which the cars were sold was completely new. Rather than building up a dealer network where Daewoo

Above: Daewoo Nexia three-door hatchback

Below: The Nexia four-door saloon

would have limited control over customer care and sales, the company sold cars direct at a fixed, no haggling, price which included all servicing and consumable service parts for three years. Using such techniques, Daewoo expected to be selling 200,000 cars a year across Europe.

This method of marketing cars was thought to be so effective that rival dealers started a boycott, refusing to take Daewoos in part exchange. No other manufacturer could compete without incurring losses.

The cars proved to be reliable but could never be described as exciting. The Nexia, based on the Opel Kadett/Vauxhall Astra, received a decent face-lift so that it at least looked passably modern, as did the Vauxhall Cavalier-based Espero.

Finally, having proved to itself that cars were worthwhile business, Daewoo launched new models, designed completely in-house, in 1997, and looked to be on target for an even brighter future.

Above: Daewoo Lanos, Nubira and Leganza   *Below: the Vauxhall Cavalier-based Espero*

DAF

Holland
1958–1975

DAF of Eindhoven, Holland, began building cars in 1958, following many years of manufacturing commercial and military vehicles. The company's first small saloon car was powered by an air-cooled, flat-twin engine of 590cc, developing 22bhp and driving the rear wheels through belt-operated 'Variomatic' transmission, which employed a centrifugal clutch and twin vee-belts. This gave constantly varying drive ratios to suit the prevailing road conditions. The DAF was first exported to the U.K. in 1961.

Further models were announced in 1962 – the 750 and the Daffodil, with 30bhp engines which allowed a top speed of around 65mph (104km/h).

In late 1966 the larger, Michelotti-styled DAF 44 was introduced, with a longer-stroke version of the flat-twin engine, now of 844cc and producing 40bhp. This gave a top speed approaching

Below: 1965 Variomatic racing car
Bottom: 1959 33, with air-cooled engine

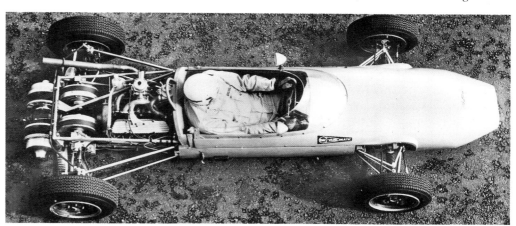

80mph (128km/h). Stability was improved by widening the track and lengthening the wheel-base.

In early 1968, the DAF 55 was announced. This retained the belt-drive transmission, but was powered by a modified four-cylinder Renault engine of 1108cc, giving 50bhp and 140km/h (87mph). This model also featured 12-volt electrics, earlier cars having six-volt systems. By 1969, estate-car variants of the 44 and 55 were available as well as a 55 Coupé.

A Marathon version of the 55 was announced during 1971, the model celebrating the success of DAFs entered in the 1968 London-to-Sydney Marathon. The production cars were uprated to give some 13bhp more than the standard 55 models, and cruised comfortably at speeds above 128km/h (80mph).

In 1972 the DAF 66 Series was introduced to replace the 55 models. The new cars had revised styling and a new, plate-type automatic clutch, while revisions were made to the 1108cc engine to give quieter operation and a little more power. A Marathon version of the 66 was produced, with improvements similar to those made on the Marathon 55. A 1300cc

Above right: DAF 66 Coupé Marathon

Below: The 750cc Daffodil was introduced in 1962, and like the earlier 600cc-engined car featured DAF's 'Variomatic' transmission.

Left: 1967 DAF 44 estate car
Above: 1974 55 Coupé Marathon

66 was introduced in 1973, although the 1100 model was still available.

In 1975 DAF ceased production, but Volvo took over and built its own, restyled version of the DAF 66, with the 1300cc engine and servo-operated clutch.

Daimler

Great Britain
1896 to date

The Daimler Motor Syndicate was formed in 1893 to build the German car of the same name under licence, but the British and German concerns went their separate ways after 1898. The first Daimlers were imported, but the Coventry factory soon began to turn out twin-cylinder models and eventually a whole range of types.

From 1904, the company began to concentrate on large and powerful four-cylinder cars with chain drive to the wheels. Before long, it was making some of the biggest and best British cars, with its prestige well established thanks to the purchase of a Daimler in 1900 by the then

Left: 1898 model, probably imported
Above: 1904 28hp Landaulette

Below: 1923 30hp Landaulette

Above: 1909 four-cylinder tourer

Prince of Wales, later King Edward VII. Royal patronage would stay with the marque until the 1950s.

Major changes took place in 1909 and 1910. In the former, Daimler changed over completely from poppet-valve engines to Knight sleeve-valve designs; in the latter, the company was bought out by the BSA Group. Thus began a period in which the Daimler name signified large, smooth and silent cars, which were dignified rather than sporting. There were no more four-cylinder cars after World War I (except for the short-lived '20' of 1922), and in 1927 the company announced the fabulous Double-Six, with a V12 engine of 7.1 litres. This was the first of many V12s,

Below: 1911 20hp Doctor's coupé

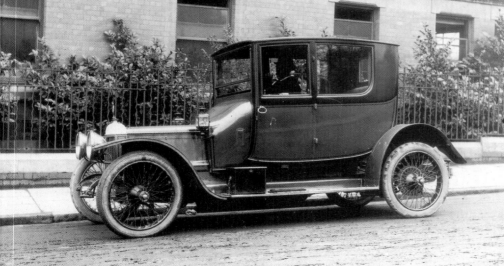

Top: 20hp Landaulette, built around 1912
Above: 1914 45hp 'special' for India
Below: 1921 Light Thirty

which ranged in size down to 1.9 litres and would remain in production until 1938.

The Daimler car range alone was enormous; but, in addition, there had been well-respected buses since 1908, and the company marketed small cars under the BSA name. A range of medium-sized cars

was added under the Lanchester name after that company was bought out in 1931. This diversification gave the company a sound commercial footing, but by the end of the 1930s it had abandoned the very top of the market to Rolls-Royce.

The Daimlers of the 1930s were characterized by Wilson-type preselector gearboxes which drove through a fluid flywheel, and this transmission was standard on all models until the 1950s. Independent front suspension appeared in 1938, but the stately Double-Six had ceased production a year earlier, its engine already reduced to 6½-litres. For 1939, the largest Daimler was the 4½-litre straight-eight first seen in 1936.

Above: 1930 Double-Six
Below: 1931 Light straight eight

Below: 1932 Fifteen Sports Coupé

Above: 1938 Light Twenty saloon
Below: 1939 DB18 saloon

Above: 1949 DE39 5.5-litre

Above: 1957 Conquest drophead coupé

After World War II, the pre-war 15 was revived with some modifications, and there were two new limousine models, one with the six-cylinder engine originally designed for an armoured car and the other with a straight-eight of 5½-litres. Lanchester production was also resumed, along with a successful range of bus and coach chassis.

The Daimlers of the 1950s were conservatively styled, although the company remained in the public eye through a series of flamboyant Show cars commissioned by its Chairman, Sir Bernard Docker. The Conquest, Majestic, and 'One-O-Four' models were well-equipped owner-driver saloons, and there was also a sports two/three-seater. After

Above: 1955 Regency Mk. II

Below: The 1959 SP250 sports car had a glassfibre body and a 140bhp overhead-valve V8 engine of 2547cc. Top speed was 197km/h (123mph). It was a departure for Daimler, and one which the firm never followed up.

1956, automatic transmission became an alternative to the fluid flywheel, and 1958's 3.8-litre Majestic Major had automatic transmission as standard. A year later, the new SP250 sports car came with either a synchromesh gearbox or a conventional automatic only.

The SP250 had a 2½-litre V8 engine, designed by Edward Turner along with a 4½-litre V8 for use in the limousine models. But, in 1960, the company was bought out by Jaguar, and that company's influence gradually came to dominate. In 1962 the 2½-litre V8 was fitted to a Mark II Jaguar body shell, and the last Majestic Major was built in 1967. After 1969, all Daimler saloons were Jaguars with trim and equipment variations. The name still survives, but the only really distinctive model is a limousine with a special body on a Jaguar floorpan and running gear.

Jaguar itself was purchased by Ford Motor Company in 1989.

Left: 1962 SP250 sports
Below left: 1968 DS420 limousine
Below centre: 1969 Sovereign
Below right: 1974 DS420 Landaulette

Above: 1977 Vanden Plas 4.2-litre
Left: 1973 Double-Six coupé

Darracq

France
1896–1920

Alexandre Darracq had a great passion for mechanical objects and over a 20-year period he designed and built a wide range of bicycles, tricycles and cars; and yet, incredibly, he did not like driving and hated being driven.

Darracq was born in 1855 in Bordeaux, south-western France, of Basque parents and he first came to prominence around 1891 when, with his partner Jean Aucoc, he formed the Gladiator cycle company, quickly cashing in on the current bicycle boom. However, some five years later his company was bought out by Adolphe Clément, and Darracq turned his hand to designing electric cabs which proved to be a complete failure.

He had more luck with his tricycles inspired by Léon Bollée and on the strength of their success he paid £10,000 for the manufacturing rights of Bollée's latest four-wheeler. This belt-driven machine was an unmitigated failure, however, with recurrent ignition problems and badly designed steering.

The year 1900 saw a change in Darracq's fortunes with the introduction of a more conventional and very handsome 6.5hp voiturette. The car had a 785cc single-cylinder engine, a propeller shaft driving a bevel-gear rear axle and a three-speed steering-column gear-change. By 1903 twin- and four-cylinder models had been added to the range, while the following year the multi-cylinder cars sported a pressed-steel platform chassis.

During this period the marque performed quite well on the racing scene, with the company's V8-engined sprint car being capable of reaching nearly 190km/h (118mph), making it one of the fastest cars of its day. Racing success continued with the works team taking second, third and seventh places in the 1908 Isle of Man Tourist Trophy race, but by this time Darracq had found a new interest in the developing sport of flying, and within two years his Suresnes factory was building light aero-engines.

The following years were marred by a series of disasters beginning with the production of steam buses which failed to sell, followed by the demise of the Milan operation with which the company had hoped to take a share of the developing

Above: 1903 20hp racer

Below: Darracqs performed well in long-distance races with their V8 engines, and were capable of reaching 193km/h (120mph), making them among the fastest cars of their day. This is a 1904 racing model.

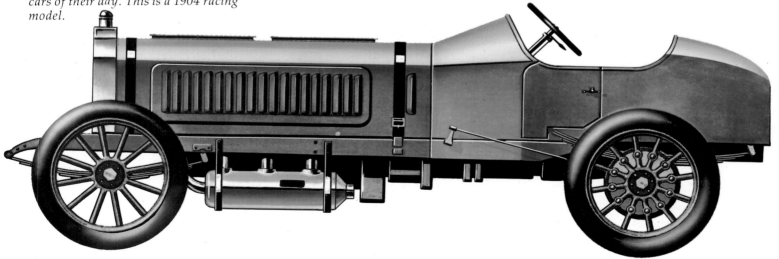

Italian market. The downward trend continued, and despite the injection of some British capital the new range of models introduced in 1912, many of which were fitted with the Henroid rotary-valve engine, did nothing to stem the company's sinking fortunes. That same year Alexandrè Darracq resigned and in 1931, at the age of 76, he died.

The company was taken over by Yorkshireman Owen Clegg who introduced a new range of cars, the Clegg-Darracqs based on his own successful Rover Twelve design. They were a great success and by the autumn of 1914 the Suresnes factory was turning out 70 cars a week, with many of the big

Top: 1903 40hp racer

Above left: 1904 8hp single-cylinder
Above right: 1904 100hp Darracq
Above: 1914 Clegg-Darracq four-cylinder

Left: 1907 16/18 tourer

four-litre models going to the French Army.

A new 4.6-litre V8 model was announced in 1919, yet despite its advanced specification – a four-speed gearbox and four-wheel braking – it did not sell well and in 1920 the ailing company was taken over by Sunbeam-Talbot. During the next two decades the cars were sold as Talbots in France and Darracqs or Talbot-Darracqs in Britain and the Empire.

Left: 1906 10/12hp
Below: 1914 16hp

Above right: 1919 4-litre tourer
Right: 1954 Lago Talbot coupé

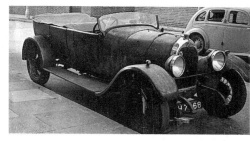

Top: 1922 16hp
Above: 1926 12/32

Below: In 1920, the ailing Darracq company was taken over by Sunbeam Talbot, and the cars were subsequently badged as Talbot-Darracqs. This 1920 six-cylinder 25hp A-type was a Darracq design, however.

Datsun

Japan 1912-1983

Many people regard Datsun as a company of the 1970s and 1980s but, in fact, its origins date back to as long ago as 1912.

American-trained engineer Masujiro Hashimoto founded the Kwaishinsha Motor Works in Tokyo and built a prototype small car. Little is known about it. However, another small car followed two years later.

Hashimoto's financiers were called K. Den, R. Aoyama and A.Takeuchi and the car was called the DAT, using the initials of their surnames. The name was particularly appropriate because 'dat' is the Japanese word for hare.

The DAT 31 came in 1915, featuring a two-litre, four-cylinder engine. The next year's model was the DAT 41 which had a 2.3-litre power unit.

Production of everything except wheels, tyres and magnetos was carried out in Japan. After a modest production run, the company turned to trucks in 1926.

A year earlier, Kwaishinsha had changed its name to DAT Motor Co., later moving to Osaka to merge with the Jitsuyo Jidosha Seizo Co.

That company continued to make the Lila light car for a short period after the

Above: 1951 Thrift four-door saloon
Below: 1951 De Luxe four-door saloon

merger. It was popular with taxi drivers in Japan because of its exceptionally narrow track, and followed an earlier three-wheeler designed by William Gorham, an American engineer who was living in Japan.

DAT was bought in 1931 by Tobata Imono, a large industrial business. Its president, Yoshisuke Ayukawa, had big plans. He wanted to offer a mass-produced Japanese car to compete with American

Below: Datsun had still not made a four-door saloon by the time of this DS model, built in 1949. Its 860cc four-cylinder engine put out 20bhp and drove the rear axle through a three-speed gearbox.

products in the export market.

His wish made a move towards reality with the 1931 DAT prototype small car. And the car started a famous name – it was called Datson; literally the son of DAT.

However, the name was soon changed to Datsun for two reasons. Primarily, it meant that the manufacturers could use the Japanese national emblem of the rising sun. And, since the word 'son' means loss in Japanese, it was totally inappropriate for a product aimed at gaining popularity.

Production started in 1932 and in that year some 150 Datsuns were made in roadster, tourer and saloon versions. With

Right: Station wagon of the early 1950s

a 495cc, four-cylinder engine which developed 10bhp, the top speed was 56km/h (35mph).

The car bore a passing resemblance to the Austin Seven and it has been suggested that it was, indeed, a copy of the Austin. But the similarity ended with appearances because, whereas the Austin used cantilever springs and bevel drive, the Datsun had semi-elliptic rear suspension and worm drive. Quite apart from that, its engine was considerably smaller than that of the British car.

Jidosha Seizo changed its name to Nissan Motor Co. Ltd. at the end of 1933 (the Nissan story is told in detail elsewhere) and production moved from Dsako to new premises at Yokohama. But the name Datsun continued and the thousandth model was built in mid-1934. Exports for that year comprised 44 cars to Spain, India and the United States.

Engine capacity was increased to 725cc in 1935 and it remained that size until after World War II.

Nissan concentrated heavily on commercial vehicles and Datsun cars took second place, a policy typified by the 860cc Thrift of 1951. The engine was used until 1958, albeit in more modern bodywork. The Thrift was replaced with the Austin-based 1.2-litre Bluebird, a name which has survived until today.

Above right: 1972 240C saloon
Below: 1970 240Z works rally car
Bottom: 1974 Cherry coupé

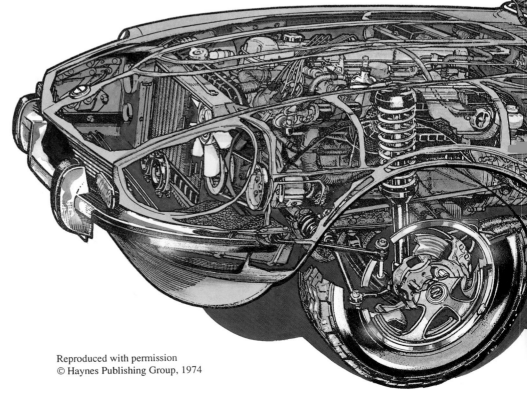

Reproduced with permission
© Haynes Publishing Group, 1974

Above: 1974 260Z coupé
Below right: 1974 160B SSS coupé

The Datsun range was growing in complexity in the 1960s with models including the Cedric, President, Fairlady and Skyline. The 240Z sports coupé of 1969 put the company in the performance-car market. It was to become the best-selling sports car in the world with sales exceeding 720,000 by the end of 1980 (including successive models).

Above: The 1969 240Z was a two-seater coupé powered by a 151bhp six-cylinder engine which drove through a five-speed gearbox. It could reach 201km/h (125mph) and started a famous line of Z-cars.

Left: 1973 120Y estate car

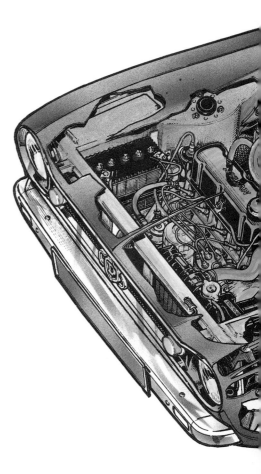

Other popular models included the original rear-wheel-drive Sunny 120Y, the front-wheel-drive Cherry and the Patrol four-wheel-drive Jeep-style vehicle.

The name Datsun was officially dropped at the end of 1983 and thereafter all the company's vehicles have been called Nissans.

Centre: 1979 Violet 160J saloon
Left: 1978 280ZX sports coupé

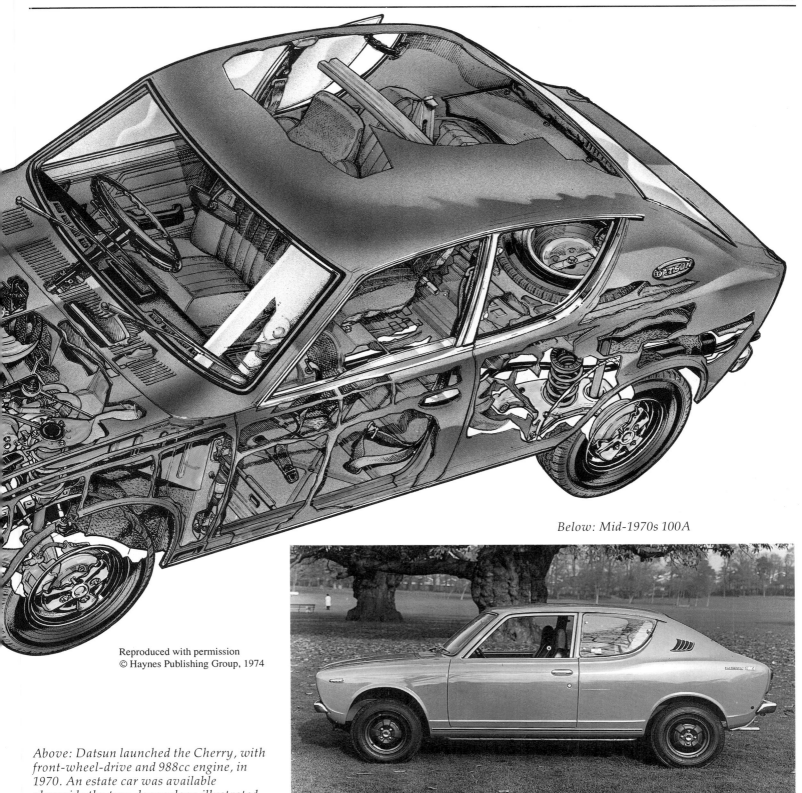

Below: Mid-1970s 100A

Reproduced with permission
© Haynes Publishing Group, 1974

*Above: Datsun launched the Cherry, with
front-wheel-drive and 988cc engine, in
1970. An estate car was available
alongside the two-door saloon illustrated
here.*

De Dietrich

France
1897–1934

The De Dietrich business was originally involved in the manufacture of railway rolling stock – wagons, axles, wheels and carriages. When Alsace and part of Lorraine changed nationality in 1871 the company, now in German territory, set up a new French factory at Lunéville.

One of the families with a controlling interest in the firm was that of Baron Edouard de Türckheim. In 1897 his son,

Above: 1904 24hp Paris-Madrid racer

Above: Lorraine-Dietrich racer, c. 1908

Adrien, acquired a licence to build Amédée Bollée's vehicles at the Lunéville plant. This then became the Société de Dietrich et Cie. de Lunéville, although Bollée cars were also built by De Dietrich in Germany.

After a disappointing performance in the 1901 Paris-Madrid event, De Dietrich progressed to vehicles designed by Léon Turcar and Simon Méry. The German operation built Georges Richard designs and the following year contracted Ettore Bugatti.

In 1904 Adrian de Türckheim left to start up Société Lorraine d'Anciens Etablissements de Dietrich et Cie., with backing from his father, brother and Turcat-Méry. The new vehicles became Lorraine-Dietrichs by 1905, production moving to the modern Argenteuil factory the following year.

In 1907 the company acquired Ariel in England and Isotta-Fraschini of Italy,

without notable effect. Two years later, recession and losses caused it to sell these acquisitions. De Groullard joined the firm around this time, introducing more-modern engines and designing the enormous 15-litre chain-driven Grand Prix racer of 1912.

Marius Barbarou joined Lorraine-Dietrich during World War I and although his initial post-war vehicle, with a sidevalve six-cylinder engine, was unexciting, the later 15CV was more successful. The firm also enjoyed some

sporting victories, including two at Le Mans, and under commercial direction from coachbuilder Gaston Grummer, stylish bodywork and slick advertising were introduced. By 1928 the marque became known simply as Lorraine.

The company's interests moved towards aero-engines in the early 1930s, leading to closure of its car department in 1934 – although Tatras were later produced under licence at Argenteuil.

This 1925 Lorraine-Dietrich 15CV tourer had an American-inspired six-cylinder engine of 3.4-litres and a three-speed gearbox. Maximum speed was 90km/h (60mph).

Above: 1907 Lorraine-Dietrich 24/30hp
Below: Late 1920s Lorraine cabriolet

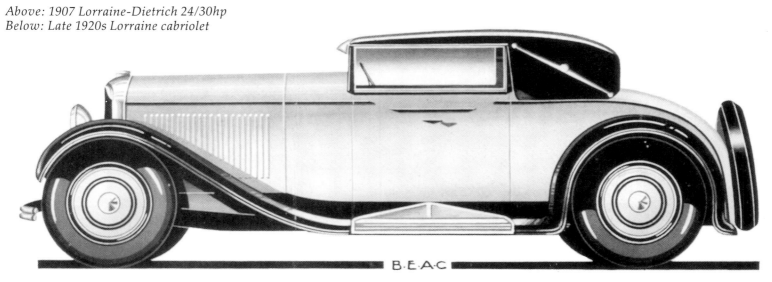

B·E·A·C

De Dion-Bouton

France
1883–1932

Count Albert de Dion went into partnership with Georges Bouton and his brother-in-law Trépardoux, makers of steam tricycles, in 1883. Although their early vehicles were mainly commercials, they built a car which was to put up the fastest time in the Paris–Rouen Trials of 1894. Trépardoux was so against this experimentation with petrol engines, however, that he resigned from the partnership that year and the De Dion-Bouton name was founded.

Before this Trépardoux had designed the famous De Dion axle system, whereby the vehicle's load-bearing structure and the drive transmission were separated.

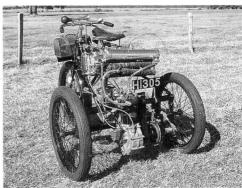

Below: This 1903 De Dion-Bouton Populaire model had its engine at the front and a steering wheel in place of the earlier tiller.

Above left: 1894 petrol tricycle
Top: 1899 single-cylinder model
Above: 1900 tricycle

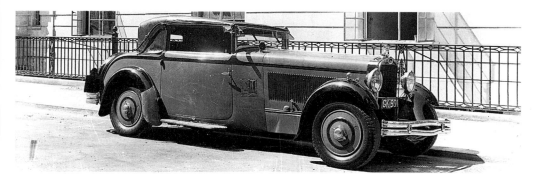

Above: 1930 D8 eight-cylinder

Above: 1935 D6 3-litre cabriolet

Below: 1938 D8 120 sports saloon

Below: From 1932 a super-sports version of the 4-litre D8 was available. Although the car pictured has elegant coachwork, the chassis was often over-bodied. A D8 super-sports took International class records at 180km/h (112mph).

Delage agent, who sold off much of the engineering side, instead making an agreement with Delahaye to build badge-engineered cars to that company's design.

Delage continued in this form until 1953 and, together with Delahaye, merged with Hotchkiss the following year.

Although he remained on the board as a figurehead, Louis Delage lost his money with his company and died poor at the age of 73.

Delahaye

France
1894–1954

Several times during its 60 years of car production, the French firm of Delahaye must have seriously considered changing its name to 'Déja vu' – as anyone attempting to trace the path the company followed would be doomed to going round in several sets of circles.

It commenced making cars in 1894 when a young engineer with experience of locomotive engines, Emile Delahaye, took over a brick-making machinery factory at Tours and successfully changed its direction to car manufacture.

This was just in time for the golden age of town-to-town racing over France's country roads, and two of the first 6hp tubular-framed rear-engined Delahayes were entered for the 1896 Paris–Marseilles–Paris event, finishing sixth and eighth respectively.

In 1898 the firm moved to Paris, and appointed as works manager the man who was to run the company until its eventual demise, Charles Weiffenbach. Emile

Delahaye himself retired in 1901 due to ill health and died four years later, leaving Weiffenbach to continue guiding the company's fortunes.

Above: Luxury for 1900, the 6hp model

He did well, continuing to enter Delahayes in road-races with a modicum of success until 1902 when racing cars grew more specialized and it was deemed too expensive to continue. The new models of that year, though, showed that the firm had gained from its experience; the Type 10B boasted a proper steering wheel, a three-speed gearbox and chain drive. Over 800 were sold, including light-van versions, and this success was followed by

The 1938 Type 135 was one of the classic Delahaye designs; its beautifully-engineered chassis with independent front suspension and its powerful 3.5-litre engine made it popular among coachbuilders.

ever-faster, more sophisticated vehicles – and usually a step up-market from their predecessors. By 1905 the top-of-the-range eight-litre car was good enough for King Alfonso of Spain, a notable connoisseur.

By the outbreak of World War I Delahaye was an undoubted success. Weiffenbach had led the company into other markets including England and Germany, other areas including fire-tender and boat-engine manufacture, and had

introduced along the way several innovative design elements like a V6 engine and pressure-lubricated suspension.

When the war ended, Weiffenbach appeared to have lost the knack of building exciting cars – the models of 1919–1930 were exceptionally average – but had acquired the desire to build an empire instead. He attempted to construct an American-style combine with Berliet (which failed) and to introduce mass-production, and then a little later he linked up with Donnet, Unic, and Chenard-Walcker.

The recession reduced sales, though, and things were looking bleak until 1933, when in a clever move the company went back to its roots in racing and started to produce powerful, lightweight sporting cars. A new young designer, Jean Francois, came up with a series of superb cars, one of which took 18 records in 1934 by averaging 172km/h (107mph) over 48 hours on the Montlhéry racetrack.

This was the beginning of a whole new era for the company. While stripped-down

versions of its cars like the famous Type 135 and 145 were winning races, coachbuilders were using the excellent chassis to produce some of the most sleek and elegant grand touring cars ever. On the way the company took over Delage, another famous name in the grand touring field.

This was definitely Delahaye's golden age, and it lasted until well after World War II – the firm survived the war

Above: Classic lines – a 1938 135M

Above: Type 44, advanced for 1911
Right: 1950 235, the essence of French auto style
Below right: Sporting and sleek, the 1938 competition roadster

building lorries, an activity it had never given up, and soon returned to racing and supplying chassis to coachbuilders. On the way the empire-building urge returned, though, and Delahaye swallowed up Simca and several truck-making firms. By the 1950s, though, the market was dwindling for large cars (partly due to French tax laws) so that side of the business suffered badly.

Its last attempt was a Jeep-type vehicle which was, sadly, too complex and sophisticated for the army who eventually settled on the U.S.A.'s simple Jeep, built under licence by Hotchkiss. And as if to add insult to injury, it was Hotchkiss that took over Delahaye in 1954 and stopped car production once and for all. Charles Weiffenbach retired at the point of the takeover and died in 1959.

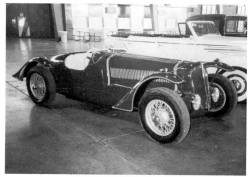

Delaunay-Belleville

France
1904–1950

Formerly a naval engineer, Louis Delaunay joined the well-known marine and locomotive boiler makers, Belleville of St. Denis, Paris, in the 1860s. He moved into a position of power in the company through marriage to the owner's daughter, adding the hyphenated Belleville name to his own in the process.

In 1903 he set up a car factory separate from the firm's other interests, called the Société des Automobiles Delaunay-Belleville, introducing his first model at the Paris Salon of 1904. Three four-cylinder cars appeared that year, designed by Marius Barbarou and Adolphe Clément, with a range of six-cylinder vehicles appearing in 1907.

Until World War I the company's cars, which had no competition history, gained much favour for their air of refined, quiet dignity – and were usually chauffeur-

Above: 1906/7 four-cylinder 20hp model

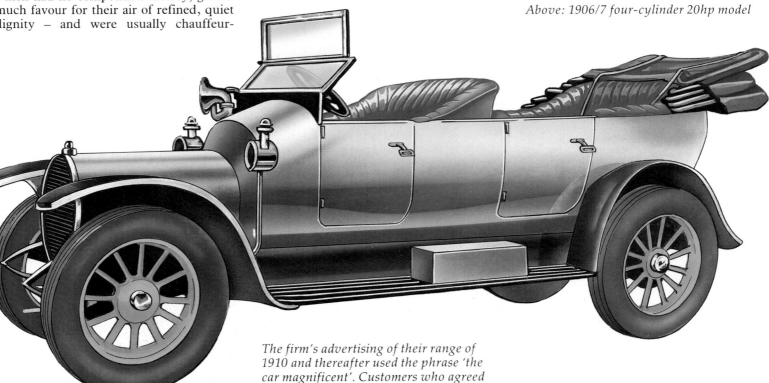

The firm's advertising of their range of 1910 and thereafter used the phrase 'the car magnificent'. Customers who agreed and bought models like this HB of 1911 included the Tsars of Russia.

driven. Tsar Nicholas II of Russia was a regular customer, as were Trotsky and Lenin after the Revolution. Louis Delaunay-Belleville died in 1912, succeeded by his sons Robert and Pierre, who offered commercial vehicles. Barbarou left to join Lorraine-Dietrich.

During the war Delaunay-Belleville manufactured Hispano-Suiza aero-engines an some heavy military vehicles, in addition to the ships' boilers of the parent company.

After World War I Delaunay continued to produce cars with rounded bonnets and

radiators, although they were now slightly pointed to follow the fashion. The company had lost credence against Hispano-Suiza and Rolls-Royce, however, and this was confirmed when American Continental engines were fitted to the cars from 1931.

Further loss of marque identity came with the 1936 R.16 – very similar to the 230 Mercedes-Benz – which was continued after World War II with an updated 'waterfall' grille.

The last cars and commercials were listed up to 1949/50, but in the initial years

after World War II the Delaunay-Belleville factory concentrated on a 450cc minicar, the Rovin; and the Delauney-Belleville name survives to this day in the shape of a factory making automotive radiators.

Above: A 15hp for the British market

Below: 1910 15hp coachbuilt special

Top: A six-cylinder 26hp model
Above: A 10hp four-cylinder landaulette

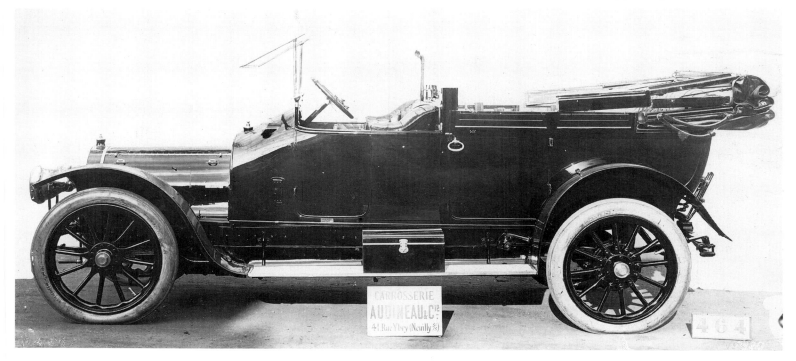

De Soto

U.S.A.
1928–1960

The De Soto was a product of the Chrysler Corporation, introduced in 1928 as a medium-priced marque to fill the gap between Plymouth and the mid-priced Dodge. The first models followed the design and styling of contemporary Chryslers and were very successful, but the marque suffered badly during the Depression and never really received the recognition which some of its models deserved. Straight-eight engines were offered in the early years, but the models of the later 1930s and 1940s had six-cylinder engines.

In 1952, an oversquare overhead-valve V8 engine arrived, based on the previous year's hemi-head Chrysler. At the same time, De Soto moved into a new market niche just above Dodge and below Chrysler itself. The last sidevalve straight-six was made in 1954, and only V8s were available in the restyled 1955 models. The less-powerful engine was known as the Firedome, and the more-powerful unit was called the Fireflite. A limited-production high-performance Adventurer hard-top

Above: 1928 Series K model

Right: 1934 Airflow saloon

Below: The 1934 De Soto Airflow was one of several similar Airflow models from Chrysler. Its body/chassis unit foreshadowed full unitary structures but the public could not live with its futuristic shape.

Above: 1961 Styline hardtop coupé   *Below: 1952 Firedome 8, model S-17*

model arrived for 1956, and in 1957 De Soto gained Virgil Exner's new 'Forward-Look' styling, along with other Chrysler products.

Less-powerful but less-expensive V8 engines were standard on the 1958 models, but De Soto was caught by a slump in the sales of medium-priced cars and in 1959 the division was merged with Plymouth.

Along with other Chrysler products (Imperial excepted), De Soto switched to unitary body construction for 1960, but poor sales resulted in the range being cut back drastically for the 1961 model year and, in fact, only a few examples had been made when De Soto production was axed altogether in November 1960.

De Tomaso

Italy
1956 to date

Alejandro de Tomaso had an unlikely background for a man who was to produce exotic sports cars.

He was born in Buenos Aires in 1928, the son of a former Prime Minister of Argentina who died when Alejandro was five.

Despite later being expected to manage the family's extensive estate he took up motor racing and fled to Italy in 1955 following political pressure.

He met the Maserati brothers and drove their OSCA cars and married American Elizabeth Haskell, herself a racing driver with a family fortune from automotive finance.

He founded De Tomaso Automobili SpA. in Modena, Italy, in 1959 and built his first racing cars around OSCA engines.

His first road-going car, the Ford-engined Vallelunga, sold just over 50 between 1963 and 1965.

An approach to American race tuner Carroll Shelby for Ford engines led to the Mangusta of 1969.

De Tomaso's wife was related to the chairman and president of Rowan Industries, of New Jersey. He persuaded them to take over coachbuilder Ghia and, as a result, he became president of that company in 1967.

Rowan Industries' investment into De Tomaso's car operations allowed room for expansion and the Mangusta was exported to America.

Sales rose to nearly £1 million in 1968, but launching the Mangusta had proved an expensive business and profits slumped.

De Tomaso's next car was the Pantera, aimed at linking Ford with the European performance market. The car was later joined by the Longchamp and Deauville.

De Tomaso had a varied career and in the 1970s bought control of Maserati from Peugeot, bought managing control of Innocenti Mini production and had interests in both boatbuilding and hotels.

The current model is the Pantera GT5-S, capable of 257km/h (160mph).

Top: The classic Ghia lines of the 1966 Mangusta
Above: The epitome of Italian style, the 1966 Pampero

The Pantera was launched in 1970 with a 5.6-litre Ford engine giving it a top speed of 257km/h (160mph). It was luxuriously equipped, with air-conditioning as standard and leather seats.

Above and below: The De Tomaso Guara, first shown in 1993, uses a mid-mounted BMW 4.0-litre V8 engine and a six-speed gearbox

Detroit Electric

U.S.A. 1907–1938

The Detroit Electric Car originated from the well-established firm of carriage builders, the Anderson Carriage Co. Its range of High School horse-drawn surreys, buggies, wagons and carriages had sold at the rate of up to 15,000 a year until the increasing prevalence of motorized vehicles had caused it to look in a new direction.

Anderson's Detroit factory was re-equipped in 1907 for the production of an electrically powered car with no trunk or hood, but rounded battery covers at both ends, which quickly became the most fashionable method of town transport.

Above: 1912-13 Electric brougham built under licence

Below: The 1909 brougham was popular with lady drivers

About this time the company bought the American branch of the British electric-motor manufacturers, Ewell-Parker, and a small number of cars were built by the Scottish Arrol-Johnston firm. The Anderson factory was, by this time, reputed to be the largest producer of such vehicles in the world. Up to World War I in excess of 1,000 cars a year were built there, although after the end of hostilities this number gradually declined.

Anderson was reorganized as the Detroit Electric Car Co. in 1919, having previously become the Anderson Electric Car Co. in 1911. Electric-powered commercial vehicles were also introduced in that year and an attempt was made to update the styling in the early 1920s, with the introduction of false hoods and radiator grilles.

By 1927 Detroit's commercial-vehicle range had been deleted and production was dwindling, being confined to specials made to order using either the pre-World War I horseless carriage styling, or more acceptable coachwork supplied by Willys-Overland.

Jamieson Handy took over the Detroit company in the mid-1930s, and after that time only a handful of the cars were produced, with orders being refused by 1938 when the firm finally closed.

D.K.W.

Germany
1928–1966

Danish-born J. S. Rasmussen started a workshop in Zschopau – now known as Karl-Marx Stadt in East Germany – in 1907, making boiler and heater fittings.

Fellow Dane Mathiessen joined him and they experimented with steam cars. They were called Dampf-Kraft Wagen – the initials of which gave birth to D.K.W.

In 1922, Rasmussen – who by now manufactured light cars and taxis – formed Metallwerke Frankenberg to make components for D.K.W.'s expanding range of motor-cycles. These were commonly known as *Das Kleine Wunder*, which means 'The Little Wonder'.

By 1927, D.K.W. was the world's largest manufacturer of motor-cycles with 40,000 produced in 1928 alone.

Rasmussen's motor company was called Zschopauer Moteren-Werke J. S. Rasmussen A.G. and it produced its first D.K.W. car in 1928. It had a two-stroke twin-cylinder engine and wooden chassis-less construction.

The company had many other interests including the manufacture of components for Audi.

D.K.W.'s first front-wheel-drive cars were the F1 and F2 which came from Audi's design department. Their transmission was soon used by other firms, including Audi and Tornax.

D.K.W. also made large V4-engined cars in Berlin-Spandau at the D-Wagen factory, and smaller cars at Zwickau, the Audi plant. The Zoschopau factory concentrated on engines and motor-cycles.

D.K.W. also built some rear-wheel-drive cars and commercials, including the F8 of 1939.

In 1934, D.K.W. commanded about 15 per cent of the German car market – second only to Opel – when Rasmussen retired.

From 1934 to 1939, D.K.W.s were made in Switzerland as Holka-D.K.W.s and immediately after the war in Sweden at Philipsson-D.K.W.s.

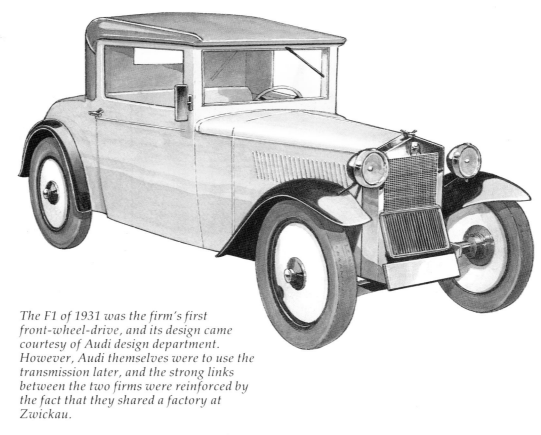

The F1 of 1931 was the firm's first front-wheel-drive, and its design came courtesy of Audi design department. However, Audi themselves were to use the transmission later, and the strong links between the two firms were reinforced by the fact that they shared a factory at Zwickau.

Below: The F1 front-wheel-drive roadster of 1930 boasted 15 horsepower

Some D.K.W.s appeared in East Germany in 1948 from the former Audi factory, and two years later they were joined by versions based on a pre-war three-cylinder F9 prototype. They were known as IFAs and production ended in 1956.

Variants of the two-cylinder Meisterklasse were followed by the F9, and two-stroke cars continued to be made until the end of D.K.W. production in 1966.

Thereafter, the company made only motorcycles and the machines mainly carry the name Hercules, although D.K.W. continues to be used in some export countries.

Above left: A 1937 model proves its strength
Left: The 1938 Reichsklasse, familiar from WWII newsreels

Top: The Berlin-built V4 of 1930
Above: 1953's two-stroke Auto Union/DKW
Below: The very American DKW 1000 of 1959

Doble
U.S.A. 1914–1931

Abner Doble, born in San Francisco in 1895, built his steam-powered car when he was only 16. His later products were considered the finest in the world, particularly in America, where the use of steam for passenger-carrying vehicles was to persist longer than anywhere else.

After studying at the Massachusetts Institute of Technology where he built what became the Model A, Doble set up his own company. The Abner Doble Motor Vehicle Co., of Waltham, Massachusetts, started in 1914, with financial backing from his parents.

Here, Doble made five model As, selling four and keeping the last for development into the Model B and C – for which he needed more money. This came from Detroit, Doble joining up with C. L. Lewis, latterly of the Consolidated Car Co., to become the General Engineering Co. by 1916.

The new vehicle, the GEC Doble, or Doble-Detroit, was due to be launched the following year, reputedly with 11,000 advance orders. Unfortunately, the war priorities of the American government would not allow Doble and Lewis the quantities of steel they required for large-scale production and the project had faded by 1918.

After the war, Doble moved west to California, setting up a new factory as the Doble Steam Motors Corporation in Emeryville, planning to restart production in 1924.

His new car was the Model E, which he showed to the public at the San Francisco Auto Show in 1923. This was a highly sophisticated car, without many of the drawbacks commonly associated with steam-powered vehicles, such as slow starting from cold. It was available with a variety of luxurious and elegant body styles made by Walter Murphy of Pasadena. Plans were for 300 cars a year to begin with, later rising to 1,000 a year.

Shortly after this Doble was extensively

Above: The luxurious Phaeton of 1923   *Below: The De Luxe Runabout version*

Right: Front view of the impressive chassis

swindled on the stock market, and faced massive debts. The Emeryville factory and land set aside for new development were either mortgaged or sold, with only a limited number of Model Es and the new F being produced. Planned production of the Doble-Simplex economy car also collapsed.

In 1931 the company went bankrupt. Doble himself worked on steam-powered commercials in Germany and on the 1950 Paxton Phoenix and the 1956 Keen, neither of which was successful.

Dodge

U.S.A.
1914 to date

The Dodge brothers, John and Horace, began as bicycle manufacturers, progressing to engine producers for Ford and becoming shareholders in that company as a result. The brothers began developing their own car in 1911, which finally came out in 1914.

The Dodge 4s were tough vehicles favoured as staff cars and ambulances during World War I. In 1915, when 45,000 were made, the company ranked third in the production stakes, rising to second behind Ford in 1920.

Left: 1915 Dodge, known for its toughness

Above: The first Dodge automobile, 1914

Above: The 1924 touring model

In that year both brothers died, and Fred J. Haynes became president. The Graham truck business began using Dodge components in large numbers. Five years later Dodge was sold to the Dillon Read & Co. firm of bankers, passing to Chrysler in 1928, with K. T. Keller replacing Haynes. At this time sales had been slipping due to competition from Chrysler marques,

Above: 1928 'Victory 6' sedan

Below: Victory 6, with hydraulic brakes

Above: The 1925 model, beginning to date
Below: The 1929 Dodge 8

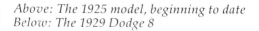

The Polara Lancer of 1960 was typical of the huge, tailfinned, heavily chrome-laden monsters of the late '50s and early '60s. It had a V8 5916cc engine and a three-speed automatic gearbox.

Top: 1954 Dodge V8
Centre: 1957 Dodge Royal
Above left: 1940s D-14 De Luxe
Above: 1959 Custom Royal

although 1927 saw Dodge commercials being assembled at Kew, Surrey, in Britain.

The Ram mascot appeared in 1931 and sales improved after the Depression, but during the 1940s Dodges became almost indistinguishable from De Sotos and luxury Plymouths.

Dodge heavy military vehicles were successful during World War II, commercial production taking place from Warren, Detroit, while the cars were still made at Hamtramck, Detroit.

The new Red Ram V8 engine appeared in 1953, and Dodge have since offered more sporting saloons, such as the Charger coupé of 1966, as well as compacts.

At the end of the 1960s came the remarkable Daytona Charger, now considered a classic; and into the early 1970s the semi-compact Dart, medium-sized Coronet and larger Polara were offered. A range of sports pickups was introduced at this time and Mitsubishi sub-compacts were also available.

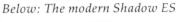

Above: The 1972 Monaco   *Below: The modern Shadow ES*

Above: Today's Dodge Colt GT
Below: The Dodge Omni

Renault took over the European commercial-vehicle side in the early 1980s, while the car side is allied closely to the Plymouth range. The startling V10 Viper concept car was displayed during 1988, with talk of production in 1990.

Right: The Dodge Grand Caravan with new 3.3-litre V6 engine

Above: 1990 Spirit LE

Below: The Daytona Shelby

Below: 1990 streamlined Daytona ES

Below: The Daytona was developed from the Chrysler K-car, a well-balanced saloon with front-wheel-drive. From the early days with just the ordinary 2.2-litre ohc four, it was developed with turbo-charging and intercooling to produce 174bhp.

The launch of the outrageous Viper in 1992 really put the Dodge badge back on the map. With a snarling, 400bhp, 8.0-litre V10 engine and massive chrome pipes, the open-topped 2-seater supercar started a bidding war among keen early customers, with some willing to cough up as much as three times the $50,000 asking price. Although it was a nineties sports car, it was distinctly low-tech compared to the competition: but this seemed to be what buyers wanted – a raw and exciting road racer. It became an instant legend and was often described as a modern-day Cobra. The V10 engine wasn't just used in the Viper, and appeared again in a monstrous and powerful pick-up, named the Dodge Ram.

Otherwise, the new-look Dodge range echoed that of Chrysler and Plymouth but with trim levels suitably adjusted to suit the targeted Dodge buyer. Although, in fact, on some markets, the Viper was Chrysler-badged.

Above right: The Dodge Viper RT/10 Roadster with 8.0-litre V10

Below: The Dodge Neon R/T

Above: Dodge Stratus

Left: 1998 Dodge Avenger

Below: Dodge Caravan

Above: 1998 Dodge Intrepid

Below Dodge Viper GTS Coupé

Duesenberg

U.S.A.
1920–1937

Fred Duesenberg began making bicycles before going on to design his famous horizontal overhead-valve engine for the Mason car. Together with his brother August he set up independently to build racing and marine engines under a variety of names.

In 1916 the Duesenberg Motors Corporation was formed in connection with J. R. Harbeck, managing director of Loew-Victor, although the Duesenberg brothers themselves put no money into the venture. A new factory was built at Elizabeth in New Jersey, in which Bugatti-designed aero-engines were manufactured during World War I.

After the war the brothers left the Duesenberg Motors Corporation and the rights to Fred's horizontal-valve engine were sold to Rochester Motors who, in turn, sold engines of that design to various luxury-car manufacturers. Instead, the brothers decided to launch a car of their own, which they did in 1920 with the Model A, having formed Duesenberg Automobile and Motors Co. Inc. in the March of that year.

Indianapolis was an important event for the Duesenberg company, because their racers (above and below) often won the event, providing both valuable publicity and engine development.

Below: The Model A, like this 1922 example, was a sound enough car for its day, but poor management and production problems led to the receivers being called in.

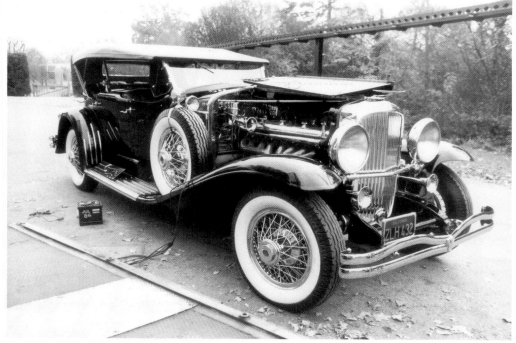

Above: 1925 Model A eight-cylinder roadster
Left: 1930 Duesenberg Model J roadster

Poor management led to the receivers being called in by 1924, but the following year the Ducsenberg Motor Co. appeared, with new finance and Fred as President. By this time the Model A was no longer so innovative and the negligibly changed Model X brought out at that time did little to revive the newer company's flagging fortunes. In 1926, however, Errett Lobban Cord, controller of Auburn Automobiles, gained control of the company with the idea of adding Duesenberg's still-successful competition name to a new prestige car.

As Duesenberg Inc. the brothers were given the brief to build an entirely new car, which came out in 1928. Called the Model J, it was the most remarkable car of its day, being very fast and of advanced design. The Duesenberg-designed engines

Above: The prestigious 1932 Model J

*The Model J, announced in 1928, was
financed by the Cord company, and thanks
to their development cash it proved to be
one of the greatest cars built in the U.S.A.
Its enormous engine had more than twice
the power of any other American car.*

were built by another company owned by Cord, Lycoming. The Model J could be bought either fully coach-built or as a chassis to take bodywork of the owner's choice. The company preferred to sell complete cars, with bodies of its own design but made by recommended builders such as Murphy, Le Baron, Derham, Bohman & Schwartz and Judkins. Model Js were owned by Al Jolson and Clark Gable.

By 1932 a supercharged version, the Model SJ, was produced. Only 36 of this model were made, but many of the earlier J cars were subsequently supercharged or merely fitted with the instantly recognizable external chrome exhausts to look like the SJ. Unfortunately, although Duesenberg survived the Depression, the Cord Corporation did not, and the final collapse of this organization in 1937 also took Duesenberg with it. The Cord-owned companies were sold off and the Duesenberg factory was turned over to Marmon-Herrington for the production of trucks until the mid-1950s.

In 1947 Augie Duesenberg was involved in an attempt to revive the famous marque but nothing ever came of it. Fred had died in a car crash in 1932 and by 1955 Augie, too, was dead.

Further attempts were made by members of the Duesenberg family to revive the marque. In 1966 Augie's son Fritz brought out a prototype for a Chrysler-powered sedan, designed by Virgil Exner and built by Ghia in Italy. In 1979 Fred's sons Harlan and Kenneth and Augie's brother Wesley tried again, this time with a limousine based on a Cadillac. Both were unsuccessful, with only one prototype car being built in each case.

It is fair to say that the marque died then, although between 1971 and 1979 the California-based Duesenberg Motor Co. (without family connection) produced around 12 replicas of the SSJ roadster. Other attempts by various outsiders have been made since to copy the famous and distinctive Duesenberg design of the 1920s.

Above right: 1931 6.9-litre, eight-cylinder Model J
Centre right: 1933 Model SJ speedster with distinctive exhaust pipes
Right: 1936 Model SJN convertible coupé

Du Pont

U.S.A.
1920–1932

E. Paul du Pont's manufacturing philosophy was to build high-quality cars in limited numbers; in the event his company built no more than 537 vehicles of all types during its 12-year lifetime, based initially in Wilmington, Delaware, and from 1923 in Moore, Pennsylvania. The very last cars were assembled and the Indian motorcycle factory in Springfield, which du Pont had acquired.

The first Du Pont was powered by a 4.1-litre four-cylinder sidevalve engine of the company's own design and manufacture, but this soon gave way to proprietary six-cylinder engines, initially made by Herschel-Spillman. Several different body styles were always available, too, built mostly by Merrimac, Waterhouse and Derham, and in touring, saloon, speedster and cabriolet configurations.

For 1925 the Model D was fitted with a five-litre six-cylinder Wisconsin straight-six producing 75bhp, a four-speed constant-mesh transmission and Lockheed hydraulic brakes all round. Its successor the Model E, was available with a supercharger if required, then in July 1928 came the Model G, arguably the best Du Pont of all and, in its distictive Speedster bodywork, certainly the best-known.

The Speedster was not a particularly good-looking car, however. It had a long, smooth hood behind a grille that concealed the radiator (the latter a pioneering feature), narrow wings or cycle-type mudguards, and Woodlite headlamps which, even if they did relatively little to illuminate the road ahead, certainly set the car apart from its contemporaries. Two- and four-seat versions were available, as well as a more conventionally styled roadster on the same chassis.

In 1931 the Model G was succeeded, logically enough, by the Model H. Mechanically, this was virtually identical to the Model G, but had a slightly longer

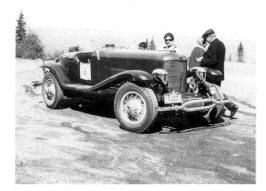

wheelbase to accommodate the flamboyant touring body with which the only three cars to be assembled were fitted.

By the end of the year falling sales had brought the company to the brink of bankruptcy. Manufacturing high-quality cars at unashamedly high prices paid off during the 1920s but the Depression brought that to an end and Du Pont, with no cheaper models to fall back on and what it saw as a reputation to protect, closed its doors for good in January 1932.

Left: 1929 Du Pont Short Roadster
Below: 1929 Du Pont Touring
Bottom: 1930 Speedster with unique radiator

Above: 1930 Model G Royal town car

*The Model G was the car which made the
marque of Du Pont famous and its 5.2-litre
straight-eight engine, which gave it a top
speed of well over 177km/h (110mph), was
just one of a series of sophisticated touches
which ensured that the few able to afford
one would appreciate this fine automobile.*

Duryea

U.S.A.
1893–1916

One of the earliest car manufacturers in America, the company was started by two brothers, Charles E. and J. Frank Duryea. Charles began his first motorized horse-buggy in 1891, but utilized Frank's mechanical skills to complete it, returning to his bicycle sale and repair job in Peoria, Illinois. This led to a long-running argument over whose invention it was!

The second prototype (Frank's work) appeared in 1895, winning the 50-mile (80-kilometre) *Chicago Times Herald* race in nine hours, and two years later the Duryea Motor Wagon Co. was formed in Springfield, Massachusetts. The brothers controlled two-thirds of the shares between them, the remainder held by local investors. Cars were also built in Peoria, where Charles still worked, by the Duryea Manufacturing Co.

By 1898 the brothers had split, Frank

Above: One offshoot included Stevens-Duryea like this 1911 model

going to the Automobile Co. of America and then to Stevens Arms in 1901, which was to produce the Stevens-Duryea. In 1906 he designed a six-cylinder engine

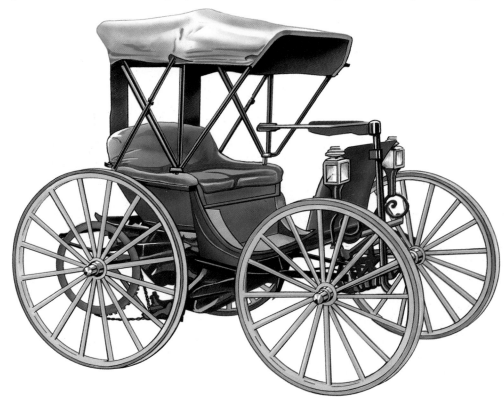

which was claimed to be the first of that type in America. Charles formed the Duryea Power Co. in Reading, Pennsylvania, continuing to manufacture the Duryea, which by this time were a variety of three- and four-wheeled vehicles with tiller controls.

The following year Henry Sturmey began building British Duryeas under licence in Coventry, which lasted until 1906. The marque was also made under licence at Waterloo in Iowa and Liège in Belgium during the period from 1899 to 1908.

In 1908 the company moved to Saginaw in Michigan, changing its name to the Duryea Motor Co. Charles, having built a three-cylinder rotary-valve model in 1907, then brought out a successful high-wheeled buggy which was listed for the next six years. He tried a Duryea cyclecar in 1914, which was actually manufactured by a Philadelphia company, Cresson-Morris. Also built in Philadelphia – by Duryea Motors Inc. – was the Duryea-Gem of 1916, which was to prove Charles Duryea's last car. He died in 1939.

Though this high-wheeled buggy of 1893 looks primitive today, the Duryea company were actually remarkably successful for their time. This model boasted a 4hp two-stroke engine and friction-drive transmission.

Excelsior

Belgium
1903–1930

Engineer Arthur de Coninck set up a modest workshop in a Brussels garage towards the end of 1903. He gave the enterprise a grand name, the Compagnie Nationale Excelsior, which it would eventually live up to, becoming the premier Belgian make alongside Minerva.

To begin with, however, de Coninck produced a range of unremarkable vehicles using French engines designed by Aster, for whom de Coninck was also the Belgian agent. Within four years he was offering three vehicles of differing engine sizes, still using Aster units. In 1907 he acquired larger premises in Liège, forming La Société Arthur de Coninck et Compagnie. At this point de Coninck also began manufacturing his own power units and transmissions.

Two years later de Coninck expanded

Below: A 1928 Imperia Monte Carlo rally car

Above: A cabriolet on an Excelsior chassis

again, this time when he bought a factory at Saventhem previously owned by the Belgica company. The name was changed to Société des Automobiles Excelsior and the first six-cylinder model, the D6, was launched from there in 1910.

De Coninck's interest in competition saw an Excelsior team entered in the 1911 Coupe des Voitures Legères. Joseph Christaens drove six-cylinder cars in the 1912 French Grand Prix. After the war they had some notable successes in Belgian endurance races and also competed at Le Mans.

Excelsior began exporting to Britain and France where the marque was popular up to the beginning of World War I. During German occupation de Coninck was deprived of his plant machinery, starting completely from scratch in 1919, although using modified D6 engines.

This was followed by the successful and prestigious Adex C, which became Excelsior's sole model. By 1927, however, the company's fortunes were failing, and it was taken over by Impéria. The marque's last public appearance was at the Brussels Salon of 1930.

Facel Vega

France
1954–1964

The name Facel was derived from Forges et Ateliers de Construction d'Eure et Loire S.A., set up in Paris in 1938 by Jean Daninos.

The company made machine-tools for the aircraft industry and under German occupation during World War II turned to manufacturing gas generators for cars.

After the war, production of aircraft-related equipment resumed and Facel made de Havilland gas-turbine components.

The company branched out and also manufactured kitchen furniture, office equipment and car bodies, mainly for Simca and Panhard.

Production of car bodies peaked in 1952 at more than 100 a day. The following year Panhard stopped using Facel but Simca bodies were made until 1961.

Daninos' own car was launched at the Paris Salon in July 1954. He called it the Vega and it was based on a prototype resembling the Ford Vendôme.

It used a 180bhp 4.5-litre De Soto Firedome V8, derived from the Chrysler Hemi, had drum brakes and tubular chassis.

The car was expensive for its day and most models were exported. A total of 46 were sold in 1954 and 1955.

The car was redesignated the Facel Vega in 1956 with a 5.4-litre engine. Later, the HK500 offered 350bhp from its 6.4 litres.

Production of a convertible in 1955 did not even reach double figures because of rigidity problems and the 1957 pillarless Excellence had similar problems – although more than 150 were made.

The compact Facellia of 1960 was a disaster, mainly because of its unreliable and noisy 1.6-litre engine designed by former Talbot man Carlo Machetti.

Daninos' last Facel was the Facel II, based on the HK500. It was a potent car but came at a time of serious financial problems.

A receiver was appointed in 1962 despite support from Mobil, Pont-à-Mousson and Hispano-Suiza.

The Volvo-engined Facel III was launched in the spring of 1963 but proved a vain attempt at a revival.

Later that year, S.F.E.R.M.A., a subsidiary of Sud-Aviation, was given a one-year management contract to rescue Facel.

The FV6 was launched with the six-cylinder Healey 3000 engine, reduced in capacity to fall within the French domestic 15hp tax cut-off. But after producing fewer than 30 cars, S.F.E.R.M.A. declined to renew its option.

The original company was declared bankrupt in 1965.

Top: The HK500, a 1958 model
Centre: The Facel II boasted even more power
Bottom: 1960's Facellia was an unsuccessful small car attempt

The Facellia was Facel Vega's attempt to go downmarket and build a smaller-engined car. Though pretty in the firm's distinctive way, production problems and reliability queries over its four-cylinder 1.6-litre engine prevented its success, and less than 500 made it to the customers.

Ferrari

Italy
1940 to date

Enzo Ferrari – the man behind one of the world's most famous names in exotic sports cars – was born in Modena, northern Italy in February 1898.

He became interested in motor racing after seeing his first event at the age of 10 and was driving the family car by 1911.

His father's railway-equipment manufacturing business was extended to motor repairs but tragedy struck in 1916 when his brother Alfredo was killed and their father died. The following year, Ferrari joined the artillery, initially as a farrier and then working on aero-engines.

He was invalided out in 1918 and made a vain attempt to get a job with Fiat. However, Ferrari found work with a Bolognese engineer called Giovanni who was converting small trucks to saloons and sports cars.

Ferrari was friendly with racing driver Ugo Sivocci and he got Ferrari a job test-driving for Construzions Meccaniche Nazionali in Milan. And this led to his first race, competing for CMN at the Parma Poggio di Berceto hillclimb in 1919.

Ferrari's enthusiasm for racing was fired and a year later he joined Alfa Romeo as a test-driver, finishing second for Alfa in the Targa Florio.

Above: 1948 Ferrari Type 166 Corsa Spider – priceless

Below: The 250GTO, the last of the Ferrari front-engined competition cars, was developed to overcome problems with the GT models, better stability at high speeds being one. During its 1962 season the GTO came second and third at Le Mans.

Ferrari enjoyed several wins, albeit minor, at the Circuit of Savio and earned the congratulations of Count Enrico Baracca, father of flying ace Francesco Baracca.

The famous pilot had been killed in 1918 and his mother, the Countess Paolina, dedicated her son's prancing-horse emblem to Ferrari. He adopted it as his badge.

Ferrari's racing career ended abruptly when his son Dino was born in January 1932. He decided to retire after being plagued by illness including a nervous breakdown in 1924.

During his racing days, he moved closer and closer to building his own cars. He left Alfa in 1929 and formed Societa Anonima Scuderia Ferrari as a limited company with partners Mario Tadini and the Caniato brothers, in Modena.

The company was mainly involved with racing Alfas. Alfa went into state ownership in 1932 but Ferrari carried on independently and was also involved in motorcycle racing.

Alfa formed Alfa Corse in 1938 with Ferrari as manager but the latter left a year later after a dispute with Spanish engineer Wilfredo Ricart. He used his golden handshake and the residual assets of Scuderia Ferrari and formed Societa Anonima Auto Avio Construzioni Ferrari. At first, the company concentrated on tool manufacture but soon began making racing cars.

The first car was called the 815 but the four-year Alfa severance conditions prevented him using the name Ferrari. It was designed by Alberto Massimino and built between December 1939 and April 1940. It featured a straight-eight engine, using some Fiat parts, with a Touring of Milan body.

Top: Sports car perfection – a 1950 166MM Barchetta
Above: 1951 Vignale Berlinetta, a more sophisticated 212 Export

The Daytona, styled by Pininfarina, was the last of the front-engined V12 Ferraris and when it was introduced in 1968 it was one of the fastest road cars ever with a top speed of 282km/h (175mph). Few have beaten that claim to this day.

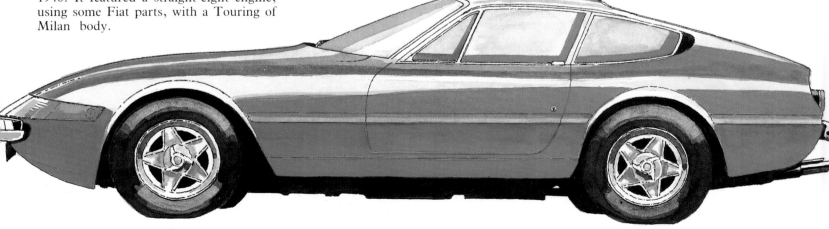

Two of the cars showed promise in the Brescia Grand Prix but both retired before completing the course.

World War II halted production and Ferrari turned to making aircraft parts and machine tools. In 1943 he moved to nearby Maranello and, despite two bombing raids on the factory, it was rebuilt in 1946 with Ferrari announcing that he would build cars for both the road and track. By now, he was allowed to call them Ferraris.

The new breed was launched with a 1½-litre V12 racing sports car, designed by Gioacchino Colombo and announced in November 1946. It made its debut at a race in Piacenza in May 1947.

Three 125s were built and then came the larger-engined 159 and 166. It was the 166 which was to form the basis of the first road-going car – the 1947 166 Inter.

Ferrari's first customer took delivery in January 1948 and then Ferrari offered the 1951 195 Inter and the later 212 model.

Although road cars were still something of a sideline, Ferrari sold over 250 Inters plus the bigger-engined 342s and 375s for the American market.

Ferrari's enterprise and flair caught the imagination of Milanese businessman Franco Cornacchia and Luigi Chinetti, both of whom injected cash into the company and helped set up America's long-standing Ferrari connection which saw Briggs Cunningham import the first of the marque, a 1949 Spider.

The Americans demanded the biggest engines and fastest cars and, with few exceptions, opted for the 400 and 410 Superamerica models of the mid-1950s, the lightweight 410 Superfast and, eventually, the 4.9-litre 500 Superfast with a 400bhp engine.

In fact, the 500 was the last of the large but comparatively crude cars made specifically for the American market from 1964 to 1966. Thereafter, export cars to America were ostensibly European models doctored to comply with local legislation and sales requirements.

Ferrari owed much of his success to racing and the marque made its Formula One debut in September 1948 in the Italian Grand Prix at Valentino Park, Turin. Raymond Sommer – part of a three-car team – finished third.

The first Formula One win came the same year at Lake Garda, with Froilan

Above: The 250MM of 1953, another sleek coupé
Below: A 1965 Ferrari 500 Superfast

Below: 1969's 365GT 2+2
Bottom: The 206GT Dino of 1968
Overleaf: 1960 Ferrari 250 SWB

Above: A luxurious 2+2 coupé, the 250GT

Left: The 1965 275GTB 'shortnose' Ferrari

Below: The BB series – named Berlinetta Boxer, the body style and the engine layout – kept the company's name on the lips of cognoscenti during the early 1970s, and kept the firm's reputation firmly intact through a number of changes in engine size and upratings of performance.

Gonzalez taking a Ferrari to its first Grand Prix win in Britain in 1951. The car was designed by Aurelio Lampredi who had rejoined Ferrari two years earlier. A Ferrari also won the Mille Miglia in 1951 and the cars went from strength to strength, so far taking world championships nine times, nine Le Mans wins and close to 100 individual wins in Formula One.

Ferrari's son Dino was a talented engineer and played a prominent role in developing the V6 racing engine which bore his name. Tragically, he died in 1956 at the age of 24.

Ford of America had long since been keen to win Le Mans to boost its sporting image and tried to buy out Ferrari in the early 1960s. Ferrari backed out when he realized that he would lose control of his racing operations – the one part of his company which had always been near to his heart.

Instead, he preferred to stick with a deal clinched in 1955 when he agreed to take over the struggling Lancia Grand Prix team with Fiat financially supporting his own team.

Ferrari had already established a fine reputation with the 250 Europa of 1954, a true GT which committed his company to road car manufacture. Production really got underway with the three-litre 250GT in 1956. And the 1961 250 range included the Lusso (which means luxury) and the 250GT 2+2, the first Ferrari with more than two seats.

Lightweight versions were made available, called Berlinetta (little saloon). And in 1962, Ferrari introduced the short-chassis 250GTO – for Gran Turismo Omologato – and only 39 were built until 1964.

In the mid-1960s, production had increased significantly and Ferrari used the Fiat connection to the full. But one project was less than successful. Ferrari developed a four-cylinder engine intended for a small touring car. It was tried in a Fiat 1100 chassis but the project was dropped because Ferrari did not have the production capacity. The engine design was sold to the De Nora family who used it to build the ASA Mille in 1964. But the car never found popularity and production ended in 1967.

The phenomenal Pininfarina-styled

Top: 1967's 275 GTB/4
Centre: Competition cars were Ferrari's forte, like this 250 GTO Berlinetta

Above: The 250GTO of 1962, very much a road racer

front-engined V12 365GTB4 Daytona was introduced in 1968. With a top speed of 281km/h (175mph) it is still one of the world's fastest production cars.

The same year saw the launch of the Dino 206GT, developed from the 1965 206GTS racing sports car. It was a direct competitor to the Porsche 911 and used a Ferrari-designed engine built by Fiat. The familiar prancing-horse emblem was missing. Instead, the car bore a Dino badge, in memory of Enzo Ferrari's late son. The Dino later came with a larger engine in the 246GT and 246GTS Spider.

Ferrari introduced his first road-going V8 engine in the Bertone-styled 308GT4 in 1973 but reverted to Pininfarina for the 1975 308GTB.

Above: 1971's 365GTS4 Daytona Spider
Below:The 208 Turbo was one of the firm's first applications of turbocharging to their familiar Berlinetta body style. It gave the already awesome power of the beautifully engineered Ferrari engine a further boost.

Top: The 1975 Dino 308GT/4 2+2   *Above: The 308GTB of 1976*

Left: 1973 Dino 246GT Spider
Above: 1973 365GT4 2+2

Below: 1972 Daytona 365GTB4

Grand Prix racing had a major influence on the 365GT4BB Berlinetta Boxer. The flat-twelve engine was mounted amidships, first as a 4.4-litre unit and then in five-litre form. The latter was known as the 512BB, signifying cubic capacity and the number of cylinders.

The 1984 GTO was a homologation special, developed from the 308 series and built as a road car, but only in sufficient numbers to satisfy the requirements of racing regulations. The Boxer was replaced by the Testarossa, a road car capable of 290km/h (180mph).

Ferrari was never complacent about his cars and he continually uprated them with larger engines for the 308 and Mondial and

The Testarossa – the name means 'red head', a reference to the colour of the cam covers, and was used in the 1950s too – has become a byword for all that is desirable in the world of high-performance motoring. Few have had the opportunity to drive one, however, and even fewer have tried its fabulous 290 km/h (180mph) top speed.

Top: *1979 400i Auto*

Above: *The BB 512 of 1979*

Above: The formula did not arrive until after 1975's 365BB
Left: More racing technology in a 1982 quattrovalvole (four-valve) Mondial
Below: 1984's Testarossa

more power for the luxurious 400i. The 308 spawned the 3.2-litre 328 in 1985, which was superseded by the new 3.4-litre 348 GTB in 1989; the 400 evolved into the 412 in early 1985.

In 1987, he announced what many enthusiasts regard as the finest Ferrari ever – the F40. It was to be his last contribution to the world of exotic cars. Enzo Ferrari died in 1988 at the age of 90, but his memory – and his cars – live on.

Right: The Mondial 8, introduced in 1981
Below: A 1988 Mondial 3.2 2+2
Below right: The civilized 412 Auto

The Ferrari F40, launched in 1988 to celebrate the firm's fortieth year of car production, is capable of 322km/h (200mph) and in the hands of an expert driver can do awesome things. Formula One ace Nigel Mansell has a party trick of spinning one in its own length using power alone. Zero to 97km/h (0-60mph) takes four seconds, but the waiting list even at astronomical prices is rather longer.

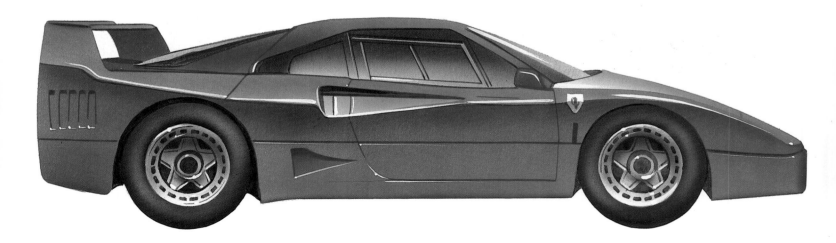

Top: 1984 Mondial Cabriolet Q/V   Above: A 1988 F40 prototype   Below: 1989 Ferrari 348 ts

Above: 1996 F355 Spider

Below: 1997 Ferrari 550 Maranello

Ferrari did not replace the 412 until 1992 when it launched the far more beautiful 456GT. Its smoother, well-balanced lines showed more than a hint of the classic 365GTB Daytona, but, with a 442bhp V12 under the hood, it could show a clean pair of heels to that seventies supercar as well as seat four in reasonable comfort.

The 348 was replaced in 1994 by the 355. Its new version of the classic Ferrari V8 engine had five valves per cylinder and produced a very healthy 380bhp. Its handling and ride was also improved over its predecessor, thanks to the use of high-tech, computer-controlled adaptive damping. Like the 348 it was available in hardtop GTB form and targa top GTS form but in 1995 a new bodystyle was introduced – the fully convertible Spider.

To celebrate 50 years of the famous marque, and as a follow-up to the great F40, Ferrari built the F50. This Pininfarina-styled stripped-out road racer was as near as one could get to driving a Grand Prix car on the road. A 60-valve, 4.7-litre, naturally

aspirated V12 gave earth-shattering acceleration and a top speed of over 200mph.

By 1996 the old Testarossa, or 512, was getting distinctly long in the tooth. Ferrari replaced it with a front-engined two-seater coupé called the 550 Maranello. A rear transaxle was used to get even weight distribution. Its performance was not far short of that of the F50.

Above: 1996 Ferrari 456GT

Below: 1996 Ferrari F355 Berlinetta

Below: Ferrari F40

Fiat

Italy
1899 to date

The F.I.A.T. company was founded in July 1899 by Giovanni Agnelli, di Bricherasio and Count Carlo Biscaretti Di Ruffia. Of the three, the entrepreneur Agnelli was the leading light behind the early commercial success of the new firm.

in 1902, followed by Mercedes-like units with the cylinders cast in pairs. Twin-cylinder engines were discontinued from 1903.

In 1904, in which year the company began to make pressed-steel chassis frames, notable new models included the 16/20hp, intended for town use, and the more sporting 24/32hp.

By 1905, the huge 60hp F.I.A.T. with a 10.2-litre four-cylinder engine was available.

Fiat (the full stops were abandoned in

Left: 1902 F.I.A.T. 8hp

Above: The first F.I.A.T. – 1899-1900

The first F.I.A.T. (*Fabbrica Italiana Automobili Torino*) was a rear-engined 3½hp flat-twin machine of 700cc capacity, based on a car produced by the Ceirano brothers. In 1900/1901 a similarly designed 6/8hp version was built. However, in 1901, a vertical-twin model was introduced, with the engine mounted at the front. In 1902 the capacity was increased from 1082cc to 1884cc, the new 8hp engine being cooled by a honeycomb radiator.

Larger engines soon appeared – a 3768cc four-cylinder unit was introduced

Above: The huge 60hp F.I.A.T. of 1905   *Below: 1911 28.3-litre Fiat S.76*

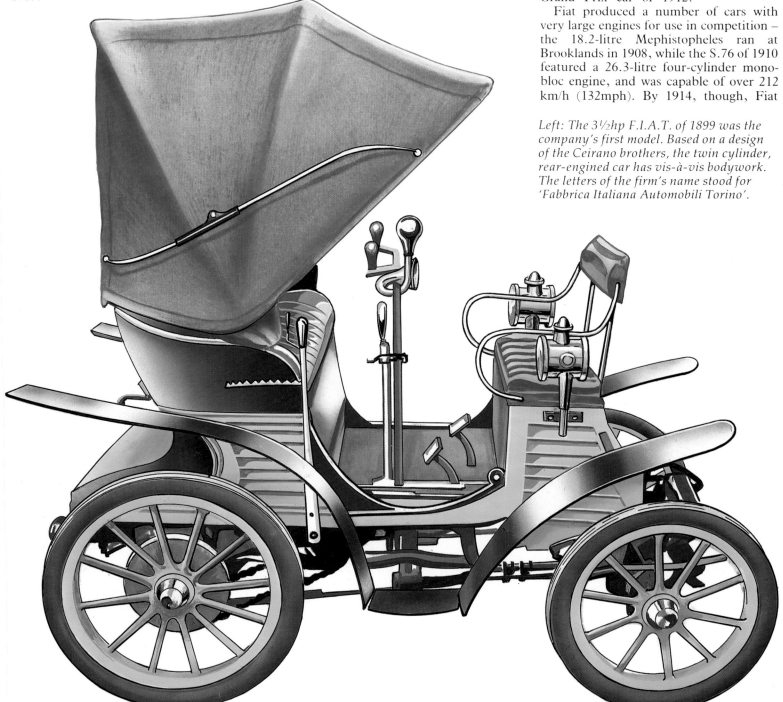

1906) employed shaft-drive for the first time in 1907 on its 14/16hp, and in the same year an 11-litre six-cylinder model was introduced.

The company's advanced thinking in engine design helped it to success in motor sport and notable victories were achieved by Fiat driver Nazarro in the Targa Florio, Kaiserpreis and French Grand Prix of 1907.

Fiat survived the European economic crisis of 1907, and its technical innovation continued, combined with a general reduction in the sizes of the company's power units. A monobloc four-cylinder two-litre 10/14hp L-head engine was introduced in 1908, with four-speed gearboxes available from 1909. The six-cylinder Type 5 models of 1908 gave way to four-cylinder versions from 1909.

Fiat was an early exponent of the use of overhead valves and overhead camshafts. The 10.9-litre racers of 1905 had engines of overhead-valve design, while the 10.1-litre 75/90hp sports car of 1911 had an overhead-cam unit, as did the 10½-litre S.61 and the chain-driven, 14½-litre Grand Prix car of 1912.

Fiat produced a number of cars with very large engines for use in competition – the 18.2-litre Mephistopheles ran at Brooklands in 1908, while the S.76 of 1910 featured a 26.3-litre four-cylinder monobloc engine, and was capable of over 212 km/h (132mph). By 1914, though, Fiat

Left: The 3½hp F.I.A.T. of 1899 was the company's first model. Based on a design of the Ceirano brothers, the twin cylinder, rear-engined car has vis-à-vis bodywork. The letters of the firm's name stood for 'Fabbrica Italiana Automobili Torino'.

was extracting 135bhp from engines as comparatively small as 4½ litres.

A wide variety of Fiats were produced before World War I intervened. From 1910, the smallest Fiat was the 1844cc Type 1B, the intermediate range was known as the Type 2, and the largest, the 3964cc Type 3. Developments of the Type 3 included, in 1912, the models 3A and 3C, and the 4, with a 5.7-litre engine. In the same year the Type 5 (Tipo 55) again became part of the range, with a 60hp nine-litre engine.

A 3.9-litre six-cylinder Tipo 57 was also produced in 1911 and 1912 (only), while the 12/15hp model – a sports version of the Type 1B – was available from 1912.

The famous Fiat Zero, built between 1912 and 1915, was a solid 15hp four-seater, with a single-block engine, and although only 2,000 were built, it was an important model for the company.

By 1914, Fiat had streamlined bodywork designs, which now incorporated oval radiators. The larger cars had electric lighting and starting, and wire wheels – all advanced features for the time.

During the war, 35,000 vehicles were produced, including the 15/20hp Type 2B, and some Type 4s, for army staff use.

Fiat's mass-produced Tipo 501 was the first post-war model to emerge, in 1919. The car, with a detachable cylinder head and 1½-litre sidevalve engine, earned a reputation for reliability. Front-wheel brakes became optional on the 501 in 1925. The 501 was built until 1926, by which time some 45,000 had been produced. Larger models along the same lines as the 501 were introduced, with 2.3-litre four-cylinder and 3.4-litre six-cylinder engines.

Between 1921 and 1923, Fiat produced a very few Superfiats, which featured an overhead-valve 6.8-litre V12 engine, and

Above: A 6.8-litre V12 'Superfiat', 1921-22
Below: The 4.8-litre Fiat 519, 1922 on

brakes on all wheels. However, the model was dropped in favour of the 4764cc six-cylinder Tipo 519. This car, built until 1929, had a power output of 77bhp, and was equipped with hydro-mechanical servo brakes.

More angular styling and flat radiators were introduced with the Superfiat and the 519, the new bodywork being cheaper to produce.

In 1925 the 990cc overhead-camshaft-engined 509 was introduced. This proved to be a popular model, with some 90,000 produced in just four years.

Two new long-stroke six-cylinder sidevalve engines were introduced with the Tipo 520 and 525 models of 1927. The 520

Above: A 1913 example of the larger Fiats
Below: The 1.8-litre Fiat 1A, 1912-1915

Above: 1922 Fiat 501; body by Bean Cars
Below right: 1927 ohc Fiat 509

had large, American-style bodywork. The 525 was fitted with hydraulic brakes from 1930.

In 1932 another important small car was introduced by Fiat – the 508 Balilla. The little car had a short-stroke 995cc engine which gave lively performance, and the model featured hydraulic brakes. By 1934

Above: 508S Balilla Sport Spider 1933-37
Right: 1932 prototype Fiat 508 Balilla

the Balilla had a four-speed synchromesh gearbox and four-door pillarless saloon bodywork. An overhead-valve sports version produced 36bhp, and made the car very competitive in motor sport.

Fiat's Tipo 508S of the mid-1930s was an attractive machine which also performed well. Sleek bodywork with a long, louvred bonnet and slanted grille, plus cut-away doors, wire wheels and a 'finned' tail, gave the car a sporting air.

The larger 518 Ardita, produced with 1750cc and 2000cc four-cylinder engines, was introduced in 1933. The following year, the long-stroke six-cylinder 527 became available, and was produced for two years in a wide range of body styles.

From 1935, the Balilla was produced under licence by Simca in France, and by Polski-Fiat in Poland until the outbreak of World War II.

In 1936 Fiat introduced the 1500, a family car with a short-stroke six-cylinder engine, to the same bore/stroke ratio as the 508 Balilla. The 1500 featured Dubonnet ('knee action') independent front suspension and aerodynamic styling.

Fiat updated the Balilla in 1937, when the independent front-suspension 508C Millecento appeared. The 508C had a 1089cc overhead-valve engine developing 32bhp and giving the car a top speed of 112km/h (70mph). A coupé capable of 145km/h (90mph) and a long-wheelbase taxi version were also produced.

Of even more significance to the company was the 570cc Tipo 500A – the famous Topolino – which was introduced in late 1936. The tiny car had two-seater cabriolet bodywork and was powered by a four-cylinder 570cc sidevalve engine which was mounted in front of the radiator. The car also had independent front suspension, hydraulic brakes and a synchromesh gearbox.

The last large Fiat to appear before the outbreak of World War II was the six-cylinder, seven-seater 2800, of which only a few examples were built. After the war,

Above: Fiat's six-cylinder 1500, 1935-38
Below: The 500 Topolino appeared in 1936

Above: The 508C, sold from 1937
Bottom: 1951 Fiat 2800 Ghia

the sidevalve Topolino continued in production until 1948, when an overhead-valve version was introduced.

Updated 1100cc and 1500cc models, with steering-column gearchange, appeared in 1949, while in 1950 an overhead-valve four-cylinder 1400cc model was introduced. This advanced car featured unitary bodywork construction and 150,000 examples were built during its nine-year production run. Many variants were available during that time, including a diesel model, the cross-country Campagnola, and a 1.9-litre luxury version.

Fiat sports models of the early 1950s included the 193km/h (120mph) two-litre V8, and a 48bhp version of the 1100.

Above: The 500C Belvedere estate, 1951-55
Right: The Fiat Multipla of the 1960s

Below: Fiat's two-litre V8, 1952-54

The much-loved Fiat 500 gave way, in 1955, to another baby car, the rear-engined 600. The new model featured unitary construction and a four-cylinder 633cc engine developing 24bhp. The car sold in large numbers (a million had been built by 1950), and continued in production into the 1970s. An interesting variant was the Multiple, a large-bodied taxi/estate.

From late 1960 the 600 was fitted with a 767cc engine, developing 29bhp, and was designated 600D.

A new (Nuova) 500 was introduced in 1957, this time with a rear-mounted, air-cooled twin-cylinder 500cc engine, developing 16½bhp, later 22bhp. Giardiniera estate-car versions, built from 1960, had the engine fitted below the rear floor. Italy's favourite car, the 500, continued in production until March 1973.

Fiat's family 1100 continued in production throughout the 1950s and 1960s, in saloon and estate-car form, and was joined in 1958 by a 1200 Full-light saloon, and by 1300 and 1500 models in 1961. The saloon bodywork changed progressively from rounded styling to more boxy designs, while the roadster versions were particularly attractive.

From 1959, Fiat built six-cylinder saloons in 1800 (75bhp) and 2100 (82bhp) form, both versions having torsion-bar suspension at the front.

Attractive sports models of the same era included the Osca-engined twin-cam 1500 Cabriolet – this produced 90bhp and was capable of well over 160km/h (100mph). It was developed into the 100bhp 1600S model, capable of 173km/h (108mph).

A particularly fast Fiat, from 1963, was the 2300. Available in saloon, coupé and estate versions, the six-cylinder car produced 117bhp in standard form, and 150bhp in 2300S Coupé guise. Maximum speeds were 175km/h (109mph) and 190km/h (118mph) respectively.

A new rear-engined Fiat was to appear in 1964 – the 850, with a lively overhead-valve 850cc power unit developing 40bhp. The car was built in two-door saloon and (later) coupé form. Semi-automatic 'Idroconvert' transmission was available on the saloons. A Sport Coupé was introduced in 1965 and from 1968 it featured a 903cc engine developing 52bhp.

Two significant family models were

Top: Fiat's 1300 saloon of the 1960s
Above: 1963 150bhp 2300S two-door coupé

Above: Fiat 2300 Lusso four-door saloon
Below: The cute 500 was built until 1973

introduced in the mid-1960s – the 1197cc overhead-valve 124 of 1966, and the 1608cc double-overhead-camshaft 125, available from late 1967. The Sport Coupé vers⁻ɑ of the 124 had a five-speed gearbox and was powered by a 1438cc twin-overhead-camshaft engine, giving 96bhp and 179km/h (106mph). The 125 featured a 90bhp engine which endowed the car with brisk performance and a top speed of 160km/h (100mph) – excellent for a family car of the time.

The Fiat Dino Coupé, also introduced in October 1967, was powered by a Ferrari-designed, twin-overhead-camshaft, triple-Weber-carburettor V6 engine of 1987cc, developing 160bhp and giving the car a top speed of some 200km/h (125mph). The rear wheels were driven via a five-speed gearbox.

Fiat introduced two significant models in 1969. These were the front-wheel-drive

Above left: The 124 Berline, 1966 on
Above: Ferrari-engined Fiat Dino Coupé

128, in 1116cc and 1290cc versions (both overhead-camshaft engines) and the three-litre V6-powered 130 luxury saloon.

Fiat replaced the 850 with the front-wheel-drive 127 from 1971, the car being available in saloon and hatchback form, and with a 903cc overhead-valve engine and, later, a 1050cc overhead-camshaft unit. The lively four-seater 127 won the European Car of the Year Award in 1972, as had the 128 in 1970 and the 124 in 1967.

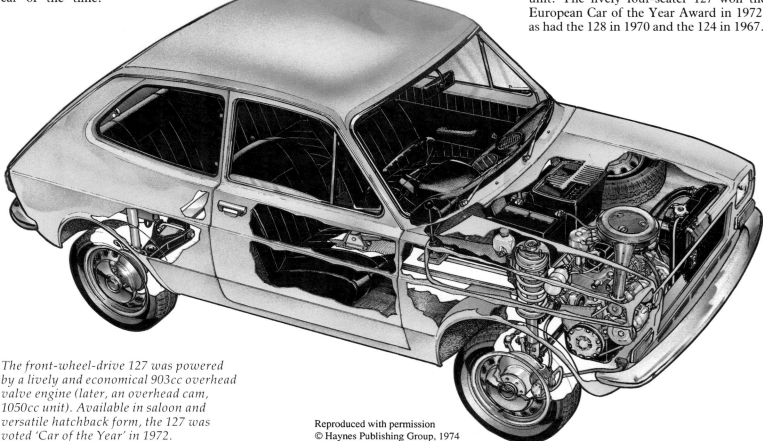

The front-wheel-drive 127 was powered by a lively and economical 903cc overhead valve engine (later, an overhead cam, 1050cc unit). Available in saloon and versatile hatchback form, the 127 was voted 'Car of the Year' in 1972.

Above: Fiat's 767cc 600D of the 1960s
Above right: Fiat 128 estate/Sport coupé

The Fiat 126 was introduced as a replacement for the 500 from 1973. It had a 23bhp twin-cylinder engine of 594cc, and in early 1989 was still, in 126 BIS guise, the cheapest new car available in Britain.

Further Fiats to be introduced in the 1970s included the 132 in 1973 (the replacement for the 125) available in 1600 and 1800cc overhead-camshaft versions; the 131 Mirafiori, in 1297cc overhead-valve and 1585cc overhead-valve overhead-cam variants; from 1975 the 850-based 133; and the two-seater sports X1/9, introduced in 1977 and produced until 1989. The up-to-the-minute Strada

Right: 1976 111bhp Fiat 132 1800ES
Below: A powerful Strada 105TC of 1982

(Ritmo) family saloon was available from 1979, in 1100, 1300, 1500, 1600 (105TC) and 2000cc (Abarth 130TC) forms. The two-litre 132 saloon was sold from 1979.

The 1980s saw the introduction of the Panda, from 1981, initially in 903cc overhead-valve form, and later (from 1986) with 769cc or 999cc overhead-cam (F.I.R.E.) engines. The short-lived two-litre Argenta was available from 1982 to 1984.

One of Fiat's most successful models ever, the Uno (Car of the Year 1984) was introduced in 1983. Petrol engines ranged from 903cc overhead-valve types to 999cc, 1116cc, 1299cc, and 1301cc overhead-camshaft units. A 1697cc diesel was also

Above: The Croma hatchback, 1986 on

available. The Uno set standards for space and fuel economy in small family cars of the early 1980s.

The Uno achieved the Car of the Year Award in 1984. The three- or five-door hatchback was available with petrol engines from 900cc to 1.3-litres capacity, or a 1.7-litre diesel. The tall bodywork provided spacious accommodation.

The Regata (saloon) and Weekend (estate) models were introduced in 1984, with a choice of 1.3-, 1.5- or 1.6-litre power, while the five-door two-litre Croma hatchback range was introduced in 1986.

The Fiat Tipo was introduced in 1988. Like the Uno, it was an innovative design in terms of space and overall design, and won the 1989 Car of the Year Award by a wide margin. The Tipo was powered by engines ranging from 1.4- and 1.6-litre petrol units to 1.7-litre and 1.9-litre (turbocharged) diesels. The Tipo's bodywork featured galvanized panels and a plastic tailgate to combat corrosion.

Above: A late 1980s Fiat Panda 4×4
Top right: A five-door Fiat Uno 70SL
Right: The Tipo – Car of the Year 1989
Below: The last X1/9 'Finale' model, 1989

Below: The Fiat X1/9 was a delightful mid-engined, two-seater sports car. Power was from a 1300cc or 1500cc overhead camshaft engine, mounted behind the cockpit. The cabin was comfortable, and the car featured two luggage compartments.

Above: 1990 Tempra SX

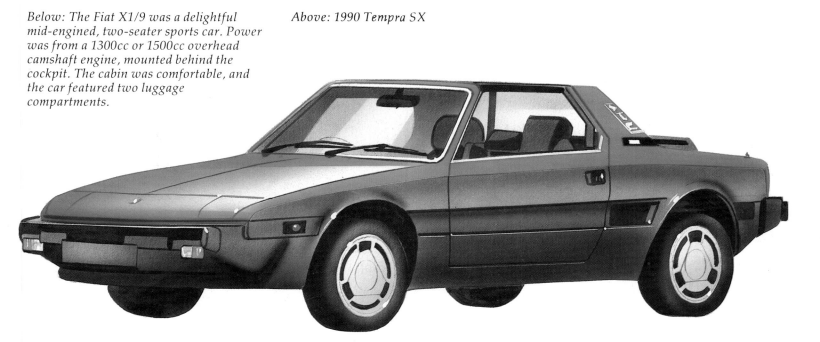

The new Tipo and Tempra helped Fiat enter the 1990s on a good note, and better was to follow. The improved build quality and design of these cars had changed the public's perception of the marque. Although some of the 1980s models remained in production, the Fiat range was almost unrecognizable by 1997.

The first new model of the 1990s was the Cinquecento. The name evoked memories of the famous Topolino and Nuova 500, and so did its diminutive size. It was built in Fiat's Polish factory and was launched at the end of 1991. An ideal town car, the Cinquecento boasted a four-seater, three-door hatchback body, extremely low fuel consumption and it cruised comfortably at 70mph. It was launched with a choice of two engines – the 899cc unit from the Uno and Panda and the two-cylinder 704cc water-cooled unit from the 126 BIS, although the smaller unit was not available in most markets. Its low price and minimal running costs made it a good seller, and the range remained unchanged until 1994 when the new Sporting model was launched. Using the 54bhp 1.1-litre engine from the Uno, the new model could reach 90mph (145km/h) and was great fun to drive. Alloy wheels, a sporty interior, spoilers and and bright colours made it the most desirable Cinquecento, with dealers unable to keep up with demand.

Fiat replaced the long-running Uno (although it was still made for the Polish market) with the stunning new Punto. This quirkily-styled hatchback was unlike anything else on the road and was even available with a six-speed gearbox on some models. As part of a new scheme by Fiat, the Punto was available in a multitude of different colours. Engines ranged from 54bhp 1.1-litre units, to a fire-breathing turbocharged 1.6-litre. As

Above: 1997 Fiat Marea Saloon

well as three- and five-door hatchbacks, there was also a cabriolet model.

Fiat's most stunning model for years also arrived in the 1990s. The new Coupé was styled in conjunction with Pininfarina and was almost more of a design statement than a mode of transport. To back up those stunning looks, the Coupé had more than adequate performance. Early four-cylinder 16-valve models were quick, but the later five-cylinder models, in particular the turbocharged version, could frighten Ferraris. The new five-cylinder engine produced 220bhp in turbocharged form and made the

Right: 1996 FiatBarchetta

Coupé the fastest car in its class with a 0-60mph (0-100km/h) time of 6.5 seconds and a top speed of over 150mph (240km/h).

The Coupé wasn't Fiat's only sports car though. The open-top Barchetta had less performance, but every bit as much style. Fiat's design centre created a well-proportioned retro-styled sports car which owed more to the original Alfa Romeo Spider, than Alfa's new Spider did.

Having done its job admirably, the competent, but ultimately bland Tipo was dropped in 1995. It was replaced by not one, but two cars, the Bravo and Brava. Identical under

Right: 1997 Fiat Coupé 20v Turbo
Below: 1996 Fiat Punto

The Marea, which used the new five-cylinder, was launched at around the same time and shared many styling features but was a bigger car to replace the Tempra.

Fiat also collaborated with Peugeot and Citroën to add a MPV to its range. Engines and a few minor styling tweaks set the Ulysse apart from the other companies' products.

Above: 1997 Fiat Marea Weekend
Below: Fiat Cinquecento Sporting

the skin, the Bravo was a 3-door hatchback, the Brava, a five-door notchback. Both benefited from Fiat's new-found innovative styling and some new engines, including the fine five-cylinder unit.

Left: 1997 Fiat Brava
Below left: 1997 Fiat Bravo
Below: Fiat Ulysse

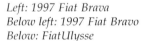

Ford

U.S.A.
1901 to date

Henry Ford, who was destined to become one of the greatest industrialists of the twentieth century, completed his first car, or 'quadricycle', during 1896. A second was running by the summer of 1899 which sufficiently impressed his financiers to form the Detroit Automobile Company. Unfortunately, the cars failed to sell and Henry's ideas differed from those of the stockholders, so he left and turned to racing.

In October 1901 his newly completed 20hp racer won a 10-mile (16km) sweepstakes race at Grosse Point race track, Detroit, averaging 43.5mph (70 km/h). Ford gained favourable publicity from the event and secured further backing which led to the formation of the Henry Ford Company in November 1901. However, Ford's interests remained with racing and this led to friction. So after just three months he left with a U.S. $900 settlement, and an agreement that the company would change its name. This it ultimately did, to Cadillac.

During 1902 Ford teamed up with Tom Cooper and built two huge 80hp racers named 'Arrow' and '999' respectively, and enlisted Barney Oldfield as a competition driver. By all accounts the cars were brutes to handle, but Oldfield drove '999' to victory in the 1902 Manufacturers' Challenge Cup, completing the five-mile (eight-kilometre) race in 5 minutes 28 seconds.

Left: Henry Ford and his 1896 'Quadricycle'
Above: The first and the 10 millionth, a 1924 Model T
Below: A very early (1902) Ford

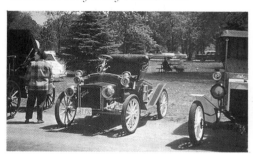

Henry Ford was, by now, well known and in a much better position to form a company that favoured his ideas, so, in June 1903 the Ford Motor Company was incorporated, and Henry could begin concentrating on producing an affordable car for the people. His mission to motorize the world had began.

The first car, the 1903 Model A, was a lightweight 8hp vehicle that could reach 30mph (48km/h). From the outset the company made a profit, U.S. $36,957 during its first 3½ months, and sales for 1903 totalled a respectable 1,708 cars.

Below: The 30mph Ford Model A of 1903

In 1904 the company offered the B, C and F models, and sales soared to 8,729 units. The Model N appeared in 1906 and proved a very good low-price car. More models followed: the R and S, essentially costlier versions of the N, and the six-cylinder K which replaced the B. The big K, advocated by Ford's partner, Alexander Malcolmson, just did not sell and was discontinued. Ford would not offer another six-cylinder car until 1941. Nevertheless, sales for 1906 reached an impressive 14,887 cars. Ford, having bought out other shareholders, now owned 58.5 per cent of the company.

Above: The Ford N (1906) preceded the 'T'
Below: The Model N sold for U.S. $600

One of the most significant landmarks in motoring history occurred on 1st October 1908, the day Ford launched the Model T. Henry Ford's (and the Model T's) success lay with his implementation of mass-production methods beginning in 1914, and the use of interchangeable precision parts, in an era when many other cars were still virtually hand-built. Ford's Highland Park, Detroit, factory was at the time the largest and most modern in the world. The company soon reaped the rewards for its efficiency and low unit costs, and Ford began cutting the price of his cars. In 1911 a Touring model cost U.S. $950, but by 1925 it was down to just U.S. $290, yet

Above: 1909 Model T Roadster
Right: 1911 'Australian' Model T Ford
Below: Cranking a 1910 Model T into life

Right: 1914 Model T

Top: Ford's six-cylinder Model K of 1906
Centre: 1909 Ford Model T Touring
Above: 1910 Model T on tour in 1967

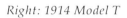

The 1908 Ford Model T was the car which literally 'put America on wheels'. By 1927, some 15 million Model Ts had been produced, all essentially similar. During 1923 alone, some 1.8 million were sold!

Ford was still averaging a U.S. $50 profit per car. Profits for 1923–24 stood at U.S. $100 million.

Apart from his customers, Henry Ford also shrewdly managed his workforce and, in 1914, introduced the celebrated U.S. $5, eight-hour working day. During this period Henry Ford became the most well-known and admired car manufacturer in the world.

Above: A distinctive 1912 Model T
Below: Timeless elegance – 1912 Model T

Top: Ford's first moving assembly line at Highland Park, Michigan in 1913
Above: 1915 Model T with twin spare tyres
Below: 1915 Ford Roadster on the 1964 Glidden Tour

Above: 1914 Ford Touring, filmed in 1964
Below: 1914 Model T wood bed pick-up

By 1926, however, Model T sales were flagging, in spite of subtle improvements and the availability of colours other than black for the first time in ten years. An increasingly unpopular aspect of the Model T was its outdated planetary transmission, which required a pedal to be held down to engage the low-speed gear or reverse. Also, as road conditions in the U.S.A. improved, customers began favouring refinement and comfort above unsophisticated raggedness. At first, Henry Ford, once so in tune with

motorists' requirements, would not accept that times were changing. However, even he could not ignore falling sales, and Model T production finally ended in May 1927.

The task of retooling for a new car was an enormous one, which took several months amidst much public speculation about the Model T's successor. It was not until December 1927 that the all-new Model A, a four-cylinder car, was finally

Above: 1915 Model T Touring – on tour!
Right: 1916 Model T Touring
Below: 1916 Model T Roadster

The Ford 18 V-8 of 1932 was developed from the Model A. The 3.6-litre V8 engine produced 70bhp and gave lively performance.

revealed to an eager public. The chassis, similar to the T, now featured a conventional three-speed transmission and four-wheel brakes. The styling, under the direction of Henry's son and company president, Edsel Ford, resembled the contemporary Lincoln (Ford having bought Lincoln in 1922). The Model A was immensely popular, and in January 1929 production worldwide totalled 159,786 units for the month. Ford was back on course.

Top: The popular Model A of 1928
Above: Model A Station Wagon

Above: 1928 Model A Tourer
Below: 1929 Model A Roadster with dickey

Above: 1926 Model T Tourer ('Swedish')
Below: 1926 Ford Roadster climbing hard
Bottom: 1928 Model A Sport Coupé

Below: 1930 Model A Roadster, hood up

Below: 1930 Model A Roadster, hood down!

March 1932 was another Ford landmark, when Henry Ford took a gamble in the midst of the Depression, and launched the first low-priced V8-powered car. Luckily, the gamble ultimately paid off, and the sidevalve flathead V8 remained Ford's primary power plant until 1953. Initially for 1932–33, the four-cylinder engine remained available. In 1937 a small-capacity V8 became optional which was subsequently replaced by a new sidevalve six in 1941.

Left: 1931 Ford Model A Convertible Sedan

Above: Stylish 1932 V-8 Roadster

Below: A De Luxe Phaeton Model A, 1930

During the 1930s Ford lost the number one sales spot to Chevrolet. This was partly because of Henry's adherence to transverse springing and outdated mechanical brakes; and partly because he alienated potential customers by his admiration for Hitler, and refused, sometimes by violent means, the unionization of his workforce.

An event that marked the end of an era for the company was the untimely death of Edsel Ford on 26 May 1943, aged 50. Edsel was very well liked and respected, and brought much to the Ford Motor Company. He made his greatest impact in the Lincoln division, and on the body styling of the Model A and V8 lines, all areas where his father showed little personal interest. Though always in his shadow, he had qualities that his father lacked, primarily fine taste and foresight.

Henry Ford, now nearly 80, and becoming increasingly eccentric, was re-elected as president while a power struggle between two key men – Charles Sorensen and Harry Bennett – went on beneath him. Bennett persuaded Ford that Sorensen, wanting to succeed Ford as president, had to go. Sorensen subsequently left to become president of Willys-Overland.

The instability at the top at Ford worried the U.S. government as Ford was a major contributor to the war effort. So, in August 1943 and aged just 26, Henry Ford II (the oldest of Edsel's three sons) was discharged from the U.S. Navy and named executive vice-president shortly after. Henry Ford was eventually persuaded by his family to resign as president in favour of Henry II in September 1945. With Henry gone the infamous Harry Bennett was on his own, and was edged out of the company the same month. Henry Ford died on 7th April 1947.

Right: 1957 Fairlane 500 Skyliner
Below: 1949 Custom Coupé

Immediately after the war the company was in turmoil, and losses ran as high as U.S. $10 million per month. Henry II was acutely aware of the situation and quickly brought in young blood and new ideas. He also knew that the first all-new post-war car had to succeed if the company was to survive. Fortunately, the 1949 Ford, the Custom Deluxe Tudor, announced in June 1948, did sell well, and the company finances rapidly returned to the black.

From 1952 Henry II set out to put Ford back in front, ahead of Chevrolet, by instigating a price-cutting war. By the mid-1950s Ford had managed to match Chevrolet model for model, but could not win the sales battle. The real losers were the small independent manufacturers: Hudson, Nash, Packard and Studebaker. They could not afford price cuts, consequently bankruptcies and mergers followed.

Above: 1953 Victoria Tudor HT
Below: Country Squire of 1954

Above: 1955 Thunderbird

Above: The 1957 Edsel Corsair

Above: The Mustang of the 1960s was a (relatively) small car, with sporting appeal, and was available in Hardtop, Fastback Coupé and Convertible versions.

Above: 1958 Edsel Pacer
Below: Fairlane 500 of 1958

Above: 1958 two-door Ford

In 1960 Henry II launched the compact Falcon range, and appointed Lee Iacocca as division general manager. Iacocca became the inspiration behind the Mustang and Ford's 'Total Performance' projects during the 1960s (before 'performance' became a dirty word in the industry), culminating with the legendary Shelby-Mustang GT 350/500 and Boss 302/429 series.

Below: 1962 Falcon Station Wagon

Below: 1964 Galaxie 500 XL

Above: Thunderbird, 1966   *Below: 1966 Ranchero Squire*

In the early 1970s the oil crisis left U.S. car manufacturers with whole ranges of largely obsolete cars, as the market swung towards economical Japanese and European cars. By 1980 the world was in an economic recession and Ford began losing vast sums of money, nearly U.S. $3.3 billion by 1982.

Fortunately for Ford, as the 1980s progressed and the company's rationalization and modernization plans took effect, things began to improve. The swing back into profit was well and truly made with the launch of the popular mid-sized Taurus range of cars in late 1985 and the aerodynamically-styled Thunderbird two years later. General Motors, on the other hand, was still struggling, and in 1986, for the first time since 1924, made less money than Ford.

Ford made a U.S. $3.7 billion profit in the first nine months of 1987, and looks well set as the company heads towards its centenary in 2003.

Below: 1974 LTD Brougham Hardtop   *Bottom: 1977 Pinto*

Above: 1972 Mustang two-door Hardtop
Below: Thunderbird, 1974; 460 c.i.d.
Bottom: 1977 Mercury Monarch Ghia

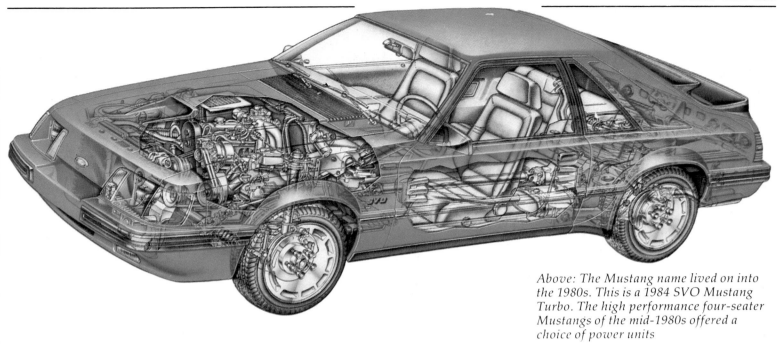

Above: The Mustang name lived on into the 1980s. This is a 1984 SVO Mustang Turbo. The high performance four-seater Mustangs of the mid-1980s offered a choice of power units

Above: 1980 two-door Fairmont

Above: 1980 Granada Ghia four-door sedan

Above: Mustang II Ghia, October 1977

Below: The 1989 Mustang was an unsophisticated but fast performer. It retained the classic front-engine rear-drive layout employed in Mustangs dating back to 1964.

Top: 1988 all-wheel-drive Tempo
Above: 1988 LTD Country Squire Wagon

Above: 1988 Thunderbird Coupé
Below: 1988 Mustang Convertible

Top: 1988 Aerostar; Eddie Bauer model
Below: The 1.3-litre Festiva, 1988
Bottom: 1989 Mustang Convertible

Ford was the only member of America's Big Three car manufacturers to get through the recession of the late-1980s without serious losses. The top-selling Taurus was a lesson to rivals and Ford's efficient manufacturing methods helped keep costs down. The company's Atlanta plant was the most efficient in the U.S., besting even the newest Japanese factories, with each Taurus taking under a minute to build. This efficiency helped Ford compete with the low-cost Japanese imports and kept the company afloat during the hard times.

Further increase in efficiency, and future stability, was gained by the company's 'Ford 2000' plan. This global reorganization of the company was intended to consolidate all its worldwide automotive units into the global Ford Automotive operation. By doing this, Ford could develop a new generation of world cars, vehicles it could sell all over the world with a minimum of modifications. These world cars could slash development costs, although there was some doubt as to how successful the plan would be. Would a car designed for German autobahns work as well driven within America's restrictive speed limits? The first true Ford world car was not expected to arrive until 1999.

Ford's small cars of the 1990s, the Aspire (Mazda 121) and Escort (Mazda 323) were developed in conjunction with Mazda (Ford owns a 25 per cent share in the Japanese company), as was the Ford Probe, which was

Top: The 1996 Ford Taurus SHO was the high-performance variant

Above: 1997 Ford Contour, was a Ford Europe Mondeo

Left: The Ford Aspire was based on the Mazda 121 or Kia Pride

Below: The U.S. -market Ford Escort was based on the Mazda 323 from 1990

more or less identical to the Mazda MX6 under the skin. Other cars were Ford through and through, with the medium-size Taurus an American sales chart success.

The mighty Mustang was replaced in 1993. Despite its modern and aerodynamic lines it still had the necessary horsepower under the bonnet and a very muscular stance. The GT model certainly had the muscle to match the looks. Its 4.6-litre V8 engine produced over 300bhp and could propel the hot Mustang to 60mph (100km/h) in under 6 seconds. The 3.8-litre V6 version was rather slower. It was also available in cabriolet form.

The Thunderbird name was kept alive in a new luxury sports grand tourer launched in 1988. The new smooth coupé styling had drag coefficient of only 0.31. With the 208bhp V8 engine it could top 130mph (210km/h).

Above: 1997 Ford Thunderbird

Left: Ford Probe

Far left: Ford F150 Lariat Supercab

Below left: 1997 Mustang GT

Below: Ford Explorer

Bottom: 1997 Ford Crown Victoria

Ford Europe

France 1947–1954

French Fords built before World War II were known as Matfords, following an agreement with the Mathis company, drawn up in 1934, under which the latter company was to produce only Ford vehicles. However, a few Fords were built in France prior to that – the Tracfords, which were essentially front-wheel-drive versions of the 8hp Model Y.

The Matfords were American in styling and origin, and featured V8 engines. The smallest engine was a 2.2-litre unit developing 63bhp. The models achieved some success in motor sport, notably in the Monte Carlo Rallies of 1936 and 1938.

The V8s continued to be built until 1939, the cars featuring vee-shaped windscreens from 1938. Their appearance was similar to that of the 22hp V8 British Ford.

In 1947 the company became known as Ford S.A.F. and the first Ford Vedette was introduced. It was fitted with the pre-war 2.2-litre V8 engine, and had an independent front suspension and hydraulic brakes. It remained in production until 1954.

In 1952 the V8-powered Comète coupé became available, with neat bodywork by Facel. A larger, 3.9-litre sidevalve engine was available from 1954. From 1955 the model was built on unitary-construction principles, and had an uprated (80bhp) engine.

Simca took over the company from Ford in late 1954 and continued building the Comète under the Simca Vedette name.

Right: The Taunus models of the mid-1970s were generally similar to the equivalent British-built Cortinas. With roomy bodywork and a range of engine sizes, they gave a wide choice to buyers. This is a 1976 example.

Germany 1931 to date

The first Fords to be assembled in Germany were Model Ts in 1925, followed by Model As from 1927. After the building of a new factory in Cologne, the German company built Model Bs under the name Rheinland, and the Model Y 8hp, known in Germany as the Köln.

The V8 engine was also built in Cologne, as were the 1157cc Eifel and the 1172cc Taunus from 1939. This car, with a sidevalve power unit similar to that used in the British Ford 10, was also built after World War II.

During the 1950s all the German Fords were known as Taunus models, and four-cylinder cars under 12M, 15M and 17M designations (denoting engine capacities; 12M indicated 1200cc) were produced.

The would-be Cortina competitor, the front-wheel-drive 12M of 1962, had a V4 engine, as did the larger-capacity 15M version. In 1964 the rear-wheel-drive 17M also used a V4 engine, of either 1.5 or 1.7 litres capacity. The 20M of the same year was powered by a two-litre V6 engine. By 1968 a 108bhp 2.3-litre V6 engine had been developed, for installation in the 20M RS.

From the late 1960s Ford of Cologne built its own versions of Fords also built in Britain and elsewhere, for example Escorts, Cortinas, Capris, Granadas and Sierras, often with minor variations in body styling and sometimes using its own V4 and V6 engines (notably in the Capris).

Right: 1975 (German) Granada Ghia Coupé

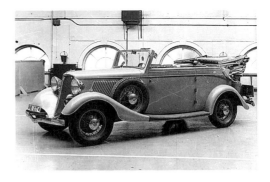

Above: 1933/4 Rheinland
Below: 1936/7 V-8 Type 48 Standard

Great Britain 1911 to date

Until 1932 British-built Fords were assembled at Trafford Park, Manchester, and were Anglicized versions of the American Models T and A. However, with the building of the vast Dagenham factory, opened in 1932, Ford of Britain was able to produce models specifically designed for use in the U.K.

The first model to emerge from the new factory was the famous 933cc 8hp Model Y, with a simple sidevalve engine, three-speed gearbox and transverse leaf-spring suspension. The car, a full four-seater, was made in two- and four-door form, and the two-door model became the first full-sized saloon to be sold for £100, in late 1935. In the same year, the 1172cc 10hp Model C was introduced, an attractive car with flowing bodywork lines.

Above: 1935 10hp Model C saloon
Below: 1937 'New Eight' (7Y)

The Dagenham plant produced V8s based on American Fords, as well as a smaller 22hp '60' V8, produced from 1937 to 1939. The Model Y was replaced, in August 1937, by the 7Y, or 'New Eight', which featured more rounded styling, 'easy clean' disc wheels and doors hinged from the front – unusual in the 1930s. In the same year the Model C was replaced by the 10hp 7W, with similar bodywork modifications as for the 7Y.

The first Ford Anglia – the 8hp E04A –

Above: A 1940 8hp Anglia E04A

was introduced in November 1939, and produced again after the war until 1948. The Anglia was similar to the 7Y, but with a larger grille. The grille was changed again in 1946, when the new E494A Anglia now featured a narrow radiator cowl with a rounded top. The E494A was built until late 1953.

Above: Prefect E93A, 10hp, c. 1940
Below: 1948 Pilot V8 (3.6-litre)

The 10hp E93A, introduced in 1936, was the first Ford to be given the Prefect designation, and was identifiable by its protruding, rounded grille and rear-hinged 'alligator'-type bonnet. As with the Popular, production recommenced in 1945. The

car was altered in 1949, and redesignated E493A on receiving a grille with vertical bars and headlamps built into the front wings. In this form it continued until 1953.

It is interesting to note that the small van derivative of the Prefect – the E83W – was produced in large numbers throughout the war years. Indeed, some 350,000 were built for the forces.

From 1953 the Popular received the 1172cc sidevalve engine of the E493A Prefect to become a more austere version of the export 10hp Anglia. In this form (designated 103E) the Popular was the cheapest car on the U.K. market. The car was produced until August 1959 and as the last of the upright Fords was the last essentially pre-war design to be built in Britain.

Above: 1949 Anglia E494A

Above: 1950-56 Zephyr Mk I
Left: Ford's 'New' Anglia 100E of 1953
Below left: The four-door Prefect 100E

In the meantime, Ford had been up-dating its larger models, and the four-cylinder 1508cc Consul and the six-cylinder 2262cc Zephyr of 1951 had sleeker, unitary bodywork, and overhead-valve engines, albeit still mated to three-speed gearboxes. In 1954 a luxury variant – the Zephyr Zodiac – was introduced. Two-door convertible versions were available, in addition to the four-door saloons. Front suspension was by Mac-Pherson strut – a feature which was to stay with Ford into the 1980s.

At the 1953 Earls Court Motor Show Ford introduced its New Anglia (two-door) and New Prefect (four-door) models, with styling similar to that used on the larger cars. Both the new models were of unitary construction, and both featured a large luggage boot. While the engines were still of 1172cc capacity, they were more powerful, and totally redesigned compared with the earlier sidevalve units. Three-speed gearboxes were still fitted. Like the larger Fords, the new Anglia and Prefect models now had MacPherson-strut front suspension and hydraulic brakes.

New (Mark II) Consul, Zephyr and Zodiac models appeared in February 1956, with 'lowline' versions being introduced in February 1959. The Consul now had a 59bhp 1703cc engine, while the six-cylinder models had a capacity of 2553cc giving 85bhp.

One of Ford's most significant models – the 105E Anglia – was introduced in 1959. Unlike earlier Fords, it featured an over-square overhead-valve engine of 997cc capacity and a four-speed gearbox. The Anglia was later also fitted with a 1200cc engine (123E), and the model continued in production until 1967, selling very well for Ford, and earning it new respect. The 100E Anglia was updated and became the latest Popular, and was sold until 1962 – the last volume-production car in the UK to be fitted with a sidevalve engine. A few thousand (100E) Prefects were fitted with the 105E's overhead-valve engine, and termed 107E.

Above right: 1959 997cc ohv Anglia 105E
Right: 1962 2.6-litre Zodiac

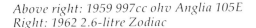

Above: 1961-3 Consul Classic

Below: 1962 1200cc Consul Cortina

The four-door 1340cc (later 1498cc) Classic and the two-door fastback Capri version were introduced in 1961, but were only sold until 1963 (Classic) and 1964 (Capri). The large Mark III Zephyrs and Zodiacs, with angular, finned styling, were introduced in 1962, and used engines of identical capacities to the earlier models, but now linked to four-speed, all-synchromesh gearboxes.

Above: Ford's mechanically 'traditional' Cortina was one of the most significant models in the history of the company. From the introduction of the Mk I in 1962,

Above: The sleek V4 Corsair, 1965

Above: 1964 Cortina Lotus in action

built, the latter having a twin-cam 1558cc engine which produced 105bhp and 174km/h (108mph).

The more luxurious 1500cc Corsair was introduced in 1963, and was fitted with a V4 engine, initially of 1663cc but of 1996cc from 1965.

April 1966 saw the introduction of the huge Mark IV Zephyrs and Zodiacs. The Zephyr Four had a two-litre V4 engine, the Zephyr Six/Zodiac, a three-litre V6. A luxury 'Executive' version of the Zodiac was available from October 1966.

Restyled Mark II versions of the Cortina were introduced in late 1966, with a choice of 1.3-litre or 1.5-litre engines. From August 1967, the Cortinas featured 'cross-flow' Kent engines, in which the inlet and exhaust manifolds were on opposite sides of the unit. Again, a Cortina Lotus was available, from March 1967. Later that year a sports/luxury version of the Cortina – the 1600E – was introduced, fitted with a GT engine developing 88bhp. More than 1,010,000 Cortinas were sold in Mark I form, and virtually the same number of Mark IIs.

The most famous family Ford of all time – the Cortina – was introduced in 1962, and proved to be a winner for Ford in sales terms. Mark I models had 1200cc or 1500cc engines, based on that of the 105E Anglia. GT and Lotus versions were also

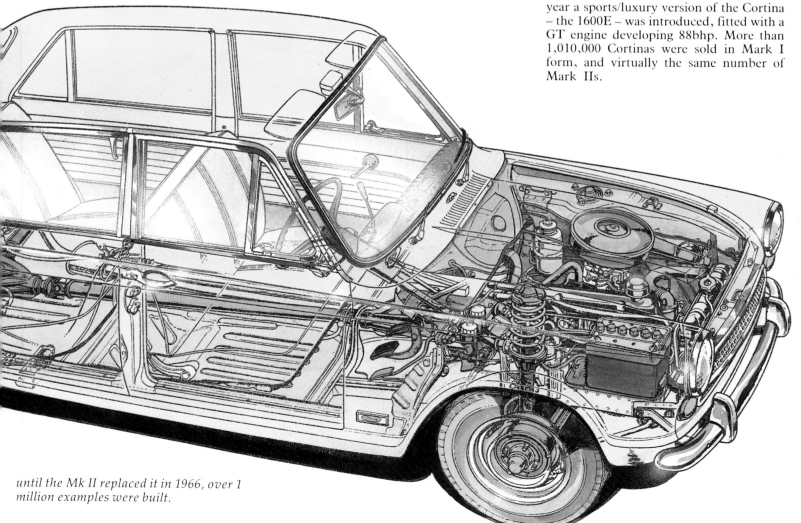

until the Mk II replaced it in 1966, over 1 million examples were built.

The Ford Anglia was replaced by the new Ford Escort at the end of 1967, the new car being available in 1.1, 1.3, 1.3GT and 1558cc Twin-Cam form, initially. Fast Mark I Escorts were to include, from January 1970, the BDA-engined twin-cam RS1600; from November 1970, the 1600cc Escort Mexico; from October 1971, the Escort Sport; and, from June 1973, the Pinto-powered RS2000. Ford's sporting image was also greatly enhanced by four victories at Le Mans in the late 1960s, regular international rallying successes in the 1970s, and 155 Grands Prix win for its Cosworth-built DFV engine between 1967 and 1983.

In January 1969, Ford introduced its sporting saloon – the Capri – at first in 1300, 1600 and 2000GT form. Three-litre V6-engined GTs were to follow.

Above: 1972 Mk III Cortina 1600XL   *Below: 1974 three-litre Capri Ghia*

The Cortina was updated and a Mark III version introduced in late 1970. The Cortinas employed overhead-camshaft 'Pinto' engines, in 1.6- and 2.0-litre versions, from 1973. A 2000E model was introduced in September 1973.

A new range of the large Consul and Granada models was introduced in 1972, using two-litre V4 or three-litre V6 engines. Series II Capris were introduced in March 1974, the new models featuring versatile hatchback bodywork.

Mark II versions of the Escort were announced in January 1975 with restyled bodywork. Sporting versions of the Mark II were later to include the RS1800, the

Left: 1976 Cortina 2000 Ghia

1600cc Mexico and the RS2000.

In July 1976 Ford produced its first small front-wheel-drive hatchback, the Fiesta, available in 957cc, 1116cc and 1298cc form, and with a wide range of trim levels. In September of the same year, a new-look Mark IV Cortina was introduced, with sleeker bodywork than the

Mark III.

Restyled Granadas were announced in August 1977, the engines now fitted being the two-litre overhead-camshaft Pinto unit, 2.3- or 2.8-litre V6s, or a 2.1-litre four-cylinder diesel made by Peugeot.

The Capri bodywork was made more aerodynamic from March 1978, and a 2.8-litre, fuel-injected V6 version was introduced in July 1981.

Increasingly, through the 1970s and 1980s, Ford's European production was spread between different centres, and factories were located in Spain, France, Belgium, Holland and Germany, as well as in Britain (notably Dagenham and Halewood).

The last Cortinas, the Mark V models, were introduced in September 1979 with a new grille and other minor changes.

Left: 1976 front-wheel-drive Fiesta
Above: Granada 2000 L, October 1977

Below: Ford Fiesta 1100S of the late 1970s

Below: Ford's front-wheel-drive Escort, introduced in 1980, gave hatchback versatility to their mid-range models. Like their predecessors, the new Escorts, available with a range of trim levels and engine sizes, were popular with buyers.

In September 1980 Ford introduced a new front-wheel-drive Escort hatchback, in three- and five-door form, with 1.1-, 1.3- or 1.6-litre engines. Sports versions designated XR3 and XR3i (fuel-injected) were also available.

The larger rear-wheel-drive Sierra hatchback was introduced as the replacement for the Cortina in October 1982 with a choice of overhead-camshaft engines of between 1.3- and 2.3-litres (the last a V6) and, later, with a 1.8-litre capacity. The fastest version, the racing-inspired Sierra RS Cosworth – with a 204bhp 2.0-litre turbocharged Pinto engine modified by Cosworth Engineering of Grand Prix fame – boasted a top speed of 241km/h (150mph) and a 0-60mph statistic of 6.7 seconds.

In 1983 a saloon version of the Escort – the Orion – became available, initially only with upmarket trim levels. From March 1986 the Escort range was updated and a 'lean-burn' overhead-camshaft 1.4-litre engine was introduced to the model.

The top-of-the-range Granadas continued throughout the 1980s, with a totally new hatchback range being announced in May 1985. The new cars were powered by overhead-camshaft four-cylinder engines of 1.8- or two-litres, a 2.8-litre V6, or a 2.5-litre diesel.

In January 1987 new 2.4-litre and 2.9-litre, overhead-camshaft four-cylinder

Below: The Sierra was the successor to the Cortina. It had hatchback bodywork, and, unlike most of its competitors of the time, retained rear-wheel-drive. Subtle changes were made to the body styling during the production life of the model.

Above: 1982 Sierra hatchback

Above: Capri S of the early 1980s
Left: 1987 Granada Scorpio hatchback
*Below: The Fiesta range was updated in
September 1983, when the styling was
revised. Engine sizes ranged from 957cc
to 1597cc (in the sporty XR2). Five-speed
gearboxes were available with 1100cc and
larger engines.*

engines were introduced to the range,
which was topped by the Scorpio 2.9i
Executive model. Saloon versions of the
Sierra – designated Sierra Sapphires – were
introduced in February 1987.

The end of an era came in March 1987,
when the last Capri – the 280 – was
introduced, with special leather trim and
based on the 2.8 Injection Special.

With the arrival of the 1990s, Ford unified its operations in Europe, with both British and German divisions making and selling the same ranges. In 1993, Ford Germany planned to cut 6,000 jobs to move the balance of power in Europe back to Britain.

Meanwhile, the Ford range was evolving steadily.

The Escort range was rejuvenated in 1990. The changes were evolutionary rather than revolutionary. Although the styling was brought up to date, the cars were still very recognizably related to their predecessors. The famous RS2000 name was brought back to life in 1991, replacing the XR3 tag. A year later the range received the all-new 16-valve Zetec engine, which was a big improvement on the crude engines previously used. Minor detail changes were made to the styling during the 1990s, with some face-lifts were more successful than others.

Ford's best-selling Fiesta was updated in 1989. New smoother styling and a five-door option helped boost sales. The pick of the Mk3 Fiestas was the RS Turbo, the first Fiesta with forced induction. Like the Escort, the Fiesta gained the Zetec engine but only in 1.8-litre guise. The smaller

Right: 1995 Fiesta Classic

Below: 1994 Ford Mondeo 24-valve V6

Top: For 1997, the U.S.-built Ford Explorer was offered to European buyers to compete with the Chrysler Cherokee and Grand Cherokee, already being imported to Europe

Above: The popular Mk4 Escort Cabriolet. This is the range-topping XR3i 16-valve model

Left: The RS2000 name was revived in 1991 for the new sporty Escort. It replaced the XR3i as the high-performance model in the Escort range. High insurance premiums made for slow sales

engines remained as before. A new Fiesta was launched in 1995 with a new range of engines. Mazda marketed the same car in Europe, as the 121.

The Sierra was replaced in 1993 by the new Mondeo. This attempt at a world car also sold in the States as the Contour. It was front-wheel-drive, unlike its predecessor, and, thanks to plenty of work by Ford engineers, the all-important NVH (noise, vibration and harshness) was kept to a minimum.

Above: Rather than design its own 4x4 to compete with Vauxhall's Frontera, Ford rebadged Nissan's Terrano as the Ford Maverick

Right: The Scorpio replaced the Granada in 1994. Its questionable styling did nothing to help the sales figures

The Mondeo was initially fitted only with four-cylinder engines but gained an all-new 2.5-litre V6 in 1994.

The old range-topper in Europe, the Granada, was replaced in 1994 by the Scorpio. This raised much comment in the press on account of its somewhat controversial styling and was often described as having been designed by committee.

In order to keep up with the current trend for MPVs, Ford, in collaboration with VW, created the Galaxy. The top-of-the-range model even used VW's VR6 engine. At the other end of the market, Ford placed a new car below the Fiesta. The Ka was very modern in its styling but used the Fiesta's old 1.3-litre engine. It was widely praised by the press but it took the buying public a little while to get used to the car's wacky looks.

The Puma was a new small coupé aimed squarely at Vauxhall's Tigra. Launched in 1997, it was dynamically a much better car than its rival. Other offerings in Europe were the Maverick, a rebadged Nissan Terrano 4x4, the American Probe coupé and the Explorer.

The Ford 2000 plan looked set to see much more commonality between European and American Ford cars by the turn of the century.

Above: Post-1996 face-lifted Mondeo estate

Above: The curiously-named Ka provided Ford with a new entry-level model. Its cheeky styling and low price helped it to appeal to youger buyers. A wheel at each corner and well-tuned suspension meant it had excellent handling

Right: The Ford Ka, was styled and priced to appeal to younger buyers

Below: The Ford Galaxy was the result of a joint project with Volkswagen

Bottom: The Ford Puma, launched in 1997, used a 1.7-litre 16-valve engine

Ford

Australia
1925 to date

Above: 1989 Orion GL   *Below: 1989 Fiesta Ghia*

Although Ford cars were available in Australia from 1908, they were actually manufactured in Canada until 1925, when the Model T and Model A bodies became Australian produced – the latter still on American-made chassis. Production was initially based in Geelong, Victoria, later with assembly plants in Granville, Brisbane, Adelaide and Fremantle. This was under the supervision of a Canadian team lead by H. C. French.

Unfortunately, the Model T was at the end of its popularity by this time and Ford was considerably behind its main rival, General Motors, for sales. The Ford V8s, which arrived in 1932, were more what the car-buying public wanted, but proved too expensive.

From 1934 onwards Australian Fords began to develop their own personality having been hitherto almost identical to the Canadian range except for a slight alteration in roof line on the Tudor sedans. Most noted of the new vehicles was the closed-cabin pickup or 'utility vehicle', a style subsequently widely copied by other manufacturers.

French retired in 1950 and was replaced by C. A. Smith, who increased the Australian-made content of the cars to over 90 per cent. Ten years later a new plant at Broadmeadows was opened for production of the six-cylinder Falcon, aimed directly at the successful Holden. The Falcon gained a V8 engine in 1966, and was joined on the market by the V8 Fairlane the following year.

The distinctive styling of these two cars was continued in the Fairmont, Fairlane and LTD V8s, separating them from the American Fords of the same name. In the 1980s the range also included smaller, Mazda-based vehicles like the Laser, Telstar and two-seater Capri convertible. Ford finally achieved its long-held ambition to take over as market leader from Holden in 1982.

Franklin

U.S.A.
1902–1934

Herbert H. Franklin was a specialist in the production of diecastings, forming his own company, the H. H. Franklin Manufacturing Co. in Syracuse, New York, in 1895. In 1901 he was introduced to John Wilkinson's air-cooled car prototypes by transmission manufacturers A. T. Brown and C. A. Lipe. Franklin ordered a Wilkinson-designed vehicle, and the following year the first Franklin car went on sale.

Franklin was to continue with air-cooled power units throughout the company's existence, and also used laminated wooden-frame chassis up until 1928.

In 1905 the first six-cylinder car was launched and Franklin tried an unsuccessful competition straight-eight. Recirculating full-pressure lubrication appeared on the 1912 models, which had Renault-style front bodywork. Four-cylinder engines were dropped in 1913, and the following year left-hand drive was standardized.

The Franklin Automobile Co. was formed in 1917. Various other firms tried to imitate the company's success, with

Above: 1929 air-cooled Franklin Six; the radiator is false
Below: 1909 Franklin Torpedo displays typically unconventional styling

10,000 cars a year sold throughout the 1920s. Bodywork by J. F. de Causse, attempting to conventionalize the new Series II's appearance by adding a false radiator, led to Wilkinson's resignation. Custom coachwork was also available by Derham, Willoughby, Holbrook and Dietrich.

Franklin's first front-wheel brakes came on the Airman series of 1928, so-named because of famous owners Charles Lindbergh and Amelia Earhart, and latching onto air-cooled aero-engine fame. Because of their comparatively light weight, Franklins were used to power aircraft during this period.

Sales plummeted in the Depression, despite worldwide exports, and management appointed by the bank cheapened the range to cut costs. The last model was the Olympic, using Reo bodywork, and the factory closed in 1934. The Franklin name was acquired by former engineers Edward Marks and Carl Dorman and a water-cooled version of the air-cooled engine was used in the 1947 Tucker.

Frazer-Nash

Great Britain 1924–1957

Archie Frazer-Nash formed Frazer-Nash Ltd. in November 1922 and his first cars were modified chain-drive vehicles bought from his former employer G.N. Ltd.

The first Frazer-Nash proper was built at the Kingston, Surrey, factory and announced in 1924. It had a 1½-litre overhead-valve Plus Power engine and then Anzani power units.

Frazer-Nash merged with William G. Thomas, converters of ex-War Department lorries, in October 1925 and the new company was known as William G. Thomas and Frazer-Nash Ltd.

The merger had lasted two years when Richard Plunkett-Greene stepped in with several thousand pounds. Frazer-Nash himself became seriously ill in 1928 and the company – now known as A.F.N. Ltd. – passed to H. J. Aldington who had been with Frazer-Nash since its earliest days.

With his brother, Bill, he went on to control Frazer-Nash until the company closed.

The Frazer-Nash changed little in 15 years. And although it was relatively crude, with chains and dog-clutches in its transmission, its following remained small but loyal.

Production remained modest with fewer than 50 cars leaving the premises in any year and the factory moved to new premises in Isleworth, Middlesex, in 1930.

Aldington collaborated with B.M.W. to produce the Frazer-Nash-B.M.W. and models sold in England included the Type 34 (B.M.W. 315), Type 40 (B.M.W. 315 or 319) and the Type 55 (315 Sports).

Sales of the chain-driven cars dropped from 1935 onwards and only one was sold in 1939. But more than 700 Frazer-Nash-B.M.W.s were sold between December 1934 and September 1939.

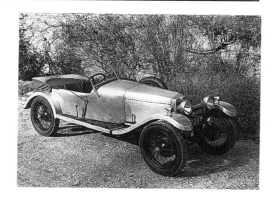

Above: 1925 Frazer-Nash Fast Tourer

Below: c. 1924 Frazer-Nash tourer

Below: Although Frazer-Nash continued to build cars like this 1934 T.T. Replica, the main source of the company's income in the '30s was the B.M.W. collaboration

The Aldington brothers served in the army during World War II, H. J. becoming involved with the Bristol Aeroplane Company.

As a result, Frazer-Nash built sports models with Bristol engines and gearboxes and, of the variety of models offered, the Le Mans replica was the most successful in competition and sales.

The last new model was the Continental coupé with a 3.2-litre B.M.W. V8 engine. It was launched in 1956 and priced at £3,751 – not competitive with the £3,076 Aston Martin DB2/4 and £1,711 Jaguar XK140 coupé.

Only two Continentals were made, the last in 1957.

A.F.N. continues to flourish as one of the U.K.'s major Porsche concessionaires.

Right: Frazer-Nash Sebring and A.F.N. staff. (L-R) Nelson Ledger, W.H. Aldington, George Sneath, H.J. Aldington, Harry Olrog

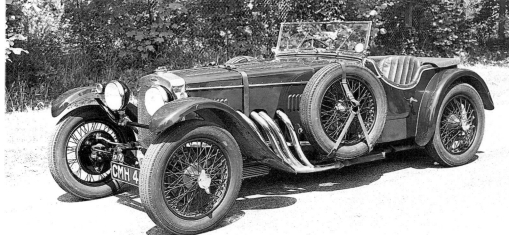

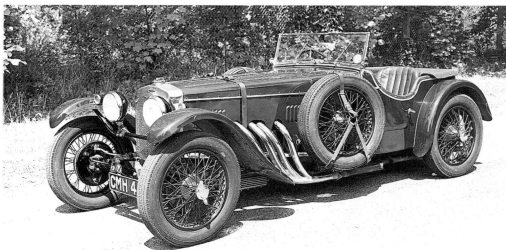

Left: Frazer-Nash T.T. Replica, built in 1935
Below left: Frazer-Nash B.M.W. Type 55, built in 1939, shortly before the outbreak of the Second World War
Below: The highly successful 1951 Frazer-Nash Le Mans Replica

FSO

Poland
1946 to date

Fabryka Samochodow Osbowych, or FSO, was set up as a state-owned company in 1946. Also known as Polski-Fiat the company started business by manufacturing the two-stroke Russian Gaz Pobieda and selling it as the Warszawa, mainly on the Polish market.

The state-owned company renewed an agreement with Fiat in 1968 and began to build the FSO 125P. The 125P used old Fiat 1300/1500 running gear and engines with newer 124 bodywork. The car lasted until 1991, by which time it was very out of date and competed with the Russian Ladas which were also an old Fiat design. Not even bargain basement pricing could disguise the grinding engines and crude suspension.

With no alternative to the aged Fiat running gear, FSO engineers set about designing its own hatchback on the 125P floorpan. The new car was called the Polonez and was launched in 1975. The narrow track looked out of place under the bulky body, but it was a brave effort given the

Above: The Caro was an updated version of the Polonez, introduced in the early 1990s, in an effort to increase sales

Below: The Polonez was FSO's first hatchback but someone forgot to tell the designers that hatchbacks should have a folding rear seat

Above: Until the 1990s, FSO had used the same Fiat pushrod engines dating from the 1950s
Right: Interiors were improved for the Caro, but it still looked ten years out of date when new
Below: As a cheap working vehicle, the Caro pick-up is in its element

ingredients. Unfortunately, someone forgot to tell the design team that a hatchback is meant to have a folding rear seat – the omission was corrected on later models.

Rock bottom pricing could not prevent FSO's decline during the early 1990s. Plunging depreciation spelled the end, before an unexpected revival in 1993 under new management.

The Polonez was updated in the early-1990s with mildly softened lines, but still with same ancient mechanicals. Now called the Caro, the car gained a Peugeot diesel engine in 1992 and even a 16-valve unit in the shape of Rover's excellent 1.4-litre, 103 horsepower K-series engine. With the latter, a brave driver could take the Caro to 100mph (160km/h). The new car was certainly a more saleable product, especially with such a low asking price and sold well enough to keep the company afloat.

GAZ

U.S.S.R.
1932 to date

GAZ, the Gorkovsky Avtomobilni Zavod or Gorky Automobile Works, was set up in 1932 at Gorky in what was then heralded as the biggest vehicle manufacturing plant in Europe. It was certainly the first major car factory in the U.S.S.R. and relied initially on assistance from Ford U.S.A. with designs for the factory buildings, machine-tools and components.

Trucks preceded cars as a priority, and both commercial and civilian models bore a close resemblance to their Ford counterparts. Not surprisingly, production runs were far longer, however, and the GAZ-A cars continued to be made until 1936, with truck versions not being replaced until 1948. Again, the A-model's successor, the M-1, was stylistically like an earlier Ford saloon, and its replacement in 1940 bore no real external evidence of stylistic progression. The engines were different, however, rising from 3.2-litre four-cylinder units to 3.4-litre straight-sixes.

Production was largely given over to building 4×4 utilities during World War II, together with trucks and a few 4×4 11-40 and 11-73 saloons.

GAZ emerged from the hostilities with a brand-new saloon, the Andrei Lipgart-designed M-20 Pobieda, or Victory, which looked not unlike the contemporary Standard Vanguard, and which remained in production until 1958. The M-20 was powered by a 2.1-litre four-cylinder engine, and of the 237,172 cars built, a number were 4×4s and convertibles. The same model was manufactured in Poland as the Warszawa, eventually using entirely Polish-sourced components; here it lasted until 1972, with about 253,000 having been made.

Alongside the M-20 was the larger 3.5-litre six-cylinder GAZ M-12 or Z1M, also designed by Lipgart, and which was made between 1951 and 1960. This car was not generally available to the public, although 21,546 units were produced, some going for export to Finland and Sweden.

From 1959, the intermediate Soviet official or professional was catered for by the Chaika, or Seagull, now fitted with 5.5-litre V8 engines. Top people rode around in the Z1S or Z1L limousines. There was a 12-year hiatus in Chaika production between 1965 and 1977, at which later date the model reappeared with the same engine but updated styling.

The M-20 Pobieda's successor was the 2.5-litre 70bhp Volga, introduced in 1955, and which, with face-lifts in 1968 and 1982, was until the mid-1980s the most numerous medium-sized car in the Soviet Union.

The Volga 3102 was widely exported, and was available with either the 2.5-litre petrol or two- and 2.2-litre Indenor diesel engines. Given the freer economic climate of the Gorbachev era, with its emphasis on profits, there will be greater efforts to market the ZAZ 1102, a 1.1-litre three-door front-wheel-drive model, developed over a six-year period and launched in 1988.

Above: 1932 Ford Model T-based GAZ-A

Below: 1940 GAZ-II-73
Bottom: 1969 Volga M.24, 2455cc, 145km/h (90mph) saloon

G.N.

Great Britain 1910-1925

H. R. Godfrey and Captain Archibald Frazer-Nash, whose surnames combined into G.N. Ltd., began business in the stables of the latter's home in Hendon, north London, where the first half-dozen or so of their cyclecars were produced.

They presented their first vehicle to the public in 1910, powered by a J.A.P. or Peugeot engine. The G.N. was one of a number of cars which brought economy motoring to large sections of the population who would previously have used a motor cycle and sidecar combination.

From 1911 Godfrey and Frazer-Nash began offering engines of their own manufacture, although built with some Peugeot parts, and until the outbreak of World War I various forms of belt and chain drive were used.

After the war, the British arm of Grégoire bought the company, which then became G.N. Motors Ltd., moving the following year to new premises at East Hill, Wandsworth, London. Extra staff were taken on, production of the aptly-named Popular model and its variants dramatically increased, and the firm even employed mobile engineers to service cus-

tomers' vehicles. Overseas, G.N. cyclecars were produced under licence by the French Salmson company between 1919 and 1922.

By 1921 the advent of the light car was eclipsing cyclecars, and falling sales led to the receivers being called in to take control of future production. The following year both the founders left after arguments over the type of vehicles to be made. Godfrey set up a G.N. servicing company and was later to form H.R.G. with E. A. Halford and Guy H. Robins. He died in 1968. Frazer-Nash founded his own famous marque from small beginnings with left-over G.N. parts in 1922.

Now making a loss, G.N. Motors Ltd. was wound up in 1923. The following year two former employees, having formed G.N. Ltd., brought out an Anzani-powered model, but by 1925 the marque had disappeared.

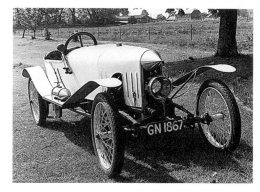

Top: A distinctive 1914 tourer
Centre: 1921 French-built GN
Above: A 1922 GN survivor

Right: A GN special named 'Spider' hillclimbed between the wars
Below: Reproductions of early 1920s racers

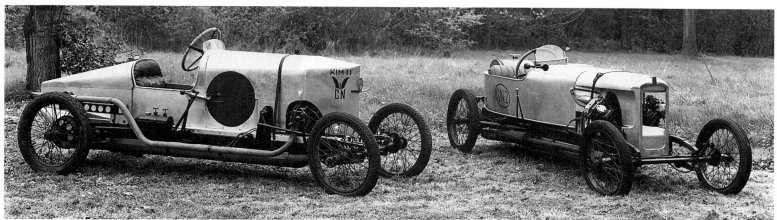

Gobron-Brillié

France
1898–1930

Although the marque was officially named Gobron-Brillié until 1919, Eugene Brillié split from Gustave Gobron in 1903, after only five years of partnership. It was he who designed their famous 'vibrationless' engine produced until 1922.

They formed the Société des Moteurs Gobron-Brillié in 1898 with premises in Paris, moving to Boulogne-sur-Seine two years later. The cars were sold in Britain as Teras and were also produced under licence in Belgium by Nagant.

The early model was doubtfully claimed to run on gin, whisky and brandy as well as petrol, and was recorded as running on alcohol in the 1902 Concours du Ministre. Indeed, the Nancéienne company won the 1901 Paris–Roubaix race for alcohol-fuelled cars with a Gobron-Brillié-designed vehicle produced under patent.

By 1903 all models were front-engined and the company had begun some forays into motor sport. The following year their 13½-litre racer officially broke the 160km/h (100mph) barrier, although its subsequent entries in the 1904/5 Gordon Bennett Eliminating Trials and the 1906/7 Grands Prix proved disappointing.

Up until World War I the company produced a variety of vehicles, including an unlikely 70/90hp six-cylinder machine. The models had a mixture of shaft and chain drive, the latter being continued as late as 1914.

After the war Gobron-Brillié moved to Levallois-Perret and became Automobiles Gobron. Sales were fairly low for the remainder of the firm's existence, despite attempts to market the cars by the Stabilia company under its own name. The rather splendid 25CV of 1922 gave way to a conventional Chapuis-Dornier-engined car, also unsuccessful.

Gobron made a final try with its supercharged Turbo-Sport model of 1928, but a very limited number were produced, and the company folded in 1930.

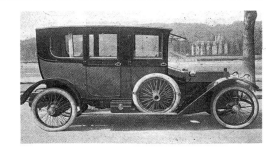

Above: The 15-20hp Gobron Berline
Below: A 1906 40/60hp model

The 1904 racer with its immense 13½-litre engine broke the 160km/h (100mph) barrier and featured mechanically-operated sidevalves on its four cylinders. However, it did not achieve much in the way of sporting success thereafter.

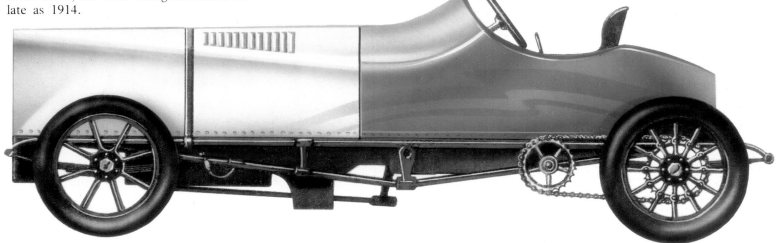

Graham-Paige

U.S.A.
1927–1940

Graham-Paige may appear to be just another fairly obscure American marque which lasted less than 20 years and produced only a few notable models. But indirectly it gave a leg up to one of the present day's largest volume-car producers and the company itself lives on today in a most unusual way.

In 1927 three brothers from Indiana, Robert, Joseph and Ray Graham, took over the Paige-Detroit Motor Company, a fairly successful firm which had made quite a name for itself since it started in 1908 with cars like the 1921 Daytona Speedster, named after a 102mph (164km/h) record-breaking run by one of its models.

The brothers themselves had made their money from agriculture, bottle-making, and assembling trucks with their own bodies on Dodge chassis and engines; a business which Dodge bought from them in 1925.

As soon as they bought the Paige concern, and its factory in Dearborn, Michigan, the three renamed it Graham-Paige and started to employ their business and salesmanship skills to good effect. They established a first-year sales record with their 1928 range, which was cannily priced and targeted within the market, and in 1929 they made nearly 80,000 cars and had to take over several more plants to cope with the demand – even opening one in Berlin.

But this phenomenal success was not to last – indeed, 1929 was to prove their best-ever year. The Depression began to affect sales badly, and the firm only just weathered the economic storm of the early 1930s which claimed so many small companies.

In 1932 it bounced back, now known simply as Graham, with its Blue Streak models, which were low (thanks to a clever chassis design), sleek, and extremely stylish. Though the cars were widely admired, they weren't as widely bought, and sales continued to slide. Even the excellent performance of the range, improved further when a supercharged model appeared in 1934, could not help to stop their fall, and the only bright spot was the sale of tools and dies for an obsolete model to Nissan of Japan, thereby temporarily saving the company and starting Nissan's rise to its present position as one of the world's biggest volume-car makers.

But nothing, it seemed, could halt the company's demise. The 1938 'Sharknose' range was a brave, if phenomenally ugly, attempt to gain attention and though they performed well, they looked like the result of a nasty crease in the blueprints and didn't sell. Floundering badly by now, the last model built, in 1940, was a mixture of Cord, Hupmobile and Graham parts which met the fate it deserved – ignominious failure.

The company stopped making cars entirely in 1940, though World War II led it briefly into aircraft and marine engines, not to mention an amphibious tractor. After the war the car-making part of the firm was absorbed into the Kaiser-Frazer corporation.

Graham made farm machinery for a while, then became involved in real estate and survives today, in spirit if not in name, as the corporation which owns and runs the giant Madison Square Gardens sporting arena.

Below: A 1939 Graham-Paige chassis with Amherst Villers body

Bottom: The 1941 Graham Hollywood

Grégoire
France
1942–1970

When Jean Albert Grégoire began the Grégoire firm in 1942, his was the second French marque to use that name, the first being in the Seine-et-Oise district of Paris between 1903 and 1924. The French designer began work on his first Grégoire model during World War II, and a running prototype was assembled by 1942.

Grégoire had already gained a great deal of experience as a manufacturer of cars. From 1926 to 1934 he had been responsible for proving the worth of front-wheel drive, both for road and competition use, with his sporting Tracta designs. After Tracta, Grégoire had worked for Amilcar, which was then under Hotchkiss control, launching the technically unusual and lightweight Compound car with all-round independent suspension. This made use of an aluminium or light-alloy casting for the chassis and unit construction. It also incorporated front-wheel drive – as did most of his vehicles – from J. A. Grégoire Tracta patents.

Grégoire's first design, built by l'Aluminium Français, was known as the Aluminium Français Grégoire, or A.F.G. It was turned down by major French manufacturers Peugeot, Simca, Citroën and Renault, but sold by Panhard as the Panhard Dyna. A few were built in England by Member of Parliament Denis Kendall under that name, and a licence

was gained by Australian Lawrence Hartnett, but little came of either venture.

In the early 1950s Grégoire designed a four-cylinder car which was produced as a joint venture with Hotchkiss, and was continued briefly after that company folded. In 1956 Grégoire tried again, this time with a supercharged model designed by Henri Chapron, and made in limited numbers until 1962 in the old Tracta factory at Asnières.

Heavy losses were incurred, however, and it was not until 1970 that Grégoire tried again, with an electric-powered prototype, but this never went into production.

Top: Grégoire's first design, sold by Panhard as the Panhard Dyna c. 1946
Above: The Socéma-Grégoire turbine car of 1954
Left: 2.2-litre convertible of 1959, one of only ten ever made

Hampton

Great Britain
1912–1931

The Hampton Engineering Company began building cars in 1912. The first model was a 1.7-litre four-cylinder 12/16, assembled using components from abroad.

Prior to World War I, a twin-cylinder, two-stroke light car was produced, followed by an 8hp cyclecar. Then came another lightweight car, powered by a 1.2-litre engine.

After the war, the firm moved from Birmingham to near Stroud, in Gloucestershire, and produced an overhead-valve 1½-litre 10/16, the new model again following established light-car chassis design.

In 1920 a 1.8-litre variant was introduced; both cars had Dorman engines, driving through gearboxes of Hampton's own manufacture.

The company was restructured in 1920, after which it had considerable success in motor sport and hill-climbs. A Hampton lapped Brooklands at around 90mph (145km/h).

Meadows engines – in 1.8- and 1.2-litre (Junior) capacities – were fitted from 1923, and the following year a 2.1-litre model became available, plus a new 1½-litre 12hp Hampton.

The company then suffered more financial problems and another restructuring, following which its 12hp model was revised.

In 1927 the company added a 1.7-litre six-cylinder 15/45 to its range, and in 1928 a 9hp model, with the mechanical components of the Junior fitted to new bodywork.

In 1929 a three-litre, 20hp model was offered with an overhead-valve six-cylinder engine.

Hampton incorporated some ingenious technical developments in its cars of the late 1920s and early 1930s. For example, adjustable rear suspension was available on its 12/40 model. The firm also worked on the Cowburn gearbox, which used coned rollers and coil springs instead of conventional gears.

By 1931 the company was facing ruinous financial problems. The last Hamptons included another 12hp model (1.2-litres), 2.2-litre straight-eights, 18hp cars with Röhr engines, and a 2.4-litre model with a six-cylinder sidevalve engine.

Top: A Hampton 14hp, c. 1926, near Stroud
Right: 1928 Hampton 12/40
Below: 1924 all-weather Hampton Junior

Healey

Great Britain 1946–1954

Donald Healey was a well-known figure in British motor sport in the 1930s, and he turned his hand to car manufacture in 1946 after working for both Riley and Triumph. The 1946 Healey used a modified 2.4-litre Riley engine and other Riley running components in a new chassis which had excellent roadholding properties.

Healeys were offered either as bare chassis or with lightweight aerodynamic two-door saloon bodywork by Elliot or convertible bodywork by Westland. These were very potent machines indeed, and one achieved a maximum speed of 111.87mph (180.03km/h) in Belgium to substantiate Healey's claim to make the fastest production car in the world. The make soon became very successful in competitive events at home and abroad.

The original models were supplemented by a rather square-rigged Sportsmobile drophead coupé in 1948, but this lasted only until 1950. In that year, the Elliot and Westland models were replaced by a Tickford-bodied saloon and an Abbott-bodied drophead. In addition, there was a lightweight two-seater model called the Silverstone, which was little short of a road-going racing car. Fearing that supplies of the Riley engine would soon dry up, Healey sought alternatives and found both the three-litre Alvis engine and the 3.8-litre Nash engine, each of which he put into new models. During 1951, he drew up plans for yet another model, with which he intended to exploit the North American sports-car market. This time, he used an Austin engine. This design was taken up by Austin's Leonard Lord as a new Austin-built car and renamed the Austin-Healey (q.v.). The last Healey, a Nash-engined car, was made in 1954.

Top: 1949 Healey Sportsmobile
Above centre: Nash Healey of 1952
Below centre: 1946-50 Healey Westland
Right: A distinctive Healey Tickford
Far right: 1950 Healey Silverstone

Hillman

Great Britain 1907–1978

William Hillman founded the Hillman Motor Car Company in 1907, in which year he produced a 25hp four-cylinder car with Louis Coatelen, to take part in the Tourist Trophy race.

From the early days Hillman built family cars, introducing a 1357cc monobloc-engined 9hp model in 1912. The company's 10hp model of 1919 had a 1593cc sidevalve engine, later reduced to 1496cc and developing 18bhp (28bhp in the sporting version).

Hillman also built bigger cars in small numbers prior to World War I, including models with two-cylinder 1.8-litre engines, four-cylinder 6.4-litre units, and six-cylinder engines of two- and 9.7-litres capacity.

The 9hp Hillman continued in production, being regularly updated, until 1925; by then the engine had grown to 1.6 litres.

Above: M. Louis Coatelen and 1907 Hillman
Left: 1931 prototype Hillman Minx

Between 1926 and 1928 Hillman built only the Fourteen, which had a sidevalve engine and a four-speed gearbox. 'Safety' versions of the car, from 1929, had toughened glass and servo-assisted brakes. A larger model of the time had a 2.6-litre straight-eight engine.

The Hillman Imp of 1963 was an innovative small car, lively and economical. The two-door, four-seater featured a rear-mounted, 875cc overhead camshaft engine, driving the rear wheels.

In 1928 the Rootes brothers bought a controlling interest in Humber, which company in turn purchased Hillman. From 1932 both firms became an integral part of the Rootes Group. In the same year the first Hillman Minx – a 10hp 1185cc family saloon – was introduced. The Minx was extremely successful and offered a freewheel and radio in 1934 (the 'Melody' Minx) and all-synchromesh gear changing in 1935.

A sports version (the 'Aero' Minx) was also sold from 1933 and this car was developed into the Talbot/Sunbeam-Talbot Tens. Hillman also built larger models in the late 1930s, including a 14hp model with hydraulic brakes.

The 1940 model Minx was continued after the war, with chassisless unitary-construction bodywork. The 1949 Minx was given lower and wider bodywork, and the engine was enlarged to 1265cc in 1950.

Hillman produced a range of models, but from 1952 the firm concentrated on a new Minx, totally restyled to celebrate the 21st anniversary of the Minx. The new car had a 1265cc engine developing 38bhp. The car was initially available in saloon, estate and convertible forms and, from 1953, a Thrupp and Maberly-bodied Californian Hardtop was available. This coupé model had a large, wrap-around rear screen, slim door pillars and only two doors.

From 1955 a new grille was fitted, and 43bhp overhead-valve engines of 1390cc were fitted to the de luxe Minx. However, the models remained essentially the same until May 1956, when a completely new Minx was announced, with badge-engineered versions being available under the Singer Gazelle (luxury version) and Sunbeam Rapier (sporting derivative) names. The power output was now 51bhp. Two-door estate versions of the Minx were designated Husky.

The Jubilee Minx of 1957 was available with two-pedal Manumatic control, while in 1960 Easidrive automatic transmission was introduced. The engine was enlarged to 1490cc for 1959 models and to 1592cc for 1962, in which year the larger-bodied Super Minx was introduced.

In 1963 the revolutionary rear-engined Imp became available. This small car, built at Linwood, Glasgow, featured an all-alloy, overhead-camshaft 875cc engine developing 39bhp, and all-round independent suspension.

A five-bearing 1725cc engine was fitted to the Minx and Super Minx in 1965, and an entirely new body shell was introduced for the Minx in 1967.

The 80bhp, 1725cc Hunter saloon ('Arrow') range replaced the Super Minx from 1957. A twin-carburettor GT version was available from October 1969.

The totally new Avenger saloon and estate-car range was introduced in February 1970, with adventurous styling and a choice of either 1248cc or 1498cc engines. High-performance GT versions were also produced. From 1973 a 1598cc engine was optional.

In September 1976 the Hillman name disappeared as the Chrysler (U.K.) organization took over the entire range.

Top left: 1927 14hp Hillman
Top right: Hillmans for Australia, 1951

Above left: 1955 Hillman Minx Mk VIII
Above: 1958 1390cc Hillman Husky

Left: 1963 Hillman Imp
Below left: 1973 Hillman Avenger GLS
Below: 1975 Hunter Topaz/Imp Caledonian

Hispano-Suiza

Spain
1904–1944

Over nearly four decades Hispano-Suiza produced a large range of high-quality cars with engines ranging in size from 3.6 to 11.3 litres, but four models stand out from the rest. These were the lightweight 3.6-litre Alfonso of 1912, the technically advanced 6.5-litre H6 of 1919, the powerful 8-litre 1924 Boulogne and the magnificent 1931 9.4-litre V12 Type 68.

Two men who were associated with the company almost from its inception were the Swiss engineer Marc Birkigt and the Spanish financier and company director Damien Mateu, who together developed a

Below: King Alfonso and his 1908 model

Top: A 1913 'Alfonso', named after the King of Spain
Above: A 1925 H6B bodied by Kellner

company which was innovative yet financially successful.

Birkigt was born in Geneva in 1878, qualified as a first-class mechanical engineer and undertook his obligatory military service in the artillery where he began to develop a lifelong interest in armaments. In 1900 he joined an engineering company in Barcelona and designed and built a small 4½hp car, before the failing company was taken over in June 1904 by Damien Mateu. The new organization was renamed 'Fabrica La Hispano-Suiza de Automobiles' indicating an amalgam of Spanish finance and leadership with Swiss engineering expertise.

A racing Hispano won the 1910 Coupe de l'Auto and from it was developed the famous 3.6-litre Alfonso, named in honour of the young King Alfonso XIII of Spain who owned some 30 Hispanos and was a long-standing patron of the company. At around this time Hispano opened a factory in Paris to assemble the Alfonso and a range of heavy luxury carriages for the more lucrative French market.

The Alfonso was probably the first true sports car, having been designed for both competiton and road use, and it came with a four-cylinder in-line 3.6-litre 64bhp engine, a three-speed (later four-speed) manual gearbox and a live rear axle. In a car weighing only 762kg (1680lb) the power-to-weight ratio was good. Another interesting feature was the very powerful gas headlights, designed and built by

The H6B of 1930 was essentially the same car that had been introduced in 1919 – a tribute to the quality of design that engineer Marc Birkigt had applied to both engine and chassis.

Blériot, the Channel aviator and manufacturer of lamps for lighthouses.

The Barcelona factory produced some rather mundane cars and commercial vehicles, while the French Hispano cars became rather more exotic, culminating in the immortal H6 (and 6B) of 1919 with its 6.5-litre 130bhp overhead-camshaft light-alloy engine and its seven-bearing pressure-lubricated camshaft. The long-stroke engine developed plenty of low-speed torque allowing the car to be driven from 16km/h to 138km/h (10mph to 86mph) in top gear. It was highly praised by the press and remained in production without major alterations until 1934.

Although not designed with competition in mind, the H6 did quite well in road-races, winning twice at Boulogne and finishing sixth in the 1924 Targa Florio. By this time a new eight-litre engine had been installed and production cars carried the name 'Boulogne' in recognition of their racing success.

Hispano-Suiza's last great fling, despite the Depression, was the production of the Type 68 (54/220CV in France) for the 1931 Paris Salon. This was the company's biggest, most complex and most expensive car to date, and although it arrived at a time of world economic depression, the huge 9.4-litre (or 11.3-litre in the Type 68 bis) V12-engined luxury saloon attracted many buyers and remained in production until Birkigt stopped manufacturing cars in 1938 to concentrate on his aircraft engines and armaments.

The Paris factory never fully recovered after World War II, and Birkigt, the quiet engineer, died peacefully in his native Switzerland in 1953.

Bodies by famous coachbuilders, like this coupé by Guiet, were the rule rather than the exception for Hispano-Suiza's moneyed clientele. This car shows off the stork mascot of the marque which commemorates French flying ace Georges Guynemer, a friend of Birkigt's killed in action during World War I.

Above: Fernandes et Darvin-bodied K6

Above: The 1927 'Barcelona'

Above: 1931's Type 68 with a V12 engine

Holden

Australia 1948 to date

Holden began as Holden and Frost in Adelaide, making coachwork for horse-drawn carriages and bodying its first car – a Lancia – in 1914. The company became Holden's Motor Body Builders Ltd. in 1920, and its work appeared on imported Morris vehicles during the following decade.

In 1931 Holden was bought by General Motors (Australia) Pty. Ltd. Subsequently, the bulk of its work was assembling British and American General Motors cars for the Australian market. In particular, this included Chevrolets and Buicks, although other makes such as Hudson, Essex, Chrysler, Plymouth, Willys, Reo and Studebaker were also provided with coachwork by Holden. The first Holden closed body appeared on an Essex in 1924.

In 1934 Sir Lawrence Hartnett became Managing Director of Holden and the company's first two-door fastback coupé

Above: 1934 coupé, just before the fastback style was introduced
Right: Holden 1937 roadster

was offered in 1938, several years before similar cars appeared on the American market. This distinctive style, built on a variety of different chassis, was known as the Sloper. It was to become Holden's trademark in the early years after World War II.

This 1967 Premier is already well known in several other guises to Europeans; many Vauxhall and Opel products ended up restyled slightly and re-badged as Holdens for the Australian market.

During the war Holden had produced military vehicles on the Canadian Military Pattern Chevrolet chassis, similar to those produced by Ford. After the war Hartnett gained the backing of the Australian government to build a new and entirely Australian car to fill the gap between the big American models and the much smaller British ones. Hartnett wanted this vehicle, a four-door sedan, to be of advanced design but General Motors vetoed the idea in favour of more-established construction and he resigned in 1947, the year before the new FX was launched.

The FX was immediately successful, and was joined by a coupé utility in 1951. Although Holden had continued to build bodies on imported chassis, the rise in price of these after the war made this an uneconomic proposition.

In May 1953 the FX was updated slightly into the FJ215, with more major changes coming with the FE of 1956. In 1954 Holden began exporting to New Zealand, and by the end of the 1950s it was building nearly half the private cars sold in Australia, leading the market until Ford took over as recently as 1982.

By 1967 the Torana had appeared, as well as larger V8-engined cars like the HK Belmont and Kingswood. Two years later the Chevrolet-engined Monaro coupé was introduced, giving Holden sporting success, and also the luxury American limousine-style Brougham. In the mid-1970s appeared the Isuzu-based Gemini, ending the idea of an entirely Australian car begun by Hartnett.

Continuing this trend was the best-selling Commodore, launched in 1979 with a variety of different engine sizes and inspired by European Vauxhall-Opel cars. The Brougham was replaced by the Statesman series, some of which were exported without engines for the Japanese market, and there fitted with Mazda rotary engines. Holden also provided Opel power units for the Swedish market since that country's emission regulations were almost identical to those of Australia, although the company never really exported to countries where General Motors already traded strongly.

More recently, Holden has marketed Japanese imports such as the Barina and the Astra which latter, although assembled

Above: The 48-215, c. 1954

in Australia, was in essence the 1.5-litre Nissan Cherry. Nissan engines were also used in other Holden models.

Besides its original plant at Woodville, which continued to supply bodies, Holden also built a body plant in Elizabeth, South Australia, and one at Acacia Ridge, Queensland, as well as its main base at Fisherman's Bend. The company ran its assembly operations at Pagewood, New South Wales; The Valley, Brisbane; Mosman Park in Perth; and Birkenhead, South Australia, employing in total over 18,000 people. In addition, it has a factory for assembly at Upper Hutt, Wellington, New Zealand.

Below: The 1948 model J in the outback

Above: 1955, start of an export boom

Below: The Gemini SL coupé of 1976

Towards the end of the 1980s, Holden launched a new range of cars that was to become the mainstay of the company for the 1990s. The Holden VS models were all based on the old Opel Senator. Unlike the Senator, however, the VS was only available with American General Motors engines: a 3.8-litre V6, a 5.0-litre V8 and a 5.7-litre V8.

The first models to be launched were the Calais, which was the luxury model, the Acclaim, the Berlina, and the sporty SS. The Statesman, Caprice and Commodore arrived in 1990. The different model designations denoted little more than trim levels. Performance from the top-of-the-range 5.7-litre V8 was astounding, with a top speed approaching 150mph(240km/h) and 60mph (100km/h) arriving in under seven seconds.

Holden held on to its second place among Australian manufacturers, with production figures not far behind those of its age-old rival Ford Australia.

Above: Holden VS Caprice

Below: Holden VS Acclaim

Above: HoldenVS Berlina

Below:: Holden VS Calais

Honda

Japan
1962 to date

The story of Honda is a classic rags-to-riches tale. Born in Iwata-gun, Japan, in 1906, Soichiro Honda was the son of a blacksmith who also repaired bicycles to supplement his income. One of nine children, of whom only four survived, his poor background denied him a formal education, but it did not dampen a spirit of enterprise and adventure, or a fascination for things mechanical.

Inheriting his father's mechanical abilities and helping with his father's main work of repairing implements he recalled years later that he was deeply stirred the first time he saw a car.

Honda joined an automobile repair shop in Tokyo after leaving school, and a few years later with his own capital set up a branch shop at Hamamatsu. He began making cast wheel spokes for cars and went on to the manufacture of piston rings by the time he was 28.

While Honda was apprenticed in Tokyo the city suffered violent earthquakes in 1923. The repair shop was destroyed through subsequent fires, but not before the workers had managed to evacuate the cars they were working on.

The emergency gave Honda his first chance to drive a car and then a motor-cycle and sidecar as he ferried people about and picked up provisions in the earthquake's aftermath. Most cars at the time had wooden spoked wheels and many were burnt away in the fires. This gave him the idea to make a better alternative in the form of metal wheels.

Meanwhile, Honda was busy learning the skills and developing resourcefulness for all aspects of vehicle repair. With parts in short supply he had to improvise. These years formed a thorough grounding from which he was to achieve success beyond imagination.

There can be little doubt that his progress would have been swifter had it not been for the Japanese tradition of seniority. Owners preferred to entrust their cars to older mechanics. Honda had to take on the cars that others said were hopeless cases, and his genius in getting these cars back into service won him the respect he deserved.

Having started his own shop with one assistant it was not long before he had built his business into a 50-man operation. His profits allowed him to indulge in some of life's luxuries. He took up speedboat racing and began to look closely at racing cars. He had already worked on preparing a racing car with his Tokyo employer Shin'ichi Sakakibara while apprenticed. Working in his own time during 1925 he helped build the machine using an 8.2-litre Curtis aircraft engine. The car was a race-winner, but Honda never drove it.

It was in 1935, the year he married, that Honda came back to the sport, this time as a driver using Ford power. His exploits in this respect were short-lived, however. A serious crash in 1936 ended his ambitions. While leading the All-Japan Speed Rally on a circuit between Tokyo and Yokohama a car moved into his path.

In the resulting crash Honda's car somersaulted three times and he did not recover consciousness until he was in hospital. The left side of his face was crushed, his left arm dislocated and his left wrist broken. It took him 18 months to recover.

Now looking for a new direction, Honda decided to go into manufacture. He applied himself to the study of casting so that he could make piston rings. It meant going back to school, for the subject was not as simple as he had at first supposed, and he almost drained his company of money because of the time taken and mistakes made before he was able to make rings of acceptable quality.

He beat the problem and even designed a machine to make rings automatically, and for Japan's war effort he produced a machine which could make an aircraft bomber propeller in 30 minutes. Until then it had required a week of manual labour.

When the war finished Honda could see the urgent need for cheap personal transport as the population tried to pick up the threads of civilian life. He started the Honda Technical Research Laboratory in 1946 having hit upon the idea of fitting small military engines, used for generators and radios, to bicycles. Petrol was in short supply, so cars were a luxury, and buses and trains were overcrowded.

With help from a younger brother, Benjiro, and Kiyoshi Kawashima (who was to become company president) Honda produced a motor-cycle entirely of his own manufacture in 1949. He called it the Dream because of his dream for speed.

The Honda story might have been different had Takeo Fujisawa not come

along. He became Honda's right-hand man, guiding the business, handling the marketing and generating fresh ideas.

In 1950 Honda and Fujisawa opened an office in Tokyo, the centre of finance and manufacturing in Japan. The following year Honda produced his first four-stroke engine. Kawashima test-rode the new model. They were thrilled with its performance and in 1952 Honda was awarded the Blue Ribbon Medal for inventions and improvements to small engines.

The company went on to become the world's biggest manufacturer of motorcycles, and it still holds that distinction today.

It was not until 1963 that the first Honda four-wheeled passenger vehicle was introduced. The previous year Honda had constructed a small sports car, the S360, with chain-drive to both rear wheels. It never went into production, but it was displayed at the 1962 Tokyo Show as a statement of intent.

The company's first four-wheeled production vehicle was a truck using the same twin-cam four-cylinder 360cc engine. This was launched in August 1963, followed in October by the 500cc version of the Tokyo Show sports car.

Below: 1963 Honda 500cc S500

Above: 1965 L700 Estate

The four-carburettor S500 was replaced in March 1964 by the S600 with a conventional rear axle instead of dual chains, and in January 1966 the S800, the first Honda car to arrive in Britain, was launched.

Quick to perceive a home market for small fuel-efficient cars as workers were beginning to enjoy higher standards of living, Honda introduced the N360 four-stroke twin-cylinder microcar. It took the Japanese market by storm in 1967.

By that time Honda had been making a name for itself on the world car-racing scene. The company's first race was the German round of the Formula One series in August 1964 with a 1.5-litre V12.

It was in Germany the following year that an S600 Coupé won its class in an endurance race at the Nürburgring. Honda's first F1 win was also in 1965, the Mexico Grand Prix in October with Richie Ginther at the wheel. This was the first F1 victory by a Japanese car.

The following year the F1 class was changed to an engine capacity of three litres. Honda built another V12 and with it John Surtees won the 1967 Italian GP.

An advocate of air-cooled engines, Honda persuaded his company to try this type and for 1968 a 120-degree V12 version producing 430bhp was produced, a very powerful machine for its time. Tragically, Jo Schlesser was killed at the French GP in the RA301 and at the end of 1968 Honda withdrew from two- and four-wheel racing.

Channelling his energies into road cars, Honda set about the problem of pollution. He personally joined the taskforce working on the CVCC (compound vortex controlled combustion) engine which came to fruition in 1973 and was first used in the Honda Civic. Honda had set up an anti-pollution centre in 1970 and his new engine met the stringent U.S. exhaust emission requirements two years before they became law.

An egalitarian who insisted that all his workers wear a white uniform to emphasize their work as a team, his honest toil nurtured an empire which helped Japan to emerge as the second largest car manufacturing country in the world.

In 1974 at the age of 67 he decided to

Below: 1965 RA 271 Formula One racing car. With this 1.5-litre V12, Honda became the first Japanese manufacturer to win in F1. The four-valve head engine would rev to 13,000rpm. Hi-tech Hondas had arrived.

Top: 1978 example of Honda Civic

Above: 1978 Accord EX-L Saloon

Below: RA 302 Formula One racing car of 1968. This 2988cc 120-degree V8 was air cooled and gave 430bhp. After making a terrific impact in racing on two and four wheels, Honda quit sport at the end of 1968 to concentrate on road vehicles.

Below: 1970 Z Coupé. This 360cc air-cooled four-stroke twin developed 36bhp. A sporty version of the highly successful N360 of 1966, the Z360 was improved by water cooling in 1971. The Japanese home market loved these tiny vehicles.

retire as president and become 'supreme advisor'. Since that time he has quietly guided his various companies as they have set up factories in various parts of the world and provided the horsepower for the public and the Formula One world champions of the 1980s.

In the 1990s, Honda plans to supplement the success of its famously competent and reliable Civic, Accord and Prelude models with cars of a more luxurious or sporty nature. These are being sold in the U.S. through a separate sales channel under the name Acura, a strategy likely to be emulated elsewhere in the world. Acura's first models, the small Integra hatchback and mid-sized Legend

Right: 1985 2.0 Accord Aerodeck
Below right: Ballade for 1985
Far right above: 1986 Integra
Far right bottom: 1986 Honda CRX

Above: 1978 Prelude two-door coupé
Right: Revised Accord of 1982

Above: 1986 Prelude 2.0

Below: Honda's 1978 Prelude evolved into an ingenious four-wheel steering version in 1988. The rear wheels turn the same way as the front at slow speeds and in the opposite direction at higher speeds.

Left: CRX coupé, launched in 1984
Above: 1.4 Civic GL 16-valve

Left: 1987 2.7 Legend coupé
Above: 1990 Civic GL saloon
Below: Concerto, launched in June 1988

Left: Latest version 2.0 injection Accord
Above: 16-valve 1.6i-16 Concerto

Above: Honda Concerto GL

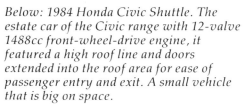

Below: 1984 Honda Civic Shuttle. The estate car of the Civic range with 12-valve 1488cc front-wheel-drive engine, it featured a high roof line and doors extended into the roof area for ease of passenger entry and exit. A small vehicle that is big on space.

Above: 2.2i Accord with sunroof
Right: Twin carburettor Concerto EX

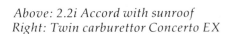

saloon and coupé, soon exceeded U.S. sales targets; the next addition to the range, the 258km/h (160mph) NS-X two-seater launched in 1989, is cause for concern for all Europe's sports car makers.

Right: 2.7 V6 air-conditioned Legend
Below: Four-wheel-drive 1.6 Shuttle
Bottom: Acura mock-up of mid-engined sports car for the U.S. market

The NSX went into production in 1990, and wowed the world. By the end of the 1980s, Honda had built up a reputation for reliable and highly competent cars, but had never really built a supercar.

The NSX used state-of-the-art technology, including a fantastic 274bhp V6 engine featuring Honda's excellent V-TEC variable valve timing. Handling, thanks to a near perfect weight distribution, was excellent. It was soon praised as the easiest supercar to drive but lacked one of the most important elements of a true supercar – passion. It was certainly an almost clinically perfect car, better in many ways than its Italian rivals, but lacking in the kind of kudos held by its competitors. If you've set your heart on a Ferrari or Lamborghini, you're never going to go out and buy a Honda instead.

The rest of the Honda range continued successfully but, due to a rather frumpy image, those models with a Rover equivalent were often outsold by their British-badged equivalent in Europe

Following BMW's takeover of the British company, Honda lost interest in Rover and its future models look set to separate themselves from those of the British firm.

Top: 1996 Honda Legend

Above: 1997 Honda CRX

Below: Honda Accord

Above: 1997 Honda Civic five-door VTi

Below: Honda Civic three-door

Right: 1997 Honda Civic Coupé

Above: 1997 NSX Targa-top

Below: 1997 Honda CR-V

Below: 1996 Honda Prelude 2.2 VTi

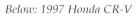

Below left: 1990 Honda Legend coupé

Below middle: 1990 Honda Legend saloon

Below: 1997 Honda Shuttle

Horch

Germany
1898–1940

August Horch gained his automotive industry experience as engineering manager with Benz at Mannheim. He left in 1899 to start his own factory in Ehrenfeld, Cologne, backed by a local cloth merchant.

Horch's first car appeared by 1900, and about ten were made. Two years later Horch moved to larger premises at Reichenbach in Vogtland to build bigger models, then in 1904 he went on to Zwickau, Saxony, with a workforce of around 300 as production increased.

In 1906 a Horch car won the Herkomer Trophy and, heartened by this, the company entered a vehicle in the first Prince Henry Trial two years later. Disagreements with his partners over the unsuccessful eight-litre engine of 1906 eventually led to Horch leaving the firm in 1909.

Top right: 1900 4/5hp voiturette
Above: 1906 18/22 model
Right: 1910 31/60 PS six

Over the next five years the extensive Horch range, under technical director Georg Paulmann, went from 1588cc to 6395cc in engine size. In 1920, Horch was taken over by Dr. Moritz Straus of Argus Motoren in Berlin. For the next two years Arnold Zoller was in charge, then Paul Daimler, which saw design improvement. Daimler's influence was still evident in the two models launched after he left the company in 1924.

The Depression seriously affected sales of Horch cars, although they were noted for combining luxury with a comparatively low price. In 1951 Argus sold the Horch factory to Auto-Union, who already owned D.K.W., Wanderer and Audi – the last of which was begun by August Horch when he left the company in 1909.

The Horch works then became home to the Porsche-designed Auto-Union competition cars, under the management of

Dr. Richard Bruhn, although the larger Horch cars continued throughout the 1930s. By 1940 production of cars was halted, but some 4×4 command cars were built for the Wehrmacht during World War II using Ford engines.

The name was revived briefly in 1956 for a six-cylinder car produced at Zwickau, but Auto-Union objected and the name was changed to Sachsenring the following year.

The luxurious cars that Horch made during the 1930s, such as this 853, were extremely well built and well engineered, featuring straight-eight engines (apart from a very few V12s) and all-independent suspension.

Top left: August Horch driving a 1914 14/35

Top right: 1931 Type 670 six-litre cabriolet
Above: The V8 range lasted until 1939

Hotchkiss

France
1903–1954

The badge of Hotchkiss features two crossed cannon – entirely appropriate for a firm which started, and was nearly finished by, munitions manufacture.

Though nominally a French company, Hotchkiss had strong links with America and, later, Britain. The firm was started in the 1870s by Benjamin Hotchkiss, an American who had made money supplying shells for the American Civil War but later moved to St. Denis, a suburb of Paris, to set up a factory there for the manufacture of munitions.

However, the skilled precision engineering that was needed to make arms and ammunition proved to be ideal for the burgeoning skill of car manufacture, and during a lull in the world arms market Hotchkiss found itself employed to provide parts to several manufacturers. The logical next step was to produce its own car, which it eventually did in 1903.

In the meantime a major reorganization had taken place; in 1885 Benjamin Hotchkiss had died and another American, Laurence Binet, took the reins, though a takeover by a British consortium happened not long after.

The first all-Hotchkiss car was designed by George Terrasse, who came from the Mors concern, and unsurprisingly it was similar to the contemporary Mors, though a neat round radiator and bonnet made the 17CV Hotchkiss recognizably individual. The following year a young draughtsman, Harry Ainsworth, joined the company – and he was the man who was to guide it for its most important years.

Though the first cars were unexceptional, engineering innovations followed including the famous Hotchkiss Drive, which was a shaft-drive transmission system with a live rear-axle layout. Sales became very respectable, considering that large, luxury cars were the firm's stock-in-trade, and in 1911 the French firm bought out its British board of directors and started making slightly less up-market

Top: 1910 model with distinctive bonnet
Below: 1926 AM2 boat-tail

Above: A well-preserved T type
Below: The AM80S of 1932

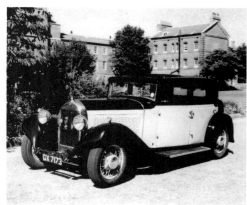

vehicles, though still retaining its reputation for accurate, precise engineering.

During World War I the armaments business flourished, and Hotchkiss acquired two satellite factories, in Coventry and Lyon, to build items like its light machine-gun. After the war the Coventry factory was bought by Morris, the Lyon one by Saurer, and meanwhile Hotchkiss moved itself to a new plant, albeit still in St. Denis.

After the war the company addressed itself firmly to the middle-class market, which proved a wise move. Its aborted AK luxury car, of which only one prototype was ever built, was firmly rejected in favour of the middle-market Type AM which lasted until 1928, when it was replaced by the three-litre AM80 and its sporty 3½-litre AM80S cousin. This proved successful on the track and, most particularly, in rallies like the Monte Carlo, which it won many times.

However, good though it was, that model was to remain, with minor changes, the mainstay of the range until 1950 – becoming an anachronism well before its final end, and that of the company. One example of the firm's intransigence is the fact that it stuck to the tradition of making

The 1936 Grand Sport was powered by a justly famous 3½-litre engine, and gained many notable rallying victories. Its classic lines were elegant when new, but dated badly, particularly as the model was in production for nearly twenty years.

right-hand-drive cars long after every other French company had abandoned the antiquated and inconvenient custom.

The company was hard-hit by the French government's decision to nationalize armaments manufacture in 1936, as the huge losses it incurred were not compensated for until several years later.

World War II was the death knell for Hotchkiss, though it was to struggle on until 1954 with almost non-existent sales. When the Germans invaded France, company head Ainsworth attempted to escape with a convoy of records, supplies and tools but only he himself made it out of the country. The factory was devastated by bombing, and the firm was criticized after the war for not working slowly enough in the German cause and so lost vital reconstruction grants.

Above: Hotchkiss 680 Monte Carlo of 1937
Below: 1938 roadster-bodied 686GS

After the war, the old 3/3½-litre was resuscitated but, already aged, its appeal was strictly limited and sales dwindled almost to nothing until 1954 when, despite mergers with Peugeot and Delahaye, car production ceased. However, U.S.-designed Jeeps were made, as were trucks, until the 1970s.

H.R.G.

Great Britain 1936–1956

Never in any way interested in volume manufacture of standard family saloons, H.R.G. was one of those classic English companies which survived by catering entirely for the lunatic fringe of flat-capped stringback-gloved sports-car fanatics.

Like Morgan, Squire and Lotus, H.R.G. was started by enthusiasts; in this case a trio comprised of racing drivers E. A. Halford and Guy Robins, and car builder H. R. 'Dan' Godfrey, who had previously been responsible, with Archie Frazer-Nash, for the first real sporting light car, the G.N. in 1910.

It was 1935 when the three established their workshop at Norbiton in Surrey, though they were to move a year later to nearby Tolworth. They took a 1500cc four-cylinder Meadows engine which had the benefit of being tuneable to produce a

very respectable power output, and built around it a car which was lightweight and had, by the standards of the day, extremely impressive handling.

The suspension could by no manner of means be described as comfortable, but allowed precise, controllable handling. There was room for two people, but you

Above: 1936 Meadows-engined 1½-litre

would have to be fairly close friends, and luxuries like heating, adequate weather-proofing and so on were strictly not on the menu.

But what the H.R.G. did offer was a feast for the enthusiast; a car equally at home in a variety of motor sports and which gave unmatched driving thrills and

The 1500 was the epitome of H.R.G. motoring, and as such the epitome of sporting British motoring both before and immediately after World War II. The cars may have been primitive but they were fast and handled well for their era.

responsive handling in any situation. Acceleration was excellent and, though the cable-operated brakes were primitive, they were effective – and adjustable while on the move.

The Meadows engine was replaced a few years later by Singer units of either one- or 1½-litre capacity, highly tuned by H.R.G. themselves. With these engines, the formerly competitive cars became even more impressively quick, winning their class at Le Mans, taking similar successes in rallies like the Alpine Rally and the RAC Rally, and were rarely out of the winners list in innumerable club hill-climbs, sprints and trials.

A milestone, though a rather lumpy one, was claimed in 1947 with the Aerodynamic model; it was the first British production sports car with full-width bodywork, which makes it something of a pioneer. However, its upright windscreen and extra weight meant that it was little faster than the normal model and it was soon withdrawn from the range.

In 1955 a new model featuring much new-fangled technology (tubular space frame structure, independent suspension and disc brakes) appeared.

This was again built around a Singer engine, and Singer themselves were getting quite interested in the idea of much closer collaboration with H.R.G., possibly including taking over the new model's manufacture and utilizing the smaller firm's tuning expertise to liven up standard Singers. However, the Rootes Group bought Singer and blocked the collaboration. Within a year the 'classic' H.R.G. had ceased production – again, partly due to Rootes' decision to discontinue the Singer SM1500 engine which was by then H.R.G.'s chosen powerplant.

The firm itself had over the years become run more and more by company secretary Grace Leather, who was sole proprietor by the time it stopped trading in 1966. By that time, however, it had been for some years merely a light-engineering and tuning-equipment company. Sadly, a prototype spaceframed sports car based around a Ford Cortina and later a Vauxhall VX4/90 engine, first shown in 1965, was abandoned on the demise of the firm. H. R. Godfrey himself died in 1968 aged 81, after a long illness.

Above: A 1939 H.R.G.
Below: 1940 Aerodynamic prototype

Bottom: In 1948 some of the mechanicals had undergone refinement

Hudson

U.S.A.
1909–1957

In 1909 the Hudson Motor Car Company, destined to become one of America's largest and most important car manufacturers during the 1920s and 1930s, was formed by a small group of people, mainly engineers, headed by Joseph L. Hudson, the owner of a large Detroit department store. Their first car, the 20bhp 2534cc four-cylinder Model 20, was launched in the same year and despite its completely orthodox design (by Howard Coffin) it became an instant best seller.

Below: Early Hudsons, such as this Hudson 37 of 1913, had four-cylinder engines. Six-cylinder machines followed with four-speed overdrive transmission.

Top: 1912 Hudson 37hp Touring Car
Above: One of the first Hudsons, 1909

Sadly 1912 saw the death of Joseph Hudson, but the birth of Hudson's first six-cylinder car, the Model 6-54, a large and handsome machine powered by a six-litre 54bhp engine. It was built in a range of both open and closed body styles and by 1914 the company was proclaiming itself to be the world's largest manufacturer of six-cylinder cars.

In 1916 the four-cylinder engines were dropped and the company adopted a one-model policy beginning with the Super-Six whose 4739cc engine remained virtually unchanged right through the 1930s. There was a wide range of body styles including sedans, cabriolets, limousines and tourers, and the car was an instant success, with President Hoover taking delivery of a Super-Six Landaulet.

In order to increase its market share, Hudson introduced in 1919, under the 'Essex' name, a less-expensive line of cars

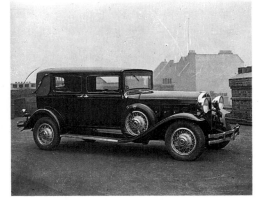

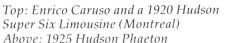
Top: Enrico Caruso and a 1920 Hudson Super Six Limousine (Montreal)
Above: 1925 Hudson Phaeton

Above: 1929 Hudson Super Eight

Below: 1934 Hudson Six

Above: 1929 Hudson Superb Sedan

powered by a 2.9-litre four-cylinder and later 2.6-litre six-cylinder engines in a range of body styles. During the peak years of 1925–29 the sales of the Essex cars greatly exceeded those of the parent company and by 1929 the Essex-Hudson combination was rated third-best seller in the U.S.A.

Another important landmark was the introduction of a straight-eight-engined car in 1930, with the engine remaining in production until 1953 by which time the power had been gradually increased from 95bhp at 3,500rpm to 128bhp at 4,200rpm. Body styles were regularly updated to compete with the big three – Ford, General Motors and Chrysler – although during the late 1930s production (and profits) ebbed and flowed with a trading loss in 1939 and 1940, followed by a small profit the following year.

After the demise of the Essex line in 1932 the Hudson and Essex Terraplane cars became almost indistinguishable. In 1935 a novel electric gear shift, the 'Electric Hand', became available as an

Below left: Four-door Hudson sedan of 1934

Above: 1935 Hudson Custom Brougham
Below: 1940 Hudson Super 6

Below: The Hudson Essex Town Sedan was a graceful machine with flowing wings. The combination of Hudson and Essex gave sales success in the late 1920s.

Left: 1946 Hudson 6-20 model

Above: 1946 Hudson ¾ ton Pick-up

Centre left: 1949 Hudson Superb
Centre right: 1950 Hudson Pacemaker
Above: 1953 Hudson Hornet

Right: 1954 prototype Hudson Italia

option, while in 1936 the 'safety engineered chassis' was developed with Bendix hydraulic brakes backed up by a mechanical system should the hydraulics fail.

During World War II the Hudson factory was turned over to manufacturing war materials and machines and it was not until 1948 that the company launched its new unitary-construction 'Step-Down Design' body-chassis unit in which one stepped down over the structural body sills on to the lowered floor. The new car line-up included the lower-priced Pacemakers with 3.8-litre 112bhp six-cylinder engines, and the top-of-the-range Commodore Eights with their 4168cc 128bhp units.

In the early 1950s sales were flagging again despite the supremacy of the five-litre Hornet in stock-car racing and the announcement of the compact 3.3-litre Jet in 1953. The latter was abandoned the following year when Hudson merged with Nash to form American Motors, and by 1957 the Hudson name had disappeared.

Top: 1951 Hudson Pacemaker Convertible   *Below: 1957 Hudson Hollywood*

Below: 1942 Hudson H21 sedan

Left: 1948 Hudson sedan

Above: 1951 Hudson Commodore 8

Humber

Great Britain
1899–1976

Humber was one of the oldest companies in the British motor industry. First established by Thomas Humber in 1867, the firm originally built bicycles.

After being involved with the production of the three-wheeled Pennington, Humber produced its first car – a single-cylinder, 3½hp model, which appeared in 1899. In the very early days Humber experimented with front-wheel-drive, and produced both three- and four-wheeled cars.

The company built motorized tricycles until 1905, as well as a voiturette and a more successful De Dion-engined 4½hp car with shaft-drive from 1901. In the following two years Humber built four-cylinder 12hp and 20hp models, and a three-cylinder machine with mechanically operated inlet valves instead of the earlier suction-activated valves.

One of the most famous cars of its time was the 1903 Humberette. This was shaft-driven via a two-speed gearbox and powered by a 600cc engine of De Dion design. The car was uprated in 1904.

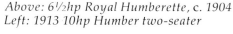
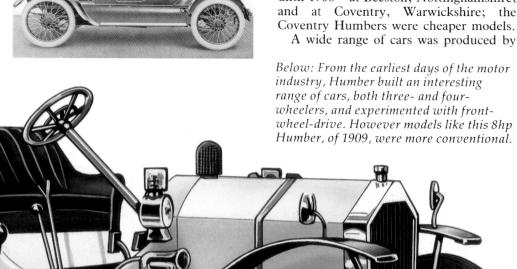

Above: 6½hp Royal Humberette, c. 1904
Left: 1913 10hp Humber two-seater

Humbers were produced at two factories until 1908 – at Beeston, Nottinghamshire, and at Coventry, Warwickshire; the Coventry Humbers were cheaper models.

A wide range of cars was produced by

Below: From the earliest days of the motor industry, Humber built an interesting range of cars, both three- and four-wheelers, and experimented with front-wheel-drive. However models like this 8hp Humber, of 1909, were more conventional.

Humber before World War I, from an 8hp to a 6.3-litre model. From 1912 the new Humberette cyclecar was available with an air-cooled 998cc engine. After the war Humber concentrated on building reliable family cars, using inlet-over-exhaust-valve cylinder-head configurations from 1923.

Above: 1923 Humber 8/18hp Chummy Car
Below: 1929 Humber saloon

Humber acquired commercial-vehicle manufacturers Commer Cars Ltd. in 1926, and took Hillman under its wing in 1928. By this time Humber had introduced an 1100cc 9/20 model, a two-litre 14/40 and a larger, six-cylinder 20/55.

Six-cylinder models introduced in 1930 included the 16/50 (2.1 litres), the Snipe (3½-litres) and a long-wheelbase Pullman version. The larger, luxury saloons then dominated the Humber range throughout the 1930s.

Humber's financial problems were solved when the Rootes Group took control of the concern in 1932. In 1933 a smaller Humber 12 was introduced, while in 1936 the largest six-cylinder model had an engine capacity of over four litres.

As World War II approached, the stately six-cylinder Humbers featured hydraulic brakes and independent front suspension, although sidevalve engines were fitted. The 4.1-litre Super Snipe was introduced at this time, and Humber

Snipes were used as staff cars by the Allies throughout the war.

When hostilities ceased, the pre-war models were reintroduced, together with a new, four-cylinder, 1.9-litre sidevalve Hawk, which owed a great deal to the 1939 Hillman Fourteen saloon.

Overhead-valve engines were used throughout the Humber range of Hawk (four-cylinder, 70bhp, 2267cc), Super Snipe and Pullman (six-cylinder, 113/116bhp, 4139cc), from 1952/3.

A rebodied, unitary construction Hawk was introduced in 1957, and a similarly styled Super Snipe (originally 2650cc, later 2965cc), in 1959. Saloon, limousine and estate-car versions of both models were produced.

The Humber Sceptre was announced in January 1963, being little more than a badge-engineered luxury version of the Hillman Super Minx/Singer Vogue, and fitted with an 85bhp 1592cc engine. The

88bhp 1725cc Sceptre was, from late 1967, the top model in the Rootes Group's Arrow range, in saloon and estate-car form.

The Humber name finally disappeared in the autumn of 1976, after the Chrysler takeover of Rootes.

Above: 1950s Hawk at the start of the overland journey to New Zealand

Below: 1964 Humber Super Snipe
Bottom: 1965 1725cc Humber Sceptre

Hyundai

Korea
1968 to date

Hyundai – Korea's largest industrial concern with interests in shipping and civil engineering – started assembling British Ford cars and trucks under licence in 1968.

By 1973 the company was building more than a third of Korea's vehicles and the next move was to graduate from assembly to production.

Most of the financial backing came from Barclays Bank in Britain and other London financial organizations.

George Turnbull, who had served his apprenticeship with the Standard Motor Co. and later became managing director of the Austin Morris division of the then British Leyland Motor Corporation, was chosen to mastermind the development and design of Hyundai's first car.

It was styled by Giugiaro and engineered by Ital Design in Turin. Bodies were partly built in France and most of the dies came from British Leyland.

The car used a 1238cc Mitsubishi engine and running gear and was announced as the Hyundai Pony in London in November 1974.

Production began late in 1975 and a target figure of 56,000 was met by the end of 1976. The figure reached 103,000 and a decade later it was close to 400,000.

A slightly revised version of the Pony was launched in 1982, still with Mitsubishi running gear, but with an optional 92bhp 1439cc engine.

The range was extended in 1983 with the introduction of the Stellar saloon with

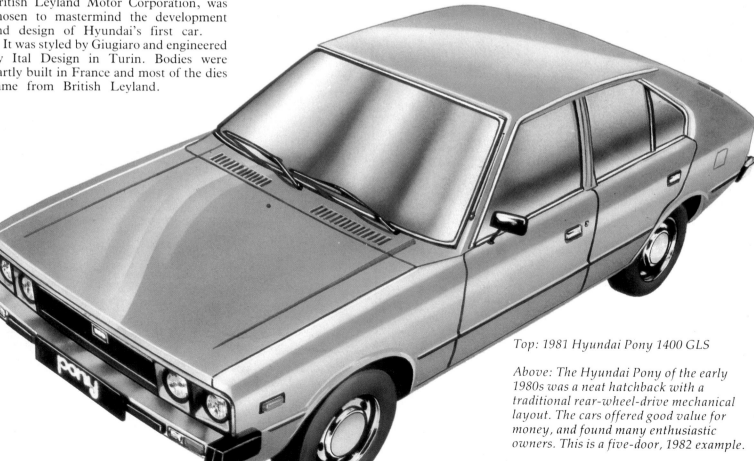

Top: 1981 Hyundai Pony 1400 GLS

Above: The Hyundai Pony of the early 1980s was a neat hatchback with a traditional rear-wheel-drive mechanical layout. The cars offered good value for money, and found many enthusiastic owners. This is a five-door, 1982 example.

Above: 1982 Hyundai Pony 1200T

either the 1439cc engine or 1597cc unit.

Hyundai made significant inroads into export markets in the mid-1980s, selling cars to Canada and becoming the fastest-growing export marque in the U.S.

The new Pony sub-compact introduced to the U.K. in 1985 (called Excel in the U.S.) was totally different from its predecessor, having front-wheel-drive with a transverse engine, and was offered in both saloon and hatchback forms.

Four years later, with export sales of its small car falling, Hyundai entered the compact market segment with its Sonata saloon. This was initially powered by a Mitsubishi-designed 2.4-litre 110bhp four-cylinder engine, but later there was the option of a single-overhead-cam V6.

Below: 1988 Hyundai Pony 1.3 Sonnet

Right: 1989 model Hyundai Stellar saloon
Below: 1984 Hyundai Stellar 1600 GSL

Like the other Korean motor manufacturers, Hyundai's foreign market image and sales improved dramatically during the nineties. In the mid-1990s, Hyundai was Korea's biggest car manufacturer, producing over a million cars per year. The old range dragged on a little past its sell-by date but was gradually replaced with all-new models.

The ancient Pony, which had previously been the company's mainstay, finally received some curves in 1994, but retained the old model's 12-valve Mitsubishi motors. The other models followed suit.

New to the range, though, was the S Coupé. It had sporting pretensions and was even available with a powerful turbo motor. Unfortunately, the chassis couldn't quite keep up and the car was not a great success. It was revamped for 1996 with new ultra-modern and curvaceous styling and vastly improved handling. The new car used Hyundai's own new 16-valve engines with

Above: 1997 Hyundai Accent 1.5 MVi

Left: Hyundai Accent 1.5 GLSi

Right: The Lantra saloon

Below: 1997 Hyundai Coupé

Above: Hyundai Sonata 2.0 CD
Left: Hyundai Lantra estate

power outputs ranging from 114 to 139bhp. It was completely transformed and universally praised by the press and soon showed itself to be popular with buyers too. The four-door Lantra shared the same floorpan as the Coupé and gained the new engines at the same time.

Above: Hyundai Sonata V6

Imperial

U.S.A.
1954–1975

Although Imperial only became a make in its own right in 1954, the name had been used for luxury Chryslers since 1926. The reason for the separation was to create a more prestigious image for Imperials, along the lines of Cadillac's De Ville series and Ford's Lincoln range.

Above: 1930 Chrysler CG Imperial 8
Right: 1972 Chrysler Imperial Le Baron
Below right: 1974 Imperial Le Baron

Basically the cars were still just big Chryslers and used the overhead-valve V8, announced in 1951. The company's products were, in the late 1940s and early 1950s, noted for being very well put together and having excellent interiors, but to be rather plainly styled. Flite Sweep

Below: Luxury Chryslers from 1926 were designated 'Imperial'. During the 1920s and 1930s, elegant Le Baron coachwork featured on the cars, and the name was revived in the 1950s for prestigious Imperial models. This is a Chrysler Imperial of 1932.

bodywork, introduced in 1955, gave the cars a more modern appearance and increased their popularity, and also in that year disc brakes were fitted as standard.

During the 1920s and 1930s the famous LeBaron firm of coachbuilders had been responsible for Imperial bodies and that name was revived in 1957 to add prestige to the more expensive models. By 1960 some models were offered with luxuries such as automatically swivelling seats and power-operated vent windows.

Unitary-construction methods came in

by 1967 and four years later anti-lock brakes were standardized, the first such system in America. Engine power had risen to 335bhp, but this dropped to 225bhp in the early 1970s.

In 1974 Chrysler made a loss of over U.S. $52 million and the following year the decision was made to discontinue the Imperial name, which was achieving only one-fifth of Lincoln's sales. The LeBaron name, however, was revived in the early 1980s using Chrysler and Mitsubishi engines and front-wheel-drive.

Invicta

Great Britain 1925–1938; 1946–1950

Noel Campbell Macklin (father of the racing driver Lance Macklin) had already built the Eric Campbell and the Silver Hawk cars before his first Invicta appeared in 1925. Macklin had been impressed by the tremendous torque of an American Doble steam car and made his own car sufficiently flexible to run most of the time in top gear.

The original 1925 Invicta, with its handsome square-cut radiator and rivets down the bonnet-hinge line, was powered by a 2.6-litre six-cylinder Meadows engine, but in 1926 the engine capacity was increased to three litres and two years later to 4½ litres in an attempt further to increase low-speed torque. The company was financed by Oliver Lyle (of Tate and Lyle) and Earl Fitzwilliam, formerly of Sheffield Simplex, with design work by William Watson.

Above: 1927 Invicta 3-litre
Below: The 'Doctor's Coupé' version of the same car

Below: The famous 4500S of 1931 was extremely capable, and in the hands of professional drivers like Donald Healey its underslung chassis for good weight distribution and torquey engine made it more than a match for Continental rally competition.

THE 4½ LITRE MULLINER SALOON

Left: 1933 4½-litre Mulliner
Above: 1933 1½-litre

In 1930 two versions of the car became available, the high-chassis model and the graceful 100mph (160km/h) underslung-chassis model. Invicta cars were kept in the public eye by Violet and Evelyn Cordery with their long-distance timed runs, and by Donald Healey who did extremely well in international events with a win in the 1931 Monte Carlo Rally and a second place the following year, driving a 4½-litre S Type.

However, the Depression was beginning to bite by this time, with production of the 4½-litre cars almost ceasing by 1935; and even the new 1½-litre six-cylinder Blackburne-powered 12/45 car launched some three years earlier was not doing well. It was overweight and underpowered and although this was to some extent remedied in the 1932 Supercharged 12/90, in 1933 Macklin sold out to Lord Fitzwilliam and helped to form the new Railton Motor Company. Three new Invictas were announced for 1936 but they were little more than rebodied French Darracqs and the project came to nothing.

The Invicta name was revived in 1946 with the introduction of the Black Prince, with its twin-overhead-camshaft three-litre Meadows engine, an untried Brockhouse automatic transmission and independent torsion-bar suspension all round, but the cars were very expensive and only a handful were sold. In 1950 the goodwill and the remaining cars and parts were bought by A.F.N. Ltd., makers of the Frazer-Nash.

Isotta-Fraschini

Italy
1900–1949

Isotta-Fraschini, not to be confused with bubble-car barons Isetta, were often thought of during their between-the-wars heyday as the ultimate practitioners of Italian automotive art.

Ironically, however, it was only their very strong and often-changing links with other countries that gave them their pre-eminence and their profits – the former surviving rather longer and more reliably than the latter.

The firm was founded in 1898 by car enthusiast Vincenzo Fraschini and moneyed lawyer Cesare Isotta, at first to import French Renault and De Dion cars into Italy. Two years later they officially named their partnership Societa Milanese d'Automobili Isotta, Fraschini & Cia and started building their first home-grown product – but from imported parts and certainly from borrowed ideas.

However, they soon started developing an identity of their own and after engineer Giustino Cattaneo, the man behind many of their best products, joined in 1905, sales boomed and models proliferated. In 1907,

however, a cash shortfall found them again looking abroad, this time to Lorraine-Dietrich who became the firm's partners until 1909.

During these years the marque was starting to build a reputation in racing, with a few notable successes, particularly in the U.S.A. These provided the foundation for sales success in America, which was capitalized on only after World

Above: A 1910 50/65hp

Above: The 1906 18/22 was competent but hardly unique
Below: The Type 8, introduced in 1919

War I which the company spent building all manner of engines for everything from armoured trucks to boats.

But soon afterwards, and by an inspired piece of marketing, they hauled themselves firmly up-market to take on the limousine makers such as Rolls-Royce and Mercedes (which the distinctive radiator grille most resembled).

American film stars, celebrities and tycoons hurried to buy the prestigious Isotta-Fraschini Type 8 which was first introduced in 1919 – with only the mechanicals being supplied by the company themselves, the variation in body styles was extensive. Italian and French styling houses vied with American and British coachbuilders to make more and more extreme and ostentatious bodies for the powerful 5.9-litre engine and quite advanced chassis which the skilled engineer Cattaneo had designed.

The names behind the company fell by the wayside in the early 1920s, with Vincenzo Fraschini leaving in 1922, a year

after his brother Oreste, also involved with the firm, died. At the same time Isotta sold his holding. The new owner, Mille Miglia founder and enthusiast Count Lodovico Mazzotti, continued with the luxury-car market but diversified into aero-engines as well, again scoring notable success in the U.S.A.

This rebounded rather negatively on the car side of the business; as the aircraft industry flourished it took more of the

Above: By 1929, the year of this model, the founders had left the company
Below right: The post-war Type 8C

firm's resources and the Type 8 was left to stagnate expensively until very nearly killed off by the Depression.

Ford expressed an interest in the firm, but some manoeuvring by Fiat stopped that partnership ever bearing fruit, and in 1933 the company effectively went

bankrupt, to be rescued by aircraft manufacturer Caproni who valued Isotta-Fraschini's aeronautical expertise.

During World War II this was put to good use by Mussolini's forces who flew Isotta-engined aircraft, drove Isotta-engineered trucks and patrolled in Isotta-powered boats. It was a tribute to the versatility of the company's designs, but a bad move in terms of post-war credibility.

They were only to return to car manufacture briefly, with the 8C Monterosa in the late 1940s. Ambitious and advanced, it nonetheless sold only six models before the firm yet again went into liquidation. The trucks and buses they had been manufacturing hadn't been enough to keep the wolf from the door, so they folded up. The company now makes engines and industrial drivetrains for all sorts of applications.

The expensive and immense Type 8 of the 1920s was the finest flowering of the company's push into the luxury car market. It was bodied by all the great coachbuilders. The price may have been high, but the steering was heavy and the brakes dubious at best.

Isuzu

Japan
1953 to date

Although the present Isuzu company dates from 1953, it can trace its ancestry back to 1916 when the Tokyo Ishikawajiama Ship Building and Engineering Company merged with the Tokyo Gas and Electric Company to produce motor vehicles. In 1918 the company signed an agreement with British manufacturer Wolseley for production and marketing rights of its cars in the Far East, and the first Japanese-built Wolseley appeared in 1922.

An independent company was set up in 1929 to build cars to original designs. This was initially called the Ishikawajiama Automotive Works Company, then the Automobile Industries Company, and it used the trade names Sumida and Chiyoda. These were later abandoned in favour of Isuzu, after the Japanese river.

Above: The 1943 PA10

In 1937 Automobile Industries became known as the Tokyo Automobile Industries Company, and in 1949 it changed identity yet again to become Isuzu Motor Ltd.

In 1953 the company reached an agreement with the British Rootes organization to build Hillman cars under licence. The first cars were assembled later the same year, and by 1957 the Minx was fully sourced and built in Japan.

Isuzu's first original design was the Bellel, launched in 1961. This was a traditional four-door saloon with obvious Western influences in its styling, and was available with either a 1471cc petrol engine or a two-litre diesel (making it the first-ever diesel-powered Japanese car).

Above: The 1963 Bellet four-door saloon   *Below: The successful coupé version*

Two years later came the slightly smaller Bellet (also available as a two-door coupé), then in 1966 appeared the attractive 117 coupé. The 1584cc Florian saloon was launched in 1967 with body design by Ghia, and a double-overhead camshaft engine with twin carburettors.

The later 1960s saw a marked downturn in Isuzu's fortunes, however. Production dropped from 39,776 cars in 1968 to 18,815 in 1970, and the company began to seek collaboration with other manufacturers in an effort to reduce its costs. Fuji, Mitsubishi and Nissan were all involved for a time, but it was not until 1971 that General Motors took a 34 per cent share in Isuzu to herald a dramatic revival of the latter's fortunes. The first car to appear as a result of this union was the 1974 Gemini, an Isuzu-built version of the contemporary Opel Kadett-Chevrolet Chevette. The car

The Isuzu Piazza, which was launched in 1981, is the most powerful Isuzu car to date with its 180bhp 1994cc four-cylinder engine and its optional turbocharger. However, it has enjoyed only moderate success despite styling by Giugiaro and favourable press coverage.

Above: The Isuzu/Aska

was powered by a 1584 or 1817cc engine and transmission was by four- or five-speed manual gearbox or a three-speed automatic.

The Gemini was revised in 1979, then in 1984 it was totally redesigned to offer front-wheel-drive in a package based on

Below: The Gemini, for export to the U.S.A.

Above: The ever-increasing off-road market is catered for too

General Motors' R-Car design. The very first front-wheel-drive Isuzu, however, was the 1983 Florian/Aska.

The only Isuzu car to be marketed in Britain (as opposed to the four-wheel-drive Trooper, and the Bedford-badged KB pickup and Midi panel van) was the Piazza (badged in the U.S.A. as the Impulse). Designed by Giorgio Giugiaro and launched in 1981, it was as dramatically styled for its time as had been the 117 coupé in 1966.

Itala

Italy
1904–1934

The Ceirano brothers had a hand in the development of over seven different makes of car, including the beginnings of Fiat. In 1903 Matteo Ceirano, looking for competition glory, left his elder brother's firm to set up his own marque with Guido Bigio, Grosso Campana, Giovanni Carenzi, Leone Fubini and Angelo Moriondo in premises in Turin.

By 1904 the company gained victory with what was essentially its first machine, driven by Ceirano in the Susa-Mont Cenisio hill-climb. The following year Giovanni Battista Raggio won the Coppa Florio in a 15.3-litre car and in 1906 an Itala took the Targa Florio with Allesandro Cagno at the wheel.

The workforce expanded as sales took off. Queen Mother Margherita of Italy owned no less than five of the cars and in 1907, Prince Scipione Borghese won the Peking-to-Paris marathon by a three-week margin. Fame also led to imitations – in particular from the British Weigel and B.S.A. companies.

Until World War I Itala offered a wide, complex range of vehicles, and was experimenting with rotary-valve engines. Bigio was killed testing one intended for the 1913 French Grand Prix. Ceirano had left the company in 1905 to start S.P.A. the following year.

Disastrous war-time contracts for Hispano-Suiza aero-engines left Itala in a perilous financial state. The 51S model won the 1922 and 1923 Targa Florio, but by 1925 Itala was being run by receivers appointed by the Italian government. Even the Tipo 61, designed by ex-Fiat man

The racing pedigree of this marque was never in doubt, even from its earliest days. Probably its finest hour was in 1907 when a 35/45 model of this type, piloted by Prince Scipione Borghese, co-driver Luigi Barzini and mechanic Ettore Guizzardi, won the Peking to Paris race by a huge margin, boosting sales immensely.

Above: Grandeur and grace – the 1907 model

Above: 1908 12-litre racing model

Below: A pair of 12hp Italas sold in 1912

Cappa, could not revive the company and a new V12 racer failed to get off the ground.

Two attempts at updating the 61 both failed, as did various reorganizations of the company in 1929 and 1931. It finally closed down at the end of 1934.

Below: 1910 75hp six-cylinder Itala

Jaguar

Great Britain
1954 to date

Jaguar's origins can be traced back to the early 1920s when William Lyons – who was later to become Sir William – set up the Swallow Sidecar Company.

He initially planned to become an apprentice at the Vickers shipyards but his father persuaded him to train with Crossley Motors in Manchester, augmenting his training with an evening engineering course at Manchester Technical College.

He again changed direction and returned to his native Blackpool to help his father's piano restoration business. Lyon's had been a keen motorcyclist for some years and later he took a job as a salesman for a Sunbeam dealer.

A chance meeting led to a further change. In 1921, William Walmsley moved into a house near Lyons' home, building aluminium sports sidecars from the garage. Lyons bought a sidecar and suggested that, as a team, they could build up the business.

Walmsley agreed reluctantly and they began working from premises on the top floor of an electrical equipment factory in Blackpool. Their company – the Swallow Sidecar Co. – was officially registered in September 1922.

Business boomed and, four years later, they formed the Swallow Sidecar and Coachbuilding Co. and moved to larger premises.

Above: Swallow sidecar of the 1920s

Lyons chose his own Austin Seven as a guinea pig and the company developed a special body for it. The car emerged in 1927 as the Austin Swallow – a two-seater with optional hinged hard top – and it quickly went into production.

It was followed soon afterwards by the Morris-based Cowley Swallow, and the company also built bodies based on Alvis and Clyno chassis.

The expansion continued and the company had 50 workers by 1928, building two cars a day and 100 sidecars a week.

More space was need and the business moved to a former ammunition works in Coventry where Lyons set a production target of 50 cars a week. Larger models were built, including several on Fiat chassis.

The company made its first appearance at the Motor Show in 1929 and two years later production was up to 30 cars a day.

October 1931 was a significant month for the company. It launched the SS1 – the first car to use a purpose-built chassis with a Swallow body. It used Standard 16hp running gear and was competitively priced at £310.

The smaller SS11 was launched at the same time, this model utilizing the 1052cc Standard Little Nine running gear. A total of 776 cars were sold in 1932.

Below: Standard Swallow of 1929
Bottom: 1936 Jaguar SS100

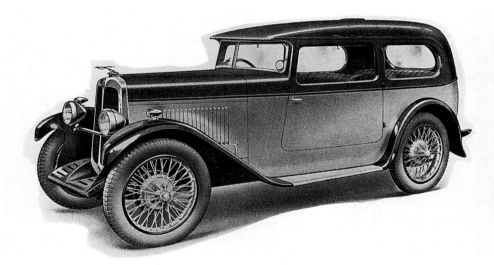

To simplify matters, the car section was separated from the sidecar operation in 1933 to become SS Cars Ltd.

The company had already produced drop-head versions of four-seaters but the first true sports car came in March 1935. It was the SS90, a two-seater with a 20hp 2663cc engine.

The Jaguar name appeared six months later with the introduction of the 2663cc overhead-valve SS100 Jaguar. The Jaguar suffix was then adopted for all SS models.

Walmsley and Lyons split up after many disagreements, Walmsley leaving to join the Airlite Trailer Co. and Lyons becoming major shareholder in SS Cars Ltd. when it was floated as a public company in January 1935.

The Swallow Coachbuilding Co. was put into voluntary liquidation and, with £10,000 nominal capital, Lyons set up the private company Swallow Coachbuilding Co. (1935) Ltd. to continue sidecar production.

By now, SS Cars was producing about 1,500 cars a year and had some 600 workers. The Sunbeam Motor Car Co. had gone bankrupt and Lyons tried to buy it but Rootes beat him to the deal.

SS1 and SS11 models were dropped in 1936. But over the following two years, plans to introduce new models were hampered by troublesome all-metal bodywork. However, SS Cars managed to

Above: 1982 XJ and 1937 SS Jaguars

make a small profit and production had exceeded 5,000 cars before the beginning of World War II.

The war years kept the factory busy making centre sections for Meteor aircraft, repairing and servicing bombers, building about 10,000 sidecars and experimenting with lightweight vehicles which could be dropped by parachute. Most of Coventry suffered tremendous damage from bombing but SS Cars escaped relatively undamaged.

A major reorganization after the war led to Jaguar Cars Ltd. being set up in March 1945. Swallow was sold to the Helliwell group (later the name was bought by Tube Investments and then Watsonian – a famous name which is still registered).

Jaguar resumed production in July 1945 but in February 1947 fire caused £100,000 worth of damage to its factory.

Jaguar's models had so far been essentially pre-war designs with 1.8-litre four-cylinder engines and 2.7-litre or 3.5-litre sixes. The sixes were Jaguar's own and the old Standard four was dropped in 1949.

Left: 1939 1.8 SS Saloon

1939 version of SS100. Introduced in 1935, the SS100 was the first model to bear the Jaguar name. The 2663cc overhead valve six-cylinder engine made the car capable of a genuine 160km/h (100mph). Jaguar and speed were now synonymous.

Lyons entrusted the engineering work to former Humber employee William Heynes who had joined SS Cars as chief engineer in 1934. Together with Harry Weslake, he first re-designed the Standard engines and later created the classic Jaguar sixes and V12 with engineers such as Claude Baily and Walter Hassan.

Jaguar created a sensation when the XK120 was launched in October 1948. It was a true 120mph (193km/h) sports car with 160bhp from a 3.4-litre double-overhead-cam engine, and all for a commendably low £1273. A total of 12,055 were sold with very few going to British customers. In fact, 92 per cent were exported and in 1952 the figure was 96 per cent, over 60 per cent of those cars going to the United States. Its replacement in October 1954 was a worthy successor – the 190bhp XK140.

Post-war sensation, the 1949 XK120 Jaguar. Its 3.4-litre double overhead cam straight six engine gave it a 193km/h (120mph) top speed – breathtaking for its time. The modern straight six Jaguar engine is a direct descendant.

Above: 1952 Long Nose C-Type

Jaguar had realized the value of the publicity which could be gained from track successes. Factory XKs were racing in the early 1950s followed by purpose-built C- and D-Type racing cars. The C-Type clocked up one Le Mans 24-Hour win in 1951 with four more victories going to D-Types in 1953, 1955, 1956 and 1957. Jaguar then withdrew from major participation in racing, partly because of its involvement in the 1955 Le Mans disaster.

The image built by the XK models and racers gave a tremendous boost to saloon-car sales. The Mark VII, launched in 1951 with the twin-cam engine as a replacement for earlier pushrod units, proved extremely popular and over 30,000 were built up to 1957. It was replaced by the improved Mark VIII and then the Mark IX with a 3.8-litre engine and power-assisted steering as standard.

Above: 1950 3½-litre Mk V dhc
Below: The Mk VII launched 1951

Profits had been healthy enough to allow the company to move into the Brown's Lane factory which had formerly been occupied by Daimler, providing over a million square feet of production area. The move took place between 1950 and 1952.

The 1950s were flourishing years for Jaguar with 1956 being particularly memorable – William Lyons was knighted.

The company had announced the unitary-construction 2.4-litre saloon at the end of 1955, later dubbing it the Mark I, and it was joined by a 3.8-engined version in 1959. The same engine was also used in the mighty XK150 which was introduced in May 1957.

Below: 1954 XK140 fhc

Below: 1956 XK140 Roadster
Below centre: 1957 XK SS

Above: 1954 XK120 Coupé

Above: 1960 XK150 dhc
Below: 1960 XK150 fhc
Bottom: 1959-61 3781cc Mk IX

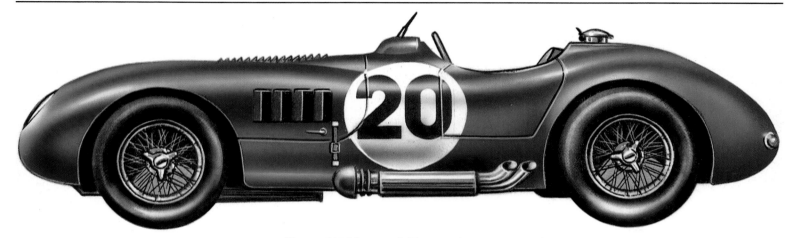

The company suffered another disastrous fire in February 1957 and almost a quarter of the factory was destroyed with damage put at £3.5 million. But to Jaguar's credit, production was back to normal within two months and in June 1960 it bought the Daimler Co. for £3.4 million from the B.S.A. group. Daimler production continued but the cars eventually became badge-engineered Jaguars.

The Mark II saloon was introduced in October 1959, eventually being available in 2.4-, 3.4- and 3.8-litre guises, and finally ending up as the 240.

One of the company's most famous cars – the E-Type – was launched in March 1961 to replace the XK150. It was mechanically similar but heavily based on the racing D-Type. It was a genuine 150mph (240km/h) sports car for less than £2,100.

Above: 1951 Jaguar C-Type racing car based on the XK120. It won the 1951 Le Mans 24-Hour race, gaining tremendous prestige for the marque. Jaguar went on to win Le Mans in 1953-55-56-57 with the subsequent D-Type version.

The saloon-car range was expanded with the cavernous Mark X in 1962 which featured independent rear suspension and unitary body construction.

Jaguar wanted to bridge the gap between the relatively compact Mark II and the larger Mark X and the company introduced the S-Type in 1964. It was basically a long-booted Mark II with the Mark X's independent rear suspension and it came with either a 3.4- or 3.8-litre engine.

Above right: 1960 Mk II Jaguar saloon
Right: 1963 S-Type saloon
Below: 1961 Series I E-Type

The famous double-overhead-cam straight-six was stretched to 4.2 litres in 1965 and was used in the Mark X and then the 420 saloon of 1967, an improved version of the S-Type. The 4.2 also replaced the 3.8-litre engine in the E-Type in 1965.

Jaguar merged with the British Motor Corporation in July 1966 to form British Motor Holdings with Sir William Lyons retaining control of Jaguar. B.M.H. merged with Leyland in May 1968 and Jaguar became part of the new British Leyland Motor Corporation.

Above: 1966 4.2-litre Mk X saloon

Below: 1968 Series II E-Type Coupé

Above: 1967 340 saloon

Below: 1966 420 saloon

Below: 1966 V12 XJ13

Below: 1967 S-Type saloon

The hugely successful XJ6 saloon was Jaguar's first product as part of British Leyland. It was introduced in September 1968 with either a 2.8- or 4.2-litre engine (the smaller unit later earning a reputation for being troublesome and subsequently being dropped) and helped the company set a new production record of 32,000 cars in 1970.

Jaguar had experimented with a rear-engined racer in the mid-1960s, using a four-cam V12 engine. The racer was stillborn but the work was not wasted because the E-Type was offered in 5.3-litre V12 form in 1971.

The XJ6 also came in for the V12 treatment and the XJ12 was introduced in 1972. It was in such demand that, for a while, secondhand models were selling for more than the new price.

A total of over 72,500 E-Types in various forms had been built when the famous model was replaced by the stylish XJ-S 5.3-litre four-seater luxury sports saloon in 1975.

Sir William Lyons retired as managing director and was succeeded by 'Lofty' England who had run Jaguar's competition department in the 1950s.

Geoffrey Robinson succeeded him in 1974 but Jaguar's independence was questioned by the government-sponsored Ryder Report in 1975 which examined Leyland's problems. Robinson resigned.

Above: 1968-69 240 saloon

Below: 1969 Series I XJ6

Below: Series III E-Type. Introduced in 1961, the 3.8-litre E-Type was the glamour car of the 1960s. Capable of over 240km/h (150mph), this triple carburettor wonder was finally produced in V12 form. E-Types were direct descendants of the racing D-Type.

Above: 1971 Series III V12 E-Type
Right: 1975 Series II XJ6
Below: 1973 Series I XJ12

Right: 1975 5.3-litre XJ Coupé
Below: 1975 V12 XJS

Below: 1968 2.8-litre XJ6. Introduced in September that year and also available in 4.2-litre form, it was voted Car of the Year.

Reproduced with permission
© Haynes Publishing Group, 1976

Le Mans 24-Hours race in 1988.

Under Egan's leadership, Jaguar greatly improved quality control which had previously lapsed and damaged the company's reputation. Sales improved in the all-important American market.

Below: 1980 Series III XJ12

Leyland enjoyed a tremendous revival under Sir Michael Edwardes and Jaguar regained its identity to such a degree that it was known simply as Jaguar Cars from 1978.

John Egan, formerly of Massey-Ferguson, became chairman of Jaguar in April 1980 with the company becoming Jaguar Cars Ltd. Sir William Lyons remained as honorary president until his death at the age of 83 in 1985, the year after Jaguar was returned from state-ownership to the private sector.

Egan treated Jaguar's individuality as a priority and his enthusiasm extended to the racing involvement with the XJ-R Sports Prototype racing cars built by Tom Walkinshaw Racing. One of these won the

Left: 1980 XJ saloon

An XJ6 replacement – the Jaguar Sovereign – was launched in October 1986 with new 2.9- and 3.6-litre engines, the latter enlarged in 1989 to 4.0-litres. And the XJ-S continued to sell well with the V12 convertible heading the range from March 1988.

But the overall success of Jaguar sales during the 1980s grew dangerously

dependent on the U.S. market, and by 1988 alterations in the dollar/pound exchange rate had seriously reduced profits. Accepting that his company lacked the resources to independently develop crucial new models, Sir John Egan entered into discussions with G.M. This prompted a 'hostile' take-over bid by Ford, and in November 1989 Jaguar Cars became a wholly-owned subsidiary of Ford of Great Britain.

Left: 1983 5.3-litre XJS HE
Below: V12 long-distance racers

Below: 1985 XJSC HE V12

Below: 1986 XJS Cabriolet

Below: 1986 3.6 Sovereign 'XJ40'

Above: 1989 2.9-litre Jaguar XJ6   *Below: 1989 5343cc V12 XJS Coupé*   *Right: Jaguar at Le Mans '89*

Below: Jaguar XJS, introduced 1975 and still in production. A luxury 2+2 two-door coupé, it featured a 5343cc ohc V12 fuel injection engine, disc brakes all round and air conditioning. A High Efficiency (HE) version was introduced in 1981.

Top left: 1988 Jaguar Sovereign

Top right: V12 XJR-S special

Above: 1997 XK8 Coupé

Below: The 4.0-litre XJ-S convertible

Following the takeover, Ford knew it would have a lot to do to get Jaguar back into profit. In 1992 Jaguar had to cut production and its workforce. This was a major embarrassment to Ford, who saw losses of a million dollars a day from a company for which it had paid $2.5 billion. The parent company bravely carried the burden and continued to contribute money and expertise to a new model programme which would see new engines and a new coupé, as well as a new small saloon by the end of the century.

A new XJ6 came in 1994 and immediately boosted Jaguar's flagging worldwide sales figures. The new car used Jaguar's AJ16 engine in an all-new, retro-styled body. Top of the range was the 4.0-litre XJR with a supercharger and 320bhp. There was also a V12 version, as well as Daimler-badged derivatives.

The replacement for the XJ-S didn't arrive until 1996. The new car was called the XK8 and used an all-new 4.0-litre V8 engine. It owed its sleek looks to its famous predecessor, the E-type, and was launched at Geneva as the E-type had been 35 years earlier. It was greatly praised by the press and sold

much better than the aged XJ-S had done. Both coupé and convertible body styles were available. The new V8 engine was fitted to the rest of the Jaguar range.

As the turn of the century draws nearer, so too does the much awaited launch of the new small Jaguar, codenamed X200. After speculation that the new car would be built outside Britain, it was revealed that a new factory would be set up in Birmingham to build the new car. It was reported in the motoring press that the new car would have retro styling, with a grille shaped like that on the old MkII.

As part of Ford 2000, Ford's plan to reduce the number of different platforms used by all of its car manufacturing divisions, it is possible that new Fords may share their underpinnings and possibly engines with the new Jaguars.

Top left: 1997 Jaguar Sovereign

Top right: 1997 Jaguar XJ12

Left: 4.0-litre XJ Sport

Below: 1990 XJ220

Jeep
USA
1963 to date

'Jeep' became a make in its own right in 1963, when Kaiser-Jeep was formed, as distinct from Willys-Overland, the Jeep's originators. At the time, and ever since, the range has consisted of two separate lines: the direct descendants of the original military workhorse (the CJ series) and the 'civilian' station wagon style Wagoneer and its offshoots. Both types have offered four, six and V8 engines at various times, though in the early '1960s, only the smaller units were available.

A V8 option (the 5.4 litre Rambler engine) joined the Wagoneer and station wagon range in 1965, which could be had with either two or four-wheel-drive – as ever, not everyone could

Above: 1975 Jeep Cherokee

Below: 1975 Jeep CJ-5

Left: 1984 Jeep Wagoneer Limited and Jeep Cherokee Chief

Below: 1984 Jeep Cherokee Chief

Below right: 1984 Jeep Wagoneer

afford or needed the expense and complication of a real 4x4, but they did appreciate the ruggedness of a vehicle with 'Jeep' in its name. Meanwhile, the wartime descendant of the Jeep soldiered on (if you'll pardon the expression) through the '1960s; cheapest of the range was the 2.2 litre 4-cylinder petrol, though there was also a diesel option (a 3.2 litre Perkins four) and a 3.7 litre Buick V6.

It's interesting to note that, such was the CJ's success that they came to be made under licence all over the world. Even in Japan, the Mitsubishi L54A was basically a CJ3 Jeep, complete with 2.2 litre petrol engine. In the United Nations, Canadian-built Jeeps did service, while in Brazil and Korea variations on the CJ5 theme appeared. Spain, Portugal, Israel and South Africa also made their own, while in India, the Mahindra company started early, assembling jeep kits from 1947. Like other Western vehicles adopted by the Indians as their own – notably the Morris Oxford car and Royal Enfield Bullet motorcycle – the Mahindra Jeep went on for ever. In the 1980s, they even started to re-export it to Europe, marketed as a bargain basement 4x4, with a 2.2 litre Peugeot diesel engine.

Meanwhile, back in the States, Kaiser-Jeep's independence was short-lived, and it merged with American Motors in 1970. It began making its own V6s at the Toledo, Ohio plant the following year, and in 1974 introduced the Cherokee, a new two door 4x4, smaller than the Wagoneer, which now came only with an automatic gearbox (Jeep was the first to marry four-wheel-drive to an auto transmission). Reflecting the times, the four-

cylinder engine had been dropped, and the range started with a 4.2 litre six, with V8s of 5.0, 5.9 and 6.6 litres, though a Perkins diesel option was introduced for export markets in 1978.

Jeeps were still selling, but the AMC parent was in a poor state, which was to eventually lead to the Jeep division being sold to Chrysler, where it stays to this day.

A four-cylinder engine (2.5 litres) returned to the range in 1981, while the following year the venerable CJ could be had with V8 power for the first time. As the '1980s progressed, the hold of diesel power on 4x4s became ever stronger, at least in Europe, and the Cherokee took on the Italian VM 2.5 litre turbo four, a torquey unit which gave this compact off-roader surprisingly good performance and economy. But even in Europe, the attraction of a Jeep was still in its American feel, which meant a big petrol V8. The CJ might have become a Wrangler, and the top of the range Grand Cherokee had air conditioning, leather upholstery and walnut trim, but a Jeep was still a Jeep.

Above: 1991 Mahindra Indian Chief (left) and limited edition "General Patton" (right).

Below: 1990 Four Doors Plus Jeep Cherokee Limited

Above: 1996 Jeep Grand Cherokee

Below: 1997 Jeep Wrangler Ancestry

Jensen

Great Britain 1935–1976

Car enthusiasts Allan and Richard Jensen were relative youngsters when their father gave them a 1923 Austin Chummy.

Yet they rebuilt it as a sporting two-seater and took it to a hillclimb at Shelsley Walsh where Standard Motor Co. chief engineer Arthur Wilde was impressed enough to ask them to build him a similar body on a Standard Nine chassis.

The car was completed in 1928 which led to Allan being asked to design a production version for Avon Bodies, called the Avon Standard.

He and his brother later joined W. J. Smith and Sons, a small bodybuilding company, and scored such a success manufacturing bodies that they took over the company as Jensen Motors Ltd. in 1934.

The first car to carry the Jensen name was a 3.6-litre Ford V8-engined four-seater tourer, launched in 1935. Customers included Clark Gable.

Top: 1937 V8 3.6-litre
Left: 1939 four-door S-Type
Above: 1950 Nash-powered PW

1938 Jensen convertible with 120bhp 3.6-litre Ford V8 engine and two speed Columbia rear axle. Film star Clark Gable indulged himself with one of these glamorous sports tourers. Jensen continued to use American engines.

The four-door S-Type was added in 1935 and continued in production until 1939. The Type H, a long-wheelbase version of the S, was also made.

World War II saw Jensen building ambulances, fire engines and amphibian tank conversions, and car production resumed after the war.

The first post-war car was the large PW saloon with a Nash engine. Jensen also formed links with Austin and eventually built bodies for the 1950 Austin A40.

Expansion dictated a move to a new factory in West Bromwich in 1956 and contracts included bodies for the big Austin-Healey and Volvo P1800 sports car.

One of the most memorable Jensens was the Chrysler-powered CV8 of 1963 which offered luxury and high performance. It was offered with Ferguson four-wheel-drive two years later and anti-lock brakes by 1966.

With the Jensen brothers approaching retirement, chief engineer Kevin Beattie orchestrated the next-generation Jensen – the Touring-designed Interceptor of 1966 – also available with four-wheel-drive in FF form.

But Jensen was in serious financial trouble for several reasons. The Rootes takeover by Chrysler saw the end of Sunbeam Alpine production which robbed Jensen of the contract to build bodies for the V8-derivative, the Tiger. Jensen was also hit by the phasing out of the Austin-Healey.

After a takeover by merchant bank William Brandt in June 1968, Donald Healey and his son Geoffrey were appointed to the board which led to the Jensen-Healey being introduced in 1972. It used the Lotus-developed 16-valve slant-four, a problematical and unreliable unit.

The car never sold well. The oil crisis had also badly hit Interceptor sales.

Jensen went into receivership in September 1975, the victim of the oil crisis, labour problems and increasing U.S. legislation. The company finally closed in May 1976.

However, the name has been kept alive with Jensen Cars, set up to produce Interceptors to customers' orders with production under way by 1986 – at a mere one a month.

Top: 1956 Jensen 541 4-litre

Above: 1963 CV8 5.9-litre

Below: 1972 Interceptor III

Left: 1974 Interceptor III convertible

Below left: 1975 Jensen-Healey GT 2.0

Top: 1973 193km/h (120mph) Jensen-Healey
Above: 1976 Lotus-powered GT
Below: 1988 Series IV Interceptor

Jowett

Great Britain
1906–1953

The Bradford, Yorkshire, firm of Jowett was started by two brothers – William and Benjamin Jowett – who made vee-twin engines for other firms before building their own vehicles. Their first car was built in 1906, and their famous flat-twin engine was to be built continuously from 1910 to 1953.

Their first designs evolved into a production two-cylinder, two-seater car in 1913. The 816cc sidevalve engine (increased in size to 907cc after World War I) drove via a three-speed gearbox.

The hard-working twin-cylinder engine performed well, and proved to be extremely reliable. It was also capable of returning excellent fuel consumption figures.

Above: 1911 Jowett 8hp two-seater

An electric starter was fitted from 1923, and a four-seater (Long Four) model was introduced, followed by a saloon version in 1926. Four-wheel brakes and a detachable cylinder head formed part of the specification in 1929, in which year the firm also introduced the fabric-bodied Black Prince model.

The Jowetts of the early 1930s, including the sporting Kestrel model of 1934 and the twin-carburettor Weasel, still had twin-cylinder engines, although four-speed transmission was fitted, together with a centrifugal clutch and freewheel assembly, from 1935.

Four cylinders first appeared in a production Jowett – the Ten saloon, with a flat-four engine of 1166cc, in 1936. However, the twins continued in production, with a slightly increased capacity from 1937 – 946cc instead of the 907cc used previously. As a comparison, the 8hp, 946cc twin-cylinder units produced 17bhp at 3,250rpm, while the 10hp four-cylinder gave 31bhp at 4,000rpm.

With the intervention of World War II, both the Eight and Ten were to disappear. However, the twin-cylinder engine, in 25bhp, 1000cc form, continued in production and was fitted to the Bradford van, which became renowned for its reliability.

A new model, the very advanced Javelin saloon, was introduced in 1947. Designed by Gerald Palmer, the streamlined and roomy Javelin featured a 1486cc flat-four engine developing 50bhp (later 53bhp). Citroën-inspired torsion-bar suspension gave excellent ride and handling qualities, and performance was brisk – sufficient to give a top speed of over 80mph (128km/h).

By the early 1950s Javelins were built at the rate of around 125 per week, together with some 135 Bradford vans.

A sophisticated sports version of the Javelin – the two-seater Jupiter – was introduced in 1950, and was capable of over 90mph (145km/h). The 100mph (160km/h) glassfibre bodied R4 Jupiter was a further development.

The Javelin-based cars competed successfully in many motor sport events,

Above: 1923 Jowett 7hp 'Short Two'
Below: A Jowett Jupiter of 1953

including the Monte Carlo Rally and Le Mans 24-Hour events.

Post-war Jowett bodies were built by Briggs Motor Bodies, in Doncaster, Yorkshire. Sadly, in 1953, Briggs was obliged to stop producing the bodies following declining Jowett sales, and the famous Bradford firm finally ceased production.

Kaiser
U.S.A.
1946–1955

The Kaiser company is generally considered to be the most successful post-war attempt by an independent manufacturer to break the Detroit-based domination of the American motor industry.

The Kaiser-Frazer Corporation was launched by Henry J. Kaiser, former World War II shipbuilder, and Joseph W. Frazer, who had been involved with both Willys-Overland and Graham-Paige.

Frazer initially rented the Willow Run premises, previously used for the war-time manufacture of B24 Liberator bombers by Henry Ford. The first prototype, shown to the public in 1946, displayed features which would later be adopted by the entire industry. Unfortunately, costs prevented Kaiser-Frazer from developing them for its first production model, the Custom Sedan. Two separate lines were offered until 1951, with Kaiser standard and Frazer luxury models.

The company did well up to 1949 when the major manufacturers introduced brand-new designs with which it simply could not compete. Sales dropped and money was borrowed to keep Kaiser-Frazer afloat. This led to arguments between the founders and Frazer all but resigned.

Left: 1948 Kaiser Special four-door sedan
Above: 1951 Frazer Vagabond three-door

Below: 1954 Kaiser Special four-door

Above: 1952 two-door Henry J. Kaiser

The launch of an economy car, the Henry J., was mistimed into a market that wanted luxury. Attempts by Sears Roebuck to boost sales with its own Allstate version had failed by 1953. The dramatically styled sedan of 1951 was an inspired design, but Kaiser-Frazer was rapidly getting left behind and was still not offering a V8 engine by 1952.

In 1954 Kaiser-Frazer merged with Willys-Overland, becoming Kaiser-Willys Sales Corporation and moving to Toledo, Ohio.

A new 161 glassfibre-bodied sports model did not succeed and in 1955 the firm closed, although the design was continued in Argentina for a further seven years.

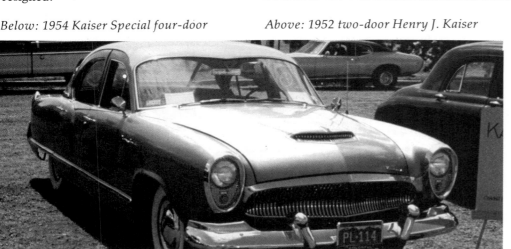

Kissel

U.S.A.
1906–1930

William and George Kissel formed the Kissel Motor Co., having built an experimental vehicle in the family agricultural factory in 1905. The name was to undergo slight changes, from Kisselkar to Kissel Kar in 1908, then became plain Kissel after World War I.

They set up production in Hartford, Wisconsin, and were joined by engineer Herman Palmer and coachbuilder J. Friedrich Werner. Commercial vehicles with Waukesha or Wisconsin engines appeared in 1908. By this time the cars were mainly powered by Kissel engines, although a V12 Weidely was tried briefly in 1917, and later Lycoming straight-eights were offered. The general emphasis was on quality.

During World War I the company built four-wheel-drive military vehicles and carried out development work on the Liberty truck. Up to that time Kissel had no sporting aspirations, although its body styles were innovative. In 1918, however,

Below: 1924 6-55 Berline   *Top: 1920 6-45 Tourster*   *Above: 1920 6-45 Speedster*

Left: 1914-20 'All-Year' KisselKar

New York dealer Conover T. Silver designed the striking Silver Special Speedster. Two years later came the Gold Bug and during the early 1920s Kissels were noted as one of the most attractive American designs, although limited in production.

Sales began to decline towards the end of the 1920s, however, leading to unsuccessful contracts for taxis, then with Archie Andrews of New Era Motors to build Ruxtons in 1930. By the end of that year the latter deal had fallen through and Kissel's only option was receivership. The company was reorganized the following year as Kissel Industries and the Hartford works was used for the production of various engine parts until 1943, when it was sold to the West Bend Aluminum Co.

Below: 1927 Kissel 8-75 Speedster.
Introduced in New York in 1919, it was
nicknamed the Gold Bug because of its
standard chrome/yellow finish, a name
that stuck for subsequent speedsters.
Power unit was a side valve 4.3-litre Six,
later enlarged to 4.7 litres.

Lada

Russia
1970 to date

Lada is the name by which the Russian Zhiguli car is know on foreign markets. The company was founded with Fiat aid in 1970. The Togliattigrad works, west of Moscow, was fitted out with most of Fiat's 124 production facility and the new factory started production of a Fiat 124-based car with a rugged Soviet-designed engine. This first car, the type 2100, also known as the Riva, was produced well into the 1990s. High demand and little competition in its home country meant that very few changes were made during the long production run.

In 1979 Lada introduced a new four-wheel-drive model, the Niva, to Western markets. The rush of small Japanese off-roaders put the Niva in the shade as far as quality was concerned. But when the going got tough, this tough little Russian left them standing. It shared the engines of the Lada Riva saloon, but used an in-house 4wd system. Amazing axle articulation gave incredible traction in impossible conditions, but on-road handling lagged a long way

behind most competitors. The car's main attraction lay in its bargain-basement price.

A more modern offering was launched in 1984. The Samara had new engines, gearbox, body and front-wheel-drive but was cursed with a dreadful interior and poor finish. It lacked much in the way of dynamic qualities, with dull performance, indifferent handling and a bouncy ride. Many buyers stuck with the old Riva.

The company made another effort at a modern car in 1996. Called the 110, it was available with a choice of engines, including a couple of 16-valve units, one a 2.0-litre, 150bhp Opel unit.

Top: 1970 Lada 1200 saloon

Below: Lada Samara five-door hatchback

Above: Late-model Lada Niva 4x4

Below: 1996 Lada Riva estate and saloon

Lagonda

Great Britain
1906 to date

American Wilbur Gunn started by building motorcycles in a small workshop at the bottom of his garden in Staines, Middlesex.

He called the operation the Lagonda Engineering Company after Lagonda Creek near his home town of Springfield, Ohio.

He then started making tricars but production stopped in 1907. A receiver was called in to wind up the company.

Meanwhile, Gunn produced a few four-wheelers, including a 10hp vee-twin and 14/ 16hp Coventry-Simplex-engined car.

A new company, Lagonda Ltd., was formed in 1913 with finance from Henry Tollemache of the brewing family and with Gunn in charge. He introduced a small Lagonda of integral construction and with a 1099cc engine. About 200 were made up to 1916.

After World War I the 1099cc Lagonda was revived and a 1420cc engine was installed in 1921.

Lagonda completely changed direction in 1926 with the new 14/60. It featured a

Below: 1913 1100cc 11.1hp convertible   *Top: 1913 11.1hp Lagonda*   *Above: 1924 12/24 Lagonda*

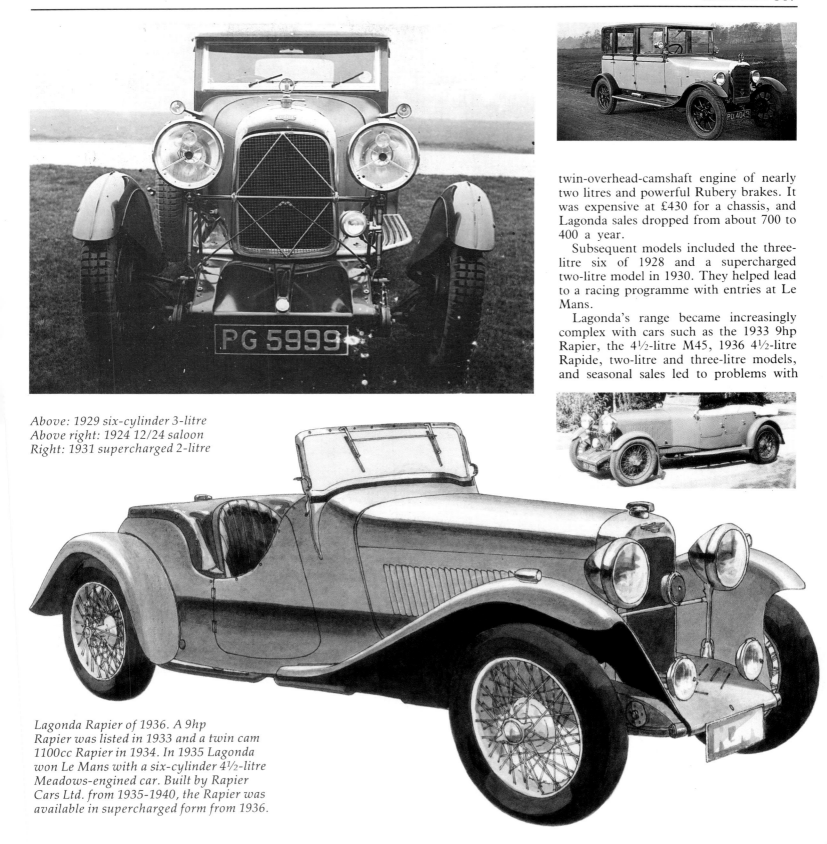

twin-overhead-camshaft engine of nearly two litres and powerful Rubery brakes. It was expensive at £430 for a chassis, and Lagonda sales dropped from about 700 to 400 a year.

Subsequent models included the three-litre six of 1928 and a supercharged two-litre model in 1930. They helped lead to a racing programme with entries at Le Mans.

Lagonda's range became increasingly complex with cars such as the 1933 9hp Rapier, the 4½-litre M45, 1936 4½-litre Rapide, two-litre and three-litre models, and seasonal sales led to problems with

Above: 1929 six-cylinder 3-litre
Above right: 1924 12/24 saloon
Right: 1931 supercharged 2-litre

Lagonda Rapier of 1936. A 9hp Rapier was listed in 1933 and a twin cam 1100cc Rapier in 1934. In 1935 Lagonda won Le Mans with a six-cylinder 4½-litre Meadows-engined car. Built by Rapier Cars Ltd. from 1935-1940, the Rapier was available in supercharged form from 1936.

cash-flow. A receiver was appointed in 1935.

The company was bought by solicitor Alan Good for £67,000, just beating Rolls-Royce. The new company was called Lagonda Motors (Staines) Ltd. and the first move was to drop the Rapier.

Lagonda's designer was W. O. Bentley and his influence was first seen in the 4½-litre LG45, a modified M45, which was later improved by fitting a Meadows engine.

Bentley and his team unveiled the 2½-litre post-war Lagonda in September 1945. It had a twin-overhead-cam six-cylinder engine and cruciform chassis. But the Lagonda company never built it.

Tractor manufacturer David Brown bought Lagonda in 1947 for £52,500 and formed Aston Martin Lagonda.

The 2½-litre Lagonda went into production in 1949 and was replaced by the three-litre, made until 1958.

There have been three revivals of the Lagonda name, the current model being the Williams Towns-designed V8 saloon, and the marque's recent history is covered in the Aston Martin section.

Above: 1936 M45 2/4 Roadster

1937 Lagonda Rapide LG45. Capable of over 160km/h (100mph), the Rapide was powered by a 4467cc six-cylinder Meadows engine originally used by Invicta cars. With cross-flow cylinder head and other modifications it developed 150bhp.

There are ambitious plans to increase production at Sant' Agata from the 350 cars per year of 1989 to 2,500 per year by 1994. Some 80 per cent of this output will be accounted for by the Jalpa replacement. Lamborghini himself returned to farming and he became a wine producer. One wine he offers is called, appropriately enough, 'Bulls' Blood'.

Above: LM002 455hp V12 off-roader

The Lamborghini Jalpa was launched in 1981 with a 3484cc V8 engine and a claimed top speed of 236km/h (147mph). This mid-engined Targa top supercar was destined for a short lifespan.

As with the Countach, the Diablo was due to have a long production run and the Lamborghini seemed stable in Chrysler's hands after it bought the company in 1987.

A year after its 1990 launch, a new model was offered alongside the standard car. The VT had four-wheel-drive, which was to put it directly into competition with Bugatti's EB110. Although grip was enhanced, it lacked the steering feel of the standard rear-wheel-drive model.

Lamborghini still had more tricks up its sleeves. In 1993, following a takeover by MegaTech in Bermuda, the Roadster was revealed. With no drop in power from the standard car's 492bhp and a negligible drop in performance, it became the fastest open-top production car in the world when it finally went into production in 1995.

1993 also marked the 30th anniversary of the creation of the company, so a special 525bhp Diablo was launched and later a new lightweight model, the SV. The 500bhp SV was widely regarded as the best driver's

Above: 1997 Diablo Roadster

Below: The fastest production convertible on earth

car in the Diablo range and was only surpassed by the rare SVR with an extra 44bhp. By 1997, the Diablo SVR was the only supercar surviving that could compete with McLaren's world-beating F1.

Above: The stripped-out SV was the ultimate Diablo evolution

Right: The four-wheel-drive Diablo VT

Below: This cutaway of the Diablo shows the mid-mounted V12 engine, whose origins date back to Lamborghini's first V12. This is the four-wheel-drive VT model

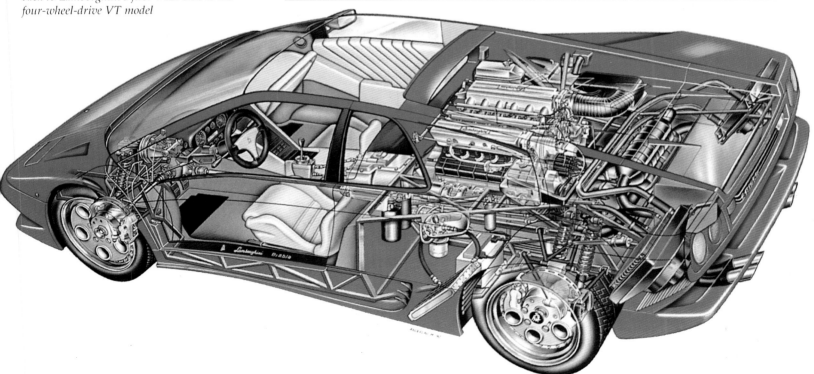

Lanchester

Great Britain 1895-1956

The first car produced by Frederick William Lanchester in 1895 was remarkable in that it was not a copy of a foreign model, nor was it an adaptation of a horse-drawn carriage, but a brilliant original design. Further prototypes followed and in late 1899 he founded the Lanchester Gas Engine Co., together with his two brothers George and Frank, who between them handled sales and publicity.

Six cars were produced by the factory in Sparkbrook, Birmingham, the year after, but cash-flow was always a problem. In 1904, just when the company was designing a new four-cylinder engine and the order books were full, it went bankrupt. George then took over the reformed Lanchester Motor Co. Ltd. from his brother Frederick, who eventually

resigned in 1913 and had no further connection with the company.

Lanchesters of that period were very distinctive, almost bonnetless with the engine mounted between the driver and

Above: 1897 8hp Lanchester two-cylinder

front-seat passenger. They also featured old-fashioned side-mounted tiller steering until 1911, when it was decided to make

Below: 1908 2470cc four-cylinder ohv three-speed 20hp Lanchester with tiller steering. The chassis design incorporated a fuel tank in its main crossmember. Good for 80km/h (50mph) it won a Gold Medal in the R.A.C.'s 1907 Vapour Emission Trials.

Above: 1902 Lanchester 8/12hp Tonneau
Below: 1908 two cylinder 12hp Lanchester

Above: 1922 40hp Sports Tourer
Below: 1923 6178cc six-cylinder Forty

Above: 1928 21hp short chassis tourer

the cars more conventional. They were extremely comfortable, and were owned by the likes of Rudyard Kipling, George Bernard Shaw and several Indian princes.

After making armoured cars during World War I, the company went into the luxury-car market with the 6.2-litre

Right: 1936 4½-litre (Vanden Plas body)
Below: 1913 38hp Torpedo Tourer
Below right: 1956 1.6-litre Sprite

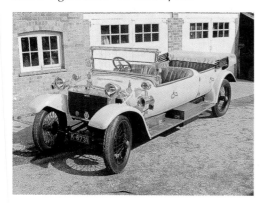

Sporting Forty, which lasted until 1929 and was given Royal patronage, but by 1931 financial troubles had struck again. The directors were forced to merge with Daimler, who wanted access to a cheaper market, and move the works to Coventry.

Frederick Lanchester continued successfully designing mechanical and electrical inventions until his death in 1946. George left the company in 1936 to join Alvis and died in 1970, ten years after his brother Frank.

Following World War II, many of the company's later cars were essentially low-price Daimlers with Lanchester radiator grilles. Two exceptions were the expensive Dauphin saloon, and an original design – the Sprite – which failed to enter production. By 1956 the once-great and respected Lanchester name had disappeared.

Lancia

Italy
1906 to date

One of Italy's oldest car manufacturers, Lancia was started in 1906. Bold and innovative, the company quickly gained a reputation for producing outstanding cars such as the 1922 Lambda and, much later, the 1972 Stratos.

Along the way the flashes of genius were tempered by some erratic performances in the field of manufacture, the terrible rust problems on the 1970s Beta range, for example, severely damaging the company's reputation.

The man behind the name was Vincenzo Lancia who was born in 1881 in Fobello, about 100 kilometres (60 miles) from Turin where his father Giuseppe based his canning business.

From an early age Vincenzo showed a mechanical aptitude and a capability for figures, so his father decided that he should study book-keeping. This led to an appointment as book-keeper for Giovanni Ceirano, importer for British Rudge bicycles.

Ceirano rented the ground floor of the Lancia family's Turin home and with engineer Aristide Faccioli had started producing his own bicycles and Welleyes car.

Young Lancia became totally absorbed in the mechanical side of the business and he had been with Ceirano for only a short period when the then recently formed F.I.A.T. made a bid for the new company.

Now 18, Vincenzo found himself appointed chief inspector for F.I.A.T. in Corso Dante and got on well with the company's secretary Giovanni Agnelli. When F.I.A.T. decided it wanted to go racing to promote its cars, Lancia was offered a drive and at Padua on 1 July 1900 he won his first race in class in a 6hp F.I.A.T. with a colleague from his Ceirano days – Felice Nazzaro – runner-up in a similar twin-cylinder model.

Regularly racing from then on, Lancia won the Coppa Florio in 1904, and finished eighth in the Gordon Bennett Cup

that year. Travelling to America for the 1905 Vanderbilt Cup races he set fastest lap and finished fourth after colliding with another car.

The following year saw him finish fifth in the first French Grand Prix, second in the Vanderbilt Cup giving F.I.A.T. a one-two, and he then went on to win the Coppa d'Oro in Milan.

Now 25 and a famous name in the

motoring world, Lancia decided to set up his own business after the 1906 racing season with fellow F.I.A.T. employee Claudio Fogolin who was to take care of sales and administration.

Their first car was ready by September 1907 – the 12hp Tipo 51 which actually

Above: 1908 Alfa 2543cc side valve
Below: 1909 Beta four-cylinder 3-litre

gave 24bhp at 1,450rpm from a 2543cc sidevalve engine.

The following year they built the six-cylinder 3815cc Dialpha. Only 23 were made, however, as the four-cylinder car was more popular and achieved 108 sales by the time production ceased in 1909.

In 1911 Lancia moved to much larger premises within Turin including room for expansion. There the 20–30hp 4080cc Delta was introduced and the overhead-cam 5030cc Eta.

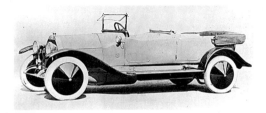

Having already displayed considerable ingenuity Lancia proved to the automotive world that there was plenty more to come. He had already patented a design for a car without a traditional chassis, his thoughts having been inspired by the hull of a ship. As well as a light and strong unit he also wanted independent front suspension. This was achieved in the shape of the 1922 2120cc V4 Lambda which was later improved with front-wheel braking and a rear-axle differential.

Above left: 1919 Kappa
Left: 1921 Dikappa produced 87bhp
Below: 1922 Trikappa 4594cc 98bhp V8

Above: 1913 Theta 4940cc

In 1918 came a 45-degree V8 and 30-degree V12 designs. The following year's V12 was tightened to a 22-degree angle allowing a one-piece cast block and featuring a single overhead camshaft. It was all very clever, but the car for which it was intended never went into production.

Below: 1913 Lancia Theta sold 1,696 examples. The 4940cc engine was already being used in Lancia IZ commercial vehicles and the unit was put to varied use during World War 1. The Theta engine was updated for use in the 1919 Kappa.

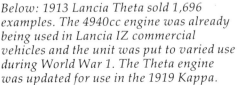

Above: 1929 3960cc V8 Dilambda Coupé

Lancia set up a factory in France which alone produced 2,500 examples. Total sales exceeded 15,000. A separate-chassis version was later produced to satisfy the coachbuilding trade and the car was made

Above: 1923 2120cc V4 Lambda
Right: 1931 2972cc V8 Astura

The car was capable of almost 112km/h (70mph), and was extremely roomy. No less than 12,530 were built in nine series during the model's 1922–31 lifespan.

Lancia then decided to tempt wealthier customers with the 1929 Dilambda with a 3960cc 24-degree V8. Built in three series up to 1932, 1,686 were made.

The Depression of the 1930s caused Lancia to look to an inexpensive model. At the 1932 Paris Motor Show he unveiled his unit-construction 18-degree 1194cc V4 Augusta. It became a best seller and

Below: The 1922 Lancia Lambda greatly enhanced Lancia's reputation, thanks to unit construction and independent pillar front suspension. The 13-degree 2120cc V4 engine was single ohc giving 49bhp at 3,250rpm.

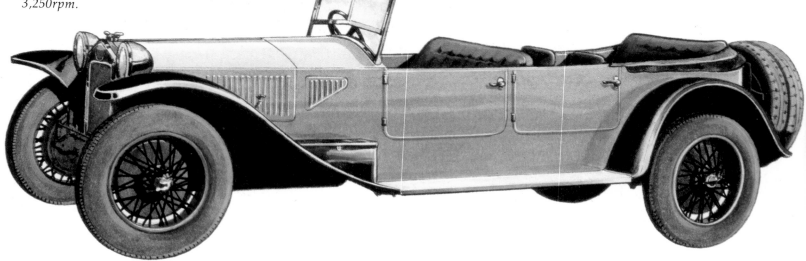

Above: 1931 Artena 1924cc V4
Right: 1933 1194cc V4 Augusta
Below: 1949 five-speed version of Ardea

until 1937 when, along with the Astura, it was phased out.

The new blade in Lancia's armoury came in the shape of the aerodynamically styled Aprilia. With a 1351cc V4 engine and low overall weight, it featured independent suspension all round and inboard rear drum brakes. Introduced to the public in 1937 it was capable of almost 128km/h (80mph) and displayed excellent roadholding for its time. Production of the new car coincided with Lancia's death in February 1937 following illness. He was 55. His wife Adèle took over as president of the company, aided by Manlio Gracco.

Arturo Lancia, a cousin of the late Vincenzo became the company's general manager in 1944, by which time the factory had moved to Bolzano following shelling of the Turin factory. After the war the Turin factory was rebuilt and Bolzano used for commercial-vehicle production.

In 1945 manufacture of the Aprilia and Ardea resumed. By 1949 23,717 Aprilias had been built. Both models were upgraded to 12-volt electrics and the Ardea received a five-speed gearbox in 1948. It was claimed to be the world's first production car so equipped. When Ardea production ceased in 1953, over 22,000 had been built.

Meanwhile a new Lancia star had emerged from the wings, the Aurelia of 1950. Masterminded by Lancia's son Gianni, who had taken command of the company in 1948, the B10 was the first production car in the world to boast a V6 engine. It also featured a Vittorio Jano-designed four-speed gearbox incorporated in the rear axle. Semi-trailing arm independent rear suspension was another world first for the unit-construction Aurelia.

Platform-chassis versions were also available for coach builders, and Pininfarina's coupé version set a trend for Gran Turismo cars featuring what was effectively a sporting car with saloon-car comfort. The GT won the 1952 Targa Florio and the GT2500 version the 1954 Monte Carlo Rally, the same year that saw the introduction of the very pretty Pininfarina Spyder version.

The V4 Appia arrived in 1953 and lasted for ten years, meanwhile Lancia was doing well in sports-car racing, moving into Formula One in 1954 with a twin-cam 260bhp V8 of 2489cc. By this time, however, Lancia was on shaky financial ground and negotiations commenced with Fiat and Ferrari. Under an agreement Lancia passed most of its D50 F1 cars to Ferrari who modified the design and won five Grands Prix in 1956.

Above: 1955 Aurelia B20 Coupé

Cement manufacturer Carlo Pesenti had taken control of Lancia in 1955. He appointed Professor Antonio Fessia as

Above: 1956 V6 Aurelia Spyder

technical head and the result was the Flaminia shown at Geneva in 1956. A luxury saloon, it was V6-powered but sold poorly and was discontinued in 1965.

Fessia had previously designed a front-wheel-drive car and pursued his conviction for this system with the Flavia, Lancia's and Italy's first front-wheel-drive car. Production of the 1500cc flat-four began in 1961 and it paved the way for Lancia's best selling Fulvia. Over 300,000 examples were sold of this small front-wheel-drive car which employed a V4 engine in various sizes starting with the

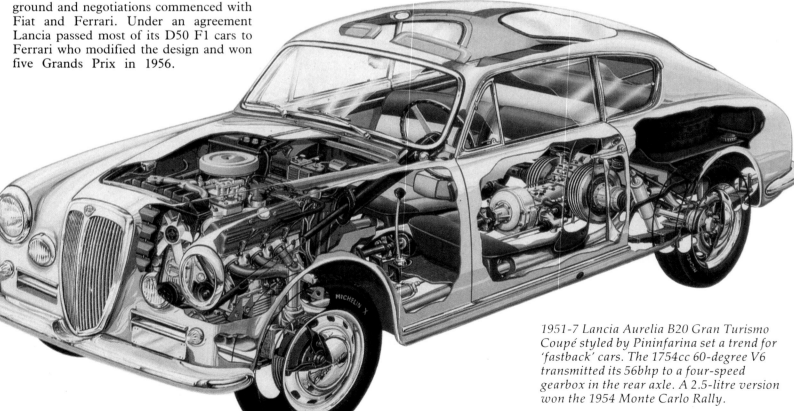

1951-7 Lancia Aurelia B20 Gran Turismo Coupé styled by Pininfarina set a trend for 'fastback' cars. The 1754cc 60-degree V6 transmitted its 56bhp to a four-speed gearbox in the rear axle. A 2.5-litre version won the 1954 Monte Carlo Rally.

Above: 1956 Flaminia Coupé 2458cc V6

1091cc unit of 1963.

A second-series coupé version was released in 1969, the year Lancia and its considerable debts were taken over by Fiat. With the Fulvia, Lancia had great success in rallying and this success was continued with the incredible-looking Stratos rally car of 1972. Styled by Bertone and powered by a 2.4-litre Ferrari Dino V6, the car won the world rally

Above: 1963 front-wheel-drive V4 Fulvia

Above right: 1971 1991cc Lancia 2000
Below right: 1972 front-wheel-drive Beta
Below: 1964 V6 Flaminia convertible

championships in 1974, 1975 and 1976.

The Beta range was introduced in 1972 powered by Fiat twin-cam four-cylinder engines of 1438cc driving the front wheels. A two-litre mid-engined version, the Beta Monte Carlo, was introduced in 1975 along with the Gamma powered by a 2484cc flat-four engine developed by Lancia.

The company's first small hatchback was the Delta of 1980. Actually made by Fiat, it was voted Car of the Year.

Two views of the 1976 four-cylinder and 2500 Gamma Coupé

Above: 1976 2-litre Monte Carlo

Below: 1976 2.5-litre Gamma saloon

1971 Lancia Fulvia Coupé 2+2. Designed by Pietro Castagnero it was first seen at the 1965 Turin Show with a 1216cc V4 power unit. A 1600cc version won the 1972 Monte Carlo Rally and World Rally championship.

Above: 1976 Lancia Stratos

Below: 1974 Stratos. With mid-mounted 1600cc HF engine, it was first shown in 1970 and produced in 1972. Later fitted with a dohc 190bhp Ferrari Dino V6 engine, it went on to claim five Monte Carlo Rally wins.

The 1995cc single-overhead-camshaft Thema replaced the Gamma in 1985. A turbocharged version and 2849cc V6 followed, resources for this car being shared between Lancia, Fiat, Saab and Alfa Romeo. Later Ferrari provided the three-litre 32-valve V8 engine for the 8.32 Thema of 1986.

In the world of hot hatchbacks none came hotter than the turbocharged HF Delta four-wheel-drive car, competition versions of which won the 1983, 1987, 1988 and 1989 world rally championships.

The tiny Y10 with Fiat's 999cc 'F.I.R.E.' engine was introduced in 1985. It is marketed in its home market as an Autobianchi.

Though part of a large conglomerate the Lancia name forges onward particularly thanks to the Delta which has taken Lancia to its seventh world rally championship, the best record of any manufacturer in this sport.

Above: 1977 Lancia Beta Coupé

Below: 1988 Delta HF 4wd Rally king

Above: 1982 Lancia Trevi 1585/1995cc

Above: 1985 999cc Y10 hatchback

Above: 1985 1049cc turbocharged Y10

Above: 1986 Lancia Prisma LX

Below: 1987 Ferrari-powered Thema 8.32

Although sales were few and far between during the recession (in fact the company had to stop exporting to Britain in 1994), Lancia survived and started to re-establish itself as Fiat's luxury car wing. The Delta gained four-wheel-drive later in life and soon proved itself to be an unbeatable rally car, in this Integrale form, with its lively turbocharged engine and fantastic grip. It was good enough to knock the Audi Quattro from the winner's podium. Initially it competed in Group B rallying with a 500bhp mid-engined version, but when Group B was banned at the end of 1986, a more conventional, front-engined car took over. The Delta Integrale, in various evolutions, completely dominated the World Rally Championship, winning it every year from 1987 to 1992.

The road version of the Delta was updated in 1993 with new smoother bodywork and engines with power outputs ranging from a 103bhp 1.6-litre to a 186bhp turbocharged 2.0-litre. A three-door version, designated HPE, was launched in 1995. Lancia never campaigned the new Delta as a rally car.

The Y10 was replaced by the stylish Y, although the Y10 continued to sell in some markets badged as an Autobianchi. The Y's clean, cropped look was very modern and adventurous, like most cars coming from the Fiat Group's design studios in the 1990s.

The Dedra, launched in 1989 to replace the Prisma of 1983, was of rather conventional design in comparison to the

Above: 1997 Lancia Y

Below: Lancia Kappa estate

Left: New Lancia Delta

Below: Lancia Dedra Station Wagon

rest of Lancia's late-1990s range. A simple three-box saloon, it was still a relatively successful seller.

The innovative Kappa saloon, which was first revealed to the public in 1994, was joined in 1996 by an estate version and a stunning two-door coupé. The Coupé's crisp styling bore a resemblance to the pretty, but ill-fated Lancia Gamma of the 1970s.

Z was Lancia's version of the PSA/Fiat MPV people carrier.

Top left: Lancia Kappa saloon

Above: Lancia Z

Left: Lancia Dedra saloon

Below: Lancia Kappa Coupé

Laurin-Klement/ Skoda

Czechoslovakia 1906 to date

Skoda, Czechoslovakia's best-known motor manufacturer, began life very humbly in the early 1890s when Vaclav Klement left his bookshop and joined mechanic Vaclav Laurin to form a bicycle-repair business in Mlada Boleslav in norther Czechoslovakia (then part of the Austro-Hungarian Empire). In 1898 they began to produce what is acknowledged to be the world's first true motor-cycle, and in 1905 unveiled their first motor car, the Model A Voiturette. It had a four-stroke twin-cylinder engine developing 7hp, a three-speed gearbox with reverse and a top speed of 48km/h (30mph).

During the following years new models were introduced including the Ds and Es with four-cylinder engines, the type B-2 motor cab and, finally, what was probably their greatest pre-World War I model, the Type FF with a 4854cc eight-cylinder engine developing 40bhp.

The company also built buses and lorries, had outlets worldwide, and gained many racing and rallying successes under the leadership of Otto Hyeronymus, an outstanding designer and experienced racing driver who joined the company in 1908.

In 1925 Laurin and Klement were taken over by Akciova Spolecnot, a manufacturer of heavy machinery and armaments, and all future cars carried the Skoda name and emblem. From 1924 to 1930 Skoda had been building Hispano-Suiza cars under licence but it was in 1928 that the first new models rolled off the production line with four-, six- and eight-cylinder engines ranging in capacity from 1944cc to 3880cc. One of the best-selling cars of this era was the Type 420 launched in 1933, with rear swing half-axles and a centre tubular chassis – a design which was to be used over the next 30 years.

The following year the 420 was given a face-lift to produce the very successful Popular, Skoda's first small family car,

Above: 1906 Type B Laurin-Klement   Below: 1907 Type F Landau Laurin-Klement

Right: Skoda factory in 1930
Below: 1929 Type 422 Skoda

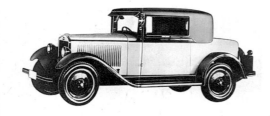

with a 903cc (later 995cc) engine developing 18bhp, and whose worldwide sales established Skoda in the international market. The other popular cars of the time were the 1165cc (later 1380cc) Rapid and the six-cylinder 2941cc Superb. During this period Skoda kept up its interest in rallying, performing well in several long-distance events including the Monte Carlo Rally.

An important change occurred in 1938 when overhead-valve engines were developed for the Popular (1089cc), the Rapid (1558cc) and the Superb (3140cc), and during this period Skoda reached its highest pre-war production figure of 6,371 cars a year.

In 1952 the Skoda 1200 was launched as a roomy four-door saloon with a 1221cc engine, followed some three years later by the similarly-powered Octavia and Felicia. From 1964 onwards, following the building of a huge new works, Skoda

Below: 1982 Skoda 120 Rapid Coupé with rear mounted 1174cc four-speed engine unit, rack and pinion steering, independent suspension, servo assisted front disc brakes, alloy wheels, halogen headlamps, front air dam and rear spoiler.

Top: 1965 Skoda Kombi Estate
Above: 1969 1000 MB De Luxe Mk II
Above left: 1950 1089cc roadster

concentrated mainly on rear-engined cars, the first being the 1000 MB (MB for Mlada Boleslav) a chassisless monocoque design with a 988cc 40bhp engine, followed by the 1100 MB with the slightly larger 1107cc engine.

Production continued through the 1970s with the S100, 110, and 120 rear-engined models of 988cc to 1147cc capacities, with the Estelle series becoming firm favourites as well as being among the cheapest cars in western Europe. The Estelle is still in production in 1989, although Skoda did finally enter the front-wheel-drive market with its long-awaited Favorit, launched in 1988 with a 1289cc all-aluminium engine and compact Bertone-designed body, thus gradually bringing to an end the 40-year reign of the rear-engined Skodas.

Below: 1977 Skoda Super Estelle 120L

Right: 1987 Skoda 130GL 1289cc

Below: 1984 Skoda 105GL four-door saloon with 1046cc ohv four-cylinder rear-mounted engine.

Above: Cabriolet Rapid introduced 1984

Below: 1989 fwd Favorit 1.3 GLX

With the introduction of the new Favorit, things looked set to change at Skoda. It was a radical departure from previous cars, distinctly more modern and consequently attracting new buyers. It also drew the attention of Volkswagen. In the early 1990s. Volkswagen bought Skoda and set about further improving the company's dowdy, downmarket image as well as bringing build quality up to Volkswagen standards.

In 1994, Volkswagen updated the Bertone styling, renaming the car Felicia. It was a westernized Skoda, with smoother, more modern lines, better build quality; somehow it was just a little bit more of a Volkswagen. The Felicia was the car that really showed the world that Skoda could make good and competitive cars, and was a completely different company to the one which had for so long been the butt of so many jokes.

To broaden the range, Skoda launched the Octavia in 1996. The name was old but the car was all new. It was available with 1.6-, 1.8- or 1.9-litre diesel engines. The base engine came from the Felicia, the more powerful 1.6 and 1.9 diesel from Volkswagen, and the 1.8 was an all-new 20-valve design, pushing out 125bhp.

Volkswagen's help was invaluable to Skoda, and the company's image had come a long way by the late 1990s, but there was still a way to go before the company could really compete with western European companies.

Above: The Felicia showed what Skoda could do with Volkswagen's help

Below: 1997 Skoda Octavia

Above: The Octavia had VW family styling

Below: Felicia Estate was a useful load carrier

Lea-Francis

Great Britain
1904 to date

Though often seen by enthusiasts as a marque that embodies the best of British sporting tradition, the fact is that Lea-Francis never set out to be a company that anything at all to do with motor racing.

Instead, their story is one of haphazardly flitting between ideas, some bad and some good, and their successes never seemed to be any more part of a premeditated plan than their failures.

R. H. Lea and G. J. Francis were both involved in the bicycle industry when they started the firm in 1895 in Coventry. And indeed bicycles were their first products. Motor-cycles also came from the company a little later, and were to continue for some time – in fact, considerably after World War I. However, they produced a car in 1904 which did not meet with a terribly enthusiastic reception, and was discontinued after only two years, only two ever sold.

In 1922, though, they returned to four wheels, and though interest was still not exactly fanatical, they persevered. Links were forged with the Vulcan company, an established car maker of the time, and after a few false starts with odd or otherwise unpalatable models, they acquired the rights to use the comparatively powerful Meadows engine in their rather lumpy cars.

However, as they gained confidence the firm tried the 1500cc Meadows powerplant in its 'Ten' model, and the combination of a light chassis and a sporting engine gave it performance well beyond the reach of most of its rivals. In the 1924 R.A.C. Six Days Small Car Trials, held in Wales, it out-climbed everything and a motor sport reputation was born.

The Meadows engine proved tuneable and reliable, and although it was used by other British sports-car makers it still remained part and parcel of the Lea-Francis legend. And it set the tone for their future products, too. Though staid

Above: The Vulcan-built LFS 14/40
Below: The 1928 'Brooklands' model

Below: A 1925 Lea-Francis four-seater

saloons were still available, the sportier end of the firm's range soon sprouted such innovatory stuff as centre-lock wire wheels, front-wheel brakes and eventually supercharging, which added another dimension to the potency of the product and made the 'Hyper' model one of the most sought-after sporting cars of the late 1920s, with many racing wins to its credit.

Abortive experiments with in-house

Below: The Hyper Sports S-Type was one of the company's finest products, bringing many competition successes and much publicity to the Lea-Francis name. Everything, in fact, but profit.

Above: 1939 Avon-bodied coupé
Below: One of the last, a 1952 saloon

Above: The 1929 TT Hyper

six-cylinder powerplants followed, which lasted several years before a useful engine, the so-called 'Ace of Spades', was developed and by 1930 the new engine was installed in a car and shown to the public. Unfortunately, despite the success of the marque in competition the company's misguided attempts to produce a luxury saloon had sent its finances spiralling downwards and it went into receivership the very same year. The company closed in 1935.

Two years later it returned, only to be confronted by the war, which resulted in crippling purchase tax, a terrible shortage of materials and threatening exhortations to export or else – not the ideal situation for a home-market-based company.

A lingering death was the inevitable result. By 1953 Lea-Francis had disappeared from the Motor Show, and by 1958 had even closed its service station. In 1960 the strangely styled Lynx, a Ford-engined effort, was launched unsuccessfully, and after a few oddities like bubble-cars and agricultural equipment, the company went down for the second time.

It reappeared in 1980 with little success, and has recently tried another expensive luxury car.

Below: The Jaguar-based 1980 version

Lexus

Japan
1988 to date

In 1988 and in order to break into the luxury car market, especially in the United States, Toyota created a new brand; the new company was called Lexus. The Lexus range was limited but the cars were loaded with almost every conceivable extra.

The mainstay of the range was the LS400. A large, five-seater saloon, the LS400 had smart, though slightly bland looks. In order to ensure good U.S. sales, a large (by Japanese or European standards) capacity V8 engine was used. Displacing nearly 4.0 litres and with two overhead camshafts per bank, the new all-alloy engine gave a healthy 264bhp by the late 1990s. Japanese build, quality and reliability, allied to transatlantic styling and without a recognizably Japanese brand name meant it was a great success,

especially in the States. It was also available in two-door coupé form.

To follow up on its success in America, Toyota created another Lexus designed for American tastes. The SC300 and SC400 coupé were launched in 1991. With either

Above: 1996 Lexus LS400

Below: Lexus GS300 Sport

the Lincoln version, the Navigator, was about the most luxurious 4x4 on the market. It arrived a yeat later than the Mercury model and was launched in 1997.

Above: 1997 Lincoln Navigator

Below: The 1997 Lincoln Town Car

Locomobile

U.S.A. 1899–1929

The Locomobile Company of America began life in Westboro, Massachusetts. The partners, A. L. Barber and J. B. Walker, produced their first vehicle in 1899, after buying the rights to the Stanley brothers' steam-powered designs. Shortly after this Walker left to start Mobile and Barber continued with Locomobile, moving to Bridgeport, Connecticut, in 1900. The two marques were remarkably similar in mechanics, differing only in bodywork.

The first model was also sold in England at this time by W. M. Letts, with some success. The following year A. L. Riker joined Locomobile as vice-president and chief engineer. Riker had begun with electric cars before producing petrol-engined Panhard-type designs. It was these Barber chose to replace his steam-driven vehicles, selling the old patents back to the Stanleys.

By 1905 the company were producing Mercedes-style cars aimed at the luxury market, and were also involved with racing. In 1908 George Robertson won the Vanderbilt Cup with a two-year-old Locomobile 'Old 16'. Five years later the company took the touring-car section of the Glidden Tour. Its most famous

Top: 1901 6hp Steamer twin cylinder
Right: 1916 six-cylinder Speedster
Below: 1900 Steam buggy
Below centre: 1901 Steam buggy
Far right: 1899-1903 Steamer Runabouts

road-going car was the 48, introduced in 1911, which was to last until 1929.

During World War I Locomobile made tank engines, staff cars and trucks. Locomobile had been producing commercials since 1912, which were badged as Rikers from 1916 until 1921 when they were phased out.

Financial problems led to the company joining the Emlen Hare's Motor Group in 1920, along with Crane-Simplex and Mercer. Two years later Locomobile's losses were running level with its assets and it was acquired by the William C. Durant empire, mainly to produce Flint cars.

Durant attempted to widen Locomobile's appeal with the cheaper Junior 8 range of 1925 which brought an increase in sales. It also lowered the tone of the marque which was unable to survive the onset of the Depression, closing in 1929.

Top: Post 1915 Model 48 Sportif
Above: c. 1915 Model 48 Gunboat Roadster

Below: 1925 Junior Eight with 3.25-litre overhead valve engine outsold larger models by eight to one, but against opposition such as Chrysler and General Motors it was expensive. The Depression finished the company.

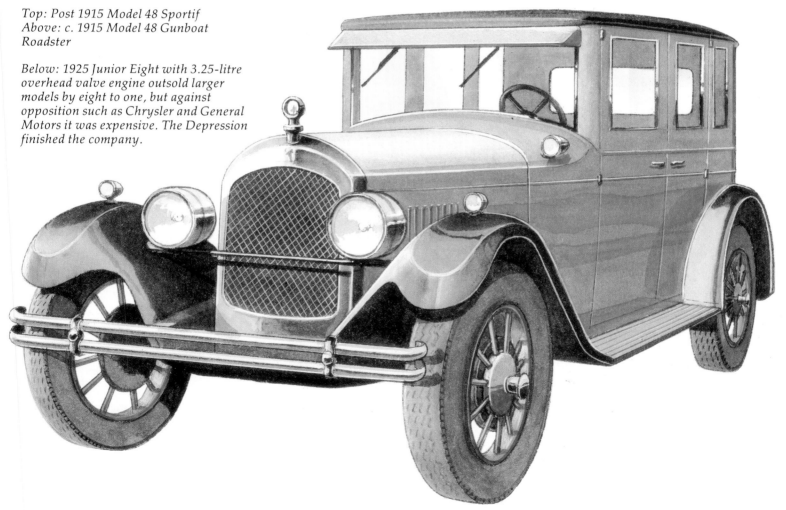

Lotus

Great Britain
1952 to date

The famous Lotus name stemmed from one man and his love of cars.

Anthony Colin Bruce Chapman was born in Richmond, Surrey, in 1928 and his first car was a 1937 Morris Eight Tourer – a Christmas gift from his parents in 1945.

He started making some extra pocket-money by buying and selling cars. But petrol rationing hit his business hard and in 1947 he decided to build a special based on a 1930 Austin Seven fabric-bodied saloon. It was completed in a lockup garage early in 1948 and used successfully in trials.

After finishing his national service with the R.A.F., Chapman worked as a constructional engineer with a London-based steel-erecting company, and later joined the British Aluminium Company as

a development engineer.

Work started on the Mark 3 in January 1951. Chapman built one for himself and two for the brothers Michael and Nigel Allen, moving to their workshop in Wood Green, north London.

He was asked to build a Mark 4 and went into partnership with Michael Allen

Above: Colin Chapman and Lotus 7

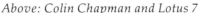

to form the Lotus Engineering Co. on 1 January 1952, moving into an old stable at Hornsey, north London. The Mark 4 was highly significant for the company – it was the first Lotus with a purpose-built spaceframe chassis (as opposed to a modified Austin frame) and it was designed for road use as well as competition.

The Mark 5 was never built but its basic design was used for the Mark 6 which had a Ford Consul engine.

The company became Lotus Engineer-

Below: Colin Chapman and 1957 Elite

Below: 1966 Lotus Ford Cortina

ing in February 1952. Allen left and Chapman's girlfriend Hazel Williams became the other director. She lent the company £25 – its total working capital. Chapman was still working for British Aluminium yet managed to make one car a fortnight.

There was to be no Mark 7 as such – although this designation was, of course, later allocated to a much more famous car – and work began on the Mark 8 in January 1954. Chapman married Hazel the following October and the next year, 1956, exhibited at the Motor Show for the first time.

Lotus's racing department was set up in 1957, by which time Chapman had gained a good reputation with Grand Prix teams such as B.R.M. and Vanwall for whom he designed suspension and chassis.

He launched the Lotus 7 at the October

1957 Motor Show and it was made by an offshoot company, Lotus Components Ltd. The car was mainly offered in kit-form to take advantage of British tax exemptions.

It was the success of the 7 which really established the Lotus name and Chapman moved to larger premises at Cheshunt, Hertfordshire, in June 1959, becoming Lotus Cars Ltd. and Lotus Components Ltd.

Most of his cars were for racing and the Mark 9, with a Coventry-Climax engine, made Lotus's Le Mans debut. The first Lotus single-seater came in 1957 – the Lotus 12 for Formula 2 events – and the 16 was the first Formula 1 car.

Stirling Moss took Lotus to its first Grand Prix win in 1960 in Rob Walker's privately entered Climax-engined 18. It was to be followed by many world-class wins.

Above left: 1951 Lotus Mk 3

Below: 1958 Lotus Mk 16

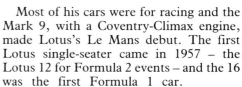

1958 Lotus 7, a spartan two-seater which made the marque into a legend. Versions included the F-model with 1172cc 36bhp Ford four-cylinder engine. The A-model accepted B.M.C.'s A-series four-cylinder unit.

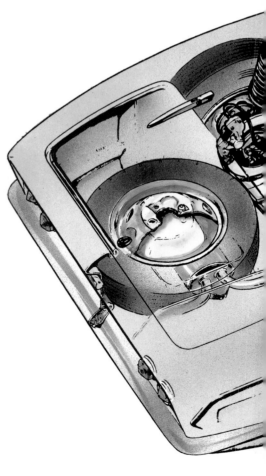

Left: 1968 Lotus Elan S4
Below left: 1973 Elan Coupé

Below: Series 2 Lotus Elan. Introduced in 1962, the Elan featured a 1558cc twin cam version of the Ford Classic engine. A top speed of 181km/h (113mph) was improved to 196km/h (122mph) with the 1971 126bhp big valve Sprint version.

Meanwhile, Chapman continued with his road cars and about 1,000 glassfibre Elites had been built by March 1964. The famous Elan was introduced in 1962, using a Ford-based twin-cam engine, and it was later joined by a fixed-head coupé, a Plus 2 version and then the powerful Sprint.

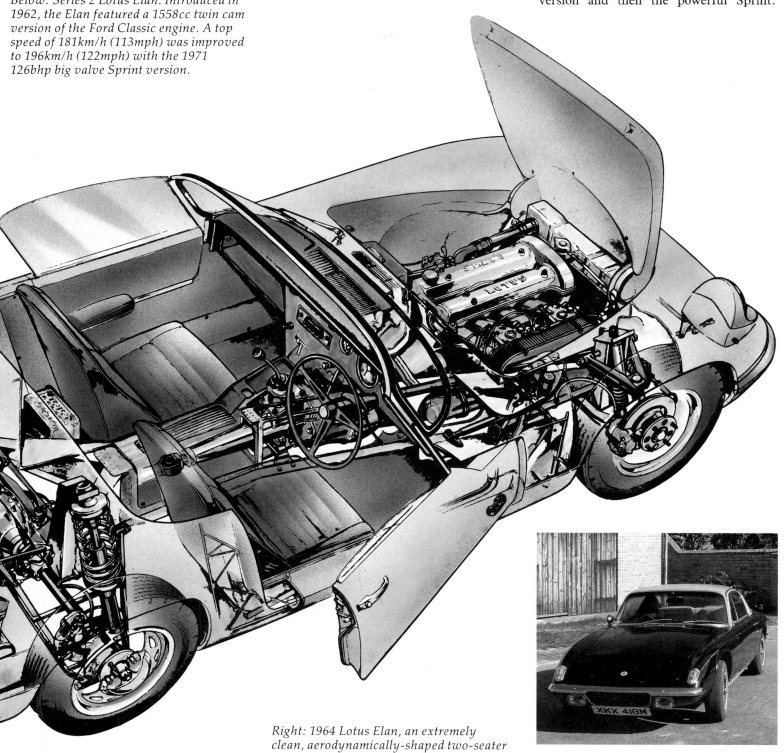

Right: 1964 Lotus Elan, an extremely clean, aerodynamically-shaped two-seater

The mid-engined Europa came in 1966 and, with its cars becoming more sophisticated, Lotus moved to a large factory at Hethel, near Norwich, and even began building its own engines.

Lotus became a public company in October 1968 with most of the ordinary shares remaining with the Chapman family, and from January 1969 Group Lotus Car Companies Ltd. was the holding company for the subsidiaries such as Lotus Cars and Lotus Components.

Left: 1972 Elan Sprint

Above: 1971 Elan +2   *Below: 1971 Europa*

The company became profitable again after a sticky period and over 4,500 cars were produced in 1969 plus about 3,000 7s, most of which were sold as kits.

The company began producing upmarket sports cars in 1974 and the public was offered the new Elite and, later, the front-engined Eclat. The stylish mid-engined Esprit was launched in 1976, first with a normally aspirated engine, and later with a turbocharged unit that could propel this tractable road car to 160mph (257 km/h). Lotus also supplied slant-four engines for the Jensen-Healey between 1972 and 1976.

Top right: 1962 Type 25
Right: 1967 Lotus 49 V8, 2993cc
Below right: 1969 Lotus 63 V8
Bottom right: 1970 Type 72 Formula 1

Below: 1974 Elite 2+2

Lotus Excel. Based on the Eclat model, the Excel was introduced in October 1982 with 2+2 fastback styling and powered by a 2172cc dohc four-cylinder front-mounted engine with a five-speed gearbox and rear-wheel drive.

Above: Lotus Eclat, launched 1975

Below: Esprit turbo, launched 1980

Below: Lotus Esprit, launched in 1975 with GRP body, 1973cc four-cylinder mid-mounted engine and disc brakes all round. The S2 was introduced in 1978, the 2174cc Turbo in 1980, the S3 in 1981, the Turbo HC in 1986, and a restyled version in 1987.

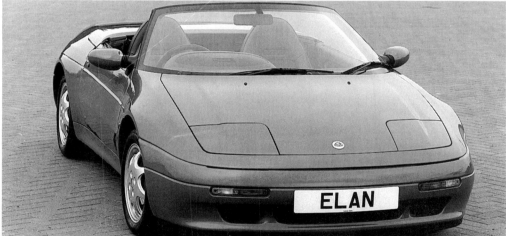

Colin Chapman died of a heart attack in December 1982 and the following year British Car Auctions bought part of the company, which was again near bankruptcy. Group Lotus was acquired by General Motors late in 1985.

Today, it continues with its own identity, producing cars such as the Excel, the all-new Elan, Esprit and stunning Esprit Turbo and conducting research into exciting new areas of vehicle design such as computer-controlled active suspension systems.

Left: 1990 Lotus Elan SE
Below: 1984 JPS Lotus 95T Formula One race car

The 1990s turned out to be an important decade for Lotus. Following a failed management buyout attempt early in the decade, the Hethel-based company, was bought in 1993 by the mysteriously wealthy Bugatti Automobili, whose chairman Romano Artioli, sold Lotuses in Italy. The company also took 200 or so unbuilt Elans, which it started to assemble and sell as the Elan S2.

Following the collapse of the Bugatti empire, Lotus was again rescued, this time by Malaysian company Proton, in 1996.

The Esprit was continually developed, or at least repackaged to keep with the times, but was perhaps the company's greatest car since the original Elan was launched in 1996.

The Elise used a 1.8-litre K-series Rover engine as used in the MGF. As in the MG it was also mid-mounted, but there the similarity ended. As with any new Lotus, it had to set new levels of handling and

Above: 1996 Lotus Elise

Below: 1997 Lotus Esprit GT3

roadholding – a job it did admirably.

With its unconventional bonded alloy chassis and finely-tuned suspension, it was praised the world over by the motoring press and was often described as the finest-handling car in the world. Despite the fact that it used only the 120bhp MGF 1.8i unit it was considerably faster than even the 143bhp MGF, due largely to its impressively light weight.

The Esprit had carried on with four-cylinder engines since its launch. It wasn't until 1997 that Lotus built its own new engine, the first since the 1970s. The new 3.5-litre V8 had a flat-plane crankshaft, common in racing engines, but almost unique in a road car. Twin turbos boosted the maximum power output to 354bhp, more than 100bhp more than the most powerful four-cylinder unit. The only drawback to the engine was that its unusual crankshaft made it sound like two four-cylinder units rather than a sporty, burbling V8. It gave the Esprit extra life to take it comfortably into the next century.

Rumours soon followed of a V8-engined Elise coupé. A car meeting this description, called the GT1, entered Le Mans in 1997.

Above right: The Lotus Esprit Sport 300 was top of the Esprit tree before the V8 arrived and was launched at the 1992 Birmingham Motor Show

Right: The GT1 used the Esprit's V8 engine in an Elise-style carbonfibre body. It competed in the Le Mans 24 Hours in 1997 but dropped out before the end

Left and below: The Esprit V8 was launched in 1996 at the Geneva Motor Show. The V8 with flat-plane crankshaft and twin turbos was Lotus' first new in-house engine since the 1970s. Power output was over 350bhp at 6,500rpm, giving a top speed of over 170mph (274km/h) and a 0-60mph (0-100km/h) time of under 4.5 seconds

Marcos

Great Britain 1959 to date

Jem Marsh and Frank Costin were the men behind Marcos and the marque was derived from their surnames.

Marsh worked in Firestone's technical department while Costin had a technical career in the aviation industry.

In 1959 Marsh founded Speedex Castings and Accessories Ltd. in Luton, Bedfordshire, to supply glassfibre shells and mechanical components to specials builders.

Costin used his knowledge of aerodynamics and skill of working with plywood to design a lightweight, high-performance two-seater car with integral body and marine ply chassis.

It had Triumph Herald front suspension and Nash Metropolitan rear.

The car was built by Marsh, who raced it successfully, and it was soon available to customers as a Marcos.

Marcos Cars Ltd. was formed in 1962 to sell the cars as kits and the following year the company moved to Bradford-on-Avon, Wiltshire.

The Marcos G.T. went on sale in 1964 with a Volvo 1800 engine, quickly followed by the 1600 G.T. with a 1.6-litre Ford engine.

The popular coupé was available later with the two-litre V4 Ford engine and the three-litre V6, eventually with a steel chassis.

The company began moving to larger premises in Westbury, Wiltshire, in 1970, and produced the four-seater Mantis. This was not a great success and only 32 were made.

Production stopped in 1972, along with the G.T., a year after the company had been sold to racing-team proprietor Rob Walker.

However, Marcos continued to build the Mini-Marcos – launched in 1965 – which used B.M.C. Mini mechanical components.

The Mini-Marcos was taken over in 1975 by D. and H. Fibreglass Techniques Ltd., of Oldham, Lancashire, and revised to become the Midas in 1978.

The company became Midas Cars and moved to Corby, Northamptonshire, in 1981 and the Metro-based Midas Gold was launched in July 1985. A fire in March 1989 destroyed Midas's production facilities, and consequent cash-flow difficulties led the company into liquidation – but hopeful of a buyer – by the end of the year.

Jem Marsh formed Jem Marsh Performance Cars at the old works in Westbury and put the Marcos G.T. back into production in 1981. By 1986 production was running at about two a week.

The latest models use Ford engines and, in the Marcos Mantula, the 3.5-litre Rover V8 unit.

Above right: 1960 Marcos GT
Right: Spyder convertibles and coupé

Top and above: The Mantula Spyder V8

Below: 1969 3-litre Marcos with V6 Ford power unit. The glassfibre body was mounted on a wood chassis. This lightweight low-slung 125bhp sports car could top 193km/h (125mph).

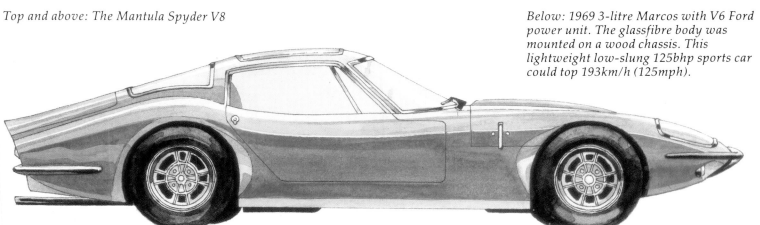

Marmon

U.S.A.
1902–1933

Howard Carpenter Marmon began producing vehicles from the family milling-machinery firm Nordyke and Marmon Co. in Indianapolis. His first car was an advanced air-cooled vee-twin developed over four years to 1902. This was not offered for sale, Marmon working instead on a four-cylinder version which appeared two years later.

Marmon stuck with V4 engines until 1908, when he went over to in-line units for ease of quantity manufacture, although he had experimented with a V6 and showed a very expensive but unsuccessful V8 at the New York Motor Show. By 1910 the Model 32 was in production, its slow start suddenly boosted by Ray Harroun's victory in the first Indianapolis 500 the following year, during Marmon's most successful competition period.

This was followed by the Model 34 in 1916, the work of two men who joined Marmon three years earlier, Frederick E. Moskovics and Alanson P. Brush. This vehicle was mainly constructed from aluminium until the outbreak of World

Above: 1911 Marmon six-cylinder
Left: 1920 Marmon Phaeton
Below: 1921 Model 34 Tourer

War I, but reappeared in 1919 with a cast-iron engine and higher price tag, although this was cut back in the early 1920s.

By 1924 the company's fortunes were failing and George M. Williams was taken on to reverse the trend, which he did by concentrating on low-cost closed models. The Marmon Motor Co. was set up in

1926, separate from the parent company, but the change in direction caused Howard Marmon to opt for semi-retirement and Barney Roos took over. Sales increased.

The Roosevelt range, offered separately from Marmon until 1930, did well until the onset of the Depression. In 1931 Howard Marmon returned plans for the Sixteen, a luxury Cadillac rival designed by Walter Darwin Teague Jr., but production delays proved fatal. In 1933 Howard Marmon personally financed a Teague-styled advanced two-door sedan design, but this failed to get off the ground. Marmon called in the receivers and the company was taken over by the American Automotive Corporation that year.

Above left: 1929 Marmon Roosevelt 3.3
Above: 1930 Marmon straight eight
Below: 1931 Marmon V16

Marmon V16 of 1931. The Model Sixteen featured an aluminium 8046cc three-speed power unit. This classic engine was Marmon's only offering for 1933. When first introduced the V16 gave 200bhp at 3400rpm.

Maserati

Italy
1926 to date

The name Maserati conjures up the same image as that evoked by Ferrari. Thoroughbred motoring in the true tradition of Italian exotica.

Though never quite in the same league as Ferrari, Maserati has nevertheless been instrumental in giving Italy its reputation for high-performance four-wheeled stallions, race-track success and motoring exclusivity.

Taking their Trident motif from the statue of Neptune in Bologna, Maserati brothers Alfieri, Bindo, Ettore, Ernesto and Mario were involved in racing cars and motor-cycles and started production of their own 1.5-litre cars in 1926, the year Alfieri had a class win in the Targa Florio.

Alfieri had been undertaking development of a racing car for Diatto of Turin. When Diatto closed down, spark plug manufacturer Alfieri of Bologna took over the straight-eight design.

The family built up a reputation for racing machinery including a V16, and in the 1930s began to look more seriously at road cars, though making very few.

Above: Nuvolari in 1934 8CM3000

Above: 1938 Maserati 8CTF

Below: 1947 1500cc A6 Spyder

Below: 1925 Diatto Tipo 20. The Maserati brothers built this 2-litre Grand Prix for Diatto of Turin before setting up in business for themselves. Sleeving the Diatto down to 1.5 litres, they won the 1926 Targa Florio.

Above: 1953/4 250F straight six Grand Prix car

In 1932 Alfieri died following a racing accident. A sixth brother, Carlo, had died in 1910, so Bindo, Ettore and Ernesto carried on the business, Mario having chosen art as his career. A seventh brother died as a child..

In 1937 industrialist Adolfo Orsi purchased a controlling interest in the company which moved to Modena the following year. By 1947 it had revealed its first true (though limited) production road car, the A6-1500 with bodywork by Pininfarina.

The brothers Maserati had signed a ten-year consultancy contract with Orsi and when this expired they decided to leave, returning to Bologna to found OSCA sports cars.

Orsi and his son Omer found a winning talent in the shape of Gioacchino Colombo who had worked with Alfa Romeo and Ferrari. Colombo helped design the Maserati 250F in 1953. This Formula One car was regarded as one of the finest racing machines of the 1950s. Many famous drivers including Stirling Moss, Mike Hawthorn and Juan Fangio enjoyed considerable success with it, Fangio winning the 1957 world title in one.

That year sealed Fangio's fifth world title (and saw the introduction of the 3500GT, an indication that Maserati was growing more serious about road cars), but many Maserati drivers were involved in serious accidents and the factory was experiencing financial troubles. So the company decided to withdraw from racing

Top: 1954 A6G Allemano

Above: 1959 2000cc 'Birdcage' Tipo 60

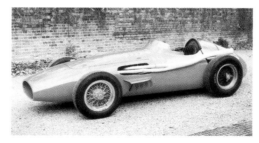

Above: 1956 twin cam 250F F1 racer

Above: 1960s 3500GT, first seen 1957

Above: 1964 Quattro Porte

Above: Mistral Coupé

and concentrate on high-performance road cars.

It found that it could not totally divorce the name from racing, however, and won the 1960 and 1961 Nürburgring 1000km race with the Maserati 'Birdcage', so called because the chassis frame was made of many lengths of small-diameter tube.

The Maserati V12 three-litre engine also powered Cooper to Grands Prix wins in 1966 and 1967.

In 1969 Orsi sold control of Maserati to Citroën of France. Citroën wanted an engine development company to work on its SM project. The result was an extremely sophisticated car with a V6 Maserati power unit.

Orsi relinquished all interest in 1971 after an argument with Citroën over policy.

In the mid-1970s luxury-car manufacturers were going through a lean time and sales of the SM were way below expectations. Citroën tried to find a buyer for Maserati, but no one was interested, so in May 1975 it was announced that the Modena factory would have to be put into voluntary liquidation.

This announcement was designed to force some interest. The result was that the company was taken over by Alejandro de Tomaso and the Italian government agency GEPI as major stockholder.

Above: 1966 Quattro Porte   *Below: 1966 Mexico V8*

Right: 1966/7 Maserati 300S
Below right: 1966 V8 Ghibli

Left: The 8C-1100 of 1931 won its class in the Mille Miglia in 1931 and 1932. Its 1078cc engine had a Roots supercharger providing a maximum speed of 185km/h (115mph).

Above: 1970 Ghibli Spyder Ghia
Right: 1968 4.7 Ghibli Spyder

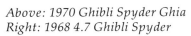

Above: 1969 V8 Indy
Left: 1971 V8 Bora
Below: 1972 line-up. From left: Bora,
Indy, Ghibli, Mexico

De Tomaso was put in charge of running the factory and for 1976 Aurelio Bertocchi was appointed general manager. Ing. (engineer) Casarini as head of design and Omer Orsi later rejoined as commercial director, but only until 1977 when he resigned.

In 1982 Maserati produced a profit, and students of the marque argue that this was probably the first time in Maserati history it had done so. That year the company produced 2,265 cars, almost five times the previous year's production, but by 1990 its future as an independent car maker looked increasingly uncertain.

Above: 1971 Maserati Bora
Right: 1980 V8 Kyalami Coupé
Far right top: 1972 V6 Citroën Maserati
Far right bottom: 1980 V8 Khamsin 2+2

Below: 1974 Maserati Merak SS with mid-mounted V6 of 2965cc. This compact cracker was dropped in 1984 when the range was 'rationalized'. Before then a 1999cc version was available. The Merak was first seen at the 1972 Paris Salon.

Above: Convertible version of the 1982 1996cc V6 Biturbo (twin turbo) giving 180bhp. Hardly striking, it has been a sales success. As a follow-up Maserati unveiled the Biturbo 430 four-door saloon with a 250bhp 2.8-litre V6 capable of 240km/h (150mph) in 1989.

Right: Front-engined Biturbo
Far right: 1989 2.5 Spyder Biturbo
Below: 2-litre Biturbo Coupé

Somehow, Maserati struggled on into the 1990s and was eventually rescued by the Fiat group. Fiat bought the company in 1993 when Alejandro De Tomaso was forced to sell his 51 per cent due to illness. By then, the existing range was looking very dated.

The first model to be modernized was the Biturbo. Reborn as the Ghibli, it remained essentially the same under the skin, but the body was all new, with much fresher styling and the build quality was greatly improved.

A new Quattroporte soon followed, the famous name being revived in a stylish new four-door saloon with the same V6 engine as the Ghibli. A new 4.2-litre V8 model followed in 1995.

Left: The Maserati Biturbo convertible was beginning to look dated by the 1990s

Below: The 1997 Maserati Ghibli Cup. Sharp styling, improved build quality, and a powerful engine helped increase sales of the new two-door Maserati coupé

1920 Mathis Type P

Mathis

Germany/France
1910–1950

Like Bugatti, the Strasbourg-based Mathis company changed from German to French nationality with the return of Alsace to France after World War I. Emile Mathis began as a dealer for Fiat, De Dietrich, Minerva and Panhard, also building a number of Hermes cars with Ettore Bugatti. It was not until 1910 that the first Mathis cars appeared, built by Stoewer of Stettin and badged as Stoewer-Mathis in Germany.

By 1912 the small Babylette car was introduced, and two years later the range consisted of five cars, some with Knight sleeve-valve engines. During World War I Mathis left the country, only returning in 1918 to rebuild his firm.

Mathis cars of the 1920s were light and very good value compared to their immediate competitors. Mathis tried some competition, but Emile wanted profit rather than prizes and this department was closed by 1925.

In the early 1930s a range of straight-eights was introduced, of between three and 5.4 litres, mainly with unexciting saloon bodywork. Sales began declining, despite advanced features such as synchromesh gears and transverse independent front suspension.

Above: 1928 'Big-Light' 10/24hp saloon
Below left: c. 1922 Mathis four-cylinder

In 1930 Mathis made a deal with William Durant to build the PY in the U.S.A., but the Depression frustrated this. Five years later Fords were also being produced at Strasboug, after Mathis formed the Matford company with Henry Ford. By 1938 Matfords were outselling Mathis and Emile Mathis sold out to Ford, although keeping the factory.

During World War II Mathis himself fled to America, running the Matam marine engine factory. Afterwards he returned again to Strasbourg to try two prototypes, the VL333 three-wheeler, and then the futuristically styled 666 saloon, both of which never really got past the prototype stage. Four years later Mathis sold his factory to Citroën, and died in an accident in 1956.

Below: 1928 six-cylinder Mathis
Below left: c. 1913 four-cylinder sports

Matra

France
1965 to date

Although it was founded before World War II, when it functioned as an aeronautical engineering contractor involved in research and development work – hence *Mécanique Aviation Traction*, from which MATRA derives – the company did not become directly involved with motor vehicles until 1964.

Led by Marcel Chassagny, the company took over the promising René Bonnet sports-car firm, having lent support to its racing activities when André Deutsch was nominal head. Matra Sports was created in 1964, and the Renault-engined René Bonnet Djet was introduced as a Matra, and produced until 1967 when Matra closed the Bonnet factory to open its own plant at Romorantin. This coincided with the launch of the striking Ford V4-engined M530 coupé. A poor dealer network caused the failure of this model, and in 1969 there was an amalgamation with Simca, itself part of Chrysler France, and a new company was formed, called Matra-Simca Division Automobile, with its headquarters at Vélizy.

Top: 1970 Matra M.S. 660
Above: 1967 Matra-Ford M.S. 7
Below: 1969 Matra M.S. 650

Under the head of Matra Sports, Jean Luc Lagardere, the company made its racing debut in 1965 at the Formula 3 races which support the Monaco Grand Prix. The company's aerospace experience was used to good effect in the design of the racing cars, and very soon Matra was dominant in Formula 2.

In 1967, Matra received substantial backing from Elf, the French national petrol company, to develop a Formula 1 car, which persuaded the French Government to enter into a three-year agreement (worth at least FF 6 million) with Matra as a means of promoting a prestigious French sports car. That Matra actually had an engine design team operational under former Simca engineer Georges Martin gave them the advantage in this deal over rivals Alpine.

The first Matra Grand Prix engine was a three-litre V12, but this was not notably successful in Formula 1; however, derivatives of this unit powered Matra sports cars to Le Mans wins in 1972, 1973 and 1974, and gave the company the World Championship for Makes in 1973 and 1974. It continued to supply Formula 1 racing engines in the early 1980s to Guy Ligier's team.

Meanwhile, the mid-engined Matra-Simca Bagheera sports coupé was launched in 1973; this had a 1.3- or 1.4-litre transverse-mounted engine and unusual three-abreast seating. This model was replaced in 1980 by the rather more attractive Murena, which was fitted with a steel rather than glassfibre body, and

which was powered by a 2.2-litre Chrysler engine. It was marketed under the Talbot banner, since Matra had become part of the giant PSA organization when this Peugeot-dominated corporation took over Chrysler's operations in Europe.

In 1983, Matra left PSA and became part of Renault, where it was to develop the concept of the trend-setting Espace people-carrier, drawing on experience gained with the front-wheel-drive Rancho estates. The joint Matra-Renault Espace programme was set to continue until 1993, and includes a four-wheel-drive version called the Quadra.

Left: 1968 Matra M530 coupé

Below left: Matra 530 coupé, c. 1969
Below centre: Matra Rancho, c. 1982
Below: 1967 Matra-Ford M.S. 5

Left: The mid-engined Matra-Simca Baghera was announced in 1973. Unusually, the driver and passengers sat three abreast.

Maybach

Germany 1921-1941

Maybach was actually two persons, father and son, who between them set the standards for German automotive engineering, from innovative brilliance to over-blown pretentiousness and thence to successful corporate anonymity.

Wilhelm Maybach, the father, was a partner and friend of Gottlieb Daimler and is credited with developing, among other things, the vertical-twin engine and the spray carburettor. There is no doubt that he was a genius, but he was financially and politically naive.

Mercedes founder Emil Jellinek offered Maybach a factory of his own and a huge salary in 1900, which he refused; in the same year Gottlieb Daimler died, leaving Maybach under Jellinek's control anyway but this time without the benefits. However, the engineer continued on his unworldly way and developed the Mercedes to perfection until, in 1907, he finally became disenchanted with the firm and left.

This was just in time to get involved in the crowning glory of pre-World War I German technology, the Zeppelin airships. Maybach developed a vast 21-litre powerplant in which he was assisted by his son Karl, and the family team proved to have the advantages of both experience and youth; their airship engines were marvels and one even went to power a racing car, the Metallique-Maybach, which still exists today. (In 1932, the vast eight-litre-engined Maybach D58 touring car came to be known as 'the Zeppelin'!)

After the war they were thanked for their pioneering efforts in aviation technology by a total ban on the German industry. So while Wilhelm gradually slipped into retirement, dying of pneumonia in 1929, Karl started the Maybach automobile company.

From the first there were no thoughts of making transport for the masses; Maybachs were always expensive and exclusive, not to mention sophisticated. Karl had obviously inherited his father's flair for engineering and the number of vacuum-driven or electrically operated devices on his magnificent cars was quite astonishing. Not, perhaps, the ideal cars for depressed post-war Germany, they nevertheless managed to find enough customers to continue as an alternative to Mercedes and Horch as a limousine for the moneyed and discerning.

The cars were huge, so it is hardly surprising that the factory's main source of capital ended up being commercial vehicles rather than limousines; the cars were heavier than many lorries, so their powerplants had to be capable of hauling great weights. Of course, during World War II those powerplants ended up in many a tank and the trickle of cars that had been made immediately preceding the war slowed to a stop.

These days, the firm is named Motoren Turbinen Union and makes heavy diesel engines, once more in partnership with its old allies and later competitors Mercedes.

Below: The 1927 Maybach W5 had a 120bhp six-cylinder engine of nearly seven litres but only two speeds. With a body by Spohn, the car weighed around three-and-a-half tons. The torque must have been immense.

Top right: The eight-litre V12 Maybach 'Zeppelin'

Above: The body was grand but heavy

Mazda

Japan
1960 to date

Although the first Mazda car was built in 1960, the company was originally established as Toyo Cork Kogyo in Hiroshima in 1920. Its early products included cork, machine tools, drilling equipment and, for a very short period, motor-cycles. By 1931 the company had changed its name to Mazda (after the founder Jujiro Matsuda and Mazda, god of light) and began production of a small delivery truck. This ultimately led to a prototype small saloon car in 1940, but further development was held up by World War II.

The factory suffered little damage during the atomic bombing of Hiroshima and production was ready to begin again

Above right: The 1967 Mazda 1000, really the first 'proper' car
Right: The Italian styling of its 1500 cousin

The Mazda 323 of 1980 was the firm's first front-wheel-drive car and, thanks to the tie-up with Ford, it was also exported to Australasia where it was very successful in the medium to small car market. This is one of the models that has made the firm so successful nowadays.

by December 1945. Manufacture of trucks recommenced during the 1950s, but it wasn't until 1960 that the company's first car appeared.

The R-360 coupé was an attractive little two-seat coupé with a rear-mounted air-cooled vee-twin engine of 356cc. Developing 16bhp at 5,300rpm, this gave the car a maximum speed of 90km/h (56mph), and it sold a creditable 23,417 units in its first year.

The P-360 Carol was launched in 1962 with a two- or four-door saloon body and immediately captured 67 per cent of the home market for cars in its class. Power was provided by an engine almost identical to the R-360's, but with water- rather than air-cooling. Developing 20bhp at 6,800rpm, this gave the Carol a maximum speed of 105km/h (65mph), then in 1964 the engine was enlarged to 586cc to provide 28bhp.

The successful Familia range was launched in 1964 as a 782cc four-door saloon. With a four-cylinder overhead-valve light-alloy engine and a four-speed manual or two-speed automatic gearbox, this led Mazda away from what would now be termed micro-cars and firmly established it as a manufacturer of full-size

The company's 717C of 1983, though it may seem an unusual departure for a company which has founded its success on workaday hatchbacks, is actually just a continuation of their racing-as-development policy.

Top: 1973/4 RX4 with a rotary engine
Above: The 1300 saloon, a big seller in the early '70s

family saloons. The Familia was later made available as a coupé with a 985cc overhead-camshaft engine producing 68bhp and capable of up to 145km/h (90mph). The range was completely restyled in 1970, when the 985cc engine became standard equipment throughout. There was also a 1272cc (87bhp) option, and even a double-rotor Wankel unit for the RX-100.

By the mid-1960s Mazda was Japan's third largest motor manufacturer, selling 54,000 cars in 1963 and just over 80,000 in 1965, and rapidly consolidated its position with the launch of the successful Luce/Cosmo 929 in 1966. Designed by Italian stylist Bertone, this had a four-cylinder 1490cc engine developing 78bhp and was capable of 150km/h (93mph). There was also a twin-rotor Wankel-engined coupé, and in 1972 both saloon and coupé models were completely restyled, the latter being fitted with a twin-rotor Wankel engine to form the highly successful 120bhp RX-4.

Mazda's interest in rotary power units had begun in 1961 when it acquired from N.S.U. a licence to build Wankel engines, although the Japanese company actually had its own prototypes running before the

Top right: 1982 323 five-door de luxe
Below: The estate variant of the 929

Above: The 1300 hatchback

Above: 1973 1000 two-door saloon

Above: 1975 818 coupé

Above: 1975 929 saloon

first engines arrived from Germany. There followed a period of intensive research and development during which the Mazda engine increasingly departed from the original N.S.U. design.

The first car to be launched as a result of this work was the 1967 Cosmo 110S coupé, the first mass-produced rotary-engined car in the world. Its 982cc twin-rotor engine developed 110bhp and gave it a maximum speed of 185km/h (115mph). Later models, with 128bhp, could reach 200km/h (124mph). The success of the 110S led to Wankel engines becoming a standard feature of many Mazda vehicles – for both normal production and competition use – and by 1978 the company had sold well over a million such engines in its cars.

Mazda began exporting to Europe and the United States in 1966 with the Familia and Luce, and by 1967 over 16 per cent of its annual production was sold abroad, this figure rising to over 30 per cent by 1969.

In 1970 the company expanded its range with the Capella 616 saloon and RX-2

Mazda's RX-7 is a fine example of a company sticking to its guns on an idea – in this case the rotary engine – and proving it to work after everyone else has given up. Launched in 1978, the RX7 has been redesigned since, but at its heart is still the rotary power plant.

Above: 1985 RX7 2+2

Above: The 626 2.0-litre GLX saloon

Above: 1985 929 estate, a bluff-fronted load carrier

Above: The perennial 323 in three-door 1985 guise

coupé, with 1490 or 1586cc piston engines and a twin-rotor 573cc Wankel engine respectively, then in 1971 appeared the Grand Familia 808. Sold as a saloon, coupé or estate car, this used four-cylinder piston engines of 1272 and 1490cc and, with a 491cc twin-rotor Wankel, was also known as the RX-3. The Cosmo 121 appeared in 1975 as a saloon or coupé and was based mechanically on the Luce. Reciprocating or rotary engines were again available, the latter's twin-rotor unit providing the equivalent of over 2.6 litres capacity and forming the RX-5.

The company suffered serious setbacks during the mid-1970s, however, and it was only with considerable financial help from the Sumimoto Bank, Toyo Kogyo's biggest shareholder at the time, that it was able to develop the Familia 323 to reverse the losses of 1975. The 323 was a conventional car with rear-wheel-drive, MacPherson strut front suspension, a live rear axle and four-cylinder engines of 1272 or 1416cc, but it sold well enough to notch up over a million units a little over two years after its launch in 1977. Revisions to the Capella range helped, too (the 626, badged in Britain as the Montrose, was introduced in 1979 as a coupé or saloon and with engines of 1586, 1769 or 1970cc, and in 1978 the rotary-engine RX-7 established Mazda as a serious manufacturer of high-performance sports cars.

Known in some markets as the Savanna (a name which had first appeared on the RX-3 in 1971), the RX-7 had a twin-rotor Wankel engine developing between 110 and 130bhp in the home market (110 and 115bhp in the U.S.A. and Europe), and a four- or five-speed manual gearbox or a three-speed automatic. A fuel-injected and turbocharged model was launched in 1983, its 165bhp allowing a maximum speed of 220km/h (137mph), and a total of nearly half a million had been built by the time of the second-generation RX-7's launch in 1986.

Toyo Kogyo's recovery was further assisted by Ford's acquisition of a 24 per cent shareholding in the company in 1979. This led directly to the opening of a new automated and highly flexible factory at Hofu in 1982, and allowed Mazda to sell its products throughout the U.S.A. and the

Right: 626 1990 2.0i GT estate

Above: 1990 RX-7 Turbo Cabriolet

Above: 1990 323 F 1.8 GT Injection

Above: 1990 121 1.3 LX Sun Top

Above: 1990 626 2.0-litre GLX Executive

Pacific badged as Fords.

The early 1980s also saw the radical development of Mazda's existing models. The revised Familia 323 became the company's first front-wheel-drive car in 1980 (selling in Australasia as the Ford Laser or Meteor), then in 1985 – at which date total Familia sales reached the two million mark – it was redesigned yet again to provide more interior space and better aerodynamics. Engines were now of 1296 or 1490cc, and there was a sporting model with four valves per cylinder, fuel injection and a turbocharger to provide 140bhp and a top speed in excess of 200km/h (125mph).

The Capella 626 was also substantially revised for 1982. Like the 323 it acquired front-wheel-drive and a transversely mounted engine, together with a brand-new range of four-door saloon, five-door hatchback or two-door coupé bodies and engines of 1587, 1789 or 1998cc. The latter was also available as a turbocharged unit producing 145bhp. Additionally, there was a 72bhp diesel variant of the 1998cc engine. The whole range marketed in some parts of Asia as the Ford Telstar.

The late 1980s saw similar advances throughout the Mazda range. The 626 and 323 were progressively developed to offer options of four-wheel steering and four-wheel drive respectively (the latter on the 323 Turbo, which proved to be a formidable competition machine); a 626 estate was launched in 1988 together with the 121, Mazda's first-ever contender in the so-called super-mini market; and for 1989 the long-running RX-7 became available as a full convertible. A brand-new 323 range was launched in the autumn of 1989 and, for 1990, there was an all-new two-seater open-top sports car, with styling reminiscent of the original Lotus Elan, called the MX-5 Miata.

Above: Mazda 323 three-door of 1997
Left: European Mazda 121
Below: Mazda 323 four-door saloon

Above: 1996 Mazda MX-6 2.5i
Right: 1997 Mazda 626 five-door
Below: Mazda 323 five-door

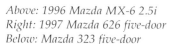

Mazda's rotary-engined sportster, the RX-7, was updated in 1991. The new model had gone up a class, both in performance and price. The rotary engine stayed but power was up 240bhp thanks to twin turbochargers. Many rated it a better car than the Porsche 968.

After the success of the MX-5, Mazda developed a taste for sports cars and quickly introduced the MX-3 and MX-6 coupés. The MX-3 was based on the 323 and the MX-6 on the 626.

Just as Ford had marketed the old 121 as one of its own models on certain markets, the next-generation 121, destined mainly for Europe, was actually a Ford Fiesta with Mazda badging.

Its new 323 was a little more inspiring. The new fastback shape was unconvention-

Above: The Mazda Xedos 6 Sport

al, but was distinctive and modern. It was available with a range of four-cylinder engines, but also a new, creamy-smooth 2.0-litre V6.

The Xedos, launched in 1991, was equally unconventional in looks. Under the skin, however, this luxury saloon was a little less adventurous, and the car relied on fairly normal underpinnings and engines from the existing Mazda range. A larger version was marketed as the Millenia in the United States. Also aimed at American buyers was the top-of-the-range 929 saloon.

Top: Mazda MX-5. Right: Mazda Xedos 9
Below: Mazda MX-3 1.6

Mercedes

Germany 1901–1926

Gottfried Daimler left the Deutz stationary-engine company in 1882 to set up in Bad Cannstatt with Wilhelm Maybach. By 1883, they had designed the world's first petrol-powered internal-combustion engine and in 1886 they put this into a modified horse-drawn carriage to create the first Daimler car. Car production began in 1890 and the first series-produced Daimler arrived in 1895. Daimler himself died in 1899, the year when the company's first four-cylinder model was introduced.

Above: Gottlieb Daimler and his 1886 car
Below: 1899 23hp Phoenix

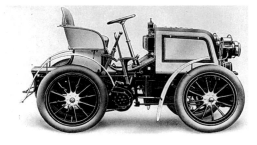

In 1900, Emil Jellinek, a wealthy diplomat and motoring enthusiast, joined the Daimler Board and encouraged the company to build a new high-performance car. The result, introduced in 1901, contained many technical innovations and its design was soon being copied all over Europe and America.

Above: 1902 Mercedes-Simplex 28/32 PS
Above right: 1907 Mercedes-Simplex 40/45

Above: 1911 tourer
Below: 1913 sleeve-valve Mercedes-Knight

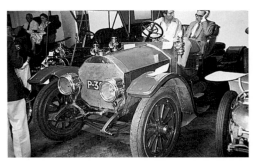

Mercedes was the name of Jellinek's daughter and was first connected with Daimler cars when Jellinek used it as a pseudonym in an 1899 speed trial. The name was adopted for Daimlers sold in France to avoid infringing licensing agreements and was adopted for all Daimler cars in 1902.

That 1901 35hp design spawned a range of successful models. In 1907, Daimler's son Paul succeeded Maybach as Chief Engineer after a spell with Austro-Daimler, the firm's Austrian subsidiary; shaft drive replaced chain drive in 1908, and Knight sleeve-valve engines arrived in 1909. Wartime saw Daimler making supercharged aero-engines, and from 1921 the company introduced superchargers on road cars. From 1922, Ferdinand Porsche was Chief Engineer, but the post-war recession forced Daimler into a co-operative agreement with Benz in 1924, and the two companies merged in 1926 (see *Mercedes-Benz*).

Above: 1922 6/25 PS Limousine
Left: 1921 supercharged 10/45/65 PS

Mercedes-Benz

Germany
1926 to date

Germany's two leading motor manufacturers, Daimler (sold as Mercedes) and Benz, merged in 1926 as a way of fighting the affects of the recession. Ferdinand Porsche, former Chief Engineer of Daimler, became the new combine's engineering head, and he chose to pursue the Daimler tradition of supercharging alongside more conventional saloon models, some carried over from the

Top left: 1928 Nurburg Pullman limousine
Top right: 1928 Mannheim 350 Pullman
Right: 1928 Type SS cabriolet
Below: 1927 Type S open sports

This short-wheelbase SSK of 1929 was typical of the Mercedes-Benz sports racers of its era. Its 7-litre six-cylinder engine developed 200bhp when the supercharger was engaged.

previously separate marques and others entirely new. Most impressive was the line of sports-racers which began in 1926 with the K and continued with the S of 1927 and the SS and SSKL of 1928.

Hans Nibel succeeded Porsche as Chief Engineer in 1928, and under him the sporting machines became more refined and elegant, with the supercharged 380 of 1933 and the formidable 500K of 1934 and 540K of 1936. A conventional saloon range remained in production, and this was significantly updated with the 170V in 1936, which quickly established itself as the company's most popular model, and with the 2600, the world's first diesel-engined production car. The early 1930s also saw a range of cars with small-capacity rear-mounted engines, though these Porsche-inspired designs never sold well.

Under the Nazi regime, Mercedes-Benz was encouraged to go Grand Prix racing, and between 1934 and 1940 the works team reigned supreme with a series of excellently engineered cars which both gathered publicity and served as test-beds for engineering developments intended for the road cars. The first cars had supercharged straight-eight engines, but

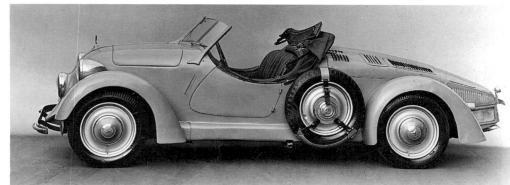

Top: 1929 SSK sports racer
Above: 1934 Type 150 rear-engined sports
Above left: 1933 supercharged type 380

Below: Most attractive of the bodies for the 1936 540K was the factory's own two-seater roadster. The straight-eight 5.4-litre engine produced 180bhp with the supercharger engaged.

when the Grand Prix formula rules were changed in 1938 – primarily to give others a chance in the face of the Mercedes-Benz team's commanding superiority – a supercharged V12 engine was developed. Finally, a small V8 powered the 1939 cars, drawn up rapidly to fit a formula changed at the last minute to suit the German team's rivals.

Above: 1935 170H rear-engined saloon

Above: 1936 540K cabriolet
Above left: 1935 260D diesel limousine
Below: 1937 W125 Grand Prix car

Below: 1939 supercharged Type 770
Bottom: 1939 W163 Grand Prix car

Production was slow to restart after World War II, for the company's factories had been bombed to rubble and were divided among the various Allied Occupation Zones. The first vehicles were light commercials based on the pre-war 170V, and the saloons of this range re-entered production in 1947, continuing through a series of modifications until 1955 and being joined by a related six-cylinder 220 model in 1951. Both ranges were offered with cabriolet and closed-coupé bodies in addition to the saloons, and chassis were available separately for coachbuilders to turn into light commercials.

The 220 was symptomatic of the company's revival, but the big 300 limousine introduced the same year showed that Technical Director Rudi Uhlenhaut had every intention of surpassing the levels of engineering achievement which had characterized pre-war Mercedes-Benz products. Although the 300 was never a large seller, it went through several versions before its demise in 1962, spawned expensive and exclusive cabriolets and coupés, and re-established the company in an important and prestigious area of the market.

Racing got under way again in 1951 with some of the pre-war cars, but the 1952 sports-racing 300SL 'Gullwing' was a new design, using the 200 limousine's big six-cylinder engine in an advanced spaceframe chassis structure. Redeveloped for production in 1954, it became the first of a long line of fuel-injected Mercedes-Benz models, and remained a coveted exotic throughout a production run which lasted until 1961, by which time

Top: 1951 Type 220 cabriolet   *Above: 1952 Type 300S roadster*

Right: 1953 Type 170S-D diesel saloon
Below: 1956 190SL roadster

the original Gullwing coupé had been replaced by an attractive roadster model. Meanwhile, the 300SL was succeeded in the racing programme by the eight-cylinder 300SLR sports-racer, but the company disbanded its racing team in 1955 after two hugely successful seasons. Mercedes returned to competition more than a decade later by supporting entries on long-distance international rallies.

A cheaper sports model appeared in the shape of the 1955 190SL, a more conventional car drawing heavily on the engineering pioneered by the 1953 Ponton saloons, which eventually superseded the 170 and 220 ranges. These were the first Mercedes-Benz models with unitary body shells and sold exceptionally well, later

pioneering fuel-injection for the company's mainstream road cars with the 1958 220SE variant. Coupé and cabriolet versions were also available.

By this time, the company's acknowledged engineering excellence, the irreproachable build-quality of its cars and its first-class service back-up were its main strengths. Next came some pioneering work in the area of passive crash-safety, and the new saloon range introduced in 1959 to replace the Pontons was the first to feature the deformable front and rear sections and reinforced passenger cell which have characterized every subsequent Mercedes-Benz.

Above: 1954 300SL Gullwing coupé

Developed initially as a works competition car, the 1954 Gullwing 300SL had a fuel-injected 2996cc six-cylinder engine and tubular spaceframe construction.

Known as the 'Fintails' after their nod in the direction of contemporary American styling trends, these cars ranged from the four-cylinder diesel 1800 beloved of taxi drivers the world over to the six-cylinder petrol-injected 300SEL with air suspension and other advanced features. Expensive coupé and cabriolet derivatives were also offered after 1963, the year in which Mercedes-Benz launched its massive and technically advanced 600 limousine. Designed to compete with Rolls-Royce models, this low-volume car was powered by a 6.3-litre V8 engine and remained the company's flagship model until its demise in 1981.

A further expansion came in 1965 when the new six-cylinder S-class range was introduced. Based on the engineering of the Fintails, this was pitched slightly further up-market and would spearhead the company's attack on the newly emerging upper-medium luxury-saloon market. It eventually spawned a remarkable 'Q'-car – the 300SEL 6.3 of 1968 – which coupled the top luxury specification to the 600 limousine's large V8 engine to give a refined saloon with ultra-high performance. Meanwhile, pagoda-roof sports cars which shared much of their engineering with the two saloon ranges had replaced the 190SL in 1963; but they put refinement before outright performance and were thus unable to replace the Gullwing-derived 300SL.

The medium-sized 'New Generation' saloons and coupés introduced at the end of the 1960s were solid if unexciting, but were notable as the range which

Right: 1974 450SE saloon
Below: 1960 220SE cabriolet

Above: 1967 250 six-cylinder saloon   *Below: 1969 300SEL 6.3 saloon*

abandoned the swing-axle rear suspension which had characterized Mercedes-Benz models since the 1930s and introduced a fully independent semi-trailing-arm suspension layout. Teutonic pride forbade the company to acknowledge publicly that there had ever been anything less than ideal about the earlier suspension, however, and so the new one was officially described as being of 'diagonal swing-axle' design!

Other technological advances, particularly in the area of crash-safety, were reserved for the new SL sports model of 1971 and for the new S-class saloons of 1974, both of which were heavily

Above: 1974 350SL roadster with roof on

Below: 1974 350SL roadster with roof off

influenced by the need to meet new fuel economy and emissions control regulations introduced in the U.S.A. which was by now a very important market for the company. (The 6.9-litre V8 powered SEL of 1975, however, was a conspicious exception, disdainful of fuel-efficiency concerns and successful partly because of this!) Diesel engines, latterly including five-cylinder and turbocharged types, were important in U.S.A. sales, but the four- and six-cylinder petrol engines remained in production throughout the 1970s, and the top models were powered by V8s.

The mid-range saloons and coupés were replaced in 1976, and the new models included an estate car for the first time after 1978. But the real innovation was reserved for the next generation of S-class cars introduced in 1979, lighter and even stronger than before and featuring enlarged but more fuel-efficient V8 engines. New the same year was the G-Wagen 4×4 range, developed in conjunction with Steyr-Daimler-Puch in

Above: 1979 280GE long-wheelbase model

The 190 range, launched in 1982, were 'compact' models, intended to broaden the Mercedes-Benz appeal without sacrificing the company's quality image. The range was hugely successful.

Austria and designed to compete with Land-Rover, Range Rover and Toyota products.

A third saloon range – known as the 190 – was introduced in 1982, and this successfully broadened the company's market by creating a cheaper entry-level model, even though the cars were, in fact, expensive medium-sized saloons. High-performance versions of the 190, using engines developed in conjunction with Cosworth in the U.K., were part of a strategy to attract younger buyers and to tackle the challenge of more sporting rival models from B.M.W. Also to rejuvenate its image, Mercedes returned to sports car racing. In 1987 the Stuttgart factory quietly provided 5.0-litre turbocharged V8 engines to the Swiss Sauber team, and in 1989 – now with three-pointed stars painted boldly on their bonnets –

Above: 1980 380SE saloon
Below: 1981 500SEC coupé

Bottom right: 1982 230E saloon

Below: 1980 500SL roadster

Below: The W107 range of roadsters arrived in 1971 and lasted until 1989. Always powered by the engines used in the big saloons, they majored on luxury and safety. This is a 1985 300SL, with a 3-litre six-cylinder engine.

Above: 1982 280TE estate car

Top left: 1982 300GD short-wheelbase
Top right: 1983 380SEC coupé

Sauber-Mercedes racers won Le Mans and the World Sports Prototype Championship.

Replacements for the company's own medium-sized saloons, estates and coupés – large cars by the standards of the 1980s – arrived in 1985, bristling with sophisticated technology and safety features. And the long-serving SL models were phased out in 1989, to be replaced by another range of hugely expensive, luxurious and technically advanced roadsters.

All these 1980s models had rather bland styling, conceived under the direction of Bruno Sacco, but technological innovation continues with the introduction of multi-valve engines, anti-lock braking systems, four-wheel drive and even traction control systems as extra-cost options on many models. Drawing on its experience of emissions-control engineering for the North American market, the company was also in the vanguard of European manufacturers attempts to produce cleaner exhausts for the 1990s.

Above: 1983 fuel-injected 190E saloon
Below: 1986 190E 2.6 six-cylinder

Above: 1984 380SEC coupé

Below: 1990 500SL roadster

The biggest news from Mercedes in 1989 was the new SL range. Topped at that time by the mighty V8 500SL, the new range was full of technical marvels, including a roll-over bar that would spring up in a fraction of a second should the car start to overturn.

Despite the launch of this fantastic but expensive car, Mercedes was hit hard by the recession, as were all the luxury car manufacturers.

The company's best-seller remained the 190, but when this was replaced by the C class in 1993, sales fell by 28 per cent. Cost-cutting in a company whose reputation was based on build quality was difficult, but somehow Mercedes managed to weather the storm and minimize its losses.

The rather bland styling of the 1980s was gradually replaced with the introduction of new, curvier models. Curviest of all was the E-class, launched in 1995, which was dynamically the match for any BMW 5-series.

Above: Mercedes C-Class Sport

Below: Mercedes C-class estate

Left: The mighty Mercedes 500SL sports car was launched in 1989 and still looked modern in the late 1990s. The car shown is fitted with the optional steel hard-top

Bottom left: The luxury S-class

Bottom middle: E-class estate

Bottom right: Mercedes E-class saloon

Despite for many years rejecting the idea of a foreign factory, claiming it would compromise quality, Mercedes set up a new plant in Vance, Alabama in America. The factory was to work on Mercedes' four-wheel-drive vehicles.

With the influx of new small sports cars in the mid-1990s, Mercedes designed its own entry to the market. Called the SLK, it was a compact convertible with the option of a supercharged engine. When it was launched at the Turin show of 1996, orders flooded in. By 1997 there was a two-year waiting list of people desperate to get their hands on the new sports car. Rather than use a conventional fabric roof, Mercedes engineers designed an amazing folding steel roof that could fold away and tuck itself into the boot at the touch of a button. Luggage space was severely limited with the roof down but for most owners it was worth it, if only for the number of heads that turned each time the roof was operated.

The new S-class, launched a few years earlier, also had ground-breaking technology. It was the first car to have double-glazed windows and could rival a Rolls-Royce with its levels of opulent luxury.

The A-class, first seen as a prototype in 1996, was a complete departure for

Right: SLK's supercharged four-cylinder engine gave 193bhp

Below: The SLK's folding steel roof was a masterpiece of engineering

Above: The V230 people carrier felt too much like a converted van to really compete in this highly competitive market

Left: Mercedes stretched the range downmarket with the A-class of 1997

Below: The handsome CLK coupé was launched in 1997

Mercedes. A miniature MPV with small, sub-2.0-litre engines, the A-class was an attempt by Mercedes to stretch its range to within the reach of a new, younger breed of Mercedes buyers.

The company also worked on the Smart microcar, in a joint project with Nicholas Hayek, inventor of the Swatch watch. The joint company, called MCC (Micro Compact Car) was 51per cent owned by Mercedes, with the other 49per cent belonging to Hayek's company, SMH.

In May 1998, the parent company Daimler-Benz entered into the £24 billion merger with Chrysler, whose marques include Plymouth, Dodge and Jeep. The split was 57% to Daimler-Benz, who will concentrate mostly on passenger cars, and 43% to Chrysler, who will develop the sport utility and pickup market, sharing platforms and development costs.

Below: 1997 Mercedes SLK

Mercer
U.S.A.
1910–1925

The Mercer Autocar Co. grew from the ashes of the Trenton-based Walter Automobile Co., which produced Roebling-Planche cars between 1906 and 1909. The new company took its name from Mercer County in New Jersey, changing it slightly to the Mercer Automobile Co. in 1910.

The first models were racing orientated and powered by Beaver engines, but in 1911 Mercer introduced its most famous and successful model, the Type 35 Raceabout. It was designed by Finlay Robertson Porter, who had joined the firm as Chief Engineer, and was short on creature comforts but long on excitement. The cars were raced at Indianapolis, and in 1914 works driver Eddie Pullen won the American Grand Prize event, the first American car and driver to do so. These competition appearances inevitably boosted sales.

Porter left the company in 1914 and the following year the Type 35 was replaced with the Type 22 design of Erik H. Delling, using a more powerful sidevalve engine. The body was far more enclosed and much of the charisma of the previous model was lost.

Mercer's financial problems led to a takeover by Hare's Motor Group in 1920. The previous year A. C. Schultz became designer, moving the cars even further away from their early sporting image, although they were still reasonably fast. By 1923 only a six-cylinder Rochester-engined machine was offered, this disappearing two years later.

There was an attempt to revive the marque in 1931, by a group of businessmen who had bought the name. Led by Harry M. Wahl, they formed the Mercer Motors Corporation in the Elcar Works, Elkhart, Indiana, but no more than half a dozen prototypes were built.

Above: 1914 Type 35 Raceabout

Below: The legendary type 35 Raceabout had a 5-litre four-cylinder Continental engine which gave only 55bhp, but the car's light weight made it good for 112km/h (70mph).

Mercury

U.S.A.
1938 to date

During the 1930s Ford U.S.A. was building its low-cost V8-engined range of cars towards the bottom end of the U.S. motoring spectrum, and the luxury Lincoln K series, often with custom bodywork, towards the top. The launch of the V12 Lincoln Zephyr for 1936 closed the gap slightly, but Ford still lacked a car in the then-growing medium-price class.

The answer, launched on 8 October 1938, was the all-new Mercury Eight. Masterminded by Edsel Ford and Ford Sales Chief Jack Davis, the new model was an instant success, selling 70,385 units worldwide during the 1939 model year.

In 1941 there appeared a new, roomier body, shared with Ford, which allowed for more body styles. By 1942 the Mercury concept was moving closer towards Lincoln in terms of appeal – a policy made official in 1945 with the formation of the Lincoln-Mercury Division of the Ford Motor Company. The first truly new post-war model, the Type 72 Coupé of

Above: 1939 convertible coupé

Above: 1952 four-door sedan

Above: 1957 Turnpike Cruiser

Below: 1954 Monterey Custom Sedan

1948, shared its basic body shell with a smaller Lincoln model, not a Ford.

During the 1950s and under the leadership of Henry Ford II, Mercury began widening its appeal and, once the Division had put the Edsel fiasco behind it, launched a 'compact' model, the Comet, in 1960 (derived from Ford's Falcon), and the mid-sized Meteor in 1962. Mercury now had a market share across the board, which has continued to the present day. In 1967 the two-door hard-top Cougar was launched, a 'personal car' in the Mustang mould.

The advent of the 1973 fuel crisis produced the sub-compact Bobcat range in 1975, replaced in 1981 by the Lynx, essentially the U.S. version of Europe's Mark III Escort. A new-generation fuel-efficient mid-range car emerged in 1978 (the Zephyr), and this was superseded by the Topaz range in 1984.

The newest Mercury, the Sable, part of Ford's U.S. $3 billion DN5 programme, has been acclaimed the design leader in the North American car industry, as it heads towards the next century.

Above: 1988 Grand Marquis sedan

Above: 1976 Grand Monarch Ghia

Above: 1976 Bobcat MPG

Above: 1988 Topaz LTS four-door

Above: 1988 Grand Marquis

Above: 1988 Merkur Scorpio

Above: 1988 Tracer hatchback

Above: 1988 high-performance Cougar

Above: 1988 3.8-litre Sable sedan
Below: The Cougar first made its appearance in 1967 as a sporty two-door hardtop. This 1969 model was a four-seater coupé powered by a 200hp 4.7-litre V8 engine with a twin-body carburettor.

Ford's Mercury division continued to offer medium-priced cars, usually higher specification Fords, fitting neatly between the Ford and Lincoln ranges.

The Cougar was still going strong in its 30th year, and was by then called the Cougar XR7. A twist of sheet metal and a touch of luxury was all that was required to turn Ford's Thunderbird into the Cougar. Mechanically, the cars were identical.

The Sable, an upmarket Ford Taurus was one of Mercury's best-sellers. The Tracer was a smartened-up American Ford Escort and was built in Hermodillo in northern Mexico. Similarly, the Mercury Mystique was based on the Contour or Mondeo. All these models were only offered with the larger engines used in the Ford-badged cars.

To get the all-important MPV in the range, Mercury borrowed Nissan's Quest minivan in 1992, complete with 3.0-litre V6 engine and autobox, and added a touch of Mercury class.

A four-wheel-drive Mercury arrived at the Detroit show in 1996 in the form of a Ford Expedition with new grille and upgraded interior trim.

Above: The Mystique was Mercury's version of the Ford Contour or Mondeo

Right: By slightly restyling the Ford Thunderbird, Mercury created the 1997 Mercury Cougar XR7

Below: The Mercury Grand Marquis was the largest car in the 1997 range

Above: Nissan's Quest minivan was converted into the Mercury Villager in 1992

Right: The Mountaineer, launched in 1996, was a more luxurious version of Ford's successful Expedition 4x4

Below: The 1997 Mercury Tracer. The entry-level Mercury was based on the American Ford Escort which itself was based on the Mazda 323. Mercury's version used only the largest, 111bhp 2.0-litre engine

M.G.

Great Britain 1924–1980; 1985 to date

Above: The first M.G., the 1924 Special

Above: 1926 M.G. 14/18 Tourer

Morris Garages in Oxford relied on the sales of production Cowleys and Oxfords, but manager Cecil Kimber began to tire of such everyday-cars, so in 1922 he mounted some Cowley chassis on special four-seater bodies made by Carbodies of Coventry. They were sold as the Chummy.

A special-bodied two-seater by Raworth of Oxford followed and then a four-seater on an Oxford chassis. It was advertised as the M.G. V-Front saloon.

It was the first time that the name M.G. had been used in an advertisement – it appeared in the *Morris Owner* magazine in March 1924 – but it is arguable whether the car or the Raworth two-seater should be considered the first M.G.

The confusion arises because, although the Raworth was advertised in May 1924 as the M.G. Super Sports Morris, the first model was sold in August 1923.

Later in 1924, Kimber built a number of sporting four-seaters on the Oxford chassis, continually improving their appearances.

Above: 1927 M.G. Sports Saloon
Above right: 1930 M.G. M Type

Below: The M Type Midget was launched at the Motor Show at Olympia in 1928. High demand for this model and the 18/20 Six allowed the company to move into larger premises in 1929.

At the time, he was operating from a workshop in Alfred Lane, Oxford, but more space was needed so he moved to a section of the Morris Motors' Radiator Branch in 1925. Two years later and with a £10,000 loan from William Morris, he moved to a new factory in Edmund Road.

The famous bull-nose radiator had been replaced with a flat type by this time and Kimber followed Morris's example.

It was also in 1927 that Morris Garages was formed as a limited company, becoming the M.G. Car Co. (Proprietors of Morris Garages Ltd.) in the spring of 1928.

The M.G. was emerging as a car in its own right and Kimber stopped buying complete rolling chassis from Morris and instead bought frames, engines and axles separately. The axles came from Wolseley.

The year 1928 was significant because M.G. had its first stand at the Motor Show in Olympia, London, exhibiting the Minor-derived Midget with an 847cc overhead-cam engine, and the 18/80 Six. The latter car's engine was a 2½-litre, overhead-cam six-cylinder unit.

Production trebled in 1929 with about 900 cars leaving the factory. Nearly 1,900 models were sold in 1930.

Increasing sales had dictated a move and in 1929 M.G. transferred to part of the Pavlova Leather Company's premises at Abingdon, about seven miles from Oxford. It turned out to be the final move.

Industry in general had a bad year in 1931 and this was reflected in M.G.'s sales which dropped to below 1,500. But they picked up to 2,400 in 1932.

M.G. began to find success on the racetrack and 1933 to 1935 are regarded as the golden years when the K3 Magnette scored many victories, including Novolari's win in the 1933 Ulster Tourist Trophy and the

Above: M.G. M Types at Brooklands

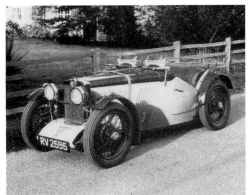

Left and below: 1932 M.G. J2 Midgets

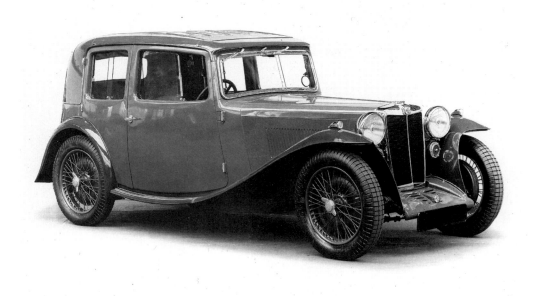

Right: 1933 K1 Magnette
Below: 1933 M.G. K3 Magnette

team prize at the 1933 Mille Miglia.

But the track fame did not always lead to profits and Kimber was under pressure to cut racing expenditure and use as many components as possible from Morris. He severed connections with Carbodies in 1933 and thereafter bought his coachwork from Morris Bodies Branch.

William Morris – who had become Lord Nuffield in 1934 – sold the M.G. Car Co. in 1935 to Yorkshireman Leonard Lord. The tough-talking businessman, who was later to head Austin, closed down the competition department as one of his first moves.

That meant a shift in emphasis on power units and the overhead-cam engines were dropped in favour of pushrod units from the Morris-Wolseley range. A 1292cc engine went into the TA Midget which was similar to the Wolseley Ten engine. And M.G. launched the SA 2-litre, with a Wolseley Super Six engine, to compete with the SS Jaguar.

By 1937, production had reached a record level and in that year some 2,850 cars were sold.

The beginning of World War II ended car production and the company concentrated on work for various ministries, its biggest contract being building front fuselage sections for the Albemarle bomber.

But Kimber's patriotic gesture led to his downfall. He had accepted the Albemarle contract without consulting the management and Miles Thomas, the Nuffield Organisation's new managing director, dismissed him in 1941.

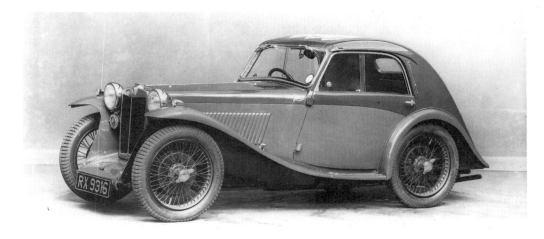

Above: Airline Coupé on 1934 PA chassis
Below: 1934 M.G. K1 four-seater

Below: M.G. SA saloon, first seen in 1935

Below: the 18/80 Mk II, which first appeared at the 1929 Motor Show, was the first M.G. to competely shed its Morris ancestry. It had a sturdier frame, better brakes and a wider track than its predecessor, the Mk I.

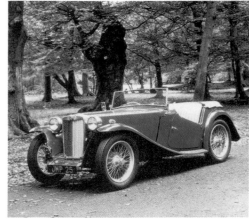

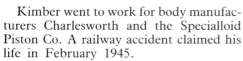

Above: 1938 M.G. TA
Top left: Mid-30s SA Tourer with
Charlesworth body
Left: Tickford drophead coupé by Salmons

Below: the last ohc Midget, the 1935/6
PB model
Bottom left: M.G. TA of 1936
Bottom right: 1939 M.G. TB

Kimber went to work for body manufacturers Charlesworth and the Specialloid Piston Co. A railway accident claimed his life in February 1945.

Development had obviously suffered during the war and M.G. had to rely on a pre-war design to recommence production in 1945. The TC Midget was announced in October and 81 were built by the end of the year.

Although it was largely based on the 1939 TB, the TC helped start a boom in sports cars and became something of a cult vehicle. Exports to the United States began early in 1947 and the influence was far-reaching because Detroit entered the same market five years later with the Chevrolet Corvette and, soon after that, the Ford Thunderbird. In fact, the Sports Car Club of America blossomed from one branch of the M.G. Car Club.

The TC was indeed successful and 10,000 had been built by the time it was replaced in March 1950. Out of those, 6,592 were exported, 2,001 to the U.S.A.

The next model, the TD, was even more successful and, in four years, 29,644 were made. Once again, many were exported

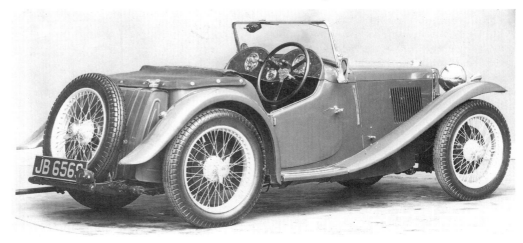

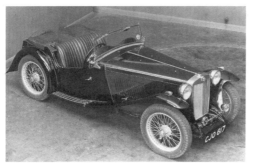

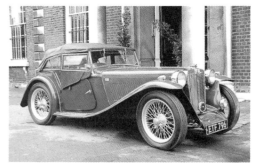

with 42 TDs being sold abroad in 1952 for every one in Britain.

The launch of the Austin-Healey 100 hit sales heavily but Leonard Lord decreed that M.G. should not bring out a brand-new Midget in 1953. He reasoned that the newly formed British Motor Corporation did not need two new sports cars.

Abingdon suffered many such snubs at the hands of B.M.C.'s top management and later British Leyland. Predictably for a large organization controlling several marques, badge-engineering became increasingly common. The ZA Magnette saloon of 1954 had the same body shell as the Wolseley 4/44 and the 'B'-series engine which was used by the Wolseley and also the Austin Cambridge.

But the MGA two-seater of 1955–62 brought encouragement for M.G. because it was significantly more individual. It featured a tuned 'B'-series engine and a streamlined sports-car body.

Sales of the MGA exceeded any previous model and 101,181 were built in seven years. These included some 2,100 of the famous twin-overhead-cam models. However, its successor did even better. The unitary-construction MGB sold right up to the end of M.G. in 1980, with over 460,000 being delivered.

M.G. offered more performance with the Healey 3000 six-cylinder engine in the MGB body, calling it the MGC. A total of around 9,000 were built. The lightweight all-aluminium Rover 3.5-litre engine later

Top right: 1939 M.G. SA saloon
Above right: The very special M.G. TC, c. 1945

Below: The MGA was launched in 1955; good aerodynamics and high gearing gave the original 1489cc model a top speed of nearly 160km/h (100mph). The coupé model below dates from 1959, when engine capacity was increased to 1588cc and disc brakes were added to the front wheels.

Above: 1947 M.G. TC
Above right: 1950 M.G. TD
Right: MGA Coupé of 1955

Below: 1953 M.G. TF 1250
Below right: MGA Twin Cam, c. 1958

found its way into the MGB body, meeting the public as the MGB GT V8.

In 1957, Austin-Healey production was moved to Abingdon, taking over the space occupied by Riley – a name associated with Abingdon since 1949.

The new Austin-Healey Sprite was launched in 1958, a distinctive car with frogeye-type headlamps (later to give the little car its popular name). The Mark II Sprite followed with the Mark I Midget as its stablemate – another badge-engineering exercise.

The first M.G. made away from Abingdon appeared in 1959. It was the Magnette III, built at Cowley and a B.M.C. Farina-styled saloon with twin carburettors and an M.G. radiator grille.

Competition from such cars as the Triumph Spitfire and Mini-Cooper hit M.G. sports-car sales in the early 1960s, and Abingdon started a useful sideline in assembling Morris Minor estates and vans.

M.G. boasted the proud record of never having sales drop below 30,000 a year in 20 years, inclusive of Rileys and Austin-Healeys. Its best year was 1972 when 55,639 sports cars were made – 39,393 of which were MGBs.

B.M.C. merged with Jaguar to form British Motor Holdings in 1968 and the M.G. Car Co. Ltd. became the M.G. Division. Shortly afterwards B.M.H. merged with the Leyland group to form British Leyland.

Ironically, Triumph had been one of M.G.'s greatest rivals. Now the company was in the same group. However, Triumph earned a higher status as part of the Standard-Triumph, Rover, Jaguar specialist-car division. Curiously, M.G. was slotted into the Austin-Morris division.

Top: Late-50s M.G. ZB Magnette 'Varitone'
Centre: 1961 948cc M.G. Midget

Below: 1962 MGA Mk II
Below right: MG 1100, introduced in 1962

B.L.'s bosses, Sir Donald Stokes and, later, Sir Michael Edwardes, were plainly not in favour of Abingdon. At least two prototype M.G.s were dropped in favour of the Triumph TR7 although the MGB still managed to outsell the TR7 on the U.S. market even when the Triumph's price was cut substantially.

The millionth M.G. left the factory in December 1975 but there was nothing new to come. The Midget was discontinued in the spring of 1979 and the closure of the Abingdon plant was announced early in 1980 with the last MGB being built in the autumn.

Below: The chrome bumper MGB soft top was made from 1962-1967. It was capable of 166km/h (103mph) and reached 96.5 km/h (60mph) in 12.2 seconds.

Above: 1967 3-litre six-cylinder MGC

Above: 1968 MG 1300

The factory was sold the following year to the Standard Life Assurance Co. for £5 million and the majority of the area was cleared in the autumn of 1981 to make way for a new industrial estate.

The M.G. EX-E prototype was shown at the 1985 Frankfurt Motor Show with the 250bhp V6 engine as used in the Metro 6R4 rally car. But it never went into production. The M.G. name lived on in the late 1980s, however, with the Metro, Metro Turbo, Maestro, Montego and Montego Turbo. But as derivatives of Austins – albeit with better performance – they are not regarded by many enthusiasts as true M.G.s.

Left: 1973 MGB GT V8

Below left: 1973 M.G. Midget Mk III

Above: 1972 MGB Roadster

Below: 1978 MGB Roadster

Above: 1980 MGB LE
Left: M.G. Metro Turbo

Below: 1988 M.G. Maestro Turbo
Bottom: 1989 M.G. Montego Turbo

Although the famous octagon never disappeared, featuring on the sports variants of Rover saloons, many had given up all hope of the famous marque ever being truly revived to build real sports cars.

In 1992, however, an MG-badged sports car was launched. The RV8 was little more than a bespoilered MGB body with a Rover V8, but it was certainly a lot nearer the mark than a badge-engineered Montego.

With Rover Group running a heritage section, it was building MGB shells for restorers, and used these for the RV8. It was a popular car, but not really a new MG, merely a warmed-over old model. Its role though, was to reinstate the MG badge on a sports car and it did its job admirably.

The real rebirth, however, came with the introduction of the MGF. A completely new car, the MGF owed nothing to Honda or BMW and used a mid-mounted 1.8-litre K-series unit, in standard 130bhp form, or with 143bhp thanks to variable valve timing. The latter model was known as the MGF VVC.

The handling was fantastic due to its ideal

Above: MG RV8 and MGB Roadster   *Below: MGF 1.8i*

Above: The MG RV8 used a Range Rover V8 engine in a modified MGB bodyshell. It was a stopgap model meant simply to revive the marque before the MGF arrived

Left: The MGF VVC was identical to the 1.8i but used a 143bhp variable valve-timing four-cylinder engine

weight distribution and interlinked Hydragas suspension. An added benefit of the unconventional suspension was a ride quality that would put many luxury saloons to shame.

The MGF was an instant success and demand far outstripped supply. A low asking price of under £20,000 helped keep orders coming in. Even in the face of much new opposition, from Lotus, Alfa Romeo, Renault etc. in the sports car market, MGF sales held up well.

Minerva

Belgium 1899–1939

Sylvain de Jong, founder of one of Belgium's most famous marques, began making Minerva and Romania cycles from his Antwerp workshops in 1897. Although he displayed voiturette and light commercial prototypes in 1899, it was not until 1902 that his first production models appeared. The following year de Jong launched Minerva Motors, going into partnership with his brother Jacques and David Citroën, who marketed the Minervette cyclecar in England.

Beginning with small one-, two- and four-cylinder vehicles, Minerva was offering a 6250cc six-cylinder by 1907, when it began a brief foray into motor sport up to 1914. During this time the Kings of Belgium, Norway and Sweden drove Minervas, as did Henry Ford. In 1909 Knight sleeve-valve engines were adopted.

After World War I de Jong revived his company remarkably quickly, exporting to America and expanding its operation to another Antwerp factory, then one in Brussels. Commercial vehicles were also produced, but de Jong's death in 1928 began Minerva's decline. The company moved away from the large prestige models towards smaller cars, but by the early 1930s even efforts by the Belgian government could not prevent heavy losses being made.

Reorganization in 1934 as the Société Nouvelle Minerva did not help and in 1935 the Mathieu Van Roggen Impéria company took control. A remarkable all-new design was shown at the 1937 Brussels Salon, but only prototypes were built. Two years later Ettore Bugatti showed interest in Minerva's factories, but World War II prevented further developments

During the hostilities Minerva produced commercial vehicles. An Armstrong-Siddeley-based revival planned in 1952 was unsuccessful, as was a Jeep-type vehicle built for a year to 1956, after which the factories were sold.

Top: 22hp tourer dating from 1906
Above: 1911 Type W 16hp

Below: 1920 saw the emergence of this six-cylinder Minerva with a 5344cc engine and a top speed of 120km/h (75mph). By the mid-1920s Minerva was exporting cars to the United States.

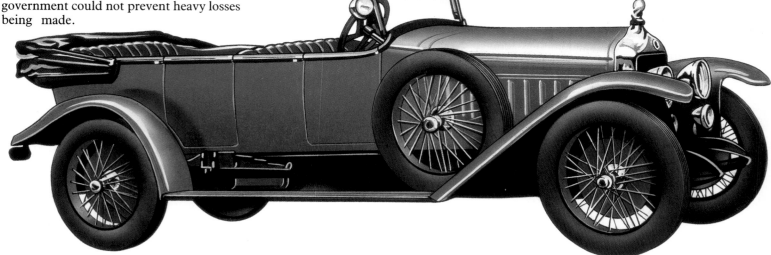

Top left: 16hp four-cylinder car, c. 1912
Top right: 1912-14 4.4-litre coupé
Centre: 1931 chassis with Rollston bodywork
Left: 1926 AK 32/34 Cabriolet with bodywork by Saoutchik
Above: 1956 Jeep-type utility vehicle

Mitsubishi

Japan
1917–1921;
1953 to date

Mitsubishi is currently one of the biggest companies in the world, employing directly or indirectly hundreds of thousands of people and having tentacles in almost every area of life. The lift you take to your office may well have been made by them, the records you buy will most probably have been recorded on their equipment and the oil you put in your car will quite probably have been transported in a Mitsubishi-built supertanker. The Mitsubishi car company is only one smallish part of a vast multi-national organization.

Top right: 1917 Fiat-based Model A
Right: The bulbous Mitsubishi 500 of 1959
Far right: Colt was the name used on later models like this 1100

Below: It is rumoured that the name Starion was kicked off by an English-Japanese pronunciation mix-up. Whether this is true or not, it is certainly the case that the car has gained respect by its performance capabilities. The 2.6-litre turbo coupé is very highly regarded by both enthusiasts and the Press.

All this goes back to 1870 when a shipping company was founded. After a few name changes when it picked up the name Mitsubishi ('three diamonds' in Japanese – hence the marque's badge) the firm had expanded into several other areas including engineering, and in 1917 produced one of the first Japanese cars, the Model A. Though the design was heavily influenced by Fiat, it started the company's involvement in internal combustion, despite selling only about 20 cars.

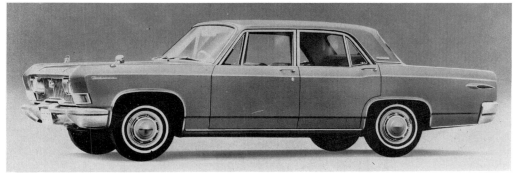

Top left: Cute Colt – a 1966 Minica
Top: A Colt saloon-car racing in 1974
Left: The big six-cylinder Debonair saloon
Above: The early Colt 800

Above: Mitsubishi's Galant, launched 1974
Right: The Galant GTO

Left: 1978 Colt Sapporo 2000 GSR with 'Astron 80' balancer engine
Above: 1985's Pajero off-roader

Trucks and buses took over after the Model A's disappearance in 1921 and, of course, wartime work (including manufacture of the infamous 'Zero' fighter plane) took over for some years.

When the smoke of battle had cleared and Japan's economy had sorted itself out to some extent, the firm regained its interest in producing passenger vehicles. Jeeps were built under licence after 1953, and in 1959 the first car appeared. This was the diminutive and fairly primitive Model 500, but at least it was a start and the company was quick to learn from its rivals. Mitsubishi's cars became rapidly more sophisticated and it absorbed a lot of American influence, making the U.S.A. a natural market for the fast-expanding company.

By the early 1970s the firm's Colt range was well established at home and it was casting around for new markets worldwide, which led to a tie-up with Chrysler to distribute the cars via the American motor giant's showrooms.

Mitsubishi has a solid foothold in most countries nowadays, its range comprising the Colt/Mirage and Lancer/Cordia subcompacts, the medium-sized Galant saloon, and the Shogun/Montero sport-utility vehicle. The Colt Starion sports coupé (also sold by Chrysler in the U.S. as the Dodge Conquest) was due to be replaced in 1991 by a new image-leader, the Mitsubishi 3000 GT/Dodge Stealth. A 2+2-seater with a 204bhp 3.0-litre twin-turbocharged V6, this was described by one magazine as 'an exotic car without the exotic price'.

Top: Shogun V6, a Land Rover challenger
Above: Galant five-door coupé

Left: Colt GTi 16V hatchback
Above: Colt 1500 GLX

Top: The Mitsubishi Space Wagon
Left: The four-wheel-drive Lancer Liftback
Above: Lancer GTi 16V saloon

Below: In 1984 Mitsubishi's extensive
range included the Shogun, a four-wheel-
drive 'off-road' diesel vehicle. In 1985 a
petrol-engine option was added.

Above: 1997 Mitsubishi Colt

Above: The popular Mitsubishi Carisma

Below: The Mitsubishi Lancer Evo III won the World Rally Championship in 1996 with Tommi Makkinen at the wheel. He beat the favourites in the Subaru Impreza

Mitsubishi was one of the few Japanese manufacturers not to be badly hit by the recession. It continued to profit and expand while those around it were suffering in the worldwide economic slump. In fact Mitsubishi was the only Japanese car manufacturer to make money in 1991-92.

The key to the company's success was not over-reaching itself, and clever product design. Every Mitsubishi model seemed to be a hit. The Shogun or Pajero 4x4, for example, was such a success that Mitsubishi had trouble keeping up with demand.

With Chrysler's stake in the company reduced from 10.99 to 5.88 per cent and the company now owning American subsidiary Diamond Star Motors outright, Mitsubishi became more and more independent and its

Above: Rear view of the Mitsubishi Colt 1.6 GLX, launched in 1995

Below: The rugged four-wheel-drive Mitsubishi Pajero, also known as the Shogun in some markets, was one of Mitsubishi's best-sellers during the 1990s

models were getting better all the time.

The Lancer was a rally winner and took the World Rally Championship with Tommi Makkinen at the wheel in 1996. The road-going version of the rally car, the EVO III had 270bhp. Mitsubishi seemed to be able to get enormous power outputs out of relatively small engines. The 1997 Colt/Mirage and Lancer range had a 1.6-litre four-cylinder producing 175 horsepower.

A new coupé was launched in 1994 to fit below the mighty 3000GT or GTO. The smaller FTO had similarly dramatic styling and power outputs of up to 200 horsepower from its four- and six-cylinder engines. Meanwhile, the GTO continued to compete with the other Japanese super coupés, such

Above: The Mitsubishi Galant received a direct-injection petrol engine in 1996

Left: The Mitsubishi Carisma 'Evolution' concept by TWR

Below: Mitsubishi 3000GT or GTO

Above: 1997 Mitsubishi Galant

as the Mazda RX-7 and Toyota Supra, all with very similar performances and prices.

The top-of-the-range Galant saloon had nearly as much power from the twin turbocharged 2.5-litre V6, but the real news in the Galant range was the event of another engine. In 1996 Mitsubishi revealed its direct-injection petrol engine. This new technology coaxed a relatively high output from the 1.8-litre engine of 150 horsepower, but the biggest benefit was in fuel consumption. The Galant with the new engine could give nearly 50mpg (18km/litre).

The company's Pajero/Shogun four-wheel-drive continued to sell well and spawned a couple of spin-offs. The first was the Pajero Mini – an amazing all-wheel-drive microcar with mini-Pajero styling and a 659cc engine. Next was the Challenger or Montero, launched in 1996. Based on the long wheelbased Pajero/Shogun, it had more modern styling.

Morgan

Great Britain
1910 to date

H. F. S. Morgan looked set for a career in the church. Both his father and grandfather were ministers. But H. F. S., as he was always known, chose to design cars.

He was born in 1884 in Herefordshire and, encouraged by his father, studied at the Crystal Palace Engineering College in London. His father later arranged for his apprenticeship as a mechanical engineer with the Great Western Railway.

After completing his training, H. F. S. bought a garage in Malvern Link, Worcestershire, selling Darracqs and Wolseleys and then started a car-hire service. But his real interest was experimenting with vehicles to his own specifications.

He built a motor-cycle in 1908 with a vee-twin Peugeot engine. Then, with the help of a Mr Stephenson-Peach, an engineering teacher at Malvern College, he built a light single-seater three-wheeler using a Peugeot engine. Features included a shaft-driven single rear wheel, two-speed transmission and independent front suspension.

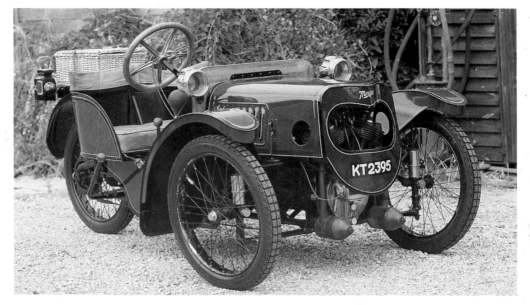

Top: 1913 Morgan vee-twin 8hp
Above: 1933 Morgan Sports Family

The Plus Four replaced the 4/4 in 1950. The new car, pictured here, was powered by a 2088cc Standard Vanguard engine, giving it a top speed of 145km/h (90mph).

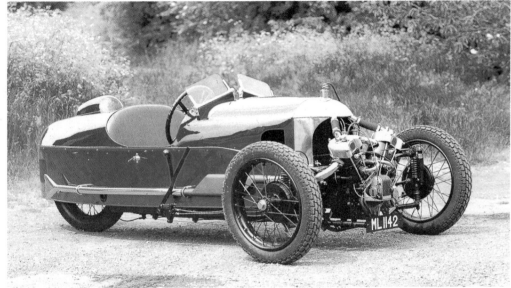

His father put up £3000 in 1910 and H. F. S. set up a small factory in Malvern Link to start production as the Morgan Motor Company. His first two J.A.P.-engined cars were shown at Olympia in November 1910. A year later he developed a two-seater and Harrods store, no less, became the first Morgan agency.

At the outbreak of World War I production was up to nearly 1,000 cars a year and sales were helped with many successes in racing and trials. H. F. S. continued to develop cars during the war, including a four-seater in 1915. However, most of the factory's efforts turned to the production of munitions.

Morgan expanded after the war and moved to Pickersleigh Road (where it has remained) with full production underway by 1923.

The four-seater Family model was available from 1919 and sales of three-wheelers continued to flourish with many winning competitions. A variety of engines was available including Anzani, Precision, Blackburne and the popular J.A.P. vee-twins.

An accident in 1924 led to the ban of three-wheelers from racing but the Morgan Club was reorganized in 1927 as the Cyclecar Club and this re-established three-wheelers in competition.

Sales of three-wheelers started to decline during the 1930s and Morgan announced his first four-wheeler in 1935– the 4/4 with

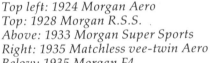

Top left: 1924 Morgan Aero
Top: 1928 Morgan R.S.S.
Above: 1933 Morgan Super Sports
Right: 1935 Matchless vee-twin Aero
Below: 1935 Morgan F4

Left: 1954 Morgan Plus Four in racing trim
Above: 1972 Morgan 4/4

Above: 1982 Morgan 4/4
Right: 1988 Morgan Plus Eight

an 1122cc Coventry-Climax engine. War halted production; it did not recommence properly until 1946 with most of the cars being exported, particularly to the U.S.A.

Morgan realized that the three-wheeler era was now declining rapidly and production of those models stopped in February 1952.

The 2088cc Standard Vanguard-engined Plus Four replaced the 4/4 in 1950 and the 4/4 was reintroduced in 1954 with a Ford 10 engine. These two cars were the foundations of the range up to 1968 with the Plus 4 using Triumph TR engines and the 4/4 eventually getting the Ford 1600GT unit.

H. F. S. Morgan died in June 1959, shortly before the company's 50th anniversary, and the company was left in trust to his four daughters and son Peter.

The Plus Eight was introduced in 1968 with the Rover 3.5-litre V8 and that helped Morgan re-enter the American market thanks to the car's excellent performance and specifications.

The range has changed little since the 1960s with the accent remaining on quality-built sports cars rather than sophisticated out-and-out performance two-seaters.

Morgan has remained loyal to Ford and the XR3 engine was introduced in 1982 in the 4/4 (the Fiat Mirafiori engine was also used in some models).

The Plus Eight continues to head the range with the Vitesse-engined petrol-injected version being the flagship.

Top: 1976 Morgan 4/4 four-seater
Left: Morgan Plus Four
Above: Morgan Plus Eight

Above: Morgan 4/4

Left: The current Morgan 4/4 is powered by the 1.6-litre overhead-camshaft engine of the Ford XR3, and is easily capable of speeds in excess of 160km/h (100mph).

Morris

Great Britain
1912–1984

William Morris (later Lord Nuffield) first built and sold motor cycles before turning his attentions to four-wheeled vehicles. The first Morris (Oxford) car, built at Cowley, Oxford, appeared in 1912, the rounded radiator design earning the car the nickname 'Bullnose'. The Oxford was powered by a 1018cc 10hp four-cylinder White and Poppe engine, and more than 1,000 were sold before World War I intervened. A larger model, the Cowley, was also built, using a 1495cc 11.9hp Continental engine from the U.S.A.

After the war the Cowley and Oxford were both sold with 1548cc 11.9hp four-cylinder Hotchkiss engines. The Cowley was the cheaper of the two models, with lower levels of standard equipment.

Above: 1913 'Bullnose' Morris Tourer

Below: Morris Cowley, 1920. The bullnose radiator design was introduced with the first Morris Oxford of 1912, and became a symbol of the marque until 1926. The Oxfords and Cowleys after World War I had 11.9hp, 1548cc Hotchkiss engines.

The company, having already built up a good reputation, started to achieve real success in the 1920s. At the 1921 Motor Show in London, the prices of all Morris cars were cut by £100, leading to a rapid increase in demand, so that annual production increased to some 65,000 cars per year.

Morris acquired the Hotchkiss company in 1923, followed by the Wrigley transmission company, and the Hillock and Pratt bodywork firm.

In 1925, the M.G. (Morris Garages) Car company was formed, to build sporting models employing Morris mechanical components.

Sales of Morris cars soared, and in the mid-1920s the 1500cc Cowley and the

Left: 1914 Morris Oxford De Luxe
Centre left: 1926 'Bullnose' Morris Cowley

Centre: 1928 Oxford 14/28 'All steel' saloon
Below: Morris Minor saloon of 1929
Bottom: 1930 Morris Cowley two-seater

1800cc Oxford were best-sellers. Both had reliable engines, driving through oil-bath clutches and three-speed gearboxes. Front-wheel brakes appeared on the Oxford in 1925. The 1802cc 13.9hp engine had been an option for the Oxford from 1923, and became a standard fitting for 1925.

The following year saw Morris's acquisition of S.U. Carburettors, and in 1927 the firm of Wolseley was taken over.

The famous bullnose radiator gave way to a flat-rad design for 1927, and in the same year Morris produced the export-model Empire Oxford, with a 2½-litre six-cylinder engine and a gate-change four-speed gearbox. A worm-driven rear axle was employed, giving high ground clearance for rough roads abroad.

The Light Six, introduced for 1928, had

an overhead-camshaft 17.7hp six-cylinder engine of 2468cc. It was built for just two years.

However, another overhead-camshaft-engined Morris was introduced in 1929 – the first Minor. This small four-cylinder car, with an engine capacity of 847cc, was very lively, and the running gear was used in the M.G. Midget. The Minor was also produced with a sidevalve engine, in which form, with basic two-seater bodywork, it was offered for just £100 in 1931.

The Morris Oxford was fitted with a sidevalve six-cylinder 14.9hp engine and hydraulic brakes from 1930. A 15.9hp engine of 2062cc was fitted from 1933, while the 1935 Oxford Twenty had a 2561cc unit.

The Cowley continued, in four-cylinder form, until 1934, with a choice of 11.9 or 13.9hp engines from 1931. The Isis was introduced for the 1930 model year, with a 2468cc 17.9hp six-cylinder engine. It was built until 1935. Another six-cylinder Morris was the Major, similar in many respects to the Cowley, which was produced from 1931 (1938cc, 14.9hp) to 1933 (1803cc, 13.9hp). For 1934 the Major was replaced by the Cowley Six, with a 1.9-litre sidevalve engine.

All Morris models had hydraulic braking by 1934, by which time the Wilcot coloured-lamp indicator system had been introduced to the range. Semaphore-type trafficators soon replaced the Wilcot units.

Top: 1931 Oxford Sportsman's saloon
Above: 1931 Morris Isis saloon

Below: 1957 Minor 1000 Convertible. The post-war Morris Minor proved to be a very popular small car, offering outstanding reliability and fuel economy, plus space for four people and their luggage.

For 1933 Morris introduced its Ten-Four, with a four-cylinder sidevalve engine of 1292cc and a four-speed gearbox. The following year a similarly-bodied Ten-Six was added to the range, the car having a longer chassis and a 1378cc engine.

A much larger model was the 1933–35 Twenty-Five, essentially an Isis with a much larger engine – a sidevalve unit of 3486cc capacity. Synchromesh gearboxes were used on all Morris models from 1934.

From 1935 Morris cars became known by horsepower rating/cylinder numbers rather than by names. A new model to appear in that year was the 1938cc Fifteen-Six, but it was produced for only a few months.

The Morris range changed significantly for the 1935 model year, and a notable new model was the Eight. This highly successful car (similar in styling but superior in specification to the Ford Eight Model-Y) had a 918ccc sidevalve engine driving through a three-speed gearbox. It was developed into Series I (mid-1935) and then Series II (late 1937) models, gaining pressed-steel wheels. The car was available in two- and four-door saloon form, and as a two- or four-seater tourer.

Morris also introduced its attractive 'Series' four-cylinder 10 and 12hp saloons in mid-1935, with four-speed gearboxes fitted from 1937. The new models had sweeping lines, even in saloon form, and a two-door coupé with 'pram irons' was

Top: 1933 Morris Oxford Special Coupé
Above: 1931-32 Morris Minor

Above: 1933 Morris Ten-Six saloon
Right: Morris Ten-Four saloon, from 1935

offered. Similarly-styled Fourteen (1818cc), Sixteen (2062cc), Eighteen (2288cc), Twenty-One (2916cc) and Twenty-Five (3485cc) sidevalve six-cylinder saloon models were also produced from 1935.

All 1938 models featured overhead-valve engines mounted within existing body styles, and in that year the Riley company became part of the Morris organization.

A new Morris Ten was introduced for 1939, with unitary-construction bodywork and an 1140cc overhead-valve engine. Production was continued for three years after World War II.

A new Morris Eight – the Series E – was also introduced just prior to the war, and featured rounded bodywork, faired-in headlamps and a four-speed gearbox. The engine was a developed version of the 918cc sidevalve unit from the earlier Eight.

Left: Series II 14/16/18hp, produced from 1935 to 1937

Like the 10M, the Series E was built until 1948.

The Alec Issigonis/A. V. Oak-designed Minor appeared at the 1948 Motor Show. This small two- or four-door four-seater saloon (or convertible) was still powered by the faithful 918cc sidevalve engine, but the car had torsion-bar front suspension, rack-and-pinion steering and unitary-construction bodywork. Its handling qualities were far superior to those offered by other small cars of the time.

Similarly-styled but far larger MO Oxford and MS Six models were also introduced for 1949. The Oxford had a 1476cc sidevalve engine, whereas the MS Six was fitted with a 2215cc overhead-camshaft six-cylinder unit developing 70bhp. Chassis design was similar to that of the Minor, but the MS had a steering box, rather than a rack-and-pinion system. The MS Six was also very similar to the Wolseley Six-Eighty of the same era.

In 1951 Morris (the Nuffield Organisation) merged with Austin to form the British Motor Corporation. As a result, Austin-sourced overhead-valve engines became used extensively throughout the Morris range. The Minor gained the overhead-valve 803cc (A-Series) engine from the Austin A30, the 1954 Cowley received the 1200cc (B-Series) engine from the A40, and the Oxford Series II received the 1489cc unit from the A50. The Cowley was fitted with the larger engine from 1956, and continued in production until 1959, as did the Oxford, in Series III and IV (estate-car) versions.

The similarly-styled six-cylinder Isis was introduced in 1955, and was produced until 1958. It used B.M.C.'s (Morris-originated) 2639cc C-Series engine, which developed 90bhp.

The Minor was updated in 1956 with the fitting of the A35's 948cc unit in 37bhp form – a strengthened and redesigned engine developed from the 803cc motor.

Morris models sold in Australia in the late 1950s included the Wolseley 1500 look-alike, the Major, and the six-cylinder Marshal.

From 1959 many Morris and Austin models became badge-engineered versions of the same cars, although the Minor continued until 1971.

The Farina-styled 1489cc Oxford family saloon/estate car was similar to the A60,

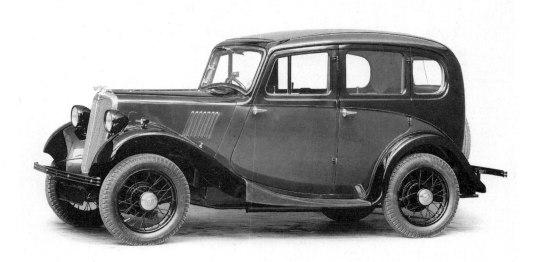

Above: 1935 Morris Eight four-door saloon

Above: Morris Ten-Four Series M, 1938

Above: 1951 Morris Minor Convertible

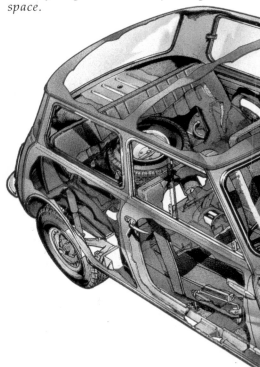

Below: The Austin Seven and Morris Mini Minor were revolutionary vehicles, designed by (Sir) Alec Issigonis. The cars featured transversely mounted four-cylinder engines, driving the front wheels. This layout gave maximum passenger space.

Left: Morris Six MS saloon, produced from 1949 to 1954

Above: Morris Mini Minor saloon of 1961
Top right: 1952 Morris Minor Traveller
Right: Morris Oxford Series II, c. 1954
Below right: Oxford Series VI Traveller, 1961

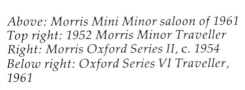

and sold well. The revolutionary front-wheel-drive Morris Mini Minor shared its boxy styling and transversely mounted engine/gearbox with the Austin Seven (later Mini). *(Variants of the Mini were introduced throughout the 1960s – see Austin section for full details.)*

Over one million Morris Minors had been built by 1961, the car being the first British model ever to achieve this figure.

For 1962 the new Series VI Oxford was fitted with a 1622cc (61bhp) version of the B-Series engine, the track was widened, and the wheelbase increased.

In late 1962 the capacity of the A-Series engine used in the Minor was increased to 1098cc (48bhp), and this engine was also used in the new front-wheel-drive four-door family saloon – the Morris 1100. In this application it was mounted transversely above the gearbox.

The 1100 became one of the most popular family cars of the 1960s, and its Hydrolastic fluid suspension gave excellent ride comfort and handling qualities.

The extremely spacious and comfortable

Right: 1962 Morris 1100
Below: 1964 Morris Oxford Series VI

Above: Mini Moke utility vehicle, 1967/8

Above: c. 1972 Morris Marina 1.3 De Luxe Coupé
Right: Mini 1000, 1976/77
Below: The 145km/h (90mph) Mini 1275 GT from 1969 on
Below right: Morris 1100, introduced in 1962

Below: 1973 Morris Marina 1.8 TC Jubilee

front-wheel-drive Morris 1800 was introduced in 1966. It too had a transversely mounted engine, here of 1798cc.

In 1967 Super De Luxe versions of the 1100 model were introduced, but fitted with the 1275cc A-Series engine, developing 58bhp. Two-door saloons joined the existing four-door models.

An uprated 1800S was announced for 1969, and a 70bhp twin-carburettor GT version of the 1300, with a top speed of 95mph (152km/h) was available from October 1969.

A significant new Morris family saloon – the Marina – was introduced in April 1971. The Marina had running gear developed from that of the Morris Minor, the last of which, in estate-car (Traveller) form, was built in the same year. Either 60bhp 1.3-litre (A-Series) or 83bhp 1.8-litre (B-Series) overhead-valve engines could be specified, and bodywork was in four-door saloon or two-door fastback coupé style. An estate model joined the range in 1976. TC (for twin carburettor) Marinas had an uprated 1798cc engine, developing 87bhp and giving a top speed of 100mph (160 km/h).

In March 1972 the Morris 2200 was introduced, with bodywork similar to that of the 1800 models but powered by a six-cylinder E-Series overhead-camshaft engine, developed from the four-cylinder unit of the Austin Maxi.

The 78bhp, 1695cc O-Series engine replaced the 1798cc B-Series unit in the more powerful Marinas, from 1979.

In July 1980 the Marina was restyled and updated, to reappear as the Morris Ital. The 1.3-litre Ital had an uprated A-Plus engine, while the higher-powered model retained the 1700cc O-Series engine.

A two-litre version, available only with an automatic gearbox, was introduced in October 1980. It was powered by the 1993cc O-Series engine from the Princess, which produced 93bhp and allowed a top speed of well over 100mph (160km/h).

The Itals were revised in September 1982, and continued in production until 1984, when the Morris name disappeared from the British Leyland range. The Ital was effectively replaced by the front-wheel-drive Austin Montego, introduced in April 1984.

Mors

France
1895–1925

In 1880 Emile Mors took over his father's Parisian electrical engineering business with his brother Louis, and by 1887 was experimenting with the steam-powered designs of Henri Brasier. They progressed to petrol-driven railway vehicles, then on to cars in 1895 which used Mors' own ignition system, changing the company name to Société d'Electricité et d'Automobiles Mors.

In 1899 Brasier-designed competition cars won the Paris–St. Malo and Paris–Bordeaux races and were beating the previous Panhard domination. The following year the company won the Paris–Toulouse–Paris and Bordeaux–Périgueux–Bordeaux events; in 1901 it won the Paris–

Left: 1899 two-cylinder Petit Duc
Above: C.S. Rolls in a 1902 Mors
Above right: 1920 Mors 14/20

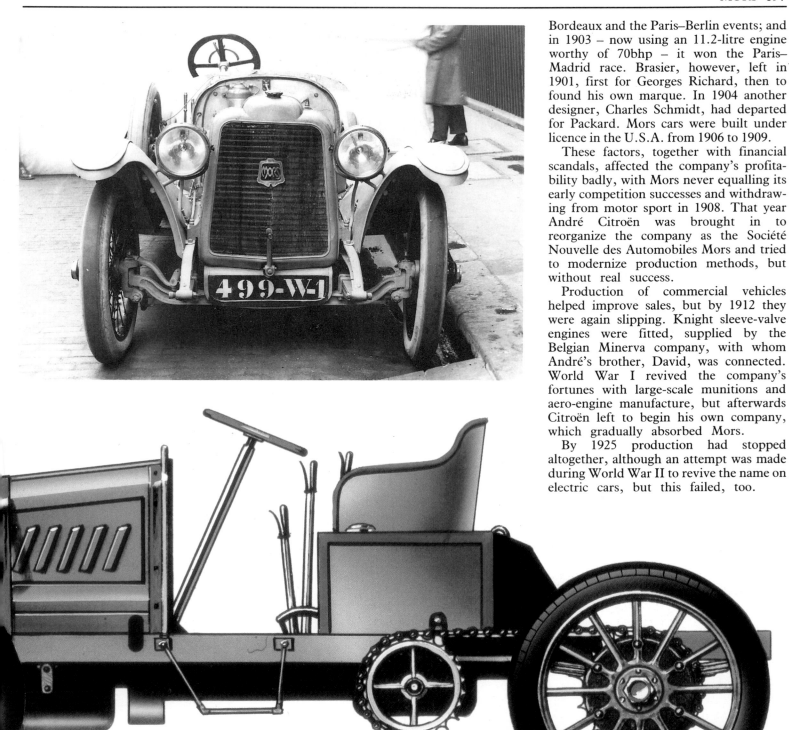

Bordeaux and the Paris–Berlin events; and in 1903 – now using an 11.2-litre engine worthy of 70bhp – it won the Paris–Madrid race. Brasier, however, left in 1901, first for Georges Richard, then to found his own marque. In 1904 another designer, Charles Schmidt, had departed for Packard. Mors cars were built under licence in the U.S.A. from 1906 to 1909.

These factors, together with financial scandals, affected the company's profitability badly, with Mors never equalling its early competition successes and withdrawing from motor sport in 1908. That year André Citroën was brought in to reorganize the company as the Société Nouvelle des Automobiles Mors and tried to modernize production methods, but without real success.

Production of commercial vehicles helped improve sales, but by 1912 they were again slipping. Knight sleeve-valve engines were fitted, supplied by the Belgian Minerva company, with whom André's brother, David, was connected. World War I revived the company's fortunes with large-scale munitions and aero-engine manufacture, but afterwards Citroën left to begin his own company, which gradually absorbed Mors.

By 1925 production had stopped altogether, although an attempt was made during World War II to revive the name on electric cars, but this failed, too.

In the first decade of this century Mors cars, such as this 60hp of 1902, made the company a force to be reckoned with. But when the motor race wins stopped, the company's fortunes went into decline and it was eventually absorbed by Citroën.

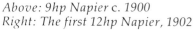

Napier

Great Britain
1900–1924

The roots of Napier cars date back to 1808 when the engineering firm of D. Napier and Son was founded, making machinery for industry.

Montague Napier – the founder's grandson – took over the business in 1895. He was a keen racing cyclist, and fellow cyclist Selwyn Francis Edge asked him to design a new engine for his 1896 Panhard. This was followed by a complete Napier car the following year, albeit an improved Panhard.

Edge formed S. F. Edge Ltd. in 1900 to build Napier's cars, and the first year's contract was for just six vehicles.

Edge successfully raced Napiers and between 1901 and 1902 8hp twins and 16hp fours were offered, customers including Prime Minister A. J. Balfour.

The small factory at Lambeth, south London, was stretched to the limit and production was transferred to larger premises at Acton, West London, in 1903.

Edge drove a 30hp four-cylinder car to victory in the Gordon Bennett Race in 1902. This was the first important win for a British car in international competition.

The 1921 40/50 limousine continued the company's tradition of building luxurious, if somewhat clumsy, cars. In the early '20s, demand for Napier cars fell, and the last were delivered in November 1924.

Above: 9hp Napier c. 1900
Right: The first 12hp Napier, 1902

Above: 1904 18/30hp Napier

Above: 1907 60hp Napier

Above: 1908 Napier six-cylinder R Type

Above: 1913 16hp Estate Wagon

Above: 1913 Type 44 Torpedo Tourer
Above right: 1922 40/50hp Napier

Right: 1920 40/50 Threequarter Cabriolet

Other cars joined the range, including the 1904 18/30hp six-cylinder, and the company also branched out to make motorboats.

The company was reorganized as S. F. Edge (1907) Ltd. in that year and a rift developed between Edge and Napier, with Edge claiming the cars were old-fashioned and of poor quality.

Legal proceedings led to the company's liquidation and Napier bought Edge's holdings.

The big Napiers in production were somewhat cumbersome but they were popular, with the 1910 catalogue listing more than 160 prominent members of the aristocracy, army and church as owners.

Napier's range was diverse, from a 10hp 1.3-litre car to the large 14-litre 90hp Six, one of its most memorable models being the 30/35 open-top coupé built between 1914 and 1916.

World War I introduced the company to aero-engines and it made the Sunbeam Arab V8 under licence.

From 1916 it developed its own Napier Lion engine. This unit later powered a number of land-speed-record cars, including Campbell's Bluebirds and Segrave's Golden Arrow.

Above: a rather special 1914 30hp Napier

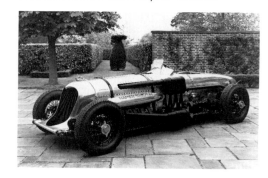

Below: 1933 24-litre Napier-Railton

Montague Napier returned to car production in 1919 and introduced the T75 luxury model with a 6.2-litre engine. Only 187 were made, however, far fewer than planned, and the last cars were delivered in November 1924. A total of 4,258 Napiers were made.

Napier continued to produce aero-engines and became part of the English Electric group in 1945.

Nash

U.S.A.
1917–1957

Although the former farm labourer Charles W. Nash rose to become President of General Motors in 1912, he had a long-standing ambition to build his own car, so in 1916 he resigned from G.M. and bought the Jeffery Motor Company.

The first Nash car, a four-litre overhead-valve six-cylinder model, appeared in 1917, while the following year roadsters and sports models were added to the already-expanding range. After a brief slump in 1920 Nash introduced a new model with an overhead-valve 2½-litre four-cylinder engine of similar design to the existing six and these two engines powered the company's nine-body line-up.

Nash was now well-established in the middle-price bracket and in order to gain a foothold in the quality-car sector, purchased La Fayette Motors who were at the time building a luxurious 5.6-litre V8. Unfortunately, the model did not sell well

Above: 1926 Nash two-door sedan

and was discontinued some two years later in 1924.

In 1928, when sales were at a record high level, Nash unveiled the Model 328, which it claimed had the lowest-priced seven-bearing six-cylinder engine on the American market. The company survived the early Depression years with its Single Six and Twin Ignition Six (both of 3378cc) and the new Twin Ignition Eight, in a 32-car range, but as the Depression deepened

sales fell and by 1932 only Nash and G.M. were in profit. In 1933 Nash car production reached an all-time low of only 14,000 units.

A further reduction in the range took place in 1935, resulting in just two six-cylinder body styles and four eight-cylinder styles, with the Advanced Six Victoria displaying the new streamlined 'Aeroform' bodywork.

Although the La Fayette line, reintroduced some years earlier, had sold quite well as the 'big car in the low-price

The Nash Four of 1921 was powered by a new four-cylinder 2.5-litre engine of similar design to the company's existing six-cylinder four-litre engine. The customer had a choice of nine different bodies.

Above: 1942 Nash 600 sedan
Right: 1953 Nash Rambler

field', it was discontinued in 1941 in favour of the new Nash 600 range. This caused quite a stir in the American press, being heralded (incorrectly) as the world's first unitary-construction body/chassis unit. However, the resultant light body, coupled to the 2.8-litre six-cylinder engine, produced excellent fuel consumption, allowing the Nash 600 to cover that number of miles (965km) on a tank of petrol – hence its name.

In 1937, Nash had merged with the Kelvinator Corporation and the combined company manufactured cars, refrigerators and air-conditioning systems for cars. Alongside the new Nash 600 range, the Ambassadors were still available in six- and eight-cylinder guise. Car production stopped in 1942 and on resumption in 1945 Ambassadors continued to be made until a redesigned range was introduced in 1949, featuring 'Airflyte' styling with semi-enclosed road wheels and a one-piece wrap-around windscreen.

An all-time production record was achieved in 1950, the year Nash unveiled 'America's first compact car', the 2.8-litre Rambler. The small-car theme was continued with the introduction of the English-built Nash-Healey with a 3.6-litre Nash Ambassador engine, and one of these cars took fourth place in the 1951 Le Mans 24-Hours race.

Just prior to the merger of Nash-Kelvinator and Hudson in 1954, Nash unveiled its sub-compact, the Metropolitan. This was based on the tiny NX1 experimental car of 1950, and built in England. It used a 1200cc overhead-valve

Below: 1954 Nash Statesman   *Bottom: 1959 Nash Metropolitan*

An assembly plant was set up in Australia in 1976 and in 1983 Nissan began production of pickup trucks in Tennessee, U.S.A.

One interesting car was the Arna – having an Italian engine and a Nissan body shell.

The Nissan Cherry body shell was also used to take an Alfasud engine and that model was known as the Nissan Cherry Europe.

The Datsun name was officially dropped at the end of 1983 and all the company's vehicles are now called Nissans.

Since 1983 Nissan has continued its dominance in the automotive industry, being Japan's second largest manufacturer and one of the biggest in the world. Models in the 1980s included the all-terrain Patrol – the Japanese Range Rover – the extremely popular Cherry and Sunny models, the Bluebird and Maxima saloons, and the supermini Micra. Two vehicles launched in 1989 showed that Nissan's products had finally caught up with those of compatriots Honda and Toyota: the 200SX/240SX 2+2 seater sports coupé was well received by critics, and in the

Top: 1983 Nissan Prairie
Right: 1990 Nissan Patrol

U.S. the 300ZX Turbo model won the prestigious *Motor Trend* Import Car of the Year award. With superb roadholding and a 300bhp twin-turbocharged V6 allowing 0-60mph acceleration in 5.6 seconds, the ZX is a credible Porsche-challenger.

Right: 1987 Nissan Silvia 1.8 Turbo

Above: 1990 Nissan 300 ZX

Left: 1989 Nissan Maxima

Cars like the Nissan Silvia, unspectacular but competent and immensely successful, are the cornerstone of the company's hugely profitable empire.

Nissan was one of the first Japanese manufacturers to move into Europe. In 1980 it took a minority interest in Motor Iberica in Spain, becoming the majority shareholder two years later. By 1983, Motor Iberica was building the Nissan Patrol 4x4 at its plant in Barcelona Zona Franca.

In 1984 Nissan founded its first new factory in Europe, in Sunderland in Britain. Nissan Motor Manufacturing Ltd. G.B. was building Bluebirds by 1986. Further outposts were set up in Holland, Belgium and Germany and, by 1993, 60 per cent of Nissans sold in Europe were produced in Europe.

By this stage, Nissan's profit-making days seemed to be over, and it was facing perhaps the bleakest period in its post-war history. While things were going well in Europe with the U.K.-built Primera and Micra, the recession was affecting the company badly on the home market.

By trying to compete with arch-rival Toyota, Nissan was having to spend huge amounts on more and more new models. To fight its way back into profit the company shut down its plant in Australia. In Japan and the U.S., though, the company stepped up production. A new Japanese plant was built and the U.S. plant at Smyrna, Tennessee was extended to take the new Altima mid-size

Top right: Nissan Micra 1.3SR

Right: Nissan Almera GTi

Below: Nissan Terrano II 2.7 TDi SR

saloon. Nissan was still making losses in 1994 though well on the road to recovery.

One of the cars to keep Nissan afloat during this crisis was the new Micra, launched in 1992. It was the first Japanese car ever to be named Car of the Year in Europe and was built in Britain. A far cry from the previous, boxy model, the new Micra had friendly curves and a cheeky look. Like its predecessor, though, it was incredibly easy to drive and unerringly reliable. It was an instant hit, especially in Europe. The British-built Primera (badged the Infiniti G20 in the U.S.) was also a good seller.

The cream of the 1990s Nissans was the Skyline GT-R, launched in 1993. This handsome four-seater coupé used a high-tech 2.6-litre straight six engine producing

Top: 1997 Nissan QX

Top right: Primera Touring Car racer

Above: 1997 Nissan Primera 2.0 SRi

Below: 1997 Nissan 200SX

280 horsepower thanks to its twin turbochargers. Viscous-coupled four-wheel-drive completed the specification of this Japanese super coupé.

The Patrol was joined by a new smaller 4x4 built in collaboration with Ford. The Terrano was built in Barcelona and aimed to take sales in the small RV market, but was outsold by most of its Japanese rivals.

By the late-1990s Nissan seemed to have steadied its finances and remained the second largest car manufacturer in Japan, second only to Toyota. It also ranked as the sixth largest manufacturer in the world.

N.S.U.

Germany
1905–1977

Christian Schmidt, a partner in a successful sewing-machine manufacturing business, branched out to make bicycles at Neckarsulm, Germany, in the early 1880s.

The operation became Neckarsulmer Fahrradwerke A.G. in 1886 and the company became suppliers of chassis to Daimler.

N.S.U. was adopted as the trademark in 1892 and used for many years for the company's famous motor-cycles.

The first car was built under licence from Belgian firm Pipe in 1905 – a luxury car with a limited market.

N.S.U. followed up with a four-cylinder 6/10 model and then a 15/24 the next year.

Until World War I, production extended to cars of up to 3.3 litres, and lorries.

After the war N.S.U. developed its small four-cylinder cars and the 1.6-litre 6/30 was particularly successful in competition.

By 1927, N.S.U.'s other factory at Heilbronn had been expanded and was in operation. But the Depression, plus poor investments, led to financial problems and car production was ended in 1929.

However, the motor-cycle side continued to make profits.

Above: NSU in 1908 Prince Henry Trials
Right: 1913 NSU 4-cylinder Torpedo
Below: The Ro80 broke new ground for NSU in 1967. The Wankel twin-rotor engine was rated at 2 litres and delivered a smooth 113bhp through the front wheels, giving a top speed of 117km/h (110mph). It proved unreliable through rotor tips wearing out.

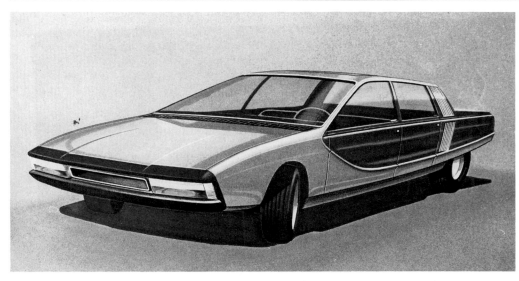

Above: 1971 Pininfarina styling for Ro80

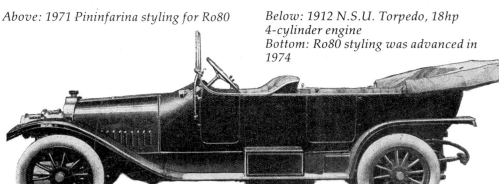

Below: 1912 N.S.U. Torpedo, 18hp 4-cylinder engine
Bottom: Ro80 styling was advanced in 1974

N.S.U. sold half of the factory to Fiat and built Fiats under licence as N.S.U.-Fiats.

The company recovered sufficiently to buy back its interests and commissioned Dr. Ferdinand Porsche to develop a people's car.

An upsurge in the motor-cycle market led to the project being shelved. But this was the beginning of the Volkswagen Beetle.

Car production resumed in 1958 and a drawn-out dispute flared up with Fiat over the use of the N.S.U. name for cars built at the Heilbronn factory. The dispute finally ended in 1966 when Fiat relinquished its claim to the name of N.S.U.-Fiat.

The new N.S.U. for 1958 was the air-cooled Prinz, which owed much to N.S.U.'s expertise with motor-cycle engines. It remained in production until the early 1970s.

Meanwhile, N.S.U. launched the first Wankel-engined car in 1963. It was called the Wankel Spyder and used a single-rotor engine conceived by Dr. Felix Wankel, going into production in a Prinz body shell in 1964.

The twin-rotor Ro80 came out in mid-1967 but cost N.S.U. a fortune in warranty claims because of the engine's excessive wear rate and initial unreliability.

It was dropped in 1977 and was the last N.S.U. The company merged with Audi in 1969.

Oldsmobile

U.S.A.
1896 to date

Ransom Eli Olds, the son of a mechanical engineer, was born in Geneva, Ohio, in 1864. When the family moved to Lansing, Michigan, Olds' father established a machine shop on River Street and, when he was 21, Olds bought into the business. By 1892 he had bought his father out and incorporated the Olds Gasoline Engine Works.

Five years later Olds had built a variety of three- and four-wheeled steam-powered vehicles, including one steamer which was sold to the Francis Times Co. of Bombay – the first American passenger car to be sold, and the first self-propelled export. In 1895 Olds began experimenting with petrol engines, forming the separate Olds Motor Vehicle Co. in August 1897 rather than gamble with the family business.

Only one example of Olds' 1897 car was built, and it was put on display at the Smithsonian Institute, Washington. It soon became apparent to Olds that Lansing could not provide the skilled labour he needed, so he moved production to Detroit, on the advice and backing of copper magnate Samuel L. Smith, who wanted to establish his two sons, Frederic and Angus, in business. Between 1899 and 1900 the new Olds Motor Works acquired all rights from the previous company.

The first vehicle offered was too complicated and costly for success, but in 1901 came the famous Curved Dash Runabout, 4,000 of which had been sold by 1903. In 1902 a fire at the Detroit plant almost wiped the company out, with only one prototype left undamaged, and production returned permanently to Lansing.

Curved Dashes were owned by Sir Thomas Lipton, Mark Twain, Theodore Roosevelt Jr., the Queen of Italy, the Krupp family of Germany, and many other famous people. By 1904 Oldsmobiles were being exported to Russia, France,

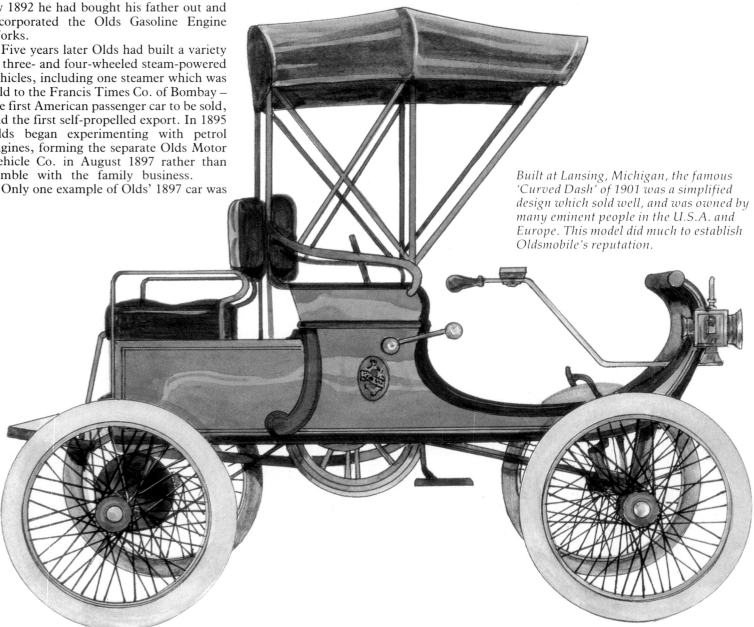

Built at Lansing, Michigan, the famous 'Curved Dash' of 1901 was a simplified design which sold well, and was owned by many eminent people in the U.S.A. and Europe. This model did much to establish Oldsmobile's reputation.

Below: Introduced in 1975, the Oldsmobile Starfire was a small economy 2+2 hatchback coupé, sharing the same bodyshell as the Buick Skyhawk and the Chevrolet Monza. It prefaced a general trend towards smaller vehicles in the U.S.A.

Top: Firenza Sedan from 1982

Left: 1978 Delta 88 Royale Sedan

Centre: 1988 Cutlass Calais 2.3 Quad 4

Above: 1989 Oldsmobile Touring Sedan

Left: 1975 Starfire GT

Like the other divisions of General Motors in the States, Oldsmobile was losing sales every year. By 1993, the company's annual production had fallen to 400,000 from a million a decade before. In an attempt to find new buyers, Oldsmobile created the Aurora, which was distinctly different from the existing range. Gone were the oversized grille and acres of chrome, and in their place simple, clean and modern styling taken from European and Asian luxury lines. For Oldsmobile, it was a matter of do or die. The company had to revitalize its image or fade away. The Aurora faced tough competition with lots of new products from Lexus, Infiniti, Mercedes, BMW, Cadillac, Lincoln and Chrysler when it made production in 1995. The gamble worked and the company managed to stay afloat.

The Intrigue, launched in 1996, had very similar styling to the Aurora, and the cars were obviously of the same family. Rather than the Aurora's V8, the Intrigue used a 200bhp V6. The Cutlass was also restyled in 1997, and continued as a good seller. The Silhouette was the Oldsmobile version of G.M.'s MPV and the Bravada was a large 4x4 based on the Chevy Blazer S.

The more traditional Oldsmobile image was still being upheld in the late 1990s by the old-fashioned-looking Regency.

Above: The 1997 Oldsmobile Bravada was based on the Chevrolet Blazer

Right: The Oldsmobile Regency looked old-fashioned compared to the rest of the 1997 range

Below: The Oldsmobile Intrigue, launched in 1996, was a smaller brother to the Aurora, with a V6 instead of the Aurora's V8

Above: Oldsmobile Achieva

Above: 1997 Oldsmobile 88 LS
Below: 1997 Oldsmobile Aurora

Above: Oldsmobile LSS

Below: 1997 Oldsmobile Cutlass Supreme

Bottom: 1997 Oldsmobile Bravada

O.M.

Italy
1905–1934

Officine Meccaniche were locomotive builders who took over the Fabbrica Automobili Züst firm in 1918. Swiss engineer Roberto Züst gained partnership in the Güller engine manufacturing business in the 1870s. By the turn of the century the firm, now under the control of his sons, was producing experimental cars, offered seriously two years later.

These early cars were Mercedes-inspired vehicles of large capacity. By 1906 a separate Brixia-Züst company had been formed in Brescia (Brixia being its Latin name) to produce cheaper cars, in particular the 1495cc three-cylinder models used as London taxis by 1910. In 1911 the name was changed again and, two years later, production of the S305 began.

O.M. continued the S305, also offering its own vehicles by Austrian designer Barratouché from 1921. O.M. used only sidevalve engines, with remarkable competition success against more advanced

Above: 1928 O.M. 15/60hp   *Below: Züst factory at Brescia, 1906*

Above: 1923 O.M. 665 Tipo Superba

machines, although the 1926 straight-eight Grand Prix car was hampered by only three forward speeds. The company's victories included the 1923 and 1924 Coppa delle Alpi, and the 1925 Tripoli Grand Prix. The firm's first six-cylinder-engined car, the Tipo 665S, won the first Mille Miglia race, in 1927.

More emphasis was placed on O.M.'s

Above: 1929 O.M. 469 1.5-litre

commercial division, which began producing vans and taxis in 1925, progressing to diesel-powered trucks under licence from the Swiss Saurer firm. In 1933 car production ceased with the firm's takeover by Fiat. From 1923 O.M. cars had been marketed in Britain by L. C.

Rawlence and Co., who also performance-tuned O.M.s which were raced in the TT. Rawlence and Co. continued to offer the cars up to 1934, built up from their stockpile of parts.

Two former employees, Augusto Coletta and Luigi Mangano, also bought parts and launched the Fiat-style OMV or Alcyone prototype in 1934, under the Esperia name, but it never went into production. Olivo Pellegatti also designed a four-cylinder O.M., but this was never built. The O.M. badge still survives on commercial vehicles, mainly of Fiat origin.

Below: Racing version of the O.M. 665 Superba, popular in England during the mid-1920s. Minoia and Morandi's 665S won the first Mille Miglia in 1927.

Opel

Germany
1898 to date

Adam Opel, born in Russelsheim, near Frankfurt, in 1837, trained as a mechanic and his first commercial venture was building sewing machines.

By 1868 business was flourishing in his purpose-built factory and it was his five sons' enthusiasm for cycling which led him to manufacture bicycles in 1886.

On his death in 1895, Opel bicycles and sewing machines were dominating the market. But the cycle market was beginning to decline and his widow Sophie and elder sons Carl and Wilhelm looked elsewhere for profitable manufacturing.

They bought the rights to the Lutzmann car – introduced in 1895 by Friederich Lutzmann, a locksmith from Dessau.

A car department was opened and the Opel-Lutzmann was shown in 1898, with a rear-mounted single-cylinder 4hp engine. The following year it was replaced by a twin-cylinder model.

Neither was successful and only a few examples were built. Lutzmann was dismissed and car production stopped.

However, in 1900 Opel became sole agent for Darracq in Germany, Austria and Hungary to build the cars under licence with German bodies. They were known as Opel-Darracqs and sold encouragingly.

Opel branched out and showed its own 10/12 1884cc model at the 1902 Hamburg Motor Show, and also launched small commercials and twin-cylinder motorcycles from 1906.

Opel's so-called 'doctor's car' in twin-cylinder 6/12 and 8/14 models was particularly popular until 1910, while at the other end of the scale the company offered the 6.9-litre 35/40 model. Many competition wins helped sales.

But fire devastated the Opel works in 1911 and Opel decided on a total commitment to cars. The company ended sewing-machine manufacture after exactly a million had been made and the plant was rebuilt for car production.

Above: 1911 Torpedo Double Phaeton
Above right: 1911 5/12hp Opel Limousine

Below and bottom: Two views of the 1912 5/12hp Opel roadster

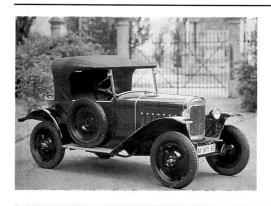

Until World War I, models included the one-litre 5/12 and 6/16 cars, up to the 10.2-litre 40/100 which had a chassis price of £800.

Opel also built trucks, trailers, a few cars and aero-engines during the war.

The post-war years were stark for Opel. Russelsheim was under French occupation, there was a shortage of raw materials and the market had slumped.

The company survived, building a few old models, but in 1924 the plant was refurbished with moving assembly lines.

Opel launched a small mass-produced car that year, copied from the Citroën 5CV. It was known as the 4/12 Laubfrosch – German for tree-frog – because of its bright-green finish. The company's fortunes blossomed and by 1928 it had about 8,000 employees.

Opel had formed an association with America's General Motors – which had an assembly plant at Berlin – and G.M. bought an 80 per cent share of the company in 1929, acquiring the other 20 per cent by 1931.

Above left: 856cc 1924 Laubfrosch (tree frog), a copy of the Citroën 5CV
Left: 1935 Olympia, a four-cylinder two-door cabriolet

Below: The Opel P4 of 1935 was the last of a generation, replaced the following year by the more elegant, rounded Olympia series. The 1279cc Olympia was timed to coincide with the Berlin Olympic Games.

Opel's 1935 1279cc Olympia – named to coincide with the Berlin Olympic Games – introduced unitary construction on a large scale to the German car industry, and the company achieved a 42 per cent share of the market that year.

Above: 1936 Opel Kadett
Below: Two-door Opel Kadett, 1936

The 1074cc Kadett was launched in 1937 and it went on to sell about 107,000 models until 1940.

Nazi control of the industry forced G.M. to relinquish control to the government in 1940 and the company turned to truck and engine production.

Car manufacturing was restarted in 1947 with the Olympia, followed by the 2473cc

Below: Opel Admiral was built 1937-39
Bottom: 1938 Opel Admiral six-cylinder four-door Cabriolet

Kapitan. G.M. resumed control in 1948.

The first real new postwar car was the 1488cc Rekord, introduced in 1953.

The one-litre Kadett – built at the new Bochum plant – was launched in 1962 with another new-generation Kadett introduced in September 1965.

The Bochum plant had produced its millionth car by October 1966 and expansion continued with another new factory at Kaiserslauten in 1966 and a proving-ground at Dudenhofen.

More sporting models appeared such as

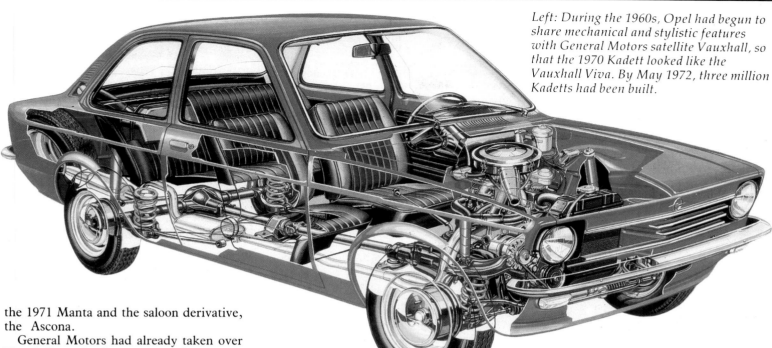

Left: During the 1960s, Opel had begun to share mechanical and stylistic features with General Motors satellite Vauxhall, so that the 1970 Kadett looked like the Vauxhall Viva. By May 1972, three million Kadetts had been built.

the 1971 Manta and the saloon derivative, the Ascona.

General Motors had already taken over Vauxhall and that company's models shared many similarities with Opels, such as the Viva and Kadett.

Opel and Vauxhall formally combined their British marketing operations in 1981 and throughout the 1980s there have been Opel and Vauxhall versions of the same models, such as the Corsa (Nova in England) and Kadett (Astra).

Two of the most popular models have been the high-performance Monza and the stylish Manta/Kadett GTE in both 1.8- and two-litre forms, the latter with fuel-injection.

Above: 1959 Olympia Rekord Saloon
Left: 1969 GT Coupé 1.9 used Kadett parts
Above right: 1972 2.8-litre Commodore GS
Right: 1972 Opel Manta SR coupé
Below: 1977 Ascona shared Manta parts

Top: Executive class, 1979 Senator CD
Above: 1981 Opel Monza, a spacious coupé
Left: 1987 Opel Ascona family saloon
Below: 1989 hot-hatch, Opel Corsa GSi

Packard

U.S.A.
1899–1958

Brothers James Ward Packard and William Doud Packard became involved with motor cars in 1898, inspired by a challenge from Alexander Winton to improve on one of his designs. They formed the New York and Ohio Automobile Company in Warren, Ohio, in 1899, launching their excellent and reliable Model A that year.

By 1901 the name had changed to the Ohio Automobile Company, altering again the year after to the Packard Motor Car Company. The company remained in Ohio, but then Henry B. Joy joined the company in 1902, bringing finance from Detroit businessmen and the firm moved there to a factory on East Grand Boulevard the following year. At this point the brothers themselves separated from their company, although James Ward Packard remained as a figurehead president until 1909.

In 1902 Packard had abandoned its insistence on single-cylinder engines, producing a flat twin. A four-cylinder model appeared in 1904, a racing version of which set speed records at Daytona and came fourth in the first Vanderbilt Cup, considerably enhancing the marque's sporting image.

Commercial-vehicle manufacture began in 1905, lasting until 1923, and the cars began to be exported to various countries around the world. By 1908 Packard had agencies in Britain, Spain, France, Cuba, Hawaii and Latin America.

Top left: Packard Touring of 1903
Top right: 1911 Packard Touring
Above: First six-cylinder car, 1911
Left: 1914 Packard Roadster

Below: The 905 of 1919 was a stripped-down racing version of the Twin Six, with a larger V12 engine. It was driven by Ralph de Palma in record-breaking runs at Daytona in 1919, and a top speed of 241.24km/h (149.9mph) was achieved.

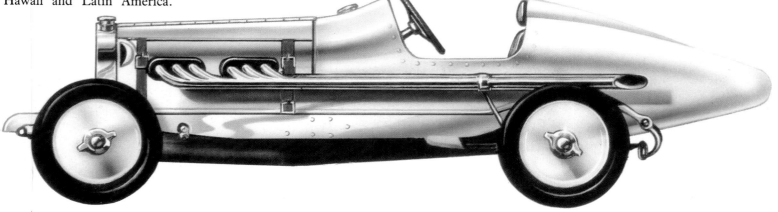

In 1911 Packard's first six-cylinder model was offered and former lawyer Alvin Macauley joined the firm, taking over as president from 1916 until 1938. He was well suited to the task, once given the accolade of being the 'only gentleman in the automotive business'. In 1913 electric lighting and starting were offered on Packard cars and the following year spiral-bevel final drive appeared.

Above: 1916 Packard Touring

Packard aimed very much for the top end of the market, its cheaper lines of this period not meeting with much success. The Twin Six, announced in 1915 for the following year, was very well received, the work of ex-Hudson man, Jesse Vincent. Vincent was also responsible for the V8 and V12 aero-engines built by Packard during World War I. During the early 1920s Packards were very much in vogue, the company ignoring the sports cars to concentrate on higher-priced prestige models. By 1928 over 50,000 cars a year were coming off the production line, outstripping Cadillac and Lincoln.

Below: 1920 Packard Twin Six

Above: 1921 Packard Twin Six Sedanca
Below: Packard Roadster of 1925

Above: 1924 Packard Roadster
Below: 1928 Packard Single Eight

Top: 1928 Single Eight with Rollston body
Above: 1930 Speedster Runabout
Right: 1930 Eight Dietrich Convertible

Below: The Packard Twelve Phaeton of 1936 was similar in concept to the 1928 model; power was provided by 7.75-litre V12 engine, giving 57hp. It had domed pistons, four-main-bearing crankshaft, with automatic valve clearance mechanism.

A Canadian outlet was opened during 1931 at Windsor, Ontario, which remained in operation for eight years. That year Prince Eugene of Belgium crossed the Sahara using two Packard Eights, which provided good publicity, but like most luxury-car manufacturers, the company was badly affected by the Depression. Sales reached a record low of just under 6,100 in 1934, with a loss of U.S. $7.3 million. The following year a new model, the relatively inexpensive 120, was brought out and helped to save Packard from early closure. Advance orders totalled somewhere around the 10,000 mark and by 1936 the firm was showing profits to the tune of U.S. $7 million and production figures of 83,226.

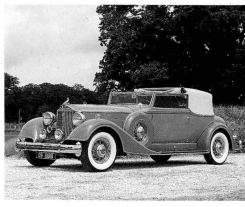

Above: 1934 Packard Twelve, Series 1107 Convertible Victoria

Above: Packard Super Eight of 1939, built on the assembly lines of the more lucrative 'junior' Packards, the six and 3.7-litre straight-eight 120. Cabriolet styling gave the car a stubby look compared with four-door models.

Above left: 1938 Packard Twelve Victoria
Above: Franay-bodied 1939 Super Eight
Left: 1941 One-eighty Sedanca prototype
Below: Post-war 180 reappearing as Ziz-110

In 1937 came the Packard Six, similar to the eight-cylinder 120, which was produced alongside the older, 'senior' Packard Eights and Twelves, on which little was changed to appeal to the old guard of customers. The new Clipper styling arrived in 1941, when the marque's first estate car was offered. Expensive models were still available at this time, with custom bodies by Darrin, LeBaron and Rollson, with such refinements as electric windows and air conditioning.

In 1942 Packard turned to war production and by the time civilian manufacture resumed in 1946 the new Clipper design had lost much of its impact – in fact, that name was dropped for a while from 1948 to 1953. The Senior Eight was also deleted from the post-war range, the production rights being sold to the U.S.S.R.

At the end of the 1940s sales began to decline and Packard decided to concentrate on the lower-priced models, totally relinquishing its place in the prestige field to Cadillac. The firm began to lag behind its competitors and was still using sidevalve in-line engines when others had long since progressed to V8s. It did, however, manage to produce its own Ultramatic automatic transmission in 1950.

Packard's slogan during its lifetime was 'Ask The Man Who Owns One', this reputedly having been said by James Packard when he was asked for publicity material on an early model. During the more enlightened 1950s, however, this was modified slightly to 'Ask The Man Who Owns One And The Woman Who Drives One'.

In 1952 former salesman James J. Nance became president, and he attempted to regain Packard's luxurious image with a new beginning, launching the Mayfair sports model and reviving the Clipper name. In 1953 came the Caribbean convertibles and a very expensive limousine range. In order to cut all ties with the past Nance reputedly threw out the parts section which was keeping the older Packards still running, and by doing so aided the downfall of the company. The following year brought the purchase of Studebaker and with it came that company's overhead-valve V8 engine, used by Nash and Hudson, by now part of

Above: 1951 Packard 300 Sedan

Above: 1952 Patrician 400
Below: Pick-up based on 1954 model

Above: 1956 Caribbean Convertible
Below: Patrician Sedan from 1956

American Motors. Studebaker's reputation had diminished, however, and in the long run it did little to help revive the public's esteem of the ailing Packard company. Another setback was the acquisition by Chrysler of Briggs, Packard's coachbuilders, and the subsequent cut-off of supply.

In 1956 Nance resigned and Studebaker-Packard was sold to Curtiss-Wright. This was the last year of the true Packards. Although the marque was still officially alive until 1958, these were, in reality, little more than rebadged Studebakers and after that time the distinguished Packard name disappeared.

Panhard

France
1891–1967

René Panhard began building experimental cars in 1888, having set up to produce engines for Gottlieb Daimler in 1886, in partnership with Emile Levassor. In 1891 the pair's first two cars were sold, and by 1893 their full-colour sales catalogue included marine engines, commercial vehicles and motor boats, and some 55 Panhard et Levassor cars had been sold, as well as 294 Daimler engines. The *Système Panhard* concept of front-wheel steering, front-mounted engine and rear-wheel drive by chain was well established by 1896; however, Levassor succumbed to injuries sustained in the previous year's Paris–Marseilles race.

In 1897, the firm was renamed Société Anonyme des Anciens Etablissements Panhard et Levassor, with a capital of FF 5 million and board members including Daimler, Hippolyte Panhard, Adolphe Clément, Arthur Krebs (designer of periscopes, balloons and carburettors), and the sportsman René de Knyff. Employees totalled 650, and production in 1898 was 336 vehicles. By 1902, manufacture had exceeded the 1,000 mark, and the cars were being sold in London by the Hon. Charles S. Rolls, who raced Panhards at the time.

Several firms copied or adopted the Panhard layout, notably Napier, Star, Locomobile, Dürkopp, M.M.C. and Germain. Prior to starting up on its own,

Hotchkiss manufactured components for Panhard. Clément left in 1903 to concentrate on his own motor business, and in 1905 the company started making aero-engines, along with an 11-litre six-cylinder car engine.

René Panhard died in 1908, and was succeeded by his son Hippolyte as head of the company. René's grandson Paul joined the firm at this point, and he controlled the family's stake in the company until 1950, when his son Jean took over.

Above: 1898 Panhard et Levassor, 2.4 twin

Sales declined badly at around this time, although the firm was able to maintain profitability, and matters gradually improved until 1913, when 2,100 vehicles

Below: 1933 Panhard coupé was right-hand-drive in the manner of all the 'grandes routieres' of the era. Chassis were huge, wheelbases long, and bodies increasingly stylish.

Above: 1908 Huntercombe, Panhard chassis
Below: Labourdette 1912 PL Skiff-torpedo

automobile side had started to decline, operating at only 60 per cent capacity.

The stylish Dynamique range introduced in 1937 under technical director Jean Panhard, with its centrally mounted steering wheel (until 1939), synchromesh gearbox, hydraulic brakes, independent torsion-bar suspension and faired-in wheels and headlamps, did much to stem

Right: 1950 Dyna-Panhard 120 cabriolet

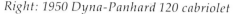

were sold. Designers were Dufresne and later Voisin, and the Knight sleeve-valve engine was by now the standard power unit. Panhard was also building four-wheel-drive, four-wheel-steering military vehicles which, along with a 15hp staff car, saw the company through World War I.

During the mid-1920s the range of engine configurations proliferated so that, by 1928, no fewer than eight different sizes were available. The commercial side was heavily involved in all sectors, producing military vehicles, half-tracks, tankers, lorries and buses, with sleeve-valve diesels appearing in the 1930s. By this time the

Above right: Curvaceous 1960 PL17
Below: Sleeve valve 1929 20/60hp PL

the downward trend, however.

Although armoured cars continued to be built in Paris during World War II, the plants at Reims and Orléans were evacuated to Tarbes. After the war and until 1950, Panhard was part of the Union Francaise Automobile, and Louis Bionnier worked on developing a successor to the Dynamique. The Dyna-Panhard, a front-wheel-drive car with a small-capacity flat-twin engine, incorporating features of the Aluminium Francaise Grégoire, appeared in 1946. This model was assembled at the Ivry, Paris, plant, with bodywork coming from Orléans and components from Reims; Arbel Chassis Pressing and Facel-Metallon made light-alloy wings and body pressings. By 1951, production had risen from 1,350 units in 1948 to 14,220. However, although several companies were using the flat-twin engine to very good effect, high prices were having an

adverse effect on sales, and spare capacity was turned over to building commercial 2CVs for Citroën.

The Dyna-Panhard of 1954 must have looked good to Citroën, with its increased use of alloys, fewer castings, and supercharged engines in the sports models, as Citroën acquired a 25 per cent stake in Panhard in 1955. Cost-cutting exercises saw a change to steel panels in 1958, although power was increased to 60bhp with the Tigre of 1961. In 1965, Panhard was taken over by Citroën, who had effectively starved it of funds for developing its own projects; Panhard was responsible for much work on the Citroën Dyane. The last Panhard car left the Ivry factory in July 1967, although Jean Panhard continues to maintain the armoured-car business from a factory at Marolles, where a Peugeot V6-powered 6X6 armoured mortar carrier is produced.

Panther

Great Britain
1972 to date

Racing enthusiast and engineer Bob Jankel worked for tuning company Superspeed Conversions in the 1960s and built cars for pleasure.

He left to join the fashion trade but sold his company in 1971 after requests to build replicas of his cars.

Jankel then founded Panther West Winds Ltd., initially working from the garage at his home in Walton-on-Thames, Surrey.

The first production Panther was the Jaguar-powered J72, looking akin to an SS100 and introduced in 1972.

A total of 45 were made in the first year and Panther moved into the former Cooper Car Co. works at Byfleet, Surrey.

A 5.3-litre version of the J72 was announced in 1973 but was dropped after 1975 in favour of the 4.2-litre straight-six.

Panther announced the V12-engined DeVille, built in the vein of the Bugatti Royale, and priced at £17,650. A drophead version was offered from 1976.

The company also produced the Rio – a Triumph Dolomite Sprint with hand-made aluminium body modifications and luxury trim – in limited numbers.

Top: 1974 Panther J72 had Jaguar 6 or V12   *Above: 1975 De Ville had V12 power*

Panther Solo 2 of 1987 used a Cosworth Sierra engine, and the aerodynamic body made much use of Kevlar and carbon fibre materials.

It was the Lima, introduced in 1976, which put Panther into the volume sales market. It had a glassfibre body and used Vauxhall Magnum mechanical components.

At the other end of the spectrum, the 1977 London Motor Show saw the launch of the six-wheeled 8.2-litre turbocharged Cadillac-powered Super Six.

A turbocharged Lima was launched in 1979 but, although sales were reasonable, the company hit financial trouble and went into receivership.

South Korean business concern Jindo Industries bought Panther in October 1980 for about £300,000. The complete range was dropped and Panther continued to produce conversions on other makes such as Mercedes and Range Rovers, mostly for the Middle East.

The J72 was relaunched as the Korean-built Brooklands in January 1982 and DeVilles were built to special order only.

The Lima was relaunched in 1982 as the Kallista with extensive improvements, and offered with 1.6-litre four-cylinder and 2.8-litre V6 Ford engines. The Kallista is now also available with the latest 2.9-litre fuel-injection Ford engine.

In 1987, Panther chairman Young C. Kim and Jindo Industries sold 80 per cent of the Panther Car Co. to Ssangyong and Dong-A Motors, South Korea's fourth-ranked vehicle maker. With fresh capital, Panther was able to develop its Solo 2 model, a mid-engined two-seater employing a two-litre turbocharged Ford Cosworth engine and Ford four-wheel-drive system.

Top: Panther 6 imitated the Tyrrell F1 car
Above left and right: Two views of the 2.9-litre Kallista, the fastest version of this classically-styled Panther to date.

Right: Fibreglass-bodied 1976 Lima
Below: Panther De Ville of 1976

Peerless

Great Britain
1957–1962

The British-built Peerless – not to be confused with the U.S. car of the same name built between 1900 and 1931 – was born out of Bernie Rodger's perception that there was no affordable GT car on the market in the mid-1950s. He obtained financial backing from Peerless Motors of Slough, who agreed that he could assemble his cars on their premises, and exhibited the alloy-bodied prototype at the Paris Motor Show in October 1957.

By the time production began in 1958, a prototype had distinguished itself by finishing 16th at Le Mans. The production Peerless GT had a multi-sectional glassfibre body on an advanced spaceframe chassis made of hollow square-section tubes, and many of its mechanical components came from the contemporary Triumph TR3 sports car. Though the front suspension was Triumph, the rear axle was a leaf-sprung De Dion type, with outboard drum brakes. Laycock-De Normanville overdrive was a recommended extra, for it was otherwise easy to over-rev the engine in the top gear of the four-speed Triumph gearbox. Despite a streamlined shape and a dry weight of no more than 1016kg (2240lb) the Peerless was nevertheless unable to exceed 107mph (172km/h) although acceleration through the gears was respectably quick.

After about 250 cars had been made, a face-lifted Phase II model with a stronger one-piece glassfibre body was introduced in August 1959. But the company ran into financial troubles early in 1960 and was liquidated after an abortive attempt to continue production in Ireland. Bernie Rodger got a further modified version of the car back into production later that year under the Warwick name, but production was slow and quality lower than the market found appropriate. Not even a 140mph (225km/h) version with Buick's 3½-litre V8 engine could rescue sales, and the company was finally wound up in 1962.

Top: 1958 Peerless 2-litre GT   *Above: The Warwick GT from 1961*

Pegaso

Spain
1951–1958

After World War II, the Empresa Nacional de Autocamiones SA was set up in Barcelona to help lift the Spanish economy out of the economic doldrums which were a legacy of the Civil War. The company was allocated space in the former Hispano-Suiza truck and aero-engine factory in Barcelona, and began producing commercial vehicles in 1946.

Technical Director and Chief Executive was Wilfredo Ricart, who had previously worked in the late 1930s as a diesel-engine consultant and technical adviser at Alfa Romeo, and at Perez and Ricart sports cars at Nacional Pescara. At Alfa Romeo he was responsible for a three-litre V16 engine and the supercharged mid-engined flat-12 Tipo 512. A personality clash with Enzo Ferrari, then in charge of the Alfa racing team, was largely responsible for Ferrari storming off to set up on his own.

Ricart brought with him to E.N.A.S.A. engineers from Alfa Romeo and Lancia, and his aim at Pegaso was to instruct his largely semi-skilled native workforce in the techniques of vehicle manufacture. To do this the plant was geared up to manufacture all the necessary components to produce a showpiece, with the only bought-in components being the Weber carburettors and licence-built 2F gearboxes. The result was one of the world's first 'supercars', and the Pegaso sports coupé was launched at the 1951 Paris Salon.

This dramatic-looking car featured an all-alloy quadruple-overhead-camshaft V8 engine which was initially produced with a capacity of 2.5 litres, later rising to 2.8 litres. Sixteen cars had bored-out 3.2-litre engines. Pegasos had de Dion axles with integral gearboxes, an arrangement redolent of the Alfetta Grand Prix cars, up to eight Weber carburettors, and dry-sump lubrication.

Bodies were panelled in steel and mounted on advanced platform-type chassis but this arrangement proved to be

Above: 1952 Z-102 Spyder

rather overweight for racing; at the 1952 Monaco Grand Prix, run for sports cars, the works cars quickly ran out of brakes. This resulted in Ricart arranging for coachbuilders Touring of Milan to produce lighter and more-elegant coupé bodies, with which 42 Pegasos were clad. Eighteen bodies were made by the French firm Saoutchik, 20 by the works, and four by Serra of Barcelona. A few of these were convertibles, and a couple were exotic styling exercises.

The three works cars, Z102BSS models, racing at the 1954 Copa Barcelona, an event which supported the Grand Prix, were fitted with superchargers, and gained the reputation of being the noisiest, if not the fastest cars present. The superchargers were of the British-made Marshall Nordec Rootes type.

Although they were very active in competition in Spain, Pegasos made very few forays into events elsewhere in Europe. For a brief period in 1953, a supercharged Le Mans Pegaso was the fastest production sports car in the world, having achieved 243km/h (151mph) over the flying kilometre in Belgium.

Wilfredo Ricart was an excellent design engineer, but the Pegaso sports car lacked consistent development. When Ricart retired in 1958, a mere 84 Z102s and a short run of restyled Z103s with 3.9-, 4.5- and 4.7-litre engines had been built.

Trucks now took precedence, and E.N.A.S.A. continued to grow in stages via a series of mergers and acquisitions, including Leyland, International Harvester, Seddon-Atkinson and DAF. In 1988, domestic sales included 65,000 buses, 15,000 vehicles were exported, and a further 20,000 military vehicles produced, accounting for 42 per cent of the Spanish commercial-vehicle market. Despite heavy losses, E.N.A.S.A. was expected to break even by 1990, with a new assembly plant in Brazil and an extended dealer network in Europe.

Below: 1952 Z-102 with Touring bodywork

Peugeot

France
1891 to date

The Peugeot family first became involved in the manufacture of ironmongery in 1810 in the Belfort region of eastern France; but it was not until 1876 that they founded the company which would eventually undertake the manufacture of cars. Cycle manufacture arrived first, in 1885, and the company's wide network of ironmongery agents all over France made this new venture successful. Armand Peugeot had for some time been doing business with Panhard over woodworking machinery, and the latter's associate, Levassor, convinced him that there was a future in self-propelled vehicles. Peugeot first investigated steam propulsion with Léon Serpollet, but their 1889 three-wheeler was not a success, and Peugeot returned to Levassor to ask for a supply of Daimler engines.

Peugeot production began at Beaulieu in 1891, and these first cars had rear-mounted vee-twin engines and chain drive. But from 1897, the company built its own

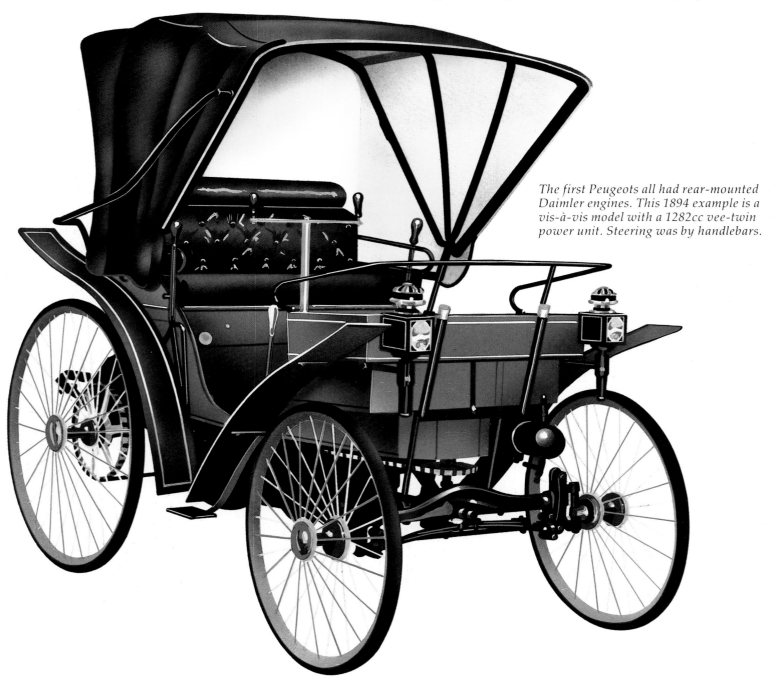

The first Peugeots all had rear-mounted Daimler engines. This 1894 example is a vis-à-vis model with a 1282cc vee-twin power unit. Steering was by handlebars.

engines. That year, a separate company was formed at Audincourt to continue car manufacure, and the range of Peugeots began to expand, embracing both small and large-engined types. Many of the latter proved successful in competitions.

As engineering and styling advances created recognizable cars from what had been simply horseless carriages before 1902, so production volumes increased. Particularly notable was the first 'Bébé' Peugeot, the 1902 Type 69 with a 652cc single-cylinder engine; at the other end of the scale was the 1908/1909 Type 105 with six-cylinder 11,150cc engine, often fitted with sporting bodywork and capable of over 128km/h (80mph). Before 1909/1910, the most popular body style was a double-phaeton, but the pre-1914 Peugeots were generally unremarkable in appearance, even though greater elegance and luxury came to characterize bodies on the larger-engined chassis after 1906.

Meanwhile, Robert Peugeot had begun to manufacture motor cycles at the old Beaulieu factory and, after 1906, he turned also to cars. Under the Lion-Peugeot name, he produced 13 basic types between then and 1915, although from 1910 the two Peugeot companies were reunited. The Lion-Peugeot models saw a great deal of competition use, unlike the products of the other Peugeot company, and were successful all over Europe. Probably the best-known Lion-Peugeot, however, was the new 'Bébé', an 856cc model designed by Ettore Bugatti and introduced in 1912.

Peugeot production continued until 1917, and then resumed slowly in 1919 with a number of pre-war models, notable among which was the 2.6-litre Type 153. While production volumes steadily increased over the next decade, however,

Top: 1892 vis-à-vis for the Bey of Tunis
Above: 1902 Type 36 Tonneau

Above: 1905 Type 77B Landaulet
Below: 1909 Type 105 Double Phaeton

Above: 1907 Lion-Peugeot voiturette

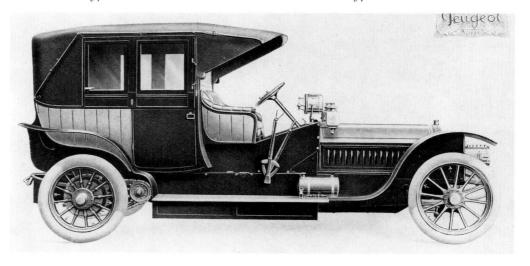

Above: 1909 20CV grand touring car

Above: 1913 6hp 'Bébé' Peugeot
Top right: 1913 Grand Prix car
Right: 1914 Grand Prix car

Below: Types 42, 43 and 44 all had a common wheelbase but engines were either 2042cc or 3635cc four-cylinders. This 1903 model had Double Phaeton coachwork.

the cars were generally worthy but staid. There were frequent changes to models. Five of the larger-engined models from this period had sleeve-valve engines; but once again the most important model was a small car, the Quadrilette of 1921, which replaced the well-loved Bébé models.

Of course, the Quadrilette was developed, gaining larger engines, a new chassis and, eventually, five-seater bodywork in place of the staggered or tandem two-seater types available at first. After 1924, and under pressure from the rival 5CV Citroën, the model evolved from what was essentially a cyclecar into an altogether more sophisticated vehicle and became more commonly known as the 5CV Peugeot. Its final versions were produced in 1931. At the other end of the range, 1927 had seen the launch of the six-cylinder 12-Six which, like many larger European cars of the period, showed American design influences. It was not a great success, however, selling slowly despite the availability of a large number of body types.

Altogether more significant was the 201 model of 1929, a small family saloon with a 6CV fiscal rating which offered more space than previous small-capacity types. Its design lay behind several new Peugeots introduced before 1936, all of which bore '01' type designations. After the 201 came the 301 in 1932, closely based on the 201 but with a longer wheelbase and a larger engine of 8CV fiscal rating. With the 301 came a new box-section chassis, also adopted by the 201 in 1932.

The next significant developments occurred in 1934, when the 201 and 301 models were modernized and two new 01

Below: 1929 201 Business Coupé
Below right: 1928 Type 183 12hp saloon

Top: 1920 Type 163 four-cylinder Torpedo　　*Above: 1921 Type 161 Quadrilette*

models were introduced. These were the 401, a 10CV type, and the 601, a luxurious medium-sized six-cylinder model. Like its predecessors, the 601 failed to catch the public imagination, partly because it offered no space advantages over the smaller Peugeots – some 301 and 401 bodies were used on 601 chassis – and partly because it was slower than its rivals from Renault. After the 601 was dropped, there would be no more six-cylinder Peugeots until 1974.

Although the last of the 01 range was not built until 1937, a new family of Peugeot cars had arrived in 1935. Like other French manufacturers, Peugeot was forced by the 1934 introduction of Citroën's advanced Traction Avant to update its range as quickly as possible. The first newcomer was the 402, an 11CV saloon with a new overhead-valve engine, a new rear suspension, and a new streamlined body shape (though some streamlined bodies were also available on 01 series

Top: 1932 Type 301C record-breaker
Above left: 1931 201 saloon
Above: 1934 401D saloon

Below: The second-generation 'Bébé' Peugeot introduced in 1913 was designed by Ettore Bugatti. The engine was a side-valve four of 850cc. These were the most popular Peugeots of their time.

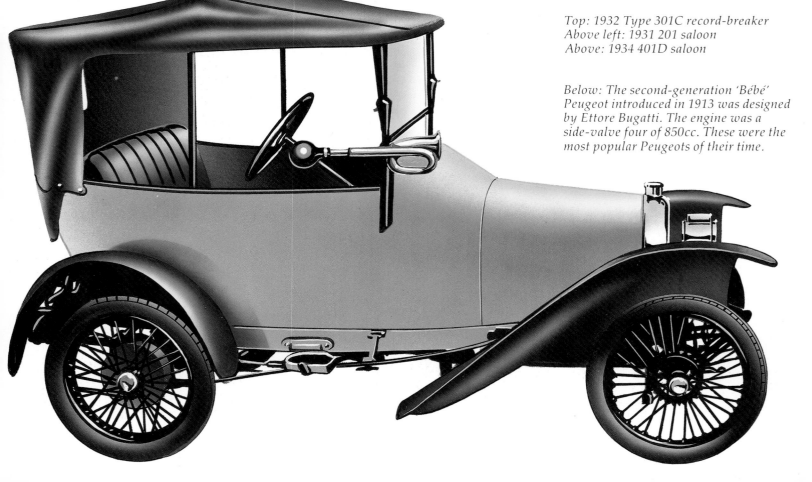

Above: 1933 301 cabriolet

Below: 1934 301D limousine

Above: 1936 302 five-seater saloon
Below: 1938 202 saloon

Peugeots). Many had the Cotal electromagnetic gearbox, which offered an overdrive top gear after 1938, when the 402 became a 402B with a larger engine rated at 12CV.

The 402 was joined in 1936 by a smaller 10CV model called the 302, and then in 1938 by a 6CV 202 which was briefly fitted with torsion-bar independent front suspension. Styling ensured that all these models bore a strong family resemblance, and Peugeot put bodies from the smaller cars on to the larger chassis to create attractive higher-performance variants like the 402B *légère* of 1938. In addition to the saloons, convertibles and closed coupé bodies were available, and there were small numbers of Darl'Mat models after 1937, with tuned engines and low-slung roadster bodywork by the Parisian Peugeot dealer Emil Darl'Mat. Many scored sporting successes.

During World War II, Peugeot built a few cars, including small numbers of a three-wheeler electric runabout called the VLV, but most of its production capacity was devoted to commercials for military use. Despite serious bombardment damage to the factory at Sochaux, post-war production resumed at the end of 1945 with the 202, but it would be 1949 before the pre-war level of production was once again attained.

Above: 1948 203 de luxe saloon   *Below: 1959 403 four-door saloon*

Below: The streamlined styling of 1935's 402 owed more than a little to the Chrysler Airflow. Its 1991cc overhead-valve engine produced 55bhp.

The first new post-war Peugeot was the 203, a bread-and-butter little saloon which was the company's first with monocoque construction. This survived with only minor modifications until 1960, and the basic saloon was joined by convertible, estate and higher-performance Darl'Mat versions, although the latter were two-door saloons without the charisma of the pre-war Darl'Mat models. There was only ever one other member of the 03 family: the 1955 403, a larger saloon which in 1959 became the first production Peugeot passenger car to have a diesel engine option. Both 03 models were tremendously successful, spawning light commercials in addition to the passenger-car versions.

The 04 family which followed was less homogeneous than those which had gone before. First of the newcomers was the Pininfarina-styled 404 of 1960, a rugged vehicle which distinguished itself in international rallies and offered the familiar range of body types, plus a diesel engine option. The car which broke the mould, however, was the 1965 204, Peugeot's first front-wheel-drive model. This was rated at 6CV and came as a saloon or estate, alongside which were offered attractive convertible and closed coupé models on a shorter wheelbase. There was also a diesel engine option. Next came the slightly larger 304 of 1969, a scaled-up 204

Top: 1972 104 four-door saloon
Above: 1972 304 cabriolet

Below: 1972 Peugeot 504 cabriolet by Pininfarina

with a larger engine and the usual range of body options.

The 404 was eventually replaced by the 1968 504, although it continued in production until 1975. The 504 was another large and rugged rear-wheel-drive saloon. Its coupé and convertible derivatives became the first Peugeot models to use the jointly designed Peugeot-Renault-Volvo V6 engine in 1974. The same power unit went into the 1975 604, a large rear-wheel-drive executive saloon. There was front-wheel-drive again on the 1972 104 range, however, a supermini with a body shell which resurfaced with a Citroën engine as that company's LN model, after the takeover by Peugeot of Citroën in 1974.

Throughout the 1970s, the Peugeot image had gradually changed and the models of the 1980s were less staid and more appealing. The new family, of course, bore an 05 designation, and the first launched was the front-wheel-drive

Below: The 1960 404 saloon had typically angular styling by Pininfarina in Italy. The cars were also remarkably tough, and showed up well in international rallies.

Above: 1977 604SL saloon

Top: 1981 305S saloon
Above left: 1988 205GTI 1.9
Above: 1988 405 saloon
Left: 1988 505GRD family estate
Below: 1988 405 Mi 16 saloon

305, which replaced the 304 in 1978. The 505 replaced the 504 a year later, but the real blockbuster was the 1983 205, a small hatchback which succeeded the 104 and secured a leading position in the 'hot hatch' market of the 1980s. Beside it, the 1987 309 (built at the former Chrysler plant in England which had belonged to Peugeot since its 1977 takeover of the European Chrysler operation) seemed merely competent. The 1987 405 demonstrated how far Peugeot had come, however, for it combined conventional engineering with state-of-the-art attractions like 16-valve engines, fuel injection and four-wheel-drive on its more expensive variants.

Peugeot followed this in 1989 with the slightly larger 605, a conservatively-styled but competent saloon, aimed at the lucrative 'upper-medium' sector of the European car market that accounts for 1.7 million sales each year.

Top: 1989 309 Special Equipment hatchback
Above: 1990 4wd 405 Mi 16×4

Below: The 205 was a market leader in the supermini sector almost from the moment it was launched in 1983. Front-wheel-drive was allied to all-independent suspension and handling was one of the car's strong suits.

Left: 1990 Peugeot 309 GR saloon
Above: 1990 Peugeot 205 GR five-door hatchback

Below: Type 905 650bhp racer for 1991 season

Above: The 106 received a face-lift in 1996 with the new corporate nose

Above: The 306 was launched in 1993

styled (with more than a hint of Ferrari 456GT) and built by Pininfarina and was available with either a 2.0-litre four or 2.9-litre V6. It was Peugeot's first real production coupé since the demise of the Pininfarina-styled 504 coupé in 1983.

To add the now obligatory MPV to the

The 605 was somewhat of a sales flop. Despite it luxurious interior and powerful V6, it looked too much like the 405 to justify the greater price. Other models continued to sell well until the early 1990s when the new '06 range started to appear.

The first, in 1991, was the 106, a small hatchback that fitted below the long-running 205. The 106 sold well and was updated in 1996. (The Citroën Saxo was the same car with a new nose and tail.) Just when everyone thought Peugeot would never come with a car that could replace the 205 GTi, the company launched the 106 GTi. With a 1.6-litre 16-valve engine in the small, light bodyshell, the new GTi could hit 60mph (100km/h) in around 8.5 seconds.

Next in the all-new range was the 306. Slightly bigger than the 205 and nearer the size of the contemporary Volkswagen Golf, the 306 was available in 3- or 5-door hatchback, four-door saloon, cabriolet and, later, estate forms. The convertible was particularly handsome and was built in conjunction with Pininfarina. One of the more popular models was the sprightly 90-horsepower turbodiesel. The GTi model never seemed as popular as its 205 predecessor.

The 406 replaced the 405 in 1995 and went straight to the top of its class. Ride and handling were astounding but performance was not too strong initially. A new 2.9-litre, 24-valve V6 remedied the problem. The Paris Show later the same year saw a surprise new variant – a coupé. The stunning new car was

Above: 1997 Peugeot 106 GTi

Below: Peugeot 406 Estate

Above: The 406 replaced the 405 in 1995

range, PSA and Fiat collaborated on a new design. There were Citroën, Fiat, Lancia and Peugeot versions. The Peugeot model was designated 806 and used a range of existing Peugeot engines.

Meanwhile, the range still contained a couple of left-overs from the 1980s. Both the much-loved Peugeot 205 (although no longer in GTi form) and unloved 605 were still in production in 1997.

Above: 1997 306 GTi had a six-speed gearbox   *Below: Pininfarina designed the 406 Coupé*

Pierce/ Pierce-Arrow

U.S.A. 1901–1938

George Norman Pierce was born in 1846, and operated a thriving business, making birdcages, ice-boxes and washing-machines, at the time when the bicycle boom hit America in the late 1880s. Children's tricycles and then bicycles were quickly added to his company's range, their gears made by Henry Leland's company in Detroit, who later went on to found Cadillac and Lincoln.

By 1895, Pierce had dropped all his other lines to concentrate on bicycles, operating from a new five-storey factory in Buffalo, N.Y. After experimenting briefly with a steam-powered car, Pierce tried a single-cylinder de Dion Bouton engine, and in 1901 began production of the Motorette. Twenty-five were sold in the first year, and 125 in the second. De Dion

Top: Pierce-Arrow Runabout of 1910
Above: 1913 66hp A-series 5-seat tourer

engines were used for the first two years, after which Pierce built its own engines.

The first car to bear the Arrow name appeared in 1903, and it was followed in 1904 by the U.S. $4,000 Great Arrow, which marked the firm's move into the ranks of the high-quality prestige makes. Some 700 cars were built in 1906, and they carried off the honours in America's premier long-distance road-race, the Glidden Tour, for four consecutive years until 1909. As production shifted to a new factory at Elmwood in 1908, the company was renamed the Pierce-Arrow Motor Car Co. Pierce's son Percy continued to build cycles and motor-cycles at the original plant.

In 1910 Pierce himself died, but not before he had seen two of his cars selected for use in the U.S. Presidential fleet. He was succeeded by George K. Birge. Production at this time stood at just under 1,000 cars a year, made up of two four-cylinder and four six-cylinder models. Pierce-Arrow was in the happy position of having sold the majority of its cars prior to their manufacture.

Like Rolls-Royce, Pierce-Arrow operated a chauffeur training-school, offering two-week courses, and its range of luxury

Below: Pierce-Arrow's mid-range 8.6-litre 48hp two-seater tourer of 1915. Pierce-Arrows were the first cars to have headlights mounted on their front mudguards, a move which provided better illumination and improved styling and aerodynamics.

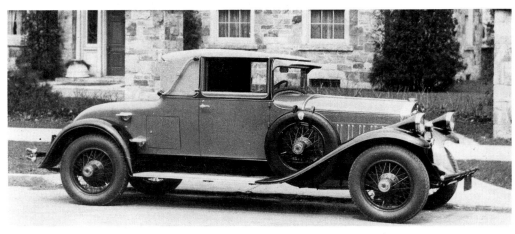

Above: Pierce-Arrow of 1915
Right: 1928 80 coupé convertible

Above: 1931 Club Sedan, Le Baron body

Above: Streamlined Silver Arrow of 1933

Above: 1937 Limousine, V12 or straight-8

models, the 38, 48 and 66, with 6.8-, 8.6- and 13.5-litre engines, reflected the likely status of potential owners. The most expensive 66 was priced at $8,200. Pierce-Arrows were the first cars to have their headlights mounted high up on the mudguards, where they gave better illumination. Right-hand drive was retained until 1921, longer than on any other U.S. make, because, it was said, the chauffeur was thus more able to open the pavement-side door for his employer.

By this time, World War I was in full spate, and Pierce-Arrow stepped up its production of two-, three- and five-ton trucks, which had begun in 1910. Several thousand were made, and the company's profits exceeded U.S.$4 million in 1915 and 1916. But with the war over, demand for trucks declined, and the emphasis of the national prosperity shifted from the eastern states across to oil-wealthy Texas and to trend-setting California.

Pierce-Arrow badly needed new engines to remain competitive. This overall situation came about because company policy was to a large extent dictated by merchant bankers rather than motoring

men, a result of the public share flotation of 1916. Nearly all the key executives had left by 1921. The recession saw sales tumble to 1,000 cars, and the company made a loss of U.S. $8 million that year.

A new model, the six-cylinder 4.7-litre 80, was introduced in 1924, and initial sales were promising. The company was not above experimentation, commissioning Laurence H. Pomeroy to design an all-aluminium car, based on the 80, in which literally everything possible would be made of alloy. Only four were built, however, and the company neglected to update the 80's styling, and it lost ground to more rivals like Cord and Packard.

In 1928, Pierce-Arrow was taken over by Studebaker, and the latter's president, Albert R. Erskine, became chairman of the Pierce board. The only technical overlap between the two companies was the casting of a new Pierce-Arrow six-litre straight-eight engine for its new 133 and 143 models at the Studebaker plant at South Bend, Indiana. Priced at U.S. $2,875 for a 133 roadster and U.S. $8,200 for a 143 French brougham, 9,840 units were sold in 1929.

But these were the Depression years, and by 1932, when Pierce-Arrow had finally produced a V12 engine, sales were down to 2,692. These were worth U.S. $8 million but some U.S. $2 million had been spent on factory improvements, and it made a net U.S. $3 million loss. Studebaker went down in 1933, and Pierce-Arrow was sold to a consortium of Buffalo businessmen for U.S. $1 million. New models which followed included the dramatically streamlined Silver Arrow, but this turned out to be more of a publicity exercise, with only five being built. The company even tried trailer-caravans with the Travelodge model in 1936 but, by 1937, there was insufficient finance available to fund new projects. Thereafter there was a steady decline until production ceased in 1938, in which year only 17 cars were sold.

The V12 engines continued to be used to power fire-engines built by the Seagrave Corporation of Columbus, Ohio, right up to 1970, and the Pierce Arrow name is still used (without the hyphen) by the Wisconsin fire-engine producers Pierce Manufacturing Co.

Plymouth

U.S.A.
1928 to date

The origins of the Plymouth name go back to 1928 when the company sales manager of the Chrysler Motors Corporation, Joseph W. Frazer, suggested Plymouth as the name for Chrysler's low-price car range to Walter Chrysler.

The name referred to the historical Plymouth Rock where the Pilgrim Fathers first set foot on American soil; and Plymouth Binder Twine was, at the time, a well-known farming product.

Right from the start the Plymouth car range was a success, being sold alongside the more expensive models through Chrysler dealers, and by 1930 Plymouth cars were also available from Dodge and DeSoto agents as well.

Although Plymouth cars were more expensive than the rival Ford and Chevrolet models, Chrysler offered more for the money. Whereas the rival makes invariably had wood-framed bodies and

Below: Now in the Harrah collection, this first Plymouth was conceived in 1928 as a cut-price Chrysler. The idea worked, for by 1935 Plymouth was regularly third in the sales ratings, beating Chrysler by a large margin.

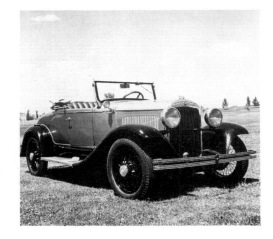

Above: One of the first, a 1928 Plymouth
Above right: 1935 Plymouth nine-passenger sedan
Below: 1955 Plymouth Plaza

mechanical brakes, for example, Plymouth followed company practice with an all-steel body and hydraulic brakes.

In 1930, in spite of a deepening economic recession, sales of the new make at 68,000 units were good enough to take it into eighth place in the sales performance league. The following year saw the launch of the first new Plymouth since the marque's inception.

The car still had the well-proven

four-cylinder engine but used the innovation of heavy rubber engine mountings to insulate it from the frame. This gave smoothness to the engine that was unheard of in such a low-priced car. The effect of this was to take Plymouth to third place in the production league, a figure it would retain for the next 23 years.

In 1932 came the introduction of a convertible model for the first time, powered by a much-improved four-cylinder engine that was giving more horsepower than many larger-capacity engines. By this time Plymouth's market share had increased considerably, particularly after the introduction of a six-cylinder engine in 1933.

Right: 1950 Plymouth Special De Luxe P20

Left: 425bhp 1970 Road-Runner Superbird
Above: 1965 Valiant V-100 two-door Sedan
Below: The 7.0-litre Barracuda, Mustang's rival

Although this engine had a smaller capacity than the four, it was more powerful. In 1936, power had been increased to 82bhp which was very respectable for a car with a price tag as low as U.S. $495. As new and revised models were introduced each year, the high specification ensured its continuing sales success.

By the time Plymouth reached its tenth year of production the model range had expanded to include the first production station wagon, and by 1940, the year Walter Chrysler died, annual production of Plymouth cars was well over 500,000 units.

In common with other U.S. car manufacturers, the war years saw Plymouth production turn to military vehicles, munitions and engines. Car production resumed in 1945, although Plymouth continued to sell its pre-war styles, reaching the half-million mark by 1949.

The sales success of Plymouth over the previous 20 years was now about to take a decline in the coming years due to the Chrysler design philosophy influenced by the new head of Chrysler, K. T. Keller. Keller didn't like the current torpedo-like styling, preferring the more practical 'three-box' style. Plymouth's new model range for 1949 reflected this, and although they gave good value for money and were reliable, they were rather dull and not particularly fast. By the early 1950s, sales figures had dropped Plymouth to fifth place.

All this changed for 1955 when Virgil Exner gave all-new styling to the Plymouth range which resulted in a more exciting-looking car and a record sales figure of over 742,000 cars. Tail fins were all the rage in 1956 and Plymouth was fully three years ahead of the competition in terms of styling.

However successful the sales figures, Plymouth could never rise above fourth place and beat Pontiac for third place, and

Above: 1977 Plymouth Gran Fury Brougham

A heavy, rear-drive, four-door saloon in the traditional manner, the angular, upright styling of the 1979 Plymouth Gran Fury was typical of the period; styling at parent company Chrysler remained static for over five years.

Above: 1990 seven-seater Grand Voyager was powered by 3.3-litre V6 engine

Above: Versatile Plymouth Colt Vista, 1990

Top: 1979 Horizon based on Sunbeam hatch
Above: 1990 mid-size front-wheel-drive Acclaim, a top-selling Plymouth

Above: Two-door Sundance with 2.5 turbo
Below: 1990 Laser with 16-valve two-litre turbocharged engine

it looked like the ups and downs of Plymouth would be repeated in the early 1960s. This was mainly due to the Plymouth management which misjudged the market trends and seemed to have the right cars but at the wrong times.

The worst year was 1962, when Plymouth anticipated a strong demand for the smaller standard cars when the public wanted larger cars. The result was falling sales and hasty facelifts, although the popularity of the compact Valiant model lifted Plymouth back to fourth in the sales league.

The turnabout for Plymouth came in 1965 when a restyled range of big cars was launched to do for the company what the Valiant model had done since the early 1960s. During the next ten years Plymouth was to produce some very successful models like the Fury and Belvedere and, in

1964, the Barracuda fastback coupé model to cash in on the sales success of the Ford Mustang and Chevrolet Corvair Monza.

Heading into the 1990s, Plymouth's range featured the Colt GT hatchback (Mitsubishi's Colt model wearing an 'Imported for Plymouth' sticker on its rump); the front-wheel-drive Acclaim LX compact saloon, with a 141bhp three-litre Mitsubishi V6 engine (also sold as the Dodge Spirit); and the front-drive Laser sports coupé, offered with 1755cc and 1997cc normally-aspirated powerplants and a 195bhp two-litre turbo. The Laser was jointly designed and developed with Mitsubishi under the Diamond Star Motors banner introduced in 1988. An all-wheel-drive version of the Laser is sold by Chrysler's Eagle division as the Talon TSi AWD, and by Mitsubishi as the Eclipse GSX.

As with Dodge, Plymouth was offering rebadged versions of the new-generation Chryslers by the early nineties. One model that really set the marque apart, however, was the outrageous Prowler.

First shown in 1993, this nineties concept car took its styling cues from the hot rods of the fifties. With such outrageous styling, few thought it possible that the Prowler would ever make it into production, but, in 1996, the production Prowler hit the highway. Powered by a 3.5-litre V6 from Chrysler's L/H range, the Prowler gave excellent performance and a fantastic exhaust note, thanks to a specially designed exhaust system. Due to its low-volume construction, Plymouth opted for an aluminium chassis,

Top: Plymouth Neon Expresso

Above: 1990 Plymouth Voyager

Left: 1998 Plymouth Breeze Expresso

clothed in mainly alloy panels. Weight was a modest 2830lb (1285kg), much lighter than it would have been with all-steel construction. Thanks to its modern suspension and wide tyres, the Prowler also handled a lot better than the hot rods from which it took its styling. Buyers could choose any colour they liked, as long as it was a striking, deep metallic burgundy.

Above: Plymouth Grand Voyager

Below: 1997 Plymouth Prowler

Pontiac

U.S.A.
1926 to date

Some 17 years after the founding of the General Motors Corporation in 1908, the Pontiac make was introduced in 1926, taking its name from the town of Pontiac, Michigan, where the car was produced.

Of the four original G.M. companion makes introduced in the mid-1920s, Pontiac is the only one to survive to the present day, although its future looked far from secure back in the early years of the Depression.

The first Pontiac model was the Pontiac Six of 1926 which was an instant sales success and outsold the popular parent Oakland model. By 1929, the division's sales were well over 200,000 units.

Above: Pontiac with rumble seat from 1929
Below: 1927 Oakland Six Sport Phaeton
Bottom: One of the first, a 1926 coupé

Above: Pontiac coupé from 1929
Below: Only 47,000 models sold in 1932

However, during the height of the Depression after the Great Crash, division sales hit rock bottom in 1932 when only 47,000 cars were sold. Most of Pontiac's original companion makes had by now ceased to exist, and the future looked bleak for Pontiac.

Pontiac's saviour was G.M. President, Alfred Sloan, whose confident and practical management policies rationalized the Pontiac and Chevrolet manufacturing facilities in 1933, thus allowing considerable cuts in tooling costs by using shared components.

Rationalization was also applied to the sales side, by consolidating the Buick, Oldsmobile, and Pontiac operations, so that existing dealers now sold all three makes. By mid-1934 these economy and efficiency measures had reduced G.M. to three main divisions: Chevrolet, Cadillac, and Buick-Oldsmobile-Pontiac.

The turnround in Pontiac's fortunes started with the Pontiac Eight in 1933, a well-styled car which helped take the

Below: 1933 straight-eight two-door sedan

Above: 1934 Pontiac coupé
Below: Pontiac's 1935 two-door sedan

Above: 1937 four-door convertible
Below: Four-door sedan from 1938
Bottom: The elegant 1939 cabriolet

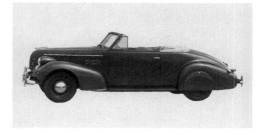

division's sales back over 200,000 by 1937, making it one of the top car producers until the mid-1940s. Much of this recovery was due to G.M.'s management team leaders; former Ford executive William S. 'Big Bill' Knudsen, chief engineer Benjamin H. Anibal (designer of the Pontiac Eight), and stylist Frank Hershey.

Part of the success of the Pontiac Eight was the new straight-eight-cylinder engine, designed by Anibal, plus G.M.'s new 'knee-action' independent front suspension. The new straight-eight was more powerful and far smoother than the V8 used in the old Oakland make, and made the cars much more sellable.

Because the engine proved very reliable, it formed the backbone of Pontiac power through the war years until the introduction of the modern high-compression V8 in 1955.

Meanwhile, the conventional Pontiac six-cylinder L-head engines were used in Chevrolet models from 1933 to 1935 but returned on a new Pontiac model range introduced in 1935. These new models inherited G.M.'s all-steel 'turret top' closed body construction and introduced the distinctive 'silver streak' trim, originated by a young designer named Virgil Exner who was later to find fame with Chrysler.

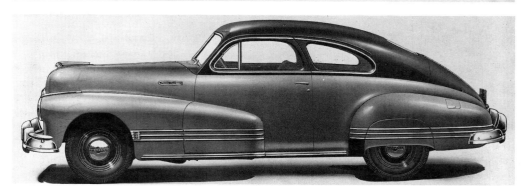

Above: 'Woody' station wagon of 1939-41
Below: 1940 Super De Luxe

It was due to the foresight of Alfred Sloan that Pontiac cars shared many common body panels with Chevrolet models but, due largely to stylist Hershey and chief body engineer Roy Milner, the Pontiac range looked distinctly different from Chevrolet models.

For the next 15 years, Pontiac styling followed industry trends with the cars becoming a more streamlined-looking torpedo shape and the increasing use of large chromed grilles and bumpers. The model range increased during this period, too, including fastbacks, wagons and coupé versions powered by either six- or eight-cylinder in-line engines.

Top: Pontiac's 1941 convertible
Above centre: 1942 Torpedo sedan
Above: 1942 Pontiac Eight sedan
Below: 1946 post-war Pontiac convertible

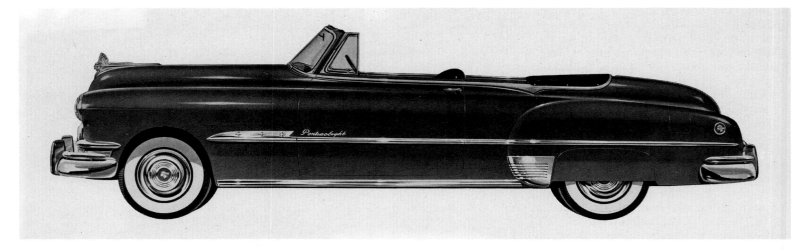

By the early 1950s, with recession and the war only a memory, Pontiac usually built the right cars at the right time, and at competitive prices. Automatic transmission was now becoming the norm, Pontiac having previously rejected using G.M.'s Hydra-Matic transmission as far back as 1946, and this option was fitted to 84 per cent of cars by 1953.

Above: 1952 Pontiac four-door sedan

The vintage year for Pontiac was 1955, when the first modern overhead-valve V8 engine was introduced, along with wrap-around windscreens, two-tone colour schemes, tubeless tyres, and 12-volt electrics, and the division sold a record 553,000 cars.

Below: Pontiac's 1955 convertible

Above: 1951 Pontiac Chieftain De Luxe
Below: Safari station wagon of 1955

By the late 1950s, Pontiac cars were becoming lower and wider and the company built some of the best-looking cars around. Gone was the image of staid family cars, and Pontiac had become synonymous with performance. The 1961 Tempest model, for example, was revolutionary by having a four-cylinder engine and a transaxle, as well as real performance.

Below: 1956 Star Chief convertible

Above: 1957 Star Chief convertible
Below: Chieftain convertible from 1958

Above: Pillarless Ventura Saloon of 1960
Right: 1961 Bonneville Safari estate car

The next decade was to be one of the most difficult for Pontiac as management decisions resulted in a succession of uninspired models which blurred the company's image. So by 1975, even Buick had come near to overtaking Pontiac's traditional number three sales spot.

The fuel crisis of the early 1970s and Federal emission legislation didn't help either, reducing the power of driver-orientated models such as the Firebird Trans Am, and Pontiac was forced to produce compact cars with a more European look.

Re-emphasizing its rule within G.M., in

Right: 1979 Firebird Trans Am

Above right: 1962 Pontiac Catalina sedan

Pontiac's Firebird was first produced in 1969, based on the Camaro platform. In 1972 the Trans Am was announced, using a 345bhp 6.5-litre V8 engine, which ironically excluded it from the championship after which it was named.

Above: 1980 Pontiac Phoenix
Right: 1980 Pontiac Grand Le Mans
Below: Pontiac Grand Am of 1980

Below: The Pontiac Fiero was a smaller, by US standards, mid-engined fibreglass coupé. Powered by transverse, mid-mounted 2.5-litre four- or 2.6-litre six-cylinder engines, the Fiero was conceptually right if not a conspicuous marketing success.

the 1980s Pontiac began to advertise "We build excitement". Some models failed to live up to that promise – notably early versions of the Fiero mid-engined two-seater, which despite its exotic format was relatively heavy and slow – but more popular models like the Grand Prix saloon helped the division weather the economic ups and downs of the decade.

Left: 1986 Pontiac Firebird SE hatchback coupé
Below: Pontiac Trans Am Turbo 1989 Indianapolis 500 Pace Car

Below: The much face-lifted Pontiac Firebird Trans Am of 1985 was descended from the earlier series cars. Although the car still looked the part, power output was somewhat restricted, now down to 90bhp, with 210bhp engines optional.

Pontiac managed to maintain its sporty image into the 1990s. The Firebird, which was completely restyled in 1992, remained the company's famous sporting flagship. With stunning, slippery styling, a 5.7-litre V8 (the only V8 left in the Pontiac range) and top speed of over 150mph (240km/h) it was second only to the Corvette in G.M.'s sports car line up. By 1997, it was one of the only Pontiacs to have rear-wheel drive.

A new entry-level Pontiac, the Sunbird, was launched in 1994. It used four-cylinder engines and had front-wheel-drive. In coupé and convertible forms it also looked very sporty and was popular as a second car or for younger buyers.

Next up was the Grand Am, a mid-sized car with a choice of four- or six-cylinder engines. The successful Grand Prix was restyled in 1996 and remained one of Pontiac's best sellers, with the turbocharged 3.8-litre V6. Perfomance was improved too.

Above: 1998 Pontiac Grand Prix GT Coupé

Left: Grand Am Coupé, this time the SE model

Far left: 1998 Pontiac Sunfire GT Coupé

Below: The Pontiac Bonneville was the largest car in the 1997 Pontiac range and used the GM 3.8-litre V6 engine

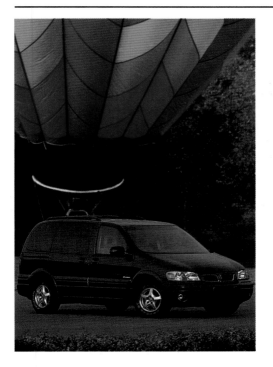

The sleek coupé was the best-looking of the Grand Prix range.

The range was completed with the luxurious Bonneville saloon and the Trans Sport MPV, which came in a choice of long or short wheelbases.

Above: 1998 Pontiac Trans Sport
Below: Pontiac Firebird Trans Am

Top: 1998 Pontiac Firebird Trans Am convertible
Right: Pontiac Sunfire SE Convertible

Porsche

Austria 1948–1950 West Germany 1950 to date

In 1930 Ferdinand Porsche set up his own design office in Stuttgart after gaining experience with first Austro-Daimler and then Steyr, Austria's biggest car manufacturer. Two potential projects came to nothing. Project 12 was for motor-cycle makers Zundapp who wanted a small car with a five-cylinder water-cooled radial engine. It was dropped because it was too costly. A similar project for N.S.U. with a flat-four air-cooled engine was completed in January 1934, but shelved when N.S.U.'s motor-cycle sales expanded.

That same year, Porsche was commissioned by Hitler to build a people's car: the story of that is told in detail in the Volkswagen section.

During the 1930s, Porsche visited America and Britain to study production techniques and met Henry Ford in 1937, keen to discuss the concept of a people's car.

Porsche did not limit his talents to the Volkswagen project and developed the mighty V16-engined Auto Union P-wagen Grand Prix car whose derivatives broke several records.

His war effort included designing the Tiger tank. It was at the onset of war that Hitler gave him the title Professor. But Porsche kept as remote from politics as possible, always referring to Hitler as Herr Hitler rather than Führer.

Porsche spent the war years in Stuttgart and was arrested by the Americans in 1945 and handed over to the French. He was imprisoned for two years. But Italian company Cisitalia paid the French authorities one million francs in return for Porsche designing the Cisitalia Grand Prix car and this secured his release in August 1947.

The decision to build sports cars which would be Porsches in their own right was taken late in 1947 and the first was called Project 356. Porsche designed a light, open two-seater based on a tuned Volkswagen 1131cc engine with V.W. suspension.

The first chassis was completed in March 1948 and the open body was added in May. Development took place at Gmünd where Porsche's operations had moved near the end of the war.

A Swiss bought the first prototype in September and in August 1948 production started in earnest with the cars getting streamlined, hand-made, coupé-type bodies. The car made its debut at the 1949 Geneva Motor Show with a 1086cc engine, despite being advertised as having an 1131cc unit.

The Gmünd plant built the first 50 cars but Porsche realized that more space was needed and eventually returned to the Stuttgart works in 1949, completing the move the following year after waiting for the American military to leave.

By now, the company had a staff of 150 and almost 300 cars were made during 1950. March 1951 saw the 500th Porsche and three months later Porsche made a stab at the world of competition, finishing 20th at Le Mans (the start of a long and illustrious racing career for the marque which was to include a record tenth Le Mans victory in 1985 and successes again in 1986 and 1987.

Porsche died after suffering a stroke in January 1952 and his son Ferry stepped in, already well versed with the job having been virtually in charge of the company since his father's imprisonment.

The 356 was gradually improved and developed with a 1500 version available in 1951, a 1600 in 1955 and, finally, the 130bhp 2000GS. The 10,000th Porsche was built in March 1956, by which time many were being exported to America, and by the end of the 1950s production had reached almost 8000 cars a year.

Above: Porsche's 1931 rear-engined car

Below: 1938 record-breaking Type 64

Above: Porsche number one at Gmünd, 1948
Below: 1955 Porsche 356A coupé
Below right: 356B, introduced in 1959

Above: 1500cc 356 cabriolet of 1952

Above: 1956 356A 1600S coupé

Below: Dr. Ferdinand Porsche had built a streamlined Volkswagen in 1939, and 1951 design study number 356 was descended from it. Using 1300cc engines, the early 356s relied on light weight, high gearing and low drag for impressive performance.

The 356 lasted until 1964, which says much for its concept, to be replaced by the famous 911 series. The 911 was launched in September of that year with a 1991cc flat-six engine. The 356C was replaced in 1965 by the 912. It used the original 1582cc flat-four with a 911 body.

Above: The Type 718 was developed into the Type RS60 for the 1960 racing season. It won the Targa Florio and the 12-Hour race at Sebring
Top right: 1963 Porsche 356 C cabriolet
Right: The original 901 of 1963 only differed from the 911 in a few minor details
Below: The rarest and fastest of the 356 C range was the 1964 Carrera 2

From then on, it was a case of continual improvement with the 911 growing in engine size and power output. Capacity went up to 2195cc in 1970 with fuel-injection being available, increasing to 2343cc in 1972 and 2687cc late the following year. Thereafter, fuel-injection became standard.

Left: 1965 four-cylinder 912

Above: 1967 flat-six 911 S

Left: 1968 targa-top 914 SC
Above: 1970 5-litre flat-12 917 K
Below: The 1973 2.7 Carrera RS

The extremely fast Carrera RS was also launched in 1973 and more than 15,000 cars were built that year. Porsche introduced a sensational 911 Turbo in 1975. The engine size grew to 3.3 litres in 1977 and it is still one of the world's fastest-accelerating production cars.

Right: 1974 Carrera RSR; only 50 built
Below: 1973 Porsche 911 RS 2.7 Carrera

Right: 1974 Porsche 911 2.7 coupé
Below: 1975 3.0 911 Turbo
Below right: 1976 911 2.7 coupé

Despite the avid following enjoyed by the 911 variants, 1975 was a bad year and sales had dropped to less than 10,000 cars, reflected by the general economic decline. But the relatively cheap 924 changed Porsche's fortunes, followed by the 928 in 1977.

Above: Porsche's luxury grand tourer, the 928, was launched in 1977. With engine capacity rising from 4.4 to 4.7 litres, and gaining 4 valves per cylinder in 1986, the V8-engined 928S4 could do 257km/h (160mph) and reach 96km/h (60mph) in 5.2 seconds.

Below: The 911 Turbo was the world's first production turbo. It ran with 7×15 front and 8×15 rear wheels, and wheel arches were widened accordingly. Handling of all the 911 models benefited from air dams and rear wings; the biggest was the 3.3 Turbo's.

Both represented a big change from previous cars, having front-mounted, water-cooled engines driving the rear wheels. But the Porsche-buying public warmed to the new offerings and the 924, for instance, reached the 100,000 mark by 1981. A turbocharged version of the 924 was launched in 1979, later being joined by the Carrera Turbo.

Above: 1978 Porsche 928, styled by Harm Lagaay

Top and above: The Porsche 928 S had 4.7-litre V8 power and bumpers that blended with the bodywork
Right: The 2.5-litre 944

Introduced as a joint venture with Volkswagen in 1975, the front-engined watercooled 2-litre 924 was a change from Porsche's customary rear-engined air-cooled cars. 924 had a rear-drive four-speed transaxle, and a large rear window formed a hatchback.

engine road car since the unfortunate VW-Porsche 914 of 1969. Thankfully, the Boxster was well received and highly regarded by the motoring press and the new cheap (about half the price of a 911) Porsche had queues of eager buyers waiting for the new car.

Meanwhile, the 911 had continued in its gradual process of evolution. It received a face-lift in 1993 and an incredible new Turbo

Above: The 911 Cabriolet, launched in 1994

Top right: 1997 911 Targa

The recession hit Porsche badly. There were fewer buyers able to afford the company's cars, and it was almost considered bad taste to be seen flaunting wealth by driving a Porsche or similar expensive car. At one stage there was even a rumour that the company was up for sale. Production figures dropped and losses increased.

Helping hands came from within the German motor industry: contracts with Mercedes and Audi kept the company afloat throughout the recession. As the recession ended and consumer confidence started to climb, so did Porsche's sales, accelerated by the launch of an all-new model.

The 944 was replaced by the 968 in 1991, with similar styling but a new 928-style front end. The new engine, based on that of the 944, was nearly as powerful in naturally aspirated form as the old engine had been with a turbo. When the 968 gained a turbocharger, it produced 305 horsepower. When the model was dropped in the mid-1990s, Porsche was left without an entry-level model.

The solution did not come until 1996, with the introduction of the new Porsche Boxster. The Boxster was the first completely new design from Porsche for years. It's 2.5-litre flat six was water-cooled and was mid-mounted. Porsche had not produced a mid-

Above: Porsche 968 Turbo

Below: 911 Turbo got four-wheel-drive in 1995

model was launched in the spring of 1995. One of most outrageous 911s ever, the car used a twin-turbocharged 3.6-litre engine giving 408 horsepower. To transfer all that power to the road it had the four-wheel-drive system developed on the Carrera 4. Acceleration off the line was fearsome with 60mph (100 km/h) coming up in less than 4.5 seconds on the way to its top speed of 180mph (290km/h).

The last year of the traditional air-cooled 911 was 1997. For 1998 Porsche were developing a restyled bodyshell to carry a new, larger version of the Boxster's water-cooled flat six.

Left: Boxster with hardtop
Below left: 1997 911 Carrera S
Below: Cutaway of Boxster shows mid-mounted, water-cooled engine

Below: 1998 911 with water-cooled engine

Proton

Malaysia
1985 to date

A 70/30 joint venture between the Malaysian Government and Mitsubishi, Proton started business in 1985. Mitsubishi supplied the know-how and the car, in the form of the old model Lancer, and the Government supplied the funding.

The first cars went west in 1989 with Britain as the first targeted European market. The car, known simply as the Mpi, was initially available with the eight-valve 1.3- and 1.5-litre engines, but a 12-valve design came in 1991. It was inexpensive to buy, easy to drive, reliable, had reasonable handling and ride, all of which gave Proton an eager market in the U.K.

If anything had been off-putting about these early cars, it was the angular styling, so Proton later launched the curvy and stylish Persona.

A third model came in 1996, in the form of the Perdana. This top-of-the-range model had a 2.0-litre 16-valve engine and a more spacious body.

In 1992, following its success on the

British market, Proton tried to push its cars into mainland Europe. Unfortunately, the company did not find such a willing market across the Channel.

Proton saved Lotus from extinction in 1996, following the disastrous events that surrounded the British company's previous owner, Bugatti Automobili SpA.

Top: 1993 Proton Mpi Aeroback

Right: 1993 Proton Persona

Below: Proton Mpi Saloon

Above: 1996 Proton Compact 1.6 SEi

Below: 1997 Proton Persona 1.8 SEi four-door

Railton

Great Britain
1933–1949

Noel Campbell Macklin, founder of Railton, was no stranger to car manufacture. He began in 1919 with the Eric Campbell, but soon left to work on the ill-fated Silver Hawk. His third venture was the Invicta, begun in 1925.

By 1933 Invicta was in financial trouble, moving to Chelsea, London, and the factory at Cobham in Surrey was taken over by Macklin's new project, Railton. Together with L. A. Cushman, Macklin planned to assemble cars designed by Reid Railton, known for his World Land Speed Record vehicles.

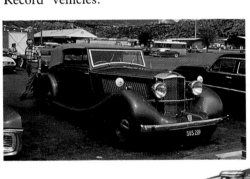

Left: c.1937 tourer in the U.S.A.

Above: 1935 Light Sports saloon

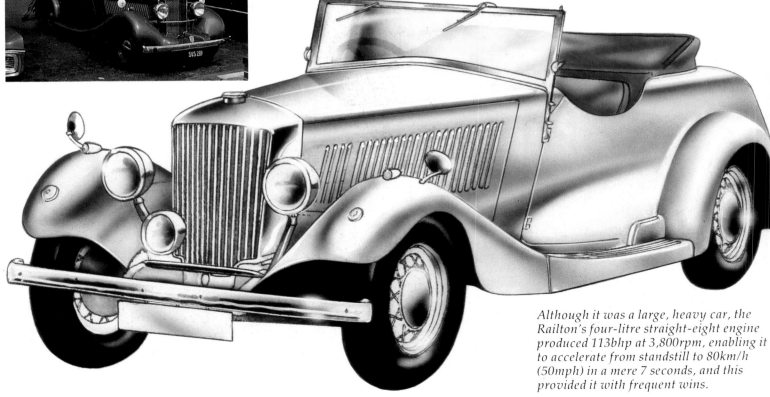

Although it was a large, heavy car, the Railton's four-litre straight-eight engine produced 113bhp at 3,800rpm, enabling it to accelerate from standstill to 80km/h (50mph) in a mere 7 seconds, and this provided it with frequent wins.

Left: 1938 Railton 10 drophead coupé
Above: 1938 2.7-litre Fairmile
Below: Jaguar-based 1989 revival

The idea was to produce cars combining British styling with typically American power units. They used the Essex Terraplane engine, designed by S. G. Baits, chief engineer for Essex.

Railtons were remarkable for their exceptional performance and relatively low price. In 1934, when 224 cars were produced, an open tourer sold for nearly £200 less than a comparable Lagonda or Alvis Speed 20. The 0–60mph (0–96km/h) acceleration figures of the 1949 Jaguar XK120 were bettered by Railton's 1935 Light Sports model. Also in that year the company achieved its highest production of 377 cars.

Hudson engines and mechanicals were used, particularly in the smaller 2723cc and 3255cc models of the late 1930s, brought out in an attempt to widen Railton's slipping appeal. In 1940 all rights were bought by Hudson Motors Ltd. in London, and Macklin's workforce moved over to war work, in particular the Fairmile gunboat, which earned him a knighthood. Reid Railton went on to work for Hudson.

Very few Railtons were built after World War II, although these did have column gear change and independent front suspension, in line with Hudson practice. The dollar-import ban and high price finally finished the marque.

Reliant

Great Britain 1935 to date

The Reliant Engineering Co. (Tamworth) Ltd. was founded in 1935, initially taking over the production of the Raleigh Cycle Company's three-wheeler van. Large wire wheels were fitted, with a single wheel at the front, suspended on motor-cycle-type forks. Raleigh's air-cooled vee-twin engine of 742cc was replaced by a sidevalve, in-line four-cylinder Austin Seven engine, of 747cc capacity and (initially) developing 14bhp. After 1938, when Austin ceased to build the engine, Reliant manufactured it under licence. It continued to power all Reliants until 1962.

Above: 1962 Reliant Sabre Six GT

In 1953, at the Earls Court Motor Show, Reliant introduced its own three-wheeled-car – the two-door, four-seater Regal. Mark 2 and Mark 3 (late 1956) versions followed, the latter being the first quantity-produced European car to have a body made entirely from glassfibre. A sturdy box-section chassis provided the backbone of the design. The Regal was available in drophead coupé, saloon and van versions.

Reliant was obliged to build its three-wheelers to an 8cwt (400kg) weight limit in order for the vehicles to qualify for road-tax and driving licence concessions in the U.K. Nevertheless, the mechanical specification and trim were constantly improved, and Mark IV, then Mark V models were produced, the latter appearing in 1959. In a light vehicle, the 17.5bhp produced by the sidevalve engine

was sufficient to give a top speed in excess of 65mph (104km/h), combined with a touring fuel consumption approaching 60mpg.

The Mark V cars featured new bodywork, with increased passenger and luggage accommodation. The comfort of rear-seat passengers was increased further in 1961 when the Mark VI, the last of the sidevalve Reliants, was introduced with an extended roof line.

A new Regal was introduced during 1962 with Reliant's own all-alloy, overhead-valve 600cc engine developing 25bhp. A van version was also produced with a capacity of 50 cubic feet (1.4 cubic metres). A luxury model – the 21E (with 21 extra fittings as standard) was announced in 1967. The 600cc engine was fitted to the four-wheeled Rebel from late 1964.

Above: 1965 Reliant Regal 3/25
Below: 1966 600cc Reliant Rebel

Below: Turkey's Anadol (by Reliant), 1974

Meanwhile Reliant had fitted its first four-wheeler – the Anglo-Israeli Sabre – with a 1700cc Ford Consul engine. By 1966 the car had been developed into the Scimitar coupé powered by Ford's 2.5-litre V6 engine, enlarged to three litres (144bhp) for 1967. The Scimitar GTE was a hatchback version, introduced in 1968. With modifications, this fast glassfibre-bodied sports tourer was produced until 1986, with a convertible (GTC) model being available from 1982.

From 1966 Reliant also produced the glassfibre-bodied Anadol saloon, designed to be built in Turkey.

A 700cc engine was fitted to the Regal 3/30 (29bhp) and Rebel (31bhp) models from 1968, and increased in size to 748cc from 1971. Production of both models ceased in October 1973.

A new three-wheeler, the Robin, was introduced in October 1973, with a 32bhp version of the 750cc engine. The capacity was increased to 848cc in late 1975, when the four-wheeled Kitten version was announced.

Above: 1976 Reliant Scimitar GTE
Below: Reliant Kitten, 1975 on

The completely revised, three-wheeled Rialto replaced the Robin in January 1982, although it still used the 848cc engine.

In February 1985 Reliant introduced its Ford-powered Scimitar SS1 two-seater sports convertible, in 1296cc (four-speed) or 1596cc (five-speed) form. In June 1986 the 1800Ti version was launched using a turbocharged, fuel-injected engine of 1800cc, and in late 1987 a 1392cc 'lean burn' model became available to meet increasingly strict exhaust emission laws.

Right: Reliant Rialto Hatch, 1982 on
Below: Fox multi-purpose vehicle, 1982
Below right: 1985 Reliant Scimitar SS1

Below: The Scimitar SS1 was introduced in February 1985, and was Britain's first new open two-seater sports car for many years. Power came from 1296cc or 1596cc Ford engines. The 1800 Ti (from June 1986) was turbocharged and fuel-injected.

Left: 1980 Reliant Scimitar GTC

Renault

France
1898 to date

Louis Renault, who was born in Paris in 1877, looked set to follow his father's footsteps as a button manufacturer. Instead, he turned to cars and built a prototype with a single-cylinder De Dion engine and propeller-shaft transmission as opposed to the more fashionable chain-drive.

It was made for his own pleasure but aroused interest among several of his friends, who ordered replicas. Renault set up his own company – Renault Frères – in March 1899 with 40,000 francs capital put up by his brothers. The car brought 60 orders when it was displayed at the Paris Automobile Salon in June.

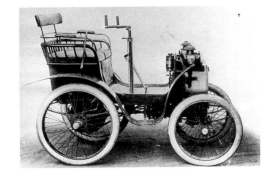

Renault then set up a factory and 179 cars were made in 1900, the first complete year of production. The little De Dion engine was later replaced by a 450cc unit and the car was offered with a coupé-type body.

Renault realized the value of racing successes and one of his cars put in the best performance in the 1899 Paris–Trouville race. Other successes included an outright victory by his brother Marcel in the 1902 Paris–Vienna race.

Louis withdrew from racing after his brother was killed in the 1903 Paris–Madrid race, but the company later returned to competition, winning the

Above left: 1898 single-cylinder Voiturette
Above: 1903 6.3-litre racer driven by Marcel Renault

first-ever Grand Prix in 1906 (over 60 years later, in 1977, another return was made to Grand Prix racing, leading to a string of successes).

Renault had begun to make its own four-cylinder engines in 1902, followed by singles and twins, although De Dion power units were also used until 1903. Production gradually expanded and, by 1905, the factory was turning out more than 2,000 cars a year.

A year earlier, Renault set a trend followed by many other car manufacturers – locating the radiator near the dashboard. The 1060cc two-cylinder AG and AX

Below: 8hp 1909 Type AX

Left: Built just before the turn of the century, the first Renault car was a single-cylinder De Dion-engined machine rated at 13/14hp. Later cars had a 450cc power unit.

models came in 1905 and, popular among taxi and light-commercial drivers, were Renault's best sellers up to 1914. Their success spread beyond France and in London, for instance, 1,100 taxis were ordered in 1907.

Renault was also doing well with its heavier commercial vehicles such as three- and five-ton trucks and the 1909 21-seater Paris bus. The company was offering six models of cars by 1907 which included the 1060cc AG and the 7429cc four-cylinder A1-C.

Above: 1913 11hp Taxi Landaulet
Below: 1914 25hp Sports Torpedo

Above: 1909 Labourdette-bodied coupé
Below: Four-cylinder limousine from 1911

Renault's fascination for machinery led him into the world of aero-engines and he built a 60hp air-cooled V8 in 1907 which, mounted in a Maurice Farman aircraft, won the 1911 Michelin Cup for a non-stop flight from Paris to Clermont-Ferrand.

Renault had reached the top of the tree by 1913, being France's largest producer of motor vehicles. Production exceeded 10,000 units a year with a workforce of nearly 4000.

That year, the factory was hit by a strike over docking of pay for inferior work. Louis Renault eventually won the battle but he was becoming increasingly remote from his employees.

World War I saw a massive expansion of his company which produced military vehicles and aero-engines. In fact, 600 of his taxis were commandeered and used to

transport men to the front in what became the Battle of the Marne. By 1918, the workforce was up to 22,500.

Part of the production had moved to Lyon in anticipation of invasion but Renault retained the factory at his home town of Billancourt which now boasted its own iron, brass, steel and aluminium foundries, assembly shops and facilities to make its own tools.

Renault's post-war range comprised three four-cylinder engines and one six, the last of which powered the famous 40CV in 1921. With a 9.1-litre engine and wooden wheels it was a huge car and, even with four-wheel braking in 1922, stopping power was notoriously poor.

The company met the challenge of the Citroën 5CV with the Model KJ (later becoming known as the NN) which ran from 1922 to 1929. Total car production had reached 46,000 by 1925.

Below: 1923 40/45hp Coupé de Maitre

Above: 1926 8.3hp NN cabriolet
Below: 1930 six-cylinder Vivastella

Commercial vehicles continued to play a significant role in the company's fortunes while Renault also produced rail-cars and tanks as well as marine, locomotive and aero-engines. The company was the world's largest manufacturer of aero-engines in 1930 with over 40,000 units to its credit in 23 years of production.

The gargantuan 40CV (known as the 45 in Britain) was replaced by the Reinastella in 1928, which used a 7.1-litre straight-eight engine, and the 4.2-litre Nervastella – also a straight-eight – was introduced two years later. In 1932, a 4.8-litre version was produced.

Above: 1933 Reinastella tourer
Below: 1934 Primastella saloon

The company also made a series of small four-cylinder cars – the Primaquatre, Monaquatre, Vivaquatre and Celtaquatre – plus a range of six-cylinder cars with the suffix 'stella'. These included the 1½-litre Monastella and the 4.1-litre Vivastella Grand Sport. The 1939 Suprastella 5.4-litre car became the official vehicle for the French president and senior ministers.

Above: 1939 Viva Grand Sport coupé

Renault's last model before World War II proved to be one of its most important. The one-litre 8CV Juvaquatre found wide appeal as a unitary-construction family saloon, with more than 27,000 being sold until the end of 1939 and several thousand more being delivered after the war. It was still available – albeit with the Dauphine engine and in van form – until 1959.

Renaults had also been assembled at Acton, west London, from 1927 to 1932 and from 1934 to 1939 and the 4CV and Dauphine were assembled there from 1949 to 1960.

The war years had taken their toll and Louis Renault had been compelled to work under German rule when France fell to the invaders. Shortly after Paris was liberated, he was arrested and accused of collaborating with the Nazis, although his only concern had been in keeping his factories operating. He was imprisoned in September 1944 and died on 23 October after a month of brutal treatment and poor medical care.

Former resistance fighter Pierre Lefaucheux had been appointed boss of the company even before Renault's death and four days after he took charge on 6 October, the first post-war truck left the factory. Renault was nationalized in February 1945 and became the Régie Nationale des Usines Renault.

Lefaucheux chose the 4CV 750cc rear-engined saloon – tested during the war – to lead Renault's post-war sales drive. But manufacture took time to build up and the Juvaquatre was the most popular passenger car until 1948.

The 40CV ultimately proved commendably successful and a total of 1,150,000 had been built when production ceased in 1961. Another post-war design was the Frégate, a front-engined two-litre saloon. But it did not sell as well as the company hoped and just 168,383 were made by the time it was withdrawn in 1958.

Above: Front-engined Frégate saloon c.1959

Above: The Floride, also a convertible

New Renault factories were opened in the 1950s including those at Flins, near Mantes, Le Mans and Choisy-le-Roi.

Lefaucheux was killed at the wheel of his Frégate in 1955 and was succeeded as director general by Pierre Dreyfus. Renault's commercial-vehicle operation merged with three other companies – Floriat, Latil and Somua – to form the Société Anonyme de Vehicules Industriels et Equipements Mécaniques (SAVIEM) became a major manufacturer of heavy vehicles by the 1970s.

The rear-engined 845cc Dauphine was introduced in 1956 and a million were sold in four years. Over 200,000 went to the U.S.A. It was also made under licence by Alfa Romeo in Italy and in Brazil by Willys-Overland. Tuner Amédée Gordini produced a high-performance version which took his name.

Below: The successful rear-engined Dauphine
Bottom: 1961 rear-engined 4 CV saloon

Above: Renault 4, launched in 1961
Below: Floride's removable hard-top

Above: 1289cc 60bhp Renault 12TL
Below: 1108cc Caravelle, introduced 1963

Above: R8 saloon, first appearing in 1963
Below: R16, one of the earliest hatchbacks

Launched in 1961 and only discontinued at the end of the 1980s, the Renault 4 was one of the company's greatest successes. It provided comfortable seating for four, outstanding economy and minimal maintenance requirements.

In 1961 the 4CV was replaced by the R4 which was planned as a more refined car than the Citroën 2CV (although Renault could hardly have known just how long the Citroën's popularity was to live on, despite its relative crudity).

The innovative Renault 16 hatchback appeared in January 1965 and was supplemented by the quicker TS version in 1968.

The 1960s also saw models such as the Renault 8 and 10 saloons and the front-wheel-drive 12 of 1969.

The Renault 5 hatchback – one of Renault's most popular models – hit the supermini market in 1972 although, tragically, designer Michel Boue never lived to see the car in production. Its universal appeal has made it the best-selling French car of all time. Engines ranged from a sedate 956cc unit to a turbocharged 160bhp power plant in the mid-engined 5 Turbo.

Below: A rare R12 Gordini from 1971

Above: 1974 Renault 5TS
Below: 1974 16 TX saloon

Below: Built from 1965 to 1980, the front-wheel-drive Renault 16 set new saloon-car standards of comfort, passenger space and performance. Later TX versions with a five-speed gearbox were good for over 160km/h (100mph).

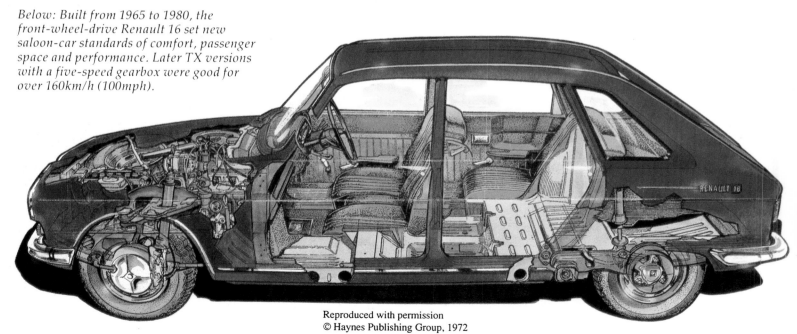

Reproduced with permission
© Haynes Publishing Group, 1972

Above: 1977 1218cc Renault 14

Above: 1977 Renault 12TL

Below: 4 TL dating from 1979

Above: 1977 Renault 6 TL
Below: 20 TS saloon c.1978

Left: Mid-engined R5 Turbo rally car in 1981
Below: 1983 Gordini Turbo road car

Launched in 1972, the Renault 5 quickly established itself as one of the new breed of front-wheel-drive small hatchbacks. The car was completely redesigned in 1985 and, with a range of engines from 956 to 1721cc, has proved just as popular.

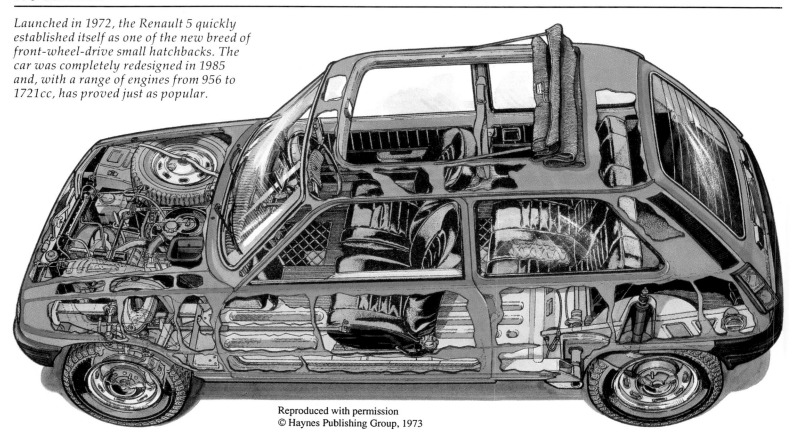

Reproduced with permission
© Haynes Publishing Group, 1973

Above: 1984 model year Renault 25
Right: 1986 GTA V6 Turbo
Below: 1984 Renault 11 Turbo

The new Renault 5 – a completely revamped yet visually similar version – was available from 1984.

The utilitarian 4 is still well-favoured while Renault has launched a host of new models this decade including the compact Renault 9 – which won a motoring journalists' Car of the Year Award – the Renault 21, the Fuego (not a successful car by the company's standards) and the high-performance GTA V6 Turbo.

Renault ran into problems in 1984 when Peugeot-Talbot-Citroën took the lead in the French market.

In January 1985, Bernard Hanon was replaced as president by Georges Besse who was brought in from Pechiney, a large state-owned chemical and iron industry. The company was stunned by his assassination outside his Paris home in November 1986. Left-wing extremists were later charged with his murder.

Above: The innovative Espace 2000 TSE

Below: 1988 9 GTX saloon

His successor was Raymond Levy, formerly chairman of the Belgian steel group Cockerill-Sambre.

Today, the company is heavily involved in American industry, such as robot technology and the manufacture of automotive electronic controls, but continues to build seven models which, in their various guises, offer customers a choice of over 50 different cars.

Below: 1990 Renault 21 GTS hatchback

Above: 1990 Renault 19 Chamade TXE

Below: By 1988 the GTA V6 Turbo Coupé was capable of 250km/h (155mph). Its turbocharged 2458cc V6 engine – mounted at the rear in unit with a five-speed transaxle – produced 200bhp at 5,750rpm.

Above: R5, completely restyled in 1985   *Below: 1989 19 TXE hatchback*

Above: Renault 25 V6 injection
Left: 1990 Renault 25 TXi
Below: Four-wheel-drive Espace Quadra

A bove: Mégane 5-door hatchback and (below) the Mégane Coupé

Louis Schweitzer took over the reins in 1993 and was able to announce that profits in 1992 had reached $980 million, an increase of no less than 84 per cent. The increase was in part due to the launch of several new models. Renault was replacing the 1980s 'numbered' models for new and stylish cars with names.

The Renault 5 was the first to be replaced in 1990. Its successor was the Clio, a chic hatchback with three or five doors. Engines ranged from a wheezy 58 horsepower 1.2-litre to a road-burning 150 horsepower 2.0-litre 16-valve unit. Unlike the Renault 5, the Clio was solidly built and had none of the flimsiness of its predecessor.

The odd Twingo mini-car, launched in 1992, was meant primarily for the home market, but many keen Francophiles elsewhere imported Twingos themselves as super-chic city cars.

Renault ditched the Alpine marque in 1992, but a new Renault-badged sports car arrived in 1995. Called the Renault Spider, the new car had an alloy chassis and race-style rose-jointed suspension. The styling was unconventional, but certainly very eye-catching. Early cars were not even fitted with windscreens, relying on a small deflector to protect driver and passenger. It was an uncompromising car, designed for driving pleasure rather than comfort, and had as little as possible that might detract from the pure driving experience. There was no heater, no carpets, no radio and only an

Above: Clio three- and five-door models

Above: Mégane Classic

Above: Laguna Estate

Above: The Renault Mégane Cabriolet was one of the last Mégane variants to be launched

Between the two World Wars, Riley built up a formidable sporting reputation, beginning in 1921 with the retrospectively named Redwinger, a rakish sporting model based on the 1919 sidevalve 11hp. But the sidevalve engines lasted only until 1928, when they were ousted by Percy Riley's new twin-camshaft engine, first shown as a 9hp four-cylinder unit in 1926. A six-cylinder version arrived in 1928. The cars powered by these engines were mostly middle-class saloons, with names like Monaco and San Remo, but there were also more glamorous models such as the

Top: 1931 14/6 saloon
Left: 1936 1½-litre Close-Coupled saloon
Above: 1934 12/4 Kestrel

Below: Notable among the sporting Rileys was the Brooklands Nine, a stylish two-seater with a 1087cc version of Percy Riley's immortal twin-cam engine.

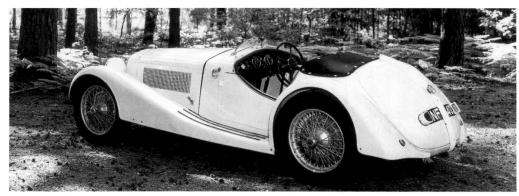

Top: 1936 Lynx four-seat tourer   *Above: 1936 Sprite sports model*

1928 Brooklands Nine, a two-seater distantly related to a notable privately built Brooklands racer.

In the early 1930s the sporting emphasis increased, and there were Imp (four-cylinder) and MPH (six-cylinder) two seaters, plus a Lynx open tourer. The saloons fed off the sporting image and were joined by the stylish fastback Kestrel. Hugh Rose enlarged the four-cylinder engine to 1½ litres in 1934 and new model names appeared – Adelphi and Falcon saloons, and Sprite two-seaters, for example. In addition, tuned Special Series or Sprite Series versions of the basic models were offered.

The middle of the decade saw Riley adding larger cars to an already confusingly varied model range. A V8 engine arrived in 1936, a 2½-litre 'Big Four' in 1937, and in 1936 a second V8 had appeared in an all-new luxury saloon marketed under the Autovia name.

But the strain on the company's resources proved too much. The Receiver was called in early in 1938 and Lord Nuffield bought the company. The huge

Below: Typical of the 1930s sporting Rileys was the Sprite. Again a two-seater model with rakish styling, it had a 1496cc version of the twin-cam engine.

model range was cut back to 12hp (1½-litre) and 16hp (2½-litre) models for 1939, both new designs bearing the scars of Nuffield influence: sporting models ceased to exist.

After World War II the company staged a remarkable comeback with widely acclaimed new 1½-litre and 2½-litre saloons. There were also short-lived drop-head and roadster variants, the latter aimed at the U.S. market. Assembly moved to the MG works at Abingdon in 1949. The saloons survived Nuffield's merger with Austin to form B.M.C. in 1952, but the Pathfinder, which replaced the 2½-litre in 1953, was an ill-developed car which shared styling and components with a big Wolseley. The 1½-litre

soldiered on until 1955, but its replacement was a larger-engined and restyled Morris Minor called the One-Point-Five. The Pathfinder gained a B.M.C. engine and re-emerged as the 2.6, but it was short-lived. The 1960s saw the Riley name added to variants of B.M.C.'s Minis, 1100s, and 1½-litre Farina saloons, but by 1969 the marque had ceased to have any real identity.

Top: 1950 2½-litre saloon, type RMB
Left: 1961 Elf with 848cc engine
Below left: 1962 4/Seventy Two saloon
Bottom left: 1965 Kestrel saloon
Below: 1961 One Point Five saloon

Rolls-Royce

Great Britain 1904 to date

The Rolls-Royce tradition stretches back to 1904, when Henry Royce's dissatisfaction with his own Decauville light car led him to produce a 10hp prototype of his own. His painstaking approach to design and construction was evident in this and subsequent three-, four-, and six-cylinder models, and greatly impressed the Hon. Charles Rolls, to whom Royce was introduced in 1904. The two concluded a marketing agreement, under which Rolls and Co. agreed to take all the cars produced by Royce and sell them as Rolls-Royce models. In 1906, the Rolls-Royce Company was founded.

In that year, the magnificent 40/50 model was announced, and Rolls-Royce settled down to a one-model policy. Commonly but mistakenly known as the Silver Ghost, after a special factory-owned example, the 40/50 was a large, expensive, and sophisticated motor car, built in chassis form only so that customers could have a body built to order by specialist coachbuilders. Several saw service with the

Right: The 1906 Silver Ghost 40/50 was an immediate success and over 6,000 were built before production ended in 1925, plus a further 1,700 at the Springfield factory. The 7036cc six-cylinder engine of early cars like this gave 80km/h (50mph) from 50bhp.

Below: The first 1904 10hp chassis

Top: 1906 Light Twenty TT car
Above: The Silver Ghost – a 1906 40/50

Above: 1909 40/50 with sporting body

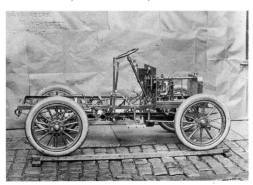

Left: 1911 40/50 Landau by Barker
Above: 1916 40/50 light armoured car
Below: 1912 40/50 Ceremonial Victoria

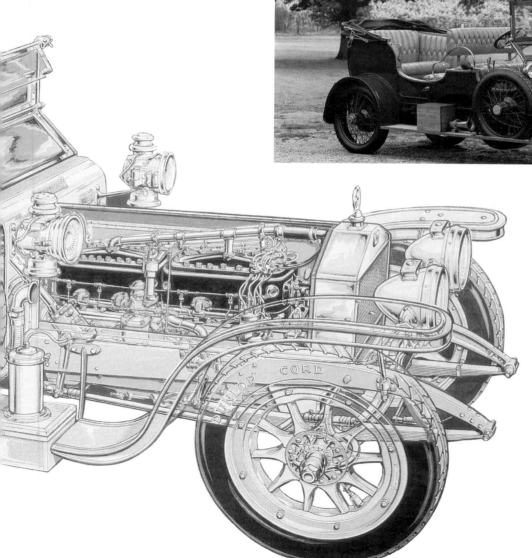

Above: 1914 40/50 tourer
Below: 1922 Springfield-built 40/50

hypoid-type rear axle permitting lower coachwork and a more powerful engine.

The Phantom II was the last car actually designed by Royce himself, who had been knighted in 1930, for he died in 1933. Legend has it that the 'RR' letters on the cars' grille badges were changed from red to black in mourning as a result; but, in fact, the change had been planned by Royce himself, who considered that the red clashed with certain bodywork colours.

The next new model was the Phantom III, introduced in 1935 and featuring a

Left: c. 1922 Twenty Doctor's Coupé
Below: 1923 20hp Barker open limousine
Centre: 1924 Phantom I by Labourdette

British Army as armoured cars during World War I.

Demand forced a move from the original Manchester premises to a larger factory in Derby during 1908, but there were no more new model announcements until 1922 brought the new 'small' Rolls-Royce, designated the Twenty and designed to meet the demands of the harsher economic climate of the time. Even so, it was an expensive and exclusive model by the standards of the average motorist.

Central to the design of the original Twenty was a new in-line six-cylinder engine of 3127cc, with pushrod-operated overhead valves instead of the inlet-over-exhaust configuration favoured on the earlier models. This was progressively enlarged in order to keep the performance of the 'small' Rolls-Royce up to scratch. Thus, 1929 saw the 20/25 model arrive with a 3680cc version of the engine, and the 1936 4257cc version turned what was still essentially the same car into a 25/30 model. This final version also went into the Wraith in 1938, and the 3½-litre and 4¼-litre types were also used in the Bentley models made at Derby after the Rolls-Royce takeover of that firm in 1931.

The 40/50 was discontinued in 1925, and the new larger Rolls-Royce was the 7.6-litre six-cylinder Phantom, the first of the company's models to have the vertical radiator shutters which have since been an essential feature of the famous Palladian radiator. Improvements turned this into a Phantom II in 1929, this time with a

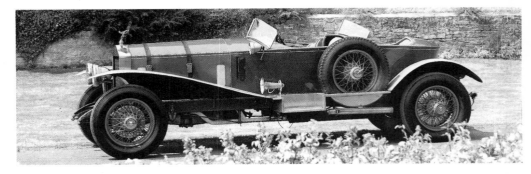

Above: c. 1922 Twenty Coupé
Left: 1926 Springfield-built Phantom I

Above: c.1925 Springfield-built Phantom I

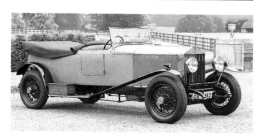

Above: 1930 R-series 20/25 sports

Above: 1930 Phantom II by Barker

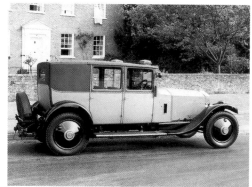

Above: 1929 Twenty with Mulliner body

Above: 1936 Phantom III by Park Ward

V12 engine which owed more than a little to the company's experience with aero-engine manufacture. Royce had initiated work on this car, with which he intended to compete with the multi-cylinder models coming out of Detroit in the early 1930s. Further Detroit influence was visible in the car's independent front suspension, based on a General Motors design by Maurice Olley, a former Rolls-Royce engineer.

Below: For the 20/25 of 1929, the Twenty's six-cylinder engine was enlarged to give 3680cc and 65bhp. Many had rather perpendicular saloon bodies, but this four-door was more stylish.

All these models were expensive and exquisitely engineered, and all were produced in chassis form only, leaving the choice of coachbuilder and body style to the customer. An exception was presented by the Rolls-Royce models built in the U.S.A. at Springfield, Massachusetts, between 1919 and 1931, which were offered as complete cars as well as in chassis form. Established to avoid high import duties on cars sold in the U.S., the Springfield factory built 40/50 models and Phantoms until a sales slump caused by the Depression forced it to close in 1931.

Since 1914, the company had also built some highly successful aero-engines, and this side of its business expanded greatly in the 1930s and during World War II. After the war, the Derby factory was turned over entirely to aero-engine manufacture, and the cars were built at Crewe, in a 'shadow' factory which the company had run on behalf of the Air Ministry during the war.

Central to the post-war models was the concept of the rationalized range, proposed by W. A. Robotham as early as 1940. The plan was to minimize manufacturing costs without compromising quality, and this was to be achieved through the use of flexible chassis and engine designs. Bentley derivatives, too, would be essentially rebadged Rolls-Royces and not separately developed models. Thus, the new inlet-over-exhaust-valve engine range introduced in 1946 came in four-, six- and eight-cylinder versions, though the four- and eight-cylinder variants would find mostly military or commercial uses.

The six-cylinder version lay at the heart of the new limousine chassis, the 1946 Silver Wraith, and of the new saloon model, the 1949 Silver Dawn, which was a detuned Mark VI Bentley. Although coachbuilt bodies were available – and all the Silver Wraiths had them – the majority of the Silver Dawns were delivered with 'standard-wheel' saloon bodies made by Pressed Steel. This apparent heresy was once again part of Robotham's rationalization policy. A third range, the Phantom IV with the eight-cylinder inlet-over-exhaust-valve engine and coach-built bodies, ran from 1950 to 1956, but was built in tiny numbers for heads of state only.

Engine changes took the six-cylinder

Top: 1934 20/25 by Gurney Nutting
Above: 1939 Wraith by Gurney Nutting

Above: 1952 Silver Dawn saloon

Above: 1954 Phantom IV by H. J. Mulliner   *Below: 1955 Silver Wraith by Hooper*

unit's capacity from 4256cc to 4566cc in 1952, and to 4887cc for the 1955 Silver Cloud. Once again, this was essentially a 'standard-steel' model, but its separate-chassis construction also gave the coachbuilders scope to produce a wide range of custom-built styles. Meanwhile, automatic transmission had become a standard feature, and refinements like air-conditioning and electric windows were beginning to appear, although only to special order. The six-cylinder engine died out in 1959, however, and in that year the Silver Cloud gained a new 6230cc V8 engine. Its V8 configuration had been

Top: 1959 Silver Cloud II
Left: 1962 Silver Cloud III
Above: 1957 long-wheelbase Silver Cloud

Below: The 1929 Phantom II was the last car designed by Sir Henry Royce. Its long bonnet covered a 7668cc six-cylinder engine which made the car much faster than any previous Rolls-Royce.

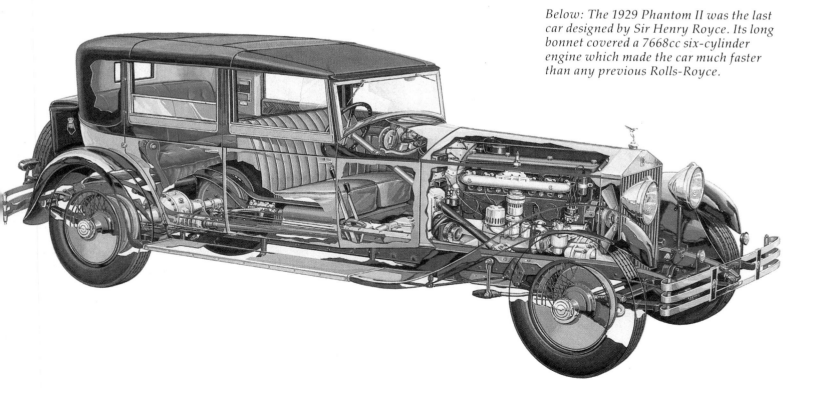

determined largely by the need to maintain sales in the U.S.A., where large and powerful V8 engines were the norm. Though the engine was indeed significantly more powerful than the older six-cylinder, it was also generally considered rather less refined.

The V8 went at the same time into the related but much larger Phantom V limousine model, itself usually sold with a 'standard-steel' body by the in-house coachbuilders Mulliner Park Ward, formed by the amalgamation of two formerly separate companies acquired by Rolls-Royce in the 1950s. The Phantom V became a Phantom VI in 1968 without drama, and this latter model remained in production, albeit in very limited numbers, at the end of the 1980s.

The Phantom V and VI shared the separate-chassis construction of the Silver Cloud models, but monocoque construction arrived with the 1965 Silver Shadow, which replaced the Silver Cloud. Powered by the V8 engine, enlarged after 1971 to 6750cc, it sold better than any previous model. Also available, after 1966, were coachbuilt coupé and convertible derivatives by Mulliner Park Ward.

The bankruptcy of the Aero-Engine Division in 1971 left the Car Division of the company unscathed; and indeed, it had always remained profitable. The coachbuilt Shadow variants were revised later that year and relaunched as Corniches, but

Above: 1960 Phantom V touring limousine   *Below: 1974 Silver Shadow saloon*

Below: This 1976 version of the Corniche drophead had coachwork by Mulliner Park Ward clothing Silver Shadow running gear. The 6750cc V8 engine gave a 193km/h (120mph) top speed.

Above: 1964 Mulliner Park Ward Cloud III
Top right: 1975 Camargue
Right: 1976 Silver Wraith II

James Young was the only outside coachbuilder to attempt series production of a Silver Shadow variant, and that not very successfully. The early Shadows had been criticized for their bias towards ride at the expense of handling, but the Series II models introduced in 1976 went some way towards restoring the balance. After 1974, a third Shadow derivative was available in the shape of the Camargue coupé, with controversial styling by the Italian Pininfarina. This was produced in relatively small numbers, and had no Bentley equivalent.

The Silver Shadow was replaced in 1982 by the Silver Spirit, again with the V8 engine, and this has been gradually refined with state-of-the-art technology like anti-lock brakes, fuel-injection and automatic ride control. Rolls-Royce models remain essentially conservative, however, and the more glamorous engineering developments of recent years have been reserved for the related Bentley models (q.v.). Unlike the Silver Shadow, the Silver Spirit has attracted the attentions of a number of high-quality coachbuilders who have produced very expensive conversions, mostly as one-offs. Series production of an ultra-long-wheelbase Silver Spur Limousine by the conversion specialists Robert Jankel did begin in 1987, however, and the relative popularity of this hugely expensive model suggests that the appeal of the Phantom VI may be on the wane.

Above: 1981 US-model Silver Spirit

Above: 1989 Corniche III
Below: 1986 Silver Spur

During the economic depression of the late 1980s and early 1990s, Rolls-Royce sales figures slumped, and Vickers, its parent company, made no secret of the fact that it would be open to offers to buy. Among the companies rumoured to be interested was BMW. Although BMW did not buy Rolls-Royce, it did assist in the development of new power units.

By 1993, the tide had turned and sales started to increase again. Also in 1993, Rolls-Royce opened a dealership in Moscow. The expansion of the Rolls-Royce marketing network to the east (there were also plans for a Chinese dealership) was evidence of how the company had reacted to the recession's devastating effect on the luxury car market.

In early June 1998, Volkswagen won the shareholders' vote by 5.1 million votes for and 109,035 against to buy Rolls-Royce from Vickers Plc for a final sum of £470m. BMW, whose V-12 engine, seats, safety equipment and electronics were already touring the world's roads in the new Rolls-Royce Silver Seraph, bid £340m. The difference, although including Cosworth Engineering in the deal for an extra £120m, has to cover re-engineering replacements for all the parts which BMW will withdraw in mid 1999.

Above: Long-wheelbase Rolls-Royce Silver Spur with division

Below: 1997 Rolls-Royce Silver Dawn

Above: Rolls-Royce Silver Spur

Below: Rolls-Royce Park Ward limousine

Rover

Great Britain
1904 to date

Rover graduated from building pedal cycles, through motor-cycles, and built its first motor car in 1904. Expansion before World War I was slow, however, and the models generally undistinguished despite a win in the 1907 Tourist Trophy race and some interesting cars built with single- and twin-cylinder sleeve-valve engines.

Above: 1908 20hp Tourist Trophy model
Below: 1922 8hp with Grose body
Right: 1925 14/45 tourer

Expansion was more rapid in the 1920s and the company offered a wide model range, starting with the air-cooled flat-twin 8hp model and going up through 14/45 and 16/50 models with complex overhead-camshaft engines. But the range was too wide and company policy lacked a clear sense of direction. At the end of the decade the economic depression left Rover in financial trouble.

Under its new General Manager, Spencer Wilks, Rover returned to profitability in the 1930s. The first of a properly planned and integrated range of cars appeared for 1934, and these made

Above: 1904 8hp model

Owen Clegg joined Rover from Wolseley in 1911 and designed the first four-cylinder model, a 12hp introduced in 1912. Its success helped the company to survive after its sleeve-valve models had sold poorly.

Above: 1933 14hp Pilot saloon
Below: 1935 10hp saloon

quality their keynote, aiming specifically at the conservative British middle classes. By the beginning of World War II the company was a respected name, offering a broad model range of saloons and coachbuilt drophead coupés from a four-cylinder 10hp up to a six-cylinder 20hp.

Rover's main Coventry factory was destroyed by bombing in 1940, and after the war the company moved into the large factory at Solihull which it had run for the Air Ministry during the hostilities, although the 1946–47 cars were revamped pre-war models, a new inlet-over-exhaust-valve engine powered the 1948 P3 saloons, and a variant of the same engine lay at the heart of the Land Rover, a lightweight 4×4 designed for agricultural and industrial uses which was inspired by the U.S. military Jeep and appeared in 1948.

Although the Land Rover had been intended only to keep the factory busy while car production picked up, its sales rapidly outstripped all projections and, for the next three decades, its profits kept the company afloat and enabled it to remain in the forefront of advanced engineering, most notably in the field of gas-turbine propulsion for road cars.

Nevertheless, Rover's image remained conservative. Despite its modern styling, the P4 saloon of 1949 managed to retain a traditional Rover flavour, and was comfortably outmoded by the time it ceased production in 1964. After 1959, it had been joined by the more luxurious P5 3-litre model, but it was not until the P6 2000 of 1963 that the mould was broken and Rover's advanced engineering was thrust to the fore. This model remained a

Top: 1947 12hp tourer
Above: 1950 P4 75 'Cyclops'
Below: 1954 T2A experimental gas turbine

Below left: 1948 Land Rover
Below: 1958 P4 90 saloon

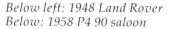

strong seller until its demise in 1976, going through several variations on the way.

In 1964, Rover acquired from General Motors the manufacturing rights to its 3½-litre light-alloy V8 engine, which went into P5 and P6 derivatives in the later 1960s and was the key to the enormously successful Range Rover, a luxury 4×4 announced in 1970. It was later used in Land Rovers and was central to the new SD1 saloon range introduced in 1976. This, however, suffered from poor quality which damaged Rover's hard-won reputation, and it failed to sell as strongly as had been hoped.

Rover took over Alvis in 1959, but was itself absorbed into the Leyland combine in 1967. Organizational reshuffles linked it with Jaguar and Triumph in the early 1970s, and after 1978 the Land Rover business was run separately. Leyland's financial difficulties meant that new Rovers for the 1980s were based on Japanese Honda designs (the 200 series of 1984) or designed jointly with Honda (the 800 series of 1986). From 1988, the former Leyland combine was renamed the Rover Group (after a brief period as Austin Rover), and in the same year it was sold by the British government to British Aerospace.

Below: The P6 was introduced in 1963 and had base-unit construction and all-disc brakes. The original two-litre four-cylinder engine was later supplemented by a 3½-litre V8. This 1974 2200TC had a 2.2-litre twin-carburettor engine.

Above: 1959 P5 3-litre saloon   *Below: 1967 P5B 3.5-litre coupé*

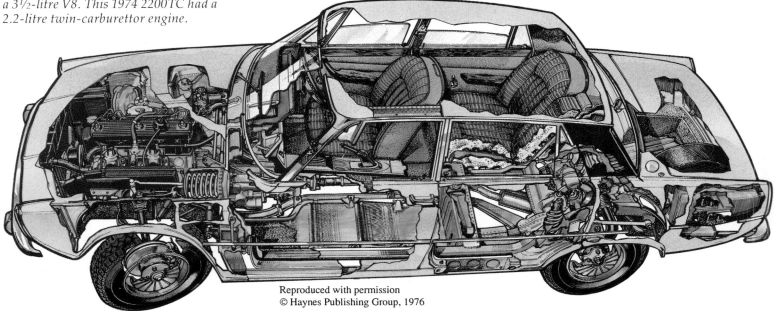

Reproduced with permission
© Haynes Publishing Group, 1976

Top: 1972 Series III Land Rover
Above: 1988 Land Rover Ninety County
Below: 1986 820Si saloon

Top: 1974 P6 3500S

Above: 1976 SD1 3500

Above: The Rover 200 series of 1984 was simply a Honda Ballade with new front and rear details. However, this 1985 216 Vanden Plas EFi had an Austin engine.

Left: 1989 Sterling 2.7-litre saloon
Below left: 1989 214SLi 16-valve

Above: 1989 214GSi 16-valve
Below: 1989 Metro (ex-Austin Metro)

Left: 1989 827Si fastback
Above: 1989 Range Rover Vogue Turbo D

Left: 1989 800-series Vitesse
Above: 1989 Land Rover Discovery Tdi

Left: 1989 216GSi 16-valve
Above: 1989 Land Rover Discovery

Left: 1990 414Si 16-valve
Above: 1989 Land Rover Discovery V8

Above: The turbocharged Rover 200 coupé was the fastest-ever Rover production model

Left: The Rover 100 was a rebadged Metro

Rover's collaboration with Honda continued into the 1990s, with Rover working to maintain and extend the individuality of its Honda-based range in order to create a separate image for its products. To this end, Rover extended the 200/400 range by introducing diesel engines, a convertible and a performance coupé, and did not follow Honda's lead when it went upmarket with the Legend.

This separation from Honda obviously worked because, in Europe, the Rover cars usually outsold their Honda equivalent. Benefiting from the strength of the yen, Rovers were even selling well in Japan, where they were being accepted as luxury Hondas. Although there was a cooling of the relationship between the two companies, the collaboration continued with the launch of the Rover 600, which was based on the Honda Accord.

Despite this success, the company was not out of the woods and lost $80 million in 1991 and $74 million in 1992, but this was mainly put down to the recession.

Meanwhile, Rover, and it successful sister company Land Rover, appeared to be up for

Above : Rover 200 convertible

sale and there were many interested potential purchasers. Honda was the favourite, with its existing 20 per cent stake, and Volkswagen and Renault were also rumoured to be interested. Sales increased in 1993 and 1994 before the company was bought by BMW. Rover had been the last major manufacturer in Britain to be British-owned.

The new BMW-owned Rover looked set for technical success with one of the best ranges of power units on the market. The engine range started with the all-alloy four-cylinder K-series in eight- and 16-valve forms. This was followed by a direct-injection diesel and then a top-level 90-degree V6, based on the K-series and designated KV6. With two cams per cylinder bank, the new 2.5-litre engine produced 175bhp.

There were still some reminders of the British Leyland era in the Rover range, in the form of the 100 (né Metro) and the Mini (which is actually pre-British Leyland). Although the 100 was to continue, the Mini, which BMW saw as a separate marque, was to be replaced by the turn of the century.

Above: The Rover 600 series was based on the Honda Accord but used Rover engines

Above: 1996 Rover Tourer 1.8

Left: 1997 Mini Cooper with Sports pack

Above: 1997 Rover 400 series

Above: 1997 Rover 200 series

Above: Rover 1.8 VVC Coupé

Above: The Rover 800 series topped the Rover range from 1986 and was face-lifted in 1992. By 1997 all engines were Rover's own

Saab

Sweden
1950 to date

Meanwhile, the 92 had been replaced by the 93 in 1956 with a three-cylinder 748cc two-stroke engine, followed by the 96 with an 841cc 42bhp engine in which Erik Carlsson scored many successes including the Monte Carlo Rally in 1962 and 1963.

Saab's policy of using two-stroke engines found great favour in Britain, America and other export countries. Ironically, most Swedish motorists wanted a less-troublesome four-stroke.

Saab responded by using the 1½-litre German Ford V4 engine in the 96 body shell. It was available from 1967 and boosted sales in Sweden where it sold 24,000 that year, compared with 500 two-strokes.

Saab made its last two-stroke in 1968 and the familiar Sason-designed two-door saloon came to an end in 1979.

Plans to replace the Sason model were being considered as early as 1963 by Saab's president Tryggve Holm.

He chose the Standard-Triumph inclined four-cylinder engine to power the new 99 which was launched at the end of 1969.

The body was designed by Sason – who sadly died seven months before the launch – and Bjorn Enwall. The 1.7-litre engine was stretched to 1854cc in 1971 and to 1985cc in 1972.

A new engine plant was opened at Sodertalje in 1972 and it used the revolutionary group assembly method – one group of workers was responsible for each engine and they rotated jobs to reduce boredom. The plant marked the end of Saab's association with Triumph.

The formation of Saab as a car manufacturer was the result of a clinical decision rather than a process of evolution.

Svenska Aeroplan A.B. was already a successful aircraft manufacturer and after the end of World War II – because of the fall in demand for aircraft – the company decided its expertise could be usefully employed in other directions.

The car department was set up under Gunner Ljungstrom who had worked for Standard and Rover in England. His car was called Project 92 and had a 764cc vertical twin two-stroke engine driving the front wheels.

Stylist Sixten Sason designed a streamlined body which resembled an aircraft wing in section.

Production began in 1950 and within a fortnight Saab engineer Rolf Melde won the Swedish Winter Rally. This was the start of a long Saab association with rallying.

By March 1954 Saab had sold about 10,000 cars, sticking with one body design until the 95 estate was introduced in 1959.

Above: Saab 93, introduced in December 1955
Below: The Saab 900 was launched in 1978 to run in parallel with the 99, and was still in production in 1990 – by that time with the option of a 16-valve double-overhead-camshaft engine and/or the ever-popular turbocharger.

Above: All-new 99 saloon for 1969
Below: New lights and bumpers for 1972

Top: 1960 model year Saab 96
Above: Triple-choke carburettor, new for 1966

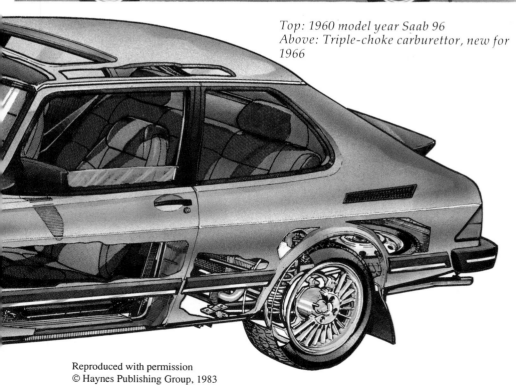

Above: Two views of the high-performance Turbo launched in 1977

By this time Saab was a massive company, having merged with the long-established truck-maker Scania-Vabis in 1968.

The launch of the 99 paved the way for more up-market Saabs. The 145bhp five-seater Turbo version was introduced in 1977 to appeal to the family man who wanted sporty motoring.

The 99 in both non-turbo and turbo forms also continued Saab's association with competition and in the 1970s was used to great effect by leading rally drivers such as Stig Blomqvist, Simo Lampinen, Tapio Rainio and Per Eklund.

The 900 model – a long-wheelbase version of the 99 – represented Saab's stab at the executive-car market in 1978. It was available in five-door form as the 900GLS.

The 90 – a modified version of the 99 – was also available as a two-door saloon.

The 1980s range of cars included the 900 – now in fuel-injected form – with a choice of saloon and hatchback bodies, the 900 Turbo and the top-of-the-range 9000 Turbo 16-valve.

A 50 per cent stake in Saab's troubled car division – though not its profitable truck or aerospace operations – was acquired for U.S. $600 million in December 1989 by General Motors. To utilize excess capacity, Saab's factories will produce some of G.M.'s bigger models during the 1990s, but by the year 2000 G.M. intends Saab to be building 200,000 luxury cars of its own each year. These will rival offerings from BMW, Jaguar and Mercedes-Benz.

Top left: 1979 five-door 900 Turbo
Top right: 1984 four-door 900 GL saloon
Above: 1984 two-door 99 GL

Below: The Saab 9000 was the company's first completely new model since the original 99. In fuel-injected form it developed 130bhp for a top speed of 185km/h (115mph); with 16 valves and a turbocharger developing 175bhp it stormed up to 215km/h (134mph).

Above: Fuel-injected 9000i from 1986

Above: High-performance 900 Turbo

Above: 1989 900 Turbo 16 Convertible

Below: Saab's 1989 CD Turbo 'S'

Above: 1989 two-door 900 Turbo

Above: 1989 9000 Carlsson

Above: The 1990 Carlsson

General Motors had to work hard to bring Saab back into profit. Efficiency was improved at the factories so that where it had taken 115 to 120 hours to build a car in 1989, it only took 34 by 1992. Saab was reorganized into two factories producing components and one assembly plant at Trollhättan, which visiting Japanese described a the best example of 'lean production' methods in Europe.

By 1992, the company looked to be heading back into profit again and planned to rebuild its product range with new up-market cars. Project 104 was the new 900, based on G.M. Vectra components; project 106 was a new 9000 with a better engine range, and project 108 was to see Saab taking over the Senator-sized G.M. range with V6 and V8 engines. The third project was put on hold in 1993, following further losses.

It wasn't until 1995 that Saab managed to make a proper profit. The success came mainly from increased U.S. sales. In 1994, nearly a quarter of Saab's sales were in the States. The company was still being held back, however, by its limited model range. Saab offered only two cars, both of which were very closely positioned in the market place. A third model (the 9-5) did not arrive until 1997, and seemed to be pitched towards the same market sector.

The new 900, launched in 1993 in five-door form, was available with the old Saab four-cylinder engine and the G.M. 2.5-litre V6. The range was completed with the introduction of the three-door and cabriolet later in the year. The four-cylinder turbo was

Above: The new 900 Turbo proved its mettle on a 25,000-mile (40,232-km) non-stop run at an average speed of over 140mph (225km/h)

Below: The 1997 Saab 9000 five-door hatchback with 2.3-litre engine

still the performance model, with 185 bhp, 15 more than the larger V6. Saab proved the capability of the Turbo at the Talladega Superspeedway, Alabama in 1996. A standard production Turbo completed a 25,000-mile non-stop journey at an average speed of over 140mph. Despite being based on the G.M. Vectra, the Saab managed to maintain its individual image.

The 9000 carried on with face-lifts and an updated engine range, but never sold as well as its smaller brother. The 3.0-litre G.M. V6 was made available in 1994, but gave less power than the 225bhp 2.3-litre turbocharged engine. The 9-5 launched in 1997 had styling similar to the 9000, but with a much improved chassis. A new generation of engines came with the new car.

Left: Saab 9000CD four-door saloon

Below: 1997 900 Convertible

Salmson

France
1921–1957

Emile Salmson began manufacturing Swiss Canton-Unné aero-engines after his attempt at building a helicopter had failed because of the engine weight. Société des Moteurs Salmson was set up at Billancourt, Seine, in 1912.

After Salmson's death at the end of World War I the firm was taken over by M. Heinrich, who had controlled Salmson's Lyon factory. He branched out into cars, producing G.N.s under licence until 1921 when the first Salmson ALs appeared, designed by Emile Petit. Petit and Heinrich were introduced by André Lombard, who initiated the distinctive St. Andrew's Cross radiator design, and after whom the AL was named.

Salmson enjoyed much sporting success during the 1920s, including the French Cyclecar Grand Prix, the Brooklands 200-Mile Race, the Targa Florio and the Le Mans 24-hour race. In 1927 Petit's 1.1-litre twin-overhead-cam twin-blown straight-eight engine was said to produce 140bhp, but was never offered commercially.

Competition entry lasted until 1929 when Heinrich shifted away from sporting racers towards touring cars, and Petit left

Above: 1925 Grand Sport taking part in a 1975 Light Car rally

Below: The Salmson Grand Sport had an enviable reputation for reliability at a time when high performance often meant quite the reverse. Its 1086cc four-cylinder double-overhead-camshaft engine enabled it to exceed 113km/h (70mph), and it was successful in many areas of motor sport.

to join Ariès. The Salmson sports models continued to be offered in Britain until 1931, but were overshadowed by the introduction of the M.G. Midget.

Salmson brought out the S4 model, usually with four-door saloon bodywork, and which was continued in various forms until 1950. The 1930s saw a revival in the company's aero-engine manufacture, although by the early 1950s its designs were outdated and it closed briefly in 1952.

At the 1953 Paris Salon Salmson introduced a new model, the aerodynamic 2300 GT Coupé, with which it won the Tulip Rally the following year and also the Lyon–Charbonnières event. Bodies for the car were supplied by Esclassan and Chapron, since Salmson itself could not provide the finance to do so. Less than 230 were built before production ceased altogether in 1957.

Above: 1927 Salmson tourer
Left: 1927 tourer (left) and 1936 saloon

Above: 1950-53 Salmson Randonnée saloon
Left: 1936 20/90 six-cylinder roadster
Below: 1955 Salmson 2300S

Serpollet
France
1887–1907

Léon Serpollet began experimenting with steam power in 1880. Within eight years he had invented an ingenious multi-tube flash boiler and was developing steam-propelled tricycles, made for him by Armand Peugeot and La Buire.

Shortly after this, Serpollet gained backing from Ernest Archdeacon and further three-wheelers were built by Jeantaud. In 1894 Serpollet turned to four-wheeled commercial vehicles, building steam-driven buses and trams. When these went over to electricity he turned to passenger cars with finance from American Frank L. Gardner, forming Gardner Serpollet in 1900. That year Power

Above: Léon Serpollet and his steam tricycle of 1887
Left: 1901 roadster

Below: The 1902 'Easter Egg', so called because of its comparatively streamlined bodywork. It was also specially geared, and in the same year it was driven by Serpollet at a speed of 120.771km/h (75.043mph) to set a new flying kilometre world record at Nice, France.

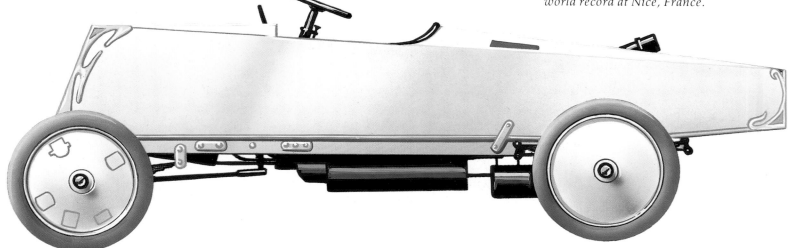

Traction & Lighting began producing Serpollets under licence in Leeds, but few were built. This was also true of Serpollet Italiana SA of Milan, Italy, between 1906 and 1908.

From works in the Rue Stendhal, Paris, Serpollet began producing cars, including racers. Serpollets were well placed in the 1902 Circuit du Nord, and competed in the Paris–Madrid race of 1903. In the 1904 Gordon Bennett Trials Serpollet fielded some six-cylinder cars, albeit unsuccessfully.

By 1906 steam-powered road cars were losing their appeal. Alexandre Darracq expressed interest in producing Serpollet-designed commercials but his plans came to nothing as in 1907, aged only 49, Serpollet died from tuberculosis. A statue to this pioneer of steam stands in the Place St. Ferdinand des Ternes, Paris.

Left: 1888 Serpollet steam tricycle
Below: 1908 11hp tourer

Simca

France
1934–1982

La Société Industrielle de Mécanique et de Carrosserie Automobile, or Simca for short, was founded in 1934 by the French importer of Fiats, Henri-Théodore Pigozzi. His aims had nothing to do with grand engineering achievements or innovatory concepts in car design; rather he wanted to run a successful business by manufacturing Fiats under licence in France.

It worked rather well, too. He took over the redundant Donnet factory in Nanterre, on the Seine, and started building the Fiat 508 and the slightly larger 518, then the 500 Topolino, called the Simca Cinq, and the 508C, badged as the Simca Huit. This latter model proved to be very amenable to tuning, and Simca had its own tame expert on improving the performance of standard cars in the person of one Amédée Gordini.

While Gordini was tuning the cars to win races, the firm itself was doing very well in business. By 1938 it was building

Right: The 1000 was first introduced as a cheap and cheerful car for the masses, although during its lifespan it gained various sporting versions and more upmarket variants. However, it was very successful at the time.

Top: A 1935 6CV Fiat/Simca collaboration   *Above: Gordini and Le Mans, 1949*

21,000 cars a year, despite a savage six-week strike. Then war broke out and the Germans invaded and seized the factory. Tiny numbers of cars continued to be made throughout the war, however, and in 1946 full-scale production resumed, still with the Cinq and Huit models.

Competition successes resumed, too, again with Gordini tweaking some of the firm's sportier models, and production took off after a slow start to better pre-war totals by 1949.

In 1951 Simca broke with its Fiat designs to introduce the Aronde (Swallow), a totally new car except for the engine design which was carried over from previous models. It sold extremely well, with overseas sales also being encouraging, and nearly 1½ million were eventually produced.

This allowed Simca some room for expansion, so it bought a succession of firms, starting with Unic in 1951, and Ford's French operation in 1954 which furnished it with more production facilities, as well as a couple of extra models which it took over from Ford.

The French subsidiary of Saurer, a Swiss commercial-vehicle company, was also taken over in 1956, and in 1959 Talbot came under Simca's wing. However, all these takeovers were mirrored by a gradual buyout of Simca itself, by Chrysler. The U.S. giant had bought 15 per cent of the firm in 1958 and by 1963 had gained a majority shareholding. Just a year later Simca's founder, M. Piggozzi, died.

New models continued to be introduced, from the very cheap Simca 1000, which was again extremely successful, to the exotic; Simca took over sports-car maker Matra in 1969 and from 1973 produced the Matra-Simca Bagheera, a high-performance coupé in the supercar style.

By 1970, however, the company was almost wholly owned by Chrysler, and thereafter it produced Rootes-designed cars, confusingly enough often for export to Britain.

In 1978 Chrysler itself suffered financial troubles and the Peugeot-Citroën company bought Simca, by now named Chrysler France SA, and renamed it Talbot, a marque name which lasted until 1982 when it was completely absorbed into the P.S.A. organization.

Above: The Vedette luxury saloon, 1954-61

Below: Simca 1100S, a 1974 economy car

Above: The Aronde Commerciale van

Below: Simca 1000 GLS

Simplex

U.S.A.
1904–1917

The Simplex Automobile Co. of New Brunswick in New Jersey was not officially formed until 1907, but actually began building cars three years earlier. A. D. Proctor Smith and Carlton R. Mabley were importers of Fiat, Renault, Panhard and Mercedes cars who began producing their own marque in 1904.

Called Simplex after their Mercedes inspiration, these vehicles were designed by Edward Franquist and built entirely in

Above: Simplex racer c.1910
Below left: 1912 Simplex on a 1964 tour
Below: 1918 Crane-Simplex Limousine

Below: 1914 Simplex 50hp tourer

Smith & Mabley's seven-storey factory on West 83rd Street, New York. Their early models included the 30/35hp and a 70hp prototype racer which was soon scrapped, although later Simplexes were raced by Joe Tracy, Al Poole and George Robertson.

In 1907 Smith & Mabley went bankrupt. Control passed to Herman Broesel, a textile importer and former customer, together with his sons Carl and Herman Jr. The firm was renamed and a new range introduced. The best of these new models was the 9.8-litre 50hp, for which bodies were made for Simplex by Quimby, Demarest, Brewster and Holbrook.

Mainly, the cars still followed the Mercedes style using flat radiators, although some had a sharply pointed V-shaped grille. Simplex was reputed to offer the last American cars to use chain drive in 1914. Up to 250 cars a year were produced.

Carl and Herman Jr. took over Simplex in 1912 on the death of their father, selling out the following year to Goodrich,

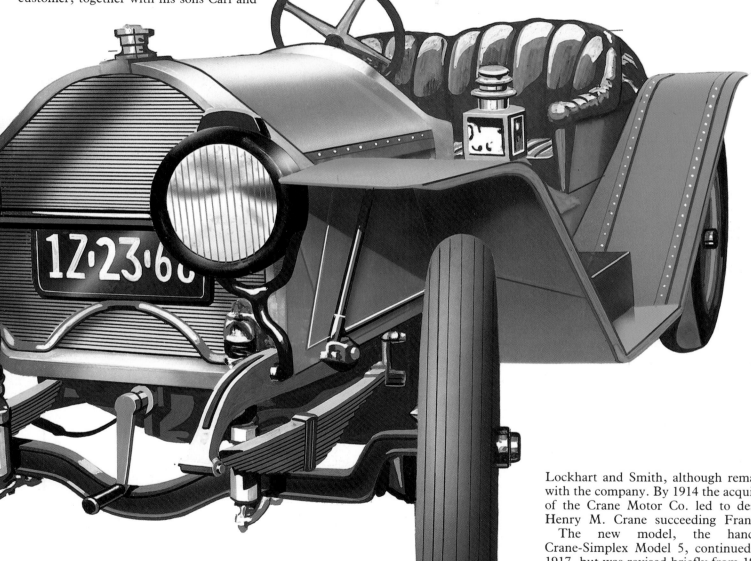

The 50hp model of 1912 was powered by a large four-cylinder T-head engine of 9.8-litres and driven by chain with various driving sprockets on offer, depending on the sort of roads to be travelled. Making great use of expensive material, this was the first car produced by Herman Broesel.

Lockhart and Smith, although remaining with the company. By 1914 the acquisition of the Crane Motor Co. led to designer Henry M. Crane succeeding Franquist.

The new model, the handsome Crane-Simplex Model 5, continued until 1917, but was revised briefly from 1922 to 1924 by the newly reorganized Crane-Simplex Co. under the ownership of Emlen Hare.

Simplex was one of four car manufacturers to bear the name, existing between 1899 and 1920, in four different countries.

Singer

Great Britain
1905–1970

George Singer, born in 1847, learned his trade in the motor industry working at Coventry Machinists. He branched out to make cycles and tricycles and his first cars were the underfloor-engined 8 and 12hp 1905 models, built under licence from Lea-Francis and designed by Alex Craig.

In the following year Singer added more conventional two-, three- and four-cylinder cars. However, the company went into receivership in 1908.

George Singer died the following year and the company was re-formed as Singer and Co. (1909) Ltd. The date was dropped from the name three years later.

Singer relied mostly on White and Poppe engines, although it built some of its own, such as the 1913 14hp unit.

The miniature 1912 1.1-litre Ten continued in production for military purposes during World War I and sales continued after the war.

Right: 1931 8hp Junior Sportsman's coupé
Below: 1915 two-seater Singer Ten

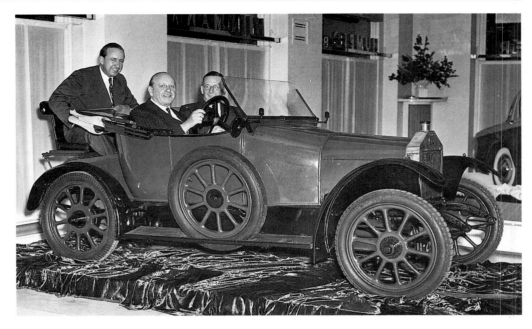

Above: 1912 10hp Singer

The two-litre six was introduced in 1922 and at the same time Singer bought motorcycle firm Coventry Premier, briefly marketing the Ten under this name.

The Calcott factory was acquired in 1926 and, by then, production stood at 100 vehicles a week.

The Ten was now known as the Senior

Below: 1933 Singer Nine sports car

and this was joined by the 848cc Junior – the first inexpensive British car with an overhead-camshaft engine.

Singer became Britain's third largest manufacturer with outputs of 11,000 cars in 1927 and 8,000 cars in 1929.

Singer bought a factory in Birmingham from B.S.A. and commenced operations in 1927, making virtually all its own components, including bodies, radiators and castings.

By 1931, capital stood at £2 million and there were 8,000 employees. Many engine types were used until 1935, probably because managing director W. E. Bullock bought a number of designs from an Italian engineer.

Singer tried diversifying into commercial vehicles but production of tractors was eventually stopped because of minimal success.

The Junior was replaced by the Nine in 1932 and production reached 4,640 in 1933.

The designing of cars had become a somewhat complex matter, with stylist Charles Beauvais being hired from Standard, A. G. Booth from Clyno designing the chassis, H. M. Kesterton

being responsible for the transmissions and L. J. Shorter, formerly of Humber, working on the engines.

Singer's quality control was excellent – with final inspection by an ex-Daimler

employee – and its cars became the most popular British vehicles in Spain.

Cars of the 1930s included a sports version of the Nine and an overhead-cam Eleven to replace the sidevalve Twelve.

Above: 1934 11hp Airstream saloon

Singer tackled the cyclecar boom with the Ten – a true car in miniature. The original Ten was launched with a three-cylinder 1358cc sidevalve engine, but by 1912 this had been replaced by a four-cylinder sidevalve of 1096cc. Production eventually rose to over 50 a week.

Sports-car sales were hit after the 1935 Tourist Trophy race when Singers suffered much-publicized steering failures.

A new version of the Ten was introduced to fill the gap between the Junior/Nine and the larger six-cylinder models but only 800 of these sidevalve cars were sold. A 1476cc sidevalve six-cylinder version suffered a similar fate.

Profits slumped after 1934 and two Coventry plants were closed in 1935. The £1 shares went down to 12s 6d in a reorganization which brought in ex-Hudson man H. M. Emery and led to a company name change in 1937 to Singer Motors Ltd.

Singer made about 5,000 cars in 1936, including the 9hp Bantam which was copied from the Morris Eight. The six-cylinder models were dropped and Singer lagged behind the 'big six' British manufacturers.

The war years saw Singer making components for military aircraft, shell cases and pumps.

Above: 1935 Singer Le Mans sports

The Nine model – launched just before World War II – went on sale again from 1946 and about 2,500 were produced until

Below: 1954 drophead coupé

The Singer Nine Le Mans was the main rival to M.G. in the cheap sports-car market of the mid-1930s. Its 972cc overhead-camshaft engine developed 45bhp at 5,500rpm and gave it a top speed of about 105km/h (65mph).

Above: 1954 SM1500 saloon
Below: 1600cc Gazelle convertible c.1961

Above: A contemporary Gazelle saloon
Below: Vogue saloon, new for 1962

1949. The pre-war Ten and Twelve were also revived and all production was based at Birmingham.

L. J. Shorter's SM1500 – with a cruciform braced chassis – made its debut in 1948 and production peaked at 6,358 in 1952.

Singer was bought by William Rootes' company in 1955 – Rootes, himself, served his apprenticeship with Singer – in a deal involving £235,000 cash plus shares.

The Rootes influence soon became apparent with the Singer Gazelle, based on the Hillman Minx, being introduced in 1957.

Badge-engineering became the norm with the Vogue, a Humber Sceptre derivative, and the Chamois, based on the Hillman Imp.

The Singer name was dropped in 1970 with Chrysler, Rootes' new owner, concentrating on other marques.

Above: 1965 Gazelle, enlarged to 1725cc   *Below: Singer Chamois Sport, c.1966*

Spyker

Holland
1900 to 1927

Jacobus Spijker and his younger brother Hendrik decided to call their cars 'Spyker's – spelt thus to aid foreign sales. Their factory at Trompenburg made cars from 1900 to 1927 and was Holland's only car manufacturer up to the outbreak of World War I.

A financial crisis in 1906 prompted Hendrik to visit their British agent and best customer to raise a loan. Spyker's entire 1904–06 output had been exported to Britain. On Hendrik's return journey to Holland with the agent a gale flung the steamer ashore. It broke up and both men perished.

To spread the Spyker name, Jacobus agreed to provide Charles Godard from Burgundy with a four-cylinder 15hp model adapted with low gears and high wheels to tackle one of motoring's greatest adventures of all time – the Peking-to-Paris race of 1907.

The open car performed extremely well and was a potential winner, but intrigue

Above: Brighton 1905. A four-wheel-drive Spyker (left) challenges a Thorneycroft.

Right: 1903 four-wheel-drive 50hp racer

Below: A 1905 version of the four-cylinder tourer which had a 2½-litre engine, three-speed gearbox and semi-elliptic leaf-spring suspension. Such a car starred in the film Genevieve *made in 1953.*

and Godard's cavalier method of raising money led to his arrest before the race was finished. Another driver got the car to Paris, but the resulting publicity did not help Jacobus. Three weeks after the race had ended, a shareholders' meeting removed him from the board.

On 1 April 1908 the company was declared bankrupt, but four months later was reconstructed with new directors and went on to flourish, producing many fine cars including taxis, many plying the streets of London. From 1906 to 1916 Spyker made cars with no less than 20 different four-cylinder engine specifications.

During World War I Spyker branched out to produce aircraft and the company's post-war cars were influenced by this, the 5.7-litre Maybach-engined C4 designed by aircraft engineer Fritz Koolhoven having vestigial tail sections, for example. It was called the 'Aerocoque'.

Spyker also attempted to market Mathis 1.2-litre cars under its own name and to assemble American-made trucks. This expansion and fragmentation of resources proved to be the company's downfall and it went out of business in 1927.

Squire

Great Britain 1934–1936

Adrian Squire, like many young men since, dreamed of designing and building his own car while he was still at school, but by 1934 – when he was still only 24 – it was a tangible reality. Sadly, no more than 15 cars were ever built – 12 by Squire himself and three by Val Zethrin who bought the company when it was liquidated in July 1936 – but as a car designed and built to the highest possible standards, regardless of price, it remains one of the real milestones in British motoring history.

After leaving school, Squire enrolled as an electrical engineering student, but after only a year he joined Bentley as an apprentice. In September 1929 he joined M.G. at Abingdon, then two years later he and G.F.A. Manby-Colegrave established Remenham Hill Filling Station near Henley-on-Thames.

This was undoubtedly the first step towards the Squire sports car; the next was the announcement in 1932 of a brand-new engine from British Anzani. With a capacity of 1496cc, twin-overhead camshafts driven by a central chain, and a series of idler gears and twin Solex carburettors, it was just what Squire was looking for. The deal was clinched when Anzani told Squire he could have his own motif cast into the camshaft covers.

Squire's next move was to equip the engine with a supercharger – a relatively easy task since it had been designed with

1936 Markham bodied Squire 'Skimpy'

just such a step in mind – and then to develop the car's chassis. By the summer of 1934, a prototype was running with a 105bhp engine, E.N.V. preselector gearbox and hydraulic brakes, and the ensuing publicity resulted in a flood of enquiries, despite the fact that the Squire was one of the most expensive British sports cars of its day.

There were initially four models – open or coupé bodies on long or short chassis – all manufactured by specialist coach-builder Vanden Plas. Ranalah built some

bodies, too, and Markham of Reading provided the so-called 'Skimpy' bodywork which Adrian Squire offered in an unsuccessful attempt to gain sales when, despite that early interest, the car's high price put it beyond the reach of all but the wealthiest of enthusiasts.

The project was finally wound up in 1936.

The 1934 Squire used a supercharged 1496cc twin overhead-camshaft British Anzani engine. With 105bhp available, performance was excellent, and the car had a top speed of 160km/h (100mph).

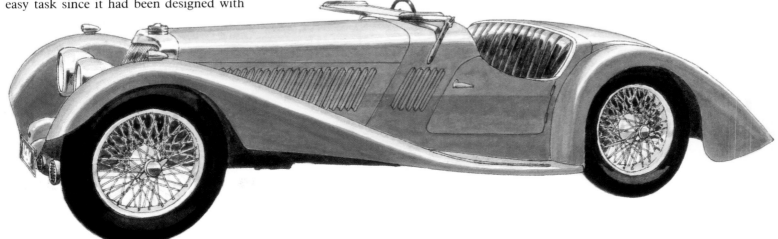

SsangYong

Korea
1954 to date

SsangYong Motors was founded in 1954 and initially specialized in commercial and 4x4 vehicles. It started its operations, like many companies, by assembling a licensed version of another company's vehicle, the Korando, a licence-built version of the Jeep CJ6.

In more recent years, SsangYong took an 80 per cent stake in Panther cars, the British specialist manufacturer. Later, in 1992, Mercedes-Benz started to show some interest in the company and took a 5 per cent stake, with an option to buy a further 5 per cent at a later date.

As a result of the Mercedes deal, SsangYong was contracted to produce 50,000 Mercedes-Benz 100 Trucks and an additional 80,000 diesel power units in 1995. These figures were expected to rise to 100,000 and 140,000 respectively by the year 2,000, with most of the diesel engines earmarked for SsangYong's own Musso

Above: SsangYong Musso 2.9D SE

Below: 1997 SsangYong Korando

Above: SsangYong Musso 2.3 Twin Cam   *Below: 1997 SsangYong Musso GX220*

luxury 4x4. A second joint venture that was planned between Mercedes and its Korean partner, was for the production of the V car, an E-class-size saloon to be built and badged by SsangYong.

The Musso was the first vehicle to be seriously marketed by SsangYong outside its native Korea. The unusual styling, carried out by a British design firm, helped, rather than hindered its sales in the West. The Mercedes diesel engine, which was initially the only engine choice for most western markets, also helped add credibility to the car. A powerful petrol-engined version arrived in 1996 giving very car-like on-road performance. Very competitive pricing compared to other large luxury 4x4s helped SsangYong's sales.

The SsangYong group is also the world's largest cement producer and comprises 24 companies. In 1986, when the car business really started, the company produced 5,759 vehicles; in 1994 they produced 46,375, representing an eightfold increase in eight years and by the turn of the century SsangYong plans further production hikes. The Musso's success gave credibility to the SsangYong name and paves the way for future models.

Standard

Great Britain
1903–1963

The first car from R. W. Maudslay's firm of Standard was a single-cylinder 6hp model built in 1903. A wide range of models followed, including large six-cylinder cars, from 1906, as well as smaller family cars such as the 9½hp Rhyl, introduced in 1912.

During the 1920s Standard built cars ranging from an overhead-valve 8hp model in 1922, to a 1.2-litre sidevalve Nine in 1928. Overhead-valve and sidevalve six-cylinder models were also produced.

Right: 1925 14hp Pall Mall
Below: The 9.5hp Rhyl of 1913

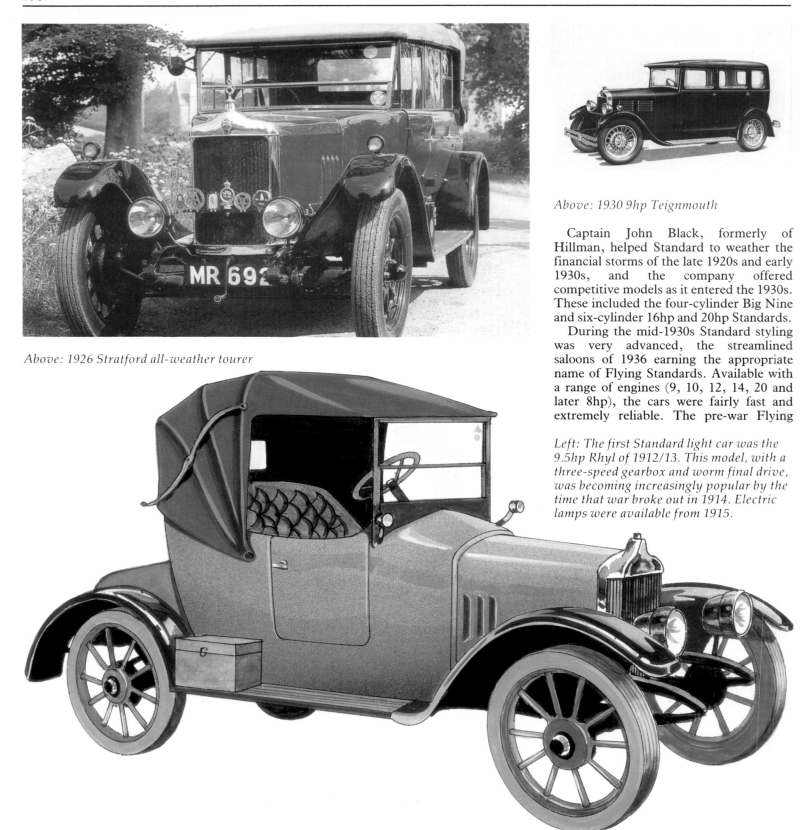

Above: 1926 Stratford all-weather tourer

Above: 1930 9hp Teignmouth

Captain John Black, formerly of Hillman, helped Standard to weather the financial storms of the late 1920s and early 1930s, and the company offered competitive models as it entered the 1930s. These included the four-cylinder Big Nine and six-cylinder 16hp and 20hp Standards.

During the mid-1930s Standard styling was very advanced, the streamlined saloons of 1936 earning the appropriate name of Flying Standards. Available with a range of engines (9, 10, 12, 14, 20 and later 8hp), the cars were fairly fast and extremely reliable. The pre-war Flying

Left: The first Standard light car was the 9.5hp Rhyl of 1912/13. This model, with a three-speed gearbox and worm final drive, was becoming increasingly popular by the time that war broke out in 1914. Electric lamps were available from 1915.

Above: 1934 Standard 12 (basic) saloon

when Standard's single new model – the beetle-shaped Vanguard – was introduced, with a two-litre overhead-valve four-cylinder engine.

In 1953 the notchback Phase II Vanguard appeared, as did the new Standard Eight, with an 803cc overhead-valve engine giving 26bhp, followed by the similarly styled Ten, with a 948cc engine developing 33bhp. This engine was later used in the Triumph Herald. A luxury version of the Ten – the Pennant – was introduced in 1957.

The four-cylinder Vanguards were updated throughout the 1950s, and a two-litre six-cylinder version was introduced in 1962. The same engine was later used to power the Triumph 2000.

Four-cylinder Ensigns were also built, with 1.7-litre engines from 1957 and, from May 1952, engines of 2.1-litres.

The Standard name and the company's own model range ceased to exist in 1963, although the Standard-Triumph concern continued under the Triumph name.

Below left: 1938 Standard Flying 8 Tourer

Below: Standard Vanguard Phase I, 1947 on

Eight was the first small British saloon to have independent front suspension. The Flying Twenty was available with a 2.7-litre V8 engine.

Standard components were also used in other models, notably engines in SS Jaguars and Morgans. The Triumph company was acquired by Standard in 1945, and post-war Standards and Triumph models were all to use Standard engines.

As with most other major manufactur-ers, in the immediate aftermath of World War II Standard marketed a reduced range of its pre-war models in revised form. These continued in production until 1948,

Stanley

U.S.A.
1897–1924

It is a well-worn cliché in the history of the automobile to say 'if only so-and-so had been a little more successful, everything would be different today'.

Probably the most use of that cliché has been on the subject of the Stanley Steamer. But here the cliché has been used wrongly, for the Stanley company was incredibly successful, at least financially, and while its steam-powered cars were sophisticated and well-made, they were quite simply not a match for the brand-new and exciting technology of the internal-combustion engine, which had caught the public's fancy rather better than the seemingly old-hat mechanics of steam.

The Stanley brothers, identical twins born in 1849 in Maine, U.S.A., started building steam cars almost by accident. They were initially violin makers, they dabbled in mathematics, and they invented various devices including an early X-ray machine and a photographic developing process – which Kodak bought for quite a large amount of money.

Above: 1899 Stanley Steam Car

Below: The 1911 10hp model was built under licence in Britain, at Gateshead. However, though sales were steady in the U.K., America's demand for steam cars had dwindled to almost nothing, and despite their fine engineering and many technical innovations this form of power was not to last.

The story of their involvement with automobiles runs like this: in 1896 they were at a fair when one of the new-fangled horseless carriages made an appearance. So unimpressed were they by its unreliability that they decided then and there to build a better one.

They ordered parts from various

names two years later with a much superior car – thanks to the U.S. $250,000 from the deal.

Performance of their cars, with their firetube boilers and twin-cylinder engines attached directly to the back axle, was good; so good, in fact, that a speed record attempt in a streamlined car called Wogglebug went disastrously wrong. At 150mph (241km/h) the primitive stream-lining turned out to induce lift rather than downforce and the car took off, smashing itself to smithereens and seriously injuring driver Fred Marriott. Though Marriott recovered, the Stanleys never raced again.

The Gentleman's Speedy Roadster, a 1907 model, showed the benefits of this development, though; it could manage 75mph (120km/h). This was the downfall of one of the twins, Freelan, who died in 1918 in a crash. The other twin, Francis, had semi-retired by this time to run a hotel.

Above left: A 1904 steamer with tiller steering
Left: A 1912 20hp model
Below: The sophisticated Stanley 735 1920 model

After World War I the company was struggling, models such as the 735 convertible of 1920 attempting to disguise the fact that they were driven by steam rather than petrol, but orders started to come in, only to be snatched from the firm's hands by the recession. The company was run by a Chicago investment group until 1924, then bought by the Steam Vehicle Corporation of America which, despite the grand name, never actually built any steam vehicles. In 1927 it closed down, and though a brief revival attempt was made about ten years later it came to nothing. The steam car had lost its battle with internal combustion.

suppliers and in 1897 their first car ran successfully. But they were still convinced that they could do better than the heavy engine and boiler they had bought, so they designed and built a lightweight power plant, mounting it on runabouts of their own design which they used for personal transport without the slightest idea of selling them commercially.

After a Stanley beat several other cars in a race, however, they were flooded with orders and decided that maybe they should

go into business. They bought an old bicycle factory and proceeded to build 200 of the lightweight buggies. However, a publisher named John Brisben Walker convinced them to sell their firm for U.S. $250,000 on condition they didn't manufacture steam cars for a year. Walker and his partner Amzi Lorenzo Barber started making cars, disagreed, and ended up splitting the company into two different firms, leaving the way clear for the Stanleys to come back under their own

Steyr

Austria
1920–1940;
1953–1978

Steyr is remarkable in one particular way; its employment of some exceptionally talented designers resulted in cars that were exceptionally average. Though the company had some reasonable sales figures, it never achieved anything like the world-beating success of ex-Steyr man Ferdinand Porsche's Volkswagen Beetle (though it had a similar model) and never managed anything as revolutionary as ex-Steyr man Hans Ledwinka's air-cooled Tatras.

However, this is perhaps not so surprising when one considers that the company first started in car manufacture out of no choice of its own. It was, in fact, an extremely successful and long-lived armaments manufacturer up until 1918. It had been the biggest maker of arms in Europe, supplying the German forces with millions of rifles, machine-guns, military aircraft engines and various other mechanisms for institutionalized slaughter, until it had the misfortune to find itself on the losing side and facing a ban on armaments manufacture.

Above: The 1925 Steyr VIII
Above right: Porsche-designed Type 30
Right: A 1929 Type 30 soft top

An earlier sideline in bicycle-making and the experience gained in aircraft-engine manufacture supplied the answer – cars. The first model was made in 1920, designed by the clever Hans Ledwinka, though it was a conventional enough car.

Ledwinka next proposed a small two-cylinder car for the masses, which was turned down, so he left to go to Tatra with the design which proved very successful. He continued to advise on the development of his original model, however, up until 1929 when another bright young designer, Ferdinand Porsche, joined the firm.

Porsche chose a bad moment to arrive. Only a few months later, as the Depression worsened and inflation spiralled, car sales at the expensive end of the market where Steyr were perched had stalled, and then the company's bank collapsed.

It was obliged to collaborate with the Austro-Daimler-Puch conglomerate, a move which forced Porsche to leave and set up his own design studio, though he, too, continued to design for the firm on a freelance basis.

In 1935 the companies merged wholly to form Steyr-Daimler-Puch, and while Austro-Daimler's production of expensive cars wound down, Steyr launched the Type 50, a cheap and successful Beetle-like machine.

However, war came round again and it was back to arms manufacture for the firm. Thanks to this, its factories were bombed to pulp by the R.A.F. and when the armistice was declared it returned to bicycles and then motor-scooters to survive. Later it built trucks and tractors and eventually, by 1949, was assembling Fiats and, a little later, producing cars that, though still Fiat-based, boasted the company's own engines. Hans Ledwinka's son, Erich, was by now in charge of the design department, and it was he who headed the development of the company's strongest seller through later years, the Haflinger four-wheel-drive mini-truck.

Steyr's last car, a Fiat 126 derivative, ceased production in 1978, although it still makes commercial vehicles.

Below: 1924 Waffenauto Type II 12/40

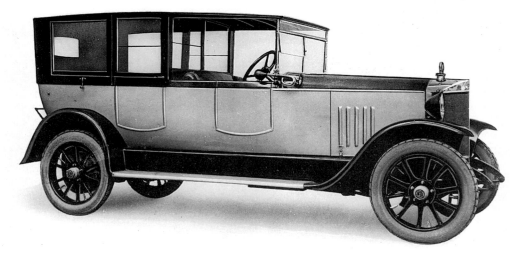

Studebaker
U.S.A.
1904–1966

The last Studebaker rolled off the assembly line in March 1966, and ended a 115-year history of horse-drawn and motorized vehicle production.

The story began in 1852 with two Studebaker brothers establishing themselves as blacksmiths and wagon builders at South Bend, Indiana. After a slow start sales of wagons and carriages reached U.S. $2 million by the 1890s.

The company showed interest in gasoline engines as early as 1895, but initially only electric runabouts were produced, the first gasoline-engined car, a 16hp, appearing in 1904. Studebaker then sold E.M.F. cars for the Everett-Metzger-Flanders Company of Detroit, but after 1912 all cars were designed, built and sold as Studebakers.

In July 1915 Albert Russel Erskine attained Presidency of the company. Though remembered as being a ruthless and overbearing man, he did have the qualities to run a large corporation, and firmly established Studebaker in the market, both at home and abroad. During the 1920s Studebaker was chasing the number-three U.S. sales spot; it had seven production plants (including a foundry and body shops); and it had an annual production capacity of 180,000 cars. In 1926 the company farsightedly opened its own 840-acre proving ground and three-mile banked test-track.

Above: The impressive 1923 Studebaker

Below: The popular Big Six 1923/4s

Below left: 1913 Model AA 27hp
Bottom left: 1913 touring model

In 1926 Delmar G. Roos ('Barney' Roos) joined the company and instigated straight-eight engines in 1928 and a less-complex independent front suspension system in 1935.

Below: The Erskine of 1926 was an attempt to make a high-volume small car for the masses; however, it could not compete with the Ford Model A. 'The Little Aristocrat' as it was dubbed eventually became just a plain Studebaker.

Above: 1929 – a classic gangstermobile
Right: 1935 Dictator Sedan

However, success was short-lived. During the early 1930s Erskine tried to operate as if the Depression had never happened and in March 1933 the company went into receivership owing U.S. $6 million in bank loans. Three months later Erskine, by now a sick and broken man, committed suicide. Luckily, under new management, with new financial backing, and the sale of Pierce-Arrow stock, Studebaker fought back, culminating with the success of the new Champion model. This sold 72,791 units in 1939.

During World War II Studebaker built military trucks, aero-engines and the Weasel – a tracked personnel-carrier powered by the Champion engine. After the war, Studebaker set trends, first in 1946 with its so-called 'coming or going' Starlight coupé, and again in 1953 with the sleek Starliner.

Again, prosperity was short-lived. The squeeze began in 1953 when Ford commenced a price-cutting war in a battle for sales supremacy. With higher unit costs and a small dealer network the

independent manufacturers simply could not compete. The last resort, it seemed, was merger. Initially Nash and Hudson combined to form American Motors, whilst Packard and Studebaker ultimately merged. Unfortunately for Packard, the ailing Studebaker Corporation rapidly consumed the former's remaining capital, and the great marque was effectively finished.

Under the direction of Harold E. Churchill, Studebaker pre-empted the 'Big Three' with the launch of the compact

Above: Commander Sedan of 1941
Below: 1948 Land Cruiser

Above: 1951 Hawk
Below: 1954 hard top coupé

Above: 1956 two-tone Golden Hawk
Below: 1963 Gran Turismo GT

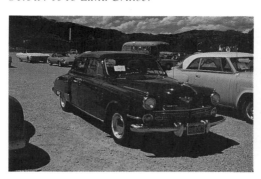

Lark series in 1959 and actually made a U.S. $28.5 million profit. However, the Studebaker directors wanted to get out of car production, and in late 1960, amongst much bad feeling, Churchill was replaced by Sherwood H. Egbert who subsequently reduced the company's car-manufacturing proportion from around 75 per cent to 50 per cent. Fortunately, Egbert considered limited car production was viable, and developed the youthful and inspiring Avanti.

The break-even point for sales in 1963 was estimated at 120,000 units, but just 44,000 were sold. The model range was a good one, but prospective customers were nervous about buying a potentially orphaned car. Production reached 86 days ahead of sales at South Bend in November 1963, and was stopped for good in December. A desperate attempt was made to continue production of just cars and station wagons (with Chevrolet engines) at the Hamilton, Ontario, plant but, sadly, this ended in March 1966.

Above: 1964 Daytona Convertible
Below: 1964 Studebaker Lark

Above: 1963 Hawk coupé

The sleek Hawk GT of 1962 was a descendant of the mid-1950s Hawk range, widely touted when it appeared as one of the most beautiful cars of all time. It was styled by design guru Raymond Loewy.

Stutz

U.S.A.
1911–1935;
1970 to date

For two decades the Stutz Motor Car Company produced some of the finest sports cars ever seen in America. Harry C. Stutz was well known for his mechanical abilities and high standard of workmanship, and his first car, built largely from other manufacturers' components, finished eleventh at his local race-track – Indianapolis – in 1911.

Three years later, the archetypal Stutz, the Bearcat, was unveiled. It was an uncompromising racer with minimal bodywork and a massive 6.4-litre Wisconsin engine and over the next five years it won many races and broke several records, including the famous trans-American record, taking 11 days, 7½ hours from San Diego to New York.

In 1919 Harry Stutz left the company and started to build his own only moderately successful H.C.S. cars but in

Below: Introduced in 1914, the Bearcat was one of the most famous Stutz models ever built. Its four-cylinder 6.4-litre Wisconsin engine developed 60bhp at 1,500rpm and endowed it with a top speed of 137km/h (85mph). The last Bearcat, a 4.7-litre Speedway Six, was built in 1924.

Top: 1913 four-cylinder 60hp Bearcat
Above: Stutz racer at Indianapolis in 1913

Above: 1919 Bearcat in road trim

Safety Stutz Vertical Eight with a single-overhead-camshaft straight-eight engine developing 92bhp at 3,200rpm. The safety features included a low-slung chassis, four-wheel hydraulic brakes and wired windscreen glass.

The Stutz Vertical Eight was one of the outstanding American cars of the day with the Black Hawk Speedster version

Below: 1927 Stutz speedster

Above: 1921 model year Bearcat roadster

1930 he died of appendicitis. Meanwhile, the company had been taken over by steel tycoon Charles Schwab and although Stutz started to build its own four- and six-cylinder engines, the basic car design changed little, with the last Bearcat, the 4.7-litre Speedway Six, rolling off the production line in 1924.

It soon became obvious that the company needed new blood and a new car, and in 1925 the Hungarian designer and great racing enthusiast Frederick E. Moskcovics, ably assisted by the Belgian designer Paul Bastien, unveiled the new

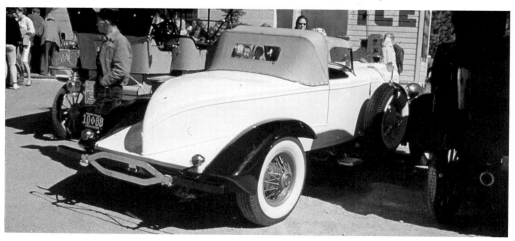

Above: Built in 1927 to make an attempt on the Land Speed Record, the Black Hawk Special had two 1½-litre supercharged Miller engines and an estimated power output of 385bhp at 7,000rpm. In 1928 it reached 327.5km/h (203.45mph) but crashed.

finishing second at Le Mans in 1928 and fifth in 1929, while in 1928 a similar car was driven at 106.5mph (171km/h) at

Right: 1928 40hp Sotheby Convertible
Below: 1930 straight-eight Black Hawk

Daytona, to set a new American stock car record.

By 1930 sales were beginning to dwindle, despite an improved version of the straight-eight and the introduction of a new, cheaper overhead-camshaft six, also marketed as a Black Hawk. At this time the American scene was beginning to be dominated by large V12 and V16 cars from Cadillac, Packard and Lincoln, so Stutz responded by producing its last great engine, the twin-overhead-camshaft eight-cylinder DV32, to power the new Stutz Bearcat of 1931. The new 5.3-litre engine had four valves per cylinder (hence the car's designation) with a power output of 155bhp, and not surprisingly each Bearcat was guaranteed a 100mph (160km/h) top speed.

Although the car's performance was terrific, the roadholding excellent and the build-quality superb, the price was simply too high to survive the financial rigours of the Depression and the marque finally succumbed in 1935, although light van production lingered on until 1938.

In 1970 the Stutz name was acquired by an American manufacturer who produced a somewhat ugly 1960s-style Bearcat designed by Virgil Exner and built in Italy by Carrozzeria of Modena. The cars currently available include the Bearcat and the Black Hawk, both with General Motors 5736cc V8 engines, and the huge Royale Limousine with its 6963cc V8 engine and optional hydraulically raised-above-the-roof throne seat.

Above: 1930 Stutz Derham roadster
Below: 1930-33 DV-32 Monte Carlo

Above: 1933 Type 29 Club sedan
Bottom: 1934 Bearcat G Type

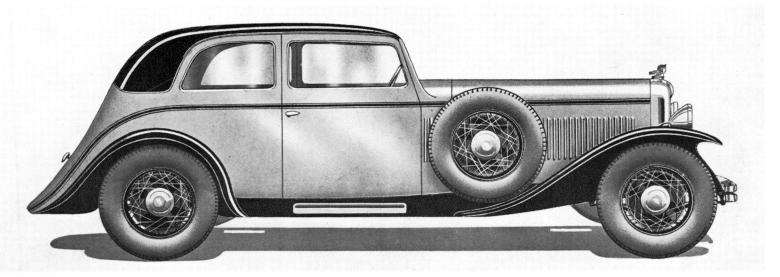

Subaru

Japan
1958 to date

Fuji Heavy Industries, a vast and impressively successful concern, was formed in 1953 from the ashes of Nakajima Aircraft, a company which had been forcibly split up by the Allied forces thanks to its involvement in the war effort.

In 1956 Fuji launched Subaru with a moped, the Rabbit. Two years later the company produced the 360 minicar, which proved considerably less sensible; though sales were reasonable, it gained much notoriety in the U.S.A. for its safety standards and proved to be slightly less than ideal as an introduction. However, the firm ploughed on regardless, improving and developing the 360.

Above: Subaru 360 minicar
Below: 1966 FF-1 with boxer engine

In 1968 it introduced its first full-sized car, the front-wheel-drive FE. It was offered in various versions and sold well on Japan's home market, gradually taking off in the U.S.A. too.

In 1968 the firm was swallowed by the Nissan group and some of its plant capacity has since been taken up in building vehicles of that name.

However, in its own right Subaru has built several models worthy of note and attracting very respectable sales. The firm's four-wheel-drive vehicles, including pickups, are well respected and its Justy hatchback has claimed a corner of the small-car market as its own.

Top: The redesigned 360, the 1970 R-2
Above: The Leone coupé of 1971

Below: Subaru's 1600 GLF 5-speed Saloon

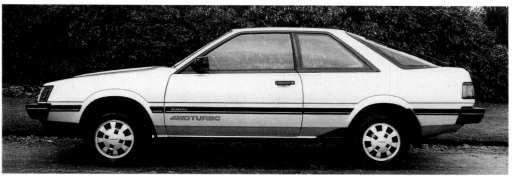

Above: 1600 four-wheel drive Estate
Left: The sporty 4WD Turbo Coupé

The company also has overseas plants, including one in New Zealand and one in Thailand, where its products are assembled for those markets; and its other interests include aircraft, commercial vehicles, trains and all sorts of industrial machinery.

Below: The XT coupé, which offers four-wheel drive and a turbocharger, is one of a number of Japanese performance coupés which offer very high levels of roadholding and performance in a well-priced package.

Despite posting losses like most companies during the recession, Subaru transformed its model range for the 1990s. At the bottom of the range was the Justy, which lost its three-cylinder motor and gained a new four-cylinder engine. It had been comprehensively restyled and was outwardly similar to the contemporary Suzuki Swift. Unlike any other Subaru, it was built in Hungary, alongside the Swift.

The Legacy, launched in 1989, replaced the aged 1980s model that had given Subaru its foothold abroad. It was campaigned successfully in Group A rallying in four-wheel-drive turbo form and sold well. It had smart and modern styling and a lusty boxer engine and in turbo form was very fast. To add appeal to the range, the Legacy Outback was born. With raised suspension and a torquey 2.5-litre boxer engine, it was a fun recreational vehicle and appealed to a new group of buyers, who were more usually attracted to the mainstream small Japanese 4x4s.

The Impreza was launched in 1992 and used a shortened Legacy floorpan. With less weight and the same power outputs (up to 280 horsepower) it became an extremely

Above: Subaru Impreza Turbo 2000 five-door

Right: 1997 Subaru Justy GX 1.3

Below: 1997 Subaru Legacy four-cam 2.5-litre, four-wheel-drive estate

Above: 1997 Impreza 2.0GL

Below: Subaru Justy four-wheel-drive five door. The Justy is built in Hungary

successful rally car, winning the championship on several occasions.

No one ever thought that the stunning SVX coupé would make production, but it soon hit the salesroom floor. Hardly a great seller, it was a great technical showcase for Subaru, and showed the world that the company was now making exciting cars, quite unlike the work-horse vehicles of the 1980s.

A brand new model came in 1997. The Forester, described by Subaru as an SUV (Sport Utility Van), was an exciting new recreational vehicle with chunky styling, raised ground clearance and a powerful 2.5-litre boxer engine giving around 170 horsepower. It looked like a cross-breed of a Jeep and a road-going estate car and entered production in the summer of 1997.

Top left: Subaru Legacy Outback

Top right: Subaru Impreza 2.0GL five-door

Left :Subaru Legacy four-cam 2.5-litre saloon

Below: The nearest you can get to the rally-winning Impreza is this Turbo 2000 saloon with a 2.0-litre turbocharged engine giving 211bhp

Sunbeam/ Sunbeam Talbot

Great Britain 1901–1976

Former sheet-metal worker and cycle enthusiast John Marston started the Sunbeamland Cycle Factory at Wolverhampton in 1887.

Eight years later he formed John Marston Ltd. to head his various business interests.

Charles Marston, a member of the family, started Villiers Engineering in 1898, making bicycle components.

John Marston allowed one of his former apprentices, Thomas Cureton, to tinker with a prototype car at the Villiers works.

The first offering – a Forman-engined 6hp twin – was displayed in 1901 and the first production cars were designed by Mabberly-Smith. They had De Dion engines, a strange diamond-pattern wheel layout and outward-facing seats and were called Sunbeam Mableys.

The motor department was taken over in 1902 by T. C. Pullinger, who acquired the rights to the 12hp Desgouttes-designed Berliets which were sold as Sunbeams from 1930.

They featured the oil-bath chaincases which had been perfected on Sunbeam cycles.

The motor section became the Sunbeam Motor Car Co. Ltd. in 1905 with a capital of £40,000 and within two years it was occupying two acres of factory space and producing the all-British 16/20, designed by Angus Shaw.

Pullinger left to join Humber and Louis

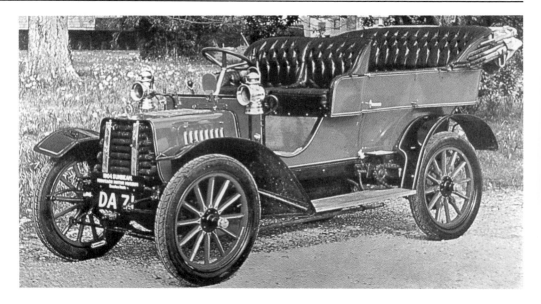

Above: 1904 12hp tourer

Below: 1912 12/16hp tourer

Below: Diamond-shaped 1902 Mabley

Coatalen became designer in 1909. He had considerable design experience on the continent plus a background with Humber and Hillman.

Coatalen joined the board in 1912 and was joint managing director with W. M. Iliff in 1914. Works manager Sidney Guy later left to form Guy Motors in 1914.

Competition successes led to improved sales and the £90 profits of 1909 rose to

£95,000 in 1913.

Sunbeam built staff cars and ambulances during the war, as well as aircraft engines.

When the war ended, Sunbeam produced the 16 and 24 at the rate of 20 a week with most parts made on the premises. By now, the factory had expanded to 30 acres.

In 1920 Sunbeam was absorbed by

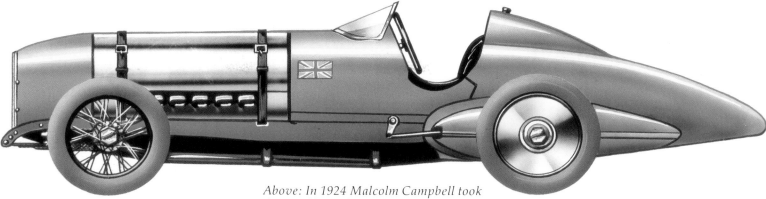

Above: In 1924 Malcolm Campbell took the World Land Speed Record at Pendine Sands, South Wales with a speed of 235.217 km/h (146.157 mph). The car was powered by an 18.3-litre, 350hp, V12 engine.

Left: 1924 4½-litre tourer
Right: 1925 Tiger Land Speed Record car
Below: 1934 Dawn saloon

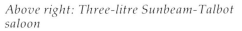

S.T.D. Motors Ltd. which included Talbot, Darracq, and commercial vehicle manufacturer W. and G. DuCros. James Todd was chairman of both Sunbeam and S.T.D. and Coatalen was the group's chief engineer and competitions director.

Sunbeam became deeply involved in racing and record-breaking but was best known for its quality and refined touring cars, some using overhead-cam Talbot engines.

The company was unable to pay dividends to shareholders in 1926 and the financial problems led to the end of the racing programme.

Experimental engineer/designer J. S. Irving and driver H. O. D. Segrave severed connections with the S. T. D. group.

Four-cylinder cars were discontinued in 1927 and the straight-eights and twin-overhead-cam six-cylinder sports models followed suit in 1930. So, too, did Sunbeam's attempt to maintain its position in the aero-engine field. Its last offering was a 1,000hp V12.

Sunbeam did better with a range of buses in 1929 which led to successful trolleybuses and the formation of Sunbeam Trolleybuses Ltd. in 1934. The firm was run jointly by Rootes and A.E.C. until

Above right: Three-litre Sunbeam-Talbot saloon
Right: 1953 Sunbeam-Talbot '90' drophead
Below: 1953 Alpine roadster

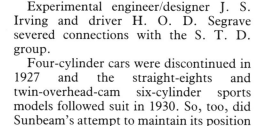

1944, eventually being bought out by engineering group Brockhouse and then being sold to Guy in 1949.

H. C. M. Stephens – formerly of Oldsmobile and Citroën – designed a new mass-appeal Sunbeam in 1932. Development cost £3.5 million and it was introduced in 1934 with independent front suspension and a 1.6-litre overhead-cam engine. But it failed to stop Sunbeam's decline.

The entire board of S.T.D. had resigned in 1931 following criticisms from shareholders over lack of co-ordination. A period of chaos followed which included a demand for the repayment of £500,000, secured to finance Coatalen's earlier Grand Prix ambitions.

Rootes had already revived Humber, Hillman and Commer. And it stepped in to salvage Sunbeam in 1935.

The Sunbeam name was coupled with Talbot – now also Rootes-owned – to offer a series of up-market and sporting versions of Hillmans and Humbers made at Talbot's London factory from 1938. They included the Minx-based Ten of which about 11,000 were made until 1948.

The Model 80 sold 3,500 from 1949–50 and the 90 about 19,000 until 1957.

The Sunbeam Rapier – based on the Hillman Minx – continued into the late 1960s, offering improved performance and

Below: Introduced in 1925, the three-litre Sunbeam Super Sports was one of the first production cars with twin overhead camshafts. Fed by twin carburettors, the six-cylinder engine developed 90bhp at 3,800 rpm, propelling the car at up to 136km/h (85mph).

Above: The new Alpine, launched in 1960

specification. It was later replaced with a fastback version.

For two-seater fans, Sunbeam produced the Alpine and a high-performance Ford V8-engined version – the Tiger. A Hillman Imp derivative, the Sunbeam Stiletto, was also offered.

The name Sunbeam was all but dead in 1968 and has occasionally been revived by subsequent owner Peugeot in a small way,

Above: 1964 Tiger rally car

such as with the Sunbeam Lotus, a Lotus-engined hatchback based on the Talbot Horizon.

Below: 1974 Rapier fastback saloon

Above left: 1964 Series IV Rapier saloon

Suzuki

Japan
1955 to date

Founded in 1909 as a textile company under the name of Suzuki Shokkuki Seisakusho, this company, which later became famous for its motorcycles, didn't enter the car market until 1955.

The first Suzuki car was the Suzulite 360 utility car, a diminutive and simply-constructed microcar. The front-wheel-drive Fronte 360 was the company's next offering, and was launched in 1967, to be followed a year later by the larger-engined Fronte 500. The Fronte remained in the range well into the eighties with only minor changes over the years.

The Cervo, also known as the SC1000 'Whizzkid', was the company's new car for 1977. This attractive 2+2 coupé used a three-cylinder two-stroke motor on the home market but was fitted with a more powerful 970-cc unit for European and other markets. By this time there was also a four-wheel-drive, Jeep-type vehicle in the range. Called the Jimny, this simple but rugged off-road utility vehicle was offered with various engines ranging from a three-cylinder 539cc

Above: For a long time, the Suzuki Jimny four-wheel-drive was the mainstay of the Suzuki range. It was also built in Spain

Left: The Suzuki Alto received a much needed restyle in 1990

Below: Suzuki's first sports car was the Cappuccino, first shown in 1991. It used a turbocharged 660cc engine

Above: Vitara 4x4

unit to a 1.3-litre four-cylinder, launched in 1982.

The four-wheel-drive market seemed a successful one for Suzuki, and in 1988 it launched the Vitara. This was a much more luxurious four-wheel-drive vehicle, designed with on-road performance in mind rather than mud-plugging. It became one of the most popular sports/leisure 4x4s, and gained a very fashionable image, especially when fitted with the full range of factory extras. The X-90 was a further extension of the on-multi-purpose 4x4 theme. Two seats and curvy styling placed it more as a stylish on-road cruiser than an off-road hauler.

Meanwhile, the road-car range had also expanded. The three-cylinder Alto had replaced the Fronte, and there was also the larger Cultus and Swift, both cars having sports variants. The Baleno, launched in 1995, was a competent and modern medium-sized saloon but was almost forgotten in the shadow of the company's now-famous 4x4 cars.

Above: Suzuki Baleno hatchback

Below: Rear view of the Alto

Below right: 1997 Suzuki Swift

Suzuki showed its first open sports car in 1989 at the Tokyo show with the production model arriving in 1991. Called the Cappuccino, it used a turbocharged 660-cc engine and a removable perspex hardtop. It was designed for the home market, but was very popular elsewhere, with many buyers importing the cars themselves.

Above: 1997 Suzuki X-90

Above: The fashionable Vitara was also available as a soft-top

Swift

Great Britain
1900–1931

Before beginning to build cars, at the turn of the century the Coventry firm of Swift were makers of sewing machines, bicycles and tricycles.

The company's first car was a single-cylinder two-speed voiturette. In early models, the de Dion-type MMC engine drove via a twin-pinion and double-geared crown-wheel system. Later cars, from 1903, had conventional transmissions.

From 1904 Swift produced its own twin-cylinder 10hp engine, also making three- and four-cylinder units and, during 1909, another single.

Above: 1914 Swift cyclecar

Above: 1908 25/30hp Limousine
Below: 1911 single-cylinder 7hp two-seater

In 1912 Swift introduced its 7hp cyclecar and a four-cylinder 10hp light car. The cyclecar had a 972cc twin-cylinder engine and a three-speed shaft-driven transmission system. The engine fitted to the four-cylinder model had a capacity of 1100cc.

This 10hp model was built after World War I when Swift also produced a similar 12hp model with a two-litre engine driving the rear wheels through a four-speed gearbox.

From 1923, the 10hp and 12hp engines were updated by being fitted with detachable cylinder heads, making maintenance and overhaul far easier.

In 1926 a 14/40hp model was introduced with a new engine, and the capacity of the

Bottom: 1925 'Q' Type tourer

10hp power unit was increased to 1.2 litres.

Swift introduced a new 10hp saloon model in 1930, featuring wire wheels and a four-speed gearbox. The following year, the company produced an 8hp Cadet model. Unfortunately, however, the company was unable to compete in business terms with the likes of Austin, Morris and Ford, and it closed down in 1931.

During their relatively short history, Swift vehicles had earned a reputation for being strong, uncomplicated and thoroughly dependable.

Talbot

Great Britain
1903–1959
1979–1986

To sell French built Cléments on the English market a syndicate between Talbot and the Earl of Shrewsbury was set up in 1903. The natural conclusion was for the new concern to make cars under its own name and by the end of the decade two-, four- and six-cylinder Talbots were available.

The company's 20hp 3.8-litre car of 1906 is generally regarded as the first of the truly British Talbots. It was one of a growing range from the company's west London factory.

In 1913 a Talbot was the first car to cover 100 miles (160km) in one hour with Percy Lambert behind the wheel at Brooklands.

Right: 1930 Talbot 75 Saloon
Below: 1909 4156cc Talbot 4T

After World War I the Talbot lineage started to become somewhat complicated. In 1920 it became part of S.T.D. (Sunbeam Talbot Darracq) Motors. After that date Darracq cars made at Suresnes, Seine, France, were sold in France as Talbots and Talbot-Darracqs in England.

In 1916 talented Swiss engineer Georges Roesch joined the company and was responsible for the 10/23 model of 1923.

Two years later Roesch was made chief executive of Clément Talbot by Louis Coatalen who was in charge of S.T.D.

Roesch produced the light six-cylinder 1.9-litre 14/45 overhead-valve model. A sophisticated and smooth design, it became Talbot's only listed model for 1929 and 1930.

Also known as the Type 65, it was followed by the 2.3-litre 75 and 90, the three-litre 95 and 105 and the 3.4-litre 110. Versions prepared for competition by Fox and Nicholls of Tolworth, Surrey, were highly successful, the assocation ending in 1932 when Fox and Nicholls decided to concentrate on Lagonda.

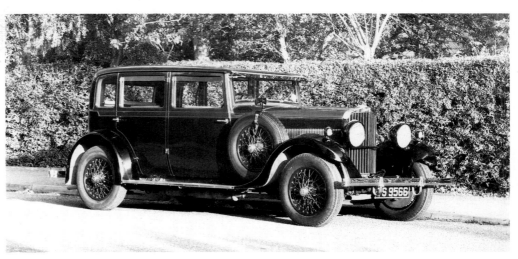

Below: 1923 10/23hp Talbot designed by Swiss engineer Georges Roesch. Based on Darracq, it was regarded as a fine four-cylinder car of side-valve design. Roesch followed up with an ohv six-cylinder car of high esteem.

Talbot finished third at Le Mans in 1930, 1931 and 1932. In the Alpine Rally Trials of 1931, 1932 and 1934 seven 105s were entered, all finishing without penalty. Alpine winners in 1932 and 1934 (jointly with Adler), Talbot also had class wins in the Irish Grand Prix, the Ulster TT and the Brooklands 500-mile (800km) race in 1930.

The S.T.D. group failed in 1935 and the Talbot and Sunbeam names were taken over by the Rootes brothers who added them to Hillman and Humber.

The inevitable cross-hatching of cars began, the Talbot Ten of 1936 being influenced by the Hillman Minx.

Roesch-designed cars were listed until 1938, but by this time Talbot's purity through its own design was now part of history and Roesch left.

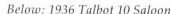

Above: 1931 Talbot '105' Brooklands

Below: 1936 Talbot 10 Saloon

Above: 1933 Talbot 90 Vanden Plas
Right: 1938 Sunbeam-Talbot dhc
Below: 1936 3½-litre Sports Saloon

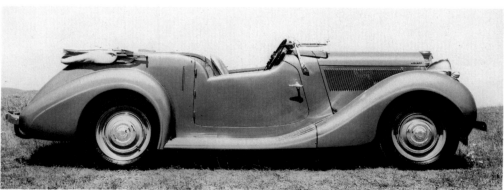

In 1938 Rootes renamed the marque Sunbeam-Talbot, fusing the two together. The post-World War II Sunbeam Talbot 80 and 90 saloon cars were well received by the British market, but the name Talbot was dropped in 1954.

Meanwhile the French Talbot factory had introduced a straight-eight 3.8-litre model in 1930. Few were made and the six-cylinder cars were the company's main source of income.

In 1935 Anthony Lago joined and used the six-cylinder engine enlarged to 4000cc to create the Talbot Lago Special.

Lago kept Talbot in France alive until 1959, producing a range of exotic machinery. His 'cross pushrod' six-cylinder engine won the 1937 Le Mans race and it was used in Grand Prix competition before and after World War II. His Talbot Record of 1946 with 4482cc displacement was to become a classic, winning at Le Mans in 1950. A smaller version, the 'Baby' Lago, was later

Above right: 1949 Talbot four-litre

Below: 1959 Talbot-Lago America Coupé powered by a 2476cc BMW V8 giving 125bhp. Claimed top speed 200km/h (125mph). It was first seen at the 1955 Paris Show powered by a 2491cc unit.

produced, and Maserati, B.M.W. and Simca engines were used to power Lago Talbots.

The Talbot name reappeared in 1979. Chrysler, who had taken over Rootes, were in trouble and thinking of backing out of

Above: 1951 Sunbeam-Talbot 90

Europe. Peugeot-Citroën stepped in and British Chryslers and French Simcas became known as Talbots.

A Talbot Sunbeam-Lotus hatchback won the 1980 R.A.C. Rally and the 1981 world rally championship.

Talbot in name had entered the 1980s but was destined not to last the decade. Sunbeam, Simca and Chrysler (still made in America) also added their names to the missing-in-Europe list, Talbot vanishing in 1986.

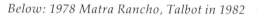

Below: 1978 Matra Rancho, Talbot in 1982

Top: 1979 2.2 Talbot Sunbeam-Lotus

Above: 1981 2.2GL Talbot Tagora

Tatra

Czechoslovakia 1923 to date

Though trucks and railway rolling stock have always been the backbone of this Czechoslovakian company's success, it is its cars that most will remember.

Of course, there is a good reason for this. They were extremely memorable, being both mechanically unusual and bodily very distinctive. And the genius engineer Hans Ledwinka put his idiosyncratic personal stamp on this firm's products, too – ensuring that they would be workable rather than weird. It is just a shame that so few Tatras have ever made their way beyond the Iron Curtain.

It all started in the mid-1800s in a small northern Moravian village called Nesseldorf, when a pair of carpenters and wheelwrights, Ignac Sustala and Adolf Raska, started a company producing carts and coaches. Business grew fast, aided by an expansion into railway-carriage construction, and in 1897 they moved into cars as well.

The motor car part of the firm was christened Nesseldorf and the first model, the President, was manufactured using a Benz engine. At the same time a truck design was started, and by the turn of the century a bus and an electric car were also being considered.

Though a racing car was built and successfully run using a Benz engine, the Nesseldorf company decided that it had to make use of its own engines. A year later it was able to offer three types, though these were at first not particularly good. Ledwinka took charge of the car direction in 1906 (rejoining after a sojourn elsewhere) and produced the S Type, a three-litre machine with many innovations for its day. Slightly later models boasted such features as four-wheel braking and overhead camshafts – before World War I.

After the war, which had found the company making mostly trucks, the firm found itself in the new state of Czechoslovakia. And not satisfied with changing its country of origin, it also changed its name to Tatra; a long-time

Above: A Type 12 of the Twenties

nickname after the mountains the development staff used to test cars in.

By 1923 Ledwinka had designed a small car for the ordinary man in the street, the Tatra 11. It was designed to be rugged and simple, and it succeeded brilliantly. It was victorious in competition and sales were excellent. By 1934, however, many variations on the theme had been tried and

Below: 1938 Tatra 57K Kubelwagen

it was time for another Ledwinka brainwave. The result was the Type 77, the world's first enclosed all-streamlined production car. Its variants, the 77A, 87 and 97, refined the theme while introducing different engines. But war was upon the horizon once again and before long the German occupation had forced the firm to discontinue car production.

After World War II the firm was taken over by the government and at first produced a trickle of pre-war models along with a flood of railway stock and commercial vehicles. In 1948, though, the Tatraplan was introduced. Basically a two-litre version of the streamlined Type 77, it was produced for only four years, mostly for party officials, before it was discontinued in favour of increasing lorry production capacity yet again.

The company bounced back in 1955 with the T603, a characteristically rounded design with a rear-mounted air-cooled V8 engine and improved suspension; a design, too, which was to survive until 1973 when the T613 came along, which had a larger version of the same engine and much more straightforward styling by Vignale.

No new models have been introduced since, however, and the truck side of the business appears to have gained the upper hand once and for all.

Above: 1940 Type 87, a futuristic oddity
Below: 613 Italian-styled body with V8

Toyota

Japan
1936 to date

Sakichi Toyoda ran a successful business making weaving looms and in 1929 sold the patent rights to a British company for £100,000.

His son Kiichiro used the money to set up a car department, having studied production methods in America and England, and the first car was launched in 1936.

It was an American-based model called the AA and used a Chevrolet chassis and transmission with a Japanese-built engine.

The Toyota Motor Company was formed in 1937, the name being changed to Toyota for several reasons including the fact that it was phonetically easier to pronounce and spell than Toyoda. The factory was located at Koromo.

By 1938 production reached about 2,000 cars, trucks and buses a month.

Truck output was 42,813 in 1941 and

Above: The first luxury car, the 1944 B
Below: 1955 RSD Crown Deluxe

soon afterwards a four-wheel-drive amphibian was added to the range.

By the end of the war the company had around 3,000 employees and production had been switched totally to trucks.

Car production resumed in 1947 at the lowly rate of 300 a year. The range included the Toyopet 27bhp light car and light four-wheel-drives.

Toyota formed Aisin Seiki and Nippondenso in 1949 to make electrical equipment for domestic and vehicle use.

The company had been seriously hit by losses and long strikes which led to the resignation of Kiichiro Toyoda.

The new management included Eiji Toyoda – who later became president – and Shoichi Saito. They had visited Ford in the United States to study the latest ideas and their enthusiasm paid dividends. Car production rose from 700 a month in 1955 to 50,000 a month ten years later.

Sales were helped by exports and, following the availability of the first English-language catalogues in 1956, Toyota enjoyed success in foreign markets.

In 1961, 3,932 cars and 7,743 commercials went abroad and ten years later the figures were 604,923 cars and 181,364 commercials.

A plant devoted solely to car production came on stream at Motomachi in 1959 by which time the one-litre Corona had made its debut.

The 1968 Corona was a good solid mass-market car with rear-wheel-drive and using a fairly aged design of engine – but it sold at a keen price.

The model proved a winner and sales of the Corona family reached five million in 1981.

Toyota's first mass-market car was the 1000 UP10 of 1961 which, in four-cylinder form, later became the Starlet.

The 1.1-litre Corolla, produced from 1966, became a top-seller in Japan.

Daihatsu came under Toyota's control in 1967 and the original loom company had, by then, diversified into making fork-lift trucks and hydraulic loading shovels.

Toyota exported its ten millionth car in 1971 and production reached 30 million by January 1980.

Traditionally, Toyota had produced rear-wheel-drive cars and the first mass-produced front-wheel-drive models were the 1.4-litre Tercel and Corsa of 1978.

Models such as the supermini Starlet and Corolla had already established Toyota as a manufacturer of dependable cars.

Above: 1975 2000, also known as Corona

Below: Crown Super saloon of 1975
Bottom: 1981 Land Cruiser diesel estate

Above: The 1985 Corolla GT was a much more sophisticated product than many of its predecessors, demonstrating the technological strides that the firm had made over the years. Engine development and chassis technology are nowadays knitted into the fabric of the company's products.

Above left: 1981 Starlet 1200 GL
Above centre: 1982 Hi-Ace minibus
Above: 1982 Tercel, an fwd first

Above left: 1983 Corolla 1.3 GL
Above: 1983 Corolla 1.3 GL with liftback

Reproduced with permission
© Haynes Publishing Group, 1983

The MR2 of 1984 earned it respect in the world of technology. The mid-engined two-seater used a 16-valve 1600cc power unit which, combined with nimble handling, made it a tempting buy for sports-car enthusiasts, particularly because of its relatively low price.

A year later Toyota had reached another milestone when the Land-Cruiser became the world's best-selling all-wheel-drive vehicle. It was sold officially in 95 countries and unofficially virtually everywhere else.

Right: 1984 MR2, a sports car milestone
Below: 1984 sporty Toyota Celica 2.0 XT liftback

Below: The MR2 T-bar has superficial resemblances to its contemporary, the Fiat/Bertone X1/9. However, it is in many ways a more sophisticated car.

Top: 1985 four-wheel-drive Tercel estate
Above: Toyota's 1985 Space Cruiser
Right: 1985 16-valve twin cam Corolla GT
Below: 1985 Camry 2.0 GLi saloon

The sporting Supra of 1986 set new performance standards with its high-tech three-litre fuel-injected engine. Even more so when the Turbo version became available early in 1989.

Also in 1989, Toyota unveiled the third-generation of its Celica coupé, with controversially individual styling, and the second-generation MR2. Bigger and faster than its predecessor, the new MR2 is offered with normally-aspirated and turbocharged two-litre four-cylinder engines that produce 167bhp and 228bhp respectively.

Current production of all vehicles is in the order of one every four seconds, maintaining Toyota's position as the world's largest motor manufacturer.

Above right: The curvaceous 1990 Celica
Right: 1990 Carina GL five-door
Below: Today's sleek Celica GT-Four

The 1989 Celica is an example of what would in early days have been called a sports coupé or even a touring car: the two-litre, fuel-injected engine gave it a strong position in the sports GT class.

Above: 1990 Toyota Land Cruiser II

Below: Toyota's Supra is, indeed, superlative, boasting a straight-six, 24-valve, twin cam, three-litre engine. It marks a shift in emphasis from mass-market models towards the top end of the luxury and high-performance market.

Toyota remained at the top of the pile throughout the 1990s, and due to its enormous wealth was under no threat from the recession, unlike many smaller companies.

The sporting Supra was comprehensively updated for 1993, with new bolder styling and even more power. The 3.0-litre straight six engine now had 24 valves and gave 224 horsepower in naturally aspirated form and a

Left: 1996 Toyota Starlet

Below left: 1996 Toyota MR2 GT

massive 330 horsepower when equipped with two turbochargers plus an intercooler.

The Toyota Carina, traditionally one of the company's biggest sellers, continued to top the sales charts and was available in two forms: the Japanese-built Carina and the British-built Carina E for Europe.

Cashing in on the late-1990s trend for mini MPVs, Toyota launched the Ipsum, called the Picnic outside Japan. The compact body could carry six adults in relative comfort.

A larger MPV came in the form of the Sienna or Avalon. Based on the Camry, the Sienna was built at Toyota's US plant and used a 3.0-litre V6 engine giving 195 horsepower.

The Camry itself was also available in two forms: the Camry J, also known as the Vista, and the European Camry, with bigger, more powerful engines.

It was this tailoring of models for specific markets that helped to keep Toyota at the head of the worldwide market throughout the 1990s.

Below: Toyota Picnic mini-MPV

Above: Post-1997 face-lifted Corolla

Above: Short-wheelbased Landcruiser

Above: 1997 Toyota Landcruiser

Right: Toyota Camry Sport Saloon

Above: 1997 Toyota Celica Cabriolet

Above left: Toyota Previa was the company's first proper MPV

Above: The Hilux 4x4 double-cab pick-up was popular in Europe as a working vehicle

Left: Toyota RAV-4 five-door

Below: The Toyota Paseo 2+2 coupé was styled in California to appeal to American buyers

Above: Carina E, built in and designed for Europe

Above: Corolla four-door saloon

Above: The Rav-4 had permanent four-wheel drive but was designed for use on road. It had good performance and handling

Left: The Celica coupé had grown a little soft by the late 1990s

Tracta

France
1926–1934

Tracta began life as an exercise in the workability of a design and its creator made very little money from the venture. During the 1920s many French manufacturers experimented with front-wheel-drive vehicles, but none met with the same success that came to Jean Albert Grégoire when he formed the Société Anonyme des Automobiles Tracta in 1926. Finance for this project was provided by the wealthy Pierre Fenaille.

Work began at Grégoire's Garage des Chantiers at Versailles, shortly moving to Asnières, in the Seine district of Paris. His first design was a two-seater powered by an S.C.A.P. engine, which he displayed to the public for the first time at the 1927 Paris Salon. That year he also began racing. In fact, Grégoire's company was unusual in that his successful forays into competition came after the launch of his production sports cars, which were, therefore, not race-developed models. In total, 142 of this type of Tracta were produced.

Grégoire managed to finish in the Le Mans 24-Hours endurance race of 1927

and the following year he took second place. Victory came in 1929, and was compounded the year after with another win, the French designer proving beyond doubt that front-wheel-drive was a viable method of transmission.

By 1930, however, Grégoire was moving away from his previous sporting image towards handsome coupé and saloon models, but of which only around 90 were

built. He also changed from S.C.A.P. engines to those of Hotchkiss and Continental, which were competitively priced.

By 1934, car production had ceased, with Grégoire satisfied that he had proved his point. Instead, he put his efforts into marketing the constant-velocity universal joint which he had developed in conjunction with Fenaille.

Top: 1929 12hp model
Above: This 1930 coupé had a 1749cc four-cylinder engine driving the front wheels, a four-speed gearbox and sliding-pillar independent front suspension.

Triumph

Great Britain
1923–1984

The Coventry-based Triumph firm began by making bicycles in 1887. Motor-cycles arrived in 1902 and by the end of World War II the marque had a first-class reputation. Until the early 1930s, the manufacture of motor-cycles remained more important than that of cars, which first appeared in 1923.

The earliest Triumph cars were mainly conventionally engineered and conservatively styled small and medium-sized saloons, although sports tourers arrived in the late 1920s and in 1925 a Triumph became the first British car to have hydraulic brakes. However, Triumph's first noteworthy car was the 1928 Super Seven, a high-quality small family saloon.

More sporting models, some with licence-built Coventry-Climax overhead-valve engines, were introduced at Managing Director Claude Holbrook's behest in the early 1930s. In 1933, Holbrook engaged Donald Healey to oversee development of new models, including the Dolomite, a supercharged straight-eight copied from the Alfa Romeo 8C 2300. But financial difficulties prevented its production or the development of other sporting Triumphs, and the production cars of the era were

Top: 1923 10/20 two-seater
Above: 1932 Super Seven pillarless saloon
Left: 1935 Gloria Southern Cross

high-quality saloons, coupés, and roadsters, mostly with handsome styling to complement their fine engineering. From 1934 there were Glorias; tuned models were known as Gloria-Vitesses and, from 1937, as plain Vitesses. That year, the Dolomite name was applied to a new range of medium-sized models which used the Gloria's chassis design and which eventually replaced both it and the Vitesse.

Too many models and too much competition bankrupted Triumph in 1939, and the company was eventually sold in

1944 to Standard. A 14hp Standard engine powered the post-war 1800cc 'razor-edge' saloon and Roadster, which shared a tubular chassis and independent front suspension, and another Standard engine went into the 1949 Mayflower, a small saloon with razor-edge styling to match that of the 1800, by then re-engined as a 2000.

The Mayflower went in 1953, and for the rest of the decade Triumph flourished as the sporting arm of Standard-Triumph. The 100mph (160km/h) TR2, introduced in 1953, was highly successful both at home and abroad, and led on to a series of open two-seaters which re-established the marque's reputation and culminated in the

Top: 1937 Vitesse drophead coupé
Above: 1939 15hp Dolomite roadster
Left: 1946 1800 roadster
Below: 1950 Renown saloon

Above: 1958 TR3 sports

earned a reputation for unreliability. Other models of the 1960s included the front-wheel-drive 1300 saloon, which failed to meet sales expectations and was later redeveloped as a rear-wheel-drive range with larger engines. Notable among these was the Dolomite Sprint, a sporting variant introduced in 1972.

TR6 of 1969. The controversial TR7 of 1975 and its TR8 derivative were designed to meet different requirements and never had the same charisma.

The success of the sports cars persuaded Standard-Triumph to badge all future models as Triumphs. The Triumph Herald accordingly replaced the small Standard saloons in 1959. This was the first Triumph styled by the Italian Michelotti, who would also design the 1963 2000 saloon and the 1970 Stag, a four-seater GT with a V8 engine which

Above: 1967 TR4A I.R.S.

Below: The TR2 initiated the famous line of affordable TR sports cars in 1952. Its engine was a 1991cc Standard four-cylinder which gave it a 161km/h (100mph) maximum speed. Sales were brisk, especially in the U.S.A.

Above: 1969 Vitesse 1.6-litre convertible
Above right: 1973 TR6 sports
Right: 1973 Stag sports tourer

Financial difficulties had overtaken the company again in the late 1950s, and in 1960 it had been bought by Leyland Motors. After 1968, Leyland's amalgamation with BMC brought Triumph into direct competition with Rover's big saloons and MG's sports cars. Several projects were cancelled, while the build-quality problems of the TR7 damaged the marque's reputation and probably sealed its fate. The last Triumph was a licence-built Honda Ballade saloon, introduced in 1981 and built until 1984.

The Spitfire was a cheap and popular sports car based on the Herald chassis and running gear. The engine in this early 1960s example was a 67bhp overhead-valve four-cylinder of 1147cc.

Left: 1973 2000 Mk II saloon
Above: 1973 Dolomite Sprint saloon
Below: 1977 TR8 V8 works rally car

TVR

Great Britain
1949 to date

Trevor Wilkinson, from whose Christian name the letters TVR were taken, was born in Blackpool in 1923, becoming an apprentice mechanic at the age of 14. After World War II he set up his own vehicle repair business, Trevcar Motors, and by late 1947 he had gone into partnership with Jack Pickard to form TVR Engineering. It was not until 1953 that he graduated from building one-off specials to a series of cars for general sale, producing 20 in kit or complete form over the next three years.

In 1956 a rolling chassis was bought by American Ray Saidel, who fitted an alloy body and Coventry-Climax engine, renaming the car a Jomar. Successful, Saidel ordered six more.

The same year Bernard Williams, who ran TVR's body suppliers, Grantura Plastics, became a director and the company expanded – too fast, in fact, since it was wound up in 1958. The following year Layton Sports Cars started, although the interruption in supplies spelled the end for Jomar in America.

Above: 1972 Triumph-engined 2500

Ford V8 engines. This continued until 1965, with TVR selling cars under its own name from 1967.

Martin Lilley pulled out in 1981, having built up the Triumph- and Ford-powered range. Chemical engineer Peter Wheeler then bought the company, initiating the use of the Rover 3.5-litre V8.

In its distinctive wedge-shaped models TVR expanded this engine to 3.9- and 4.2-litres (for the 390i and 420 SEAC models respectively), before returning to a more traditional style for the 2.9-litre Ford V6-powered S roadster, and relaunching the Tuscan name of the early 1970s.

Above: 1982 2.8-litre Tasmin
Below: Tasmin fixed-head coupé

Below: 1986 Rover-engined 350i
Bottom: 1983 TVR Series 2

Above: 1960 1588cc Grantura Mk II

In 1961 two TVR dealers, Keith Aitchison and Brian Hopton, took control and a brief foray into motor sport was attempted. Around that time Trevor Wilkinson left to start manufacturing glassfibre car accessories. Layton gave way to Grantura Plastics in 1962, then Martin Lilley took over three years later. Meanwhile, American dealer Jack Griffith was ordering cars to sell as Griffiths, fitting

Top left: 1989 Tuscan race car
Top: 1989 2.9-litre S2C
Above: V8-engined 420 SEAC

Above: 1989 450 SE Convertible

The 1989 TVR S has a two-seater body made from glassfibre, carbon fibre and Kevlar on a tubular-steel spaceframe chassis. The car is powered by a fuel-injected 3528cc V8 engine developing 225bhp and is claimed to be capable of 250km/h (155mph).

In 1990 TVR showed the new Griffith model, which went into production a year later. It combined stunning good looks with the use of high-tech materials, such as Kevlar and carbonfibre, to keep weight to a minimum. The Griffith was powered by a range of Rover V8-based engines but was later only available with a 5.0-litre unit with 340 horsepower.

Replacing the previous angular V8s was the Chimaera, launched at the Birmingham Motor Show in 1992. It was another fine-looking car with the Rover V8 engine (itself based on a Buick unit) with capacities ranging from 3.9 to 5.0-litres. TVR seemed to be master with this unit and managed to endow it with one of the loveliest exhaust notes ever to have graced a British car.

The Rover engine had its limits, however, and in 1994, TVR launched a new coupé with an engine of its own design and manufacture. The new 75-degree V8 in the Cerbera was a high-tech unit of 4.2 litres, with a flat-plane crankshaft (usually reserved for race engines) and a power output of over 350 horsepower. Performance was earth-shattering with 60mph (100km/h) coming up in around four seconds and a top speed of over 170mph (274km/h).

Above: The Griffith was the first of the new-style TVRs with well-balanced looks and a very powerful V8 engine. This is a late-model Griffith 500, with a 5.0-litre version of the Rover V8

Below: The 400SE was looking very dated by the 1990s but had served the company well through the 1980s

Above: 1997 TVR Cerbera   *Below: TVR Chimaera*

Vauxhall

Great Britain
1903 to date

The Vauxhall Iron Works Ltd. made marine engines from 1857, but the first Vauxhall car appeared in 1903. In 1904 an improved single-cylinder 6hp model was produced, with wire wheels and a reverse gear. In 1905 the firm moved from London to Luton, and it has been based in the Bedfordshire town ever since.

Above: 1911 Vauxhall Prince Henry　　　*Below: Vauxhall 14/40, 1922 on*

Above: 1904 6hp Vauxhall
Right: 1923 OE Type 30/98

The famous fluted radiator and bonnet, which were to be identifying features of Vauxhalls until the 1950s, were first used in 1906, on the company's 3.3-litre model.

Vauxhall produced a number of cars in the early years, including several three-cylinder models, the 3.3-litre four-cylinder car, and the three-litre (later four-litre) Prince Henry. In addition, a smaller A type, plus D and (six-cylinder) B types were produced. Vauxhalls were successful in motor sport at this time, with 4½-litre Grand Prix models producing some 130bhp.

In 1913 the famous 4½-litre 30/98 was introduced. The car was built until 1928, by which time the car had an

overhead-valve engine and hydraulic brakes. The 30/98 tourers were capable of more than 80mph (128km/h) in 1919.

The 14/40 was introduced in 1922, with a detachable cylinder head for its 2.3-litre engine. The car gained a four-speed gearbox from 1925, and a Wilson preselector gearbox was optional in 1927.

Vauxhall came under the control of the American General Motors concern in 1926, after financial problems. The

Above: 1924 Vauxhall Phaeton
Below: 1933 Light Six A type

General Motors-influenced Vauxhall 20/60 was produced from 1927 until 1929, and in the following year the two-litre six-cylinder Cadet was introduced – the first British car to have a synchromesh gearbox. The four-speed 12hp and 14hp Light Sixes replaced the Cadet in 1933. Larger six-cylinder models were produced at the same time.

The advanced Vauxhall 10 of 1937 was built on unitary-construction principles, and also featured torsion-bar front suspension and, in common with other Vauxhalls of the time, overhead valves. The 1203cc engine produced 35bhp and gave lively performance.

Larger Vauxhalls introduced the same year included the massive and luxurious six-cylinder 25 model. Vauxhall Twelve and Fourteen models were also produced, the 1781cc Fourteen producing 48bhp and having a top speed of 70mph (112km/h). Hydraulic brakes were fitted to all Vauxhalls in 1939.

Above: 1934 Light Six ASY 12hp (Tickford)
Below: 1939 Vauxhall 14 J type

The elegant E type Prince Henry Vauxhall 30/98 of 1913 was an impressive performer for its time. Power came from a 4½-litre sidevalve engine. Overhead valves were employed from 1922 (OE type), giving a top speed of 129km/h (80mph).

After World War II, during which Vauxhall produced munitions and the 12-cylinder-engined Churchill tank, the company initially reintroduced its pre-war Ten, Twelve and Fourteen models. However, in 1948 it introduced new models with overhead-valve engines. These were the six-cylinder, 2275cc L Type Velox and the four-cylinder, 1442cc Wyvern, giving 54 and 35bhp respectively.

In 1952 the cars were given new body designs and the shorter-stroke engines now fitted had capacities of 2262cc or 1507cc, producing 65 or 40bhp respectively. In 1955 the models were updated, and a luxury version of the Velox was introduced under the name Cresta.

Above: 1952/3 Velox E type
Below: 1954/5 Cresta

The first Vauxhall Victor – the F Series – was introduced in 1957, with transatlantic styling and a 1508cc overhead-valve engine. In the same year the PA Series Velox and Cresta were introduced, both cars having American-influenced body styling. The engine capacity of these six-cylinder models was increased to 2651cc from August 1960.

Below: 1961 FB Victor Estate

The FB Victor replaced the F Series from September 1961, at first with the 1508cc engine, increased in size to 1595cc from late 1963. The VX4/90 was the twin-carburettor, disc-brake sports version of the Victor saloon, the 1508cc version giving 81bhp, compared with 56bhp from the standard Victor. The six-cylinder Velox and Cresta models were similarly rebodied in late 1962, and designated the PB Series.

Vauxhall's first post-war small car, the HA Viva saloon, was introduced in late 1963, with roomy passenger and luggage accommodation and a lively overhead-valve 1057cc engine developing 44bhp. A Bedford Beagle estate-car version was available from late 1964.

Above: 1970 Viva HC

In October 1964 the 101 Series (PC) Victors appeared with larger, more rounded bodywork. This model was built until it was replaced in October 1967 by the overhead-camshaft 1599cc or 1975cc New Victor (FD). At the same time, new overhead-valve 3294cc Velox and Cresta models were introduced, the luxurious Viscount derivative of the Cresta becoming available in June 1966, and the high-specification Ventora in February 1968. The 3.3-litre engine was optionally available on Victors from May 1968.

In September 1966 the restyled Viva (HB) was introduced, with a 56bhp 1159cc engine. Either two- or four-door bodywork could be specified. SL and De Luxe 90 versions developed 69bhp. Other Vivas included the 1599cc and 1957cc overhead-camshaft models. The HB Viva was replaced by the HC in October 1970, the new car having restyled, larger bodywork and, from September 1971, a 1256cc engine. The HC Viva was also

available with 1759cc or 2279cc overhead-camshaft engines. Derivatives included the Firenza fastback coupé and the Magnum. The Victors were again updated in 1973, and the new models included a 2.3-litre VX4/90.

The 1256cc Chevette range (hatchback/saloon/three-door estate) was introduced in late 1975, and continued in production until 1983.

Above: VX 4/90 of 1973
Below: 1975 Chevette

The Victor's replacement was the Cavalier, launched in October 1975, with up-to-the-minute styling and a choice of 1584cc or 1897cc overhead-camshaft engines; the overhead-valve 1256cc Chevette unit became an optional fitting from late 1977.

Below: 1975 Cavalier 1900 GL Coupé

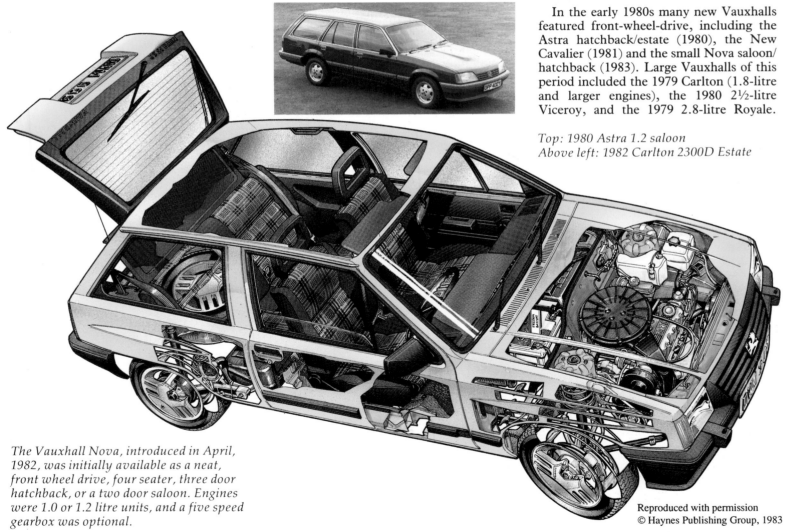

In the early 1980s many new Vauxhalls featured front-wheel-drive, including the Astra hatchback/estate (1980), the New Cavalier (1981) and the small Nova saloon/hatchback (1983). Large Vauxhalls of this period included the 1979 Carlton (1.8-litre and larger engines), the 1980 2½-litre Viceroy, and the 1979 2.8-litre Royale.

Top: 1980 Astra 1.2 saloon
Above left: 1982 Carlton 2300D Estate

The Vauxhall Nova, introduced in April, 1982, was initially available as a neat, front wheel drive, four seater, three door hatchback, or a two door saloon. Engines were 1.0 or 1.2 litre units, and a five speed gearbox was optional.

Reproduced with permission
© Haynes Publishing Group, 1983

The 2.5 and 3.0 litre Senator saloons were introduced, and the Astra range restyled, in October 1984, with the addition of a Belmont saloon version in January 1986.

The Carlton (still rear-wheel-drive) was revised for 1987, as was the Senator for 1988, and in October 1988 a totally new Cavalier range was introduced, to include, from 1989, a four-wheel-drive version.

Right 1989 Calibra Coupé
Below: 1989 Cavalier GSi 2000 16v 4×4

Above and below: 1989 Vauxhall Carlton GSi 3000 24-valve

Bottom left: 1989 Astra GTE 16v on the Lombard RAC International Rally

Above: 1989 Senator 2.5i saloon
Below: 1989 Special Edition Nova 'Sting'

Vauxhall began the 1990s with one of its most outrageous cars ever. The Lotus Carlton was a Carlton that had been heavily breathed on by Lotus to produce a 170mph executive saloon. Flared wheel arches and wide alloy wheels were all that told you that this was no ordinary run-of-the-mill Vauxhall. Unfortunately, adverse press reports questioning the wisdom of a car capable of such high speeds did nothing for sales, and the cars were slow to leave the dealer's forecourt.

By the 1990s, GM had ordained that Vauxhall and Opel products would be almost completely identical, and by the mid-1990s, even the model names were the same in Germany as in the U.K.

The company's Spanish-built super-mini, the Nova, was replaced by a new model in 1993. Now called the Corsa by both Opel and Vauxhall, the new car had rounded styling and was a good seller. A few years later it was falling behind the competition in terms of ride and handling, so Vauxhall employed Lotus engineering to retune the suspension. At the same time a new engine was added to the range: an economical 12-valve three-cylinder, with an output of 54bhp. The result was a car that was back on even terms with its competitors.

The Astra was restyled in 1991 and continued unchanged, apart from a new range of engines in 1995, well into the 1990s. As before, the cabriolet version was built by Bertone. The four-door saloon version was now badged as an Astra, rather than Belmont, as the previous model had been.

Top: 1996 Vauxhall Vectra

Above: 1991 Vauxhall Astra

Right: 1997 Vauxhall Corsa

Below: 1991 Vauxhall Frontera 4x4

Opel also took up the Astra name for the model, dropping the old Kadett label that it had used since the 1930s.

The Calibra, launched in 1989, was a completely new model based on the Cavalier floorpan. The sleek two-door coupé styling proved popular with the buyers and performance was good too. At first the car was fitted with 2.0-litre engines in various states of tune from the 115bhp eight-valve to the 150bhp turbocharged model. In 1993 the model gained Vauxhall's new 2.5-litre V6 which was fitted to the flagship model. This 170bhp unit was beginning to push the car's humble chassis to its limits. Four-wheel-drive versions improved handling, but most were sold in front-wheel-drive form. Another coupé came in 1993. The small Tigra used 1.4- and 1.6-litre engines and had quirky but attractive styling. It was later overshadowed by the superior small coupés of Renault and Ford, the Mégane and Puma.

The Cavalier remained largely unchanged until 1995, but received the new V6 in 1993.

Above: 1991 Astra GSi 16-valve

Below: 1997 Vectra SRi V6 saloon

Above left: 1997 Vauxhall Frontera SWB

Above: The Vectra estate came a year after the saloon

Far left: The Vauxhall Monterey was a rebadged Isuzu Trooper

Left: Vauxhall Omega estate

Below: The slippery Calibra coupé

The all-new 1995 model was renamed Vectra and was praised for its smooth styling. The range of engines gave Vauxhall a competitor for the Mondeo at every level, from 1.6 to 2.5 litres. An estate version came later and was launched in 1996.

The Omega was the replacement for the Carlton and Senator models and retained its predecessor's engine and rear wheel drive.

A new departure for the company was a four-wheel-drive leisure vehicle, the Frontera. Designed more with on-road performance in mind, the Frontera wasn't so happy on the rough stuff.

Vauxhall entered the MPV market quite late with the Sintra, launched in 1996. Developed in conjunction with General Motors, it was also built in America.

Above: The Lotus Carlton was the fastest production car with four doors when it was launched in 1989. A top speed of 170mph was deemed excessive by some and adverse press reports didn't help sales

Right: The Vauxhall Sintra was developed in cooperation with parent company, General Motors. Unlike the other Vauxhall/Opel offerings, the Sintra was built in America

Below: The Vauxhall Tigra was launched at the 1993 Frankfurt Motor Show. The large back window was tinted to protect passengers and prevent heat build-up in the cabin

Voisin
France
1919–1939

Famous for his aircraft, Gabriel Voisin built his first experimental car with his brother Charles in 1899, several years before he took to the air. Charles was killed in a road accident in 1912, and their aeroplane manufacturing business halted. After World War I Gabriel set up again, returning to motor vehicles in 1919, having looked at steam power, with an Artaud & Dulfresne design previously turned down by Citroën. Called the Type C1, this employed an engine of 3969cc displacement.

Voisin was as outspoken and eccentric as his cars, disliking chrome, and all things American. He favoured unusual, light-weight, aerodynamic bodywork, often so ugly that it limited sales, although Voisins often attracted rich and famous owners.

By the mid-1920s Voisin was developing Knight double-sleeve-valve engines for his

Above: Voisin C4 Tourer of 1925/6
Below: 1924 C3 (Totnes Motor Museum)

cars, aided by designers Marios Bernard and André Lefèbvre. He spent much money and effort pursuing easy gear changing, trying both Sensaud de Lavaud and Cotal systems on larger, more flexible engines to achieve this.

Belgian Impérias were built under licence in the Issy-les-Moulineaux factory in the early 1930s, when Voisin also produced a number of unusual prototypes, including a front-wheel-drive V8 and an in-line twelve-cylinder engine with the rear two cylinders protruding into the cockpit. This experimentation proved very costly, however, and in 1937 a financial group took over the company.

The Graham-engined model introduced during this period so horrified Voisin that by 1939 he had regained control. He turned to manufacturing a variety of commercial and electrically powered vehicles, and also the aero-engines of Gnome et Rhône, who now owned the company. Voisin remained as president until after World War II, when Gnome et Rhône became part of S.N.E.C.M.A., who discontinued the name by the end of the 1950s.

Gabriel Voisin went on to design the Spanish Biscuter and died in 1973, at the age of 93.

This magnificent Voisin C14 of 1932 was just one example of a range of interesting cars produced by the firm. These included models with V8 and V12 engines, and with distinctive styling. Innovative design was a Voisin feature.

Volkswagen

Germany/West Germany; 1936 to date

Volkswagen – meaning literally 'people's car' – was founded from the ambitions of two totally different characters.

Adolf Hitler was a car enthusiast – although he never learned to drive – who saw motor sport as a way of speeding up technology. He was also intent on having a car for the masses. Austrian-born engineer Dr. Ferdinand Porsche shared the ambition of building a people's car but, having absolutely no interest in politics, had little else in common with Hitler.

Porsche, who was born in 1875, designed his first small car in 1922 – the Austro-Daimler Sascha. Count Sascha Kolowrat privately financed it because Austro-Daimler showed no interest in Porsche's ideas for small cars.

Porsche persevered with his plans for a mass-market car and in 1930 he founded his own design office. The first project was for German manufacturer Wanderer and it heralded the introduction of Porsche's innovative torsion-bar suspension.

However, he wanted to build a larger vehicle with reasonable performance and endurance at an affordable price. A planned deal with motor-cycle manufacturer Zundapp eventually came to nothing. Porsche based his design on Project 12, a car he began working on in 1931, but Zundapp insisted that he use a complex five-cylinder radial engine which was totally contrary to Porsche's objective of simplicity. Zundapp pulled out when the motor-cycle market picked up.

Porsche then found himself a firm ally in Hitler. The latter had plans for an autobahn network and wanted to have a car built which could take advantage of the new roads and sell for under 1000 Deutschmarks. That was less than half the price of the cheapest equivalent vehicle available.

Hitler had heard of Porsche though his Auto Union racing designs and in May 1934 he invited the engineer to submit proposals for a people's car, allowing him a year to complete his presentation.

Porsche saw the price and deadline as daunting propositions. Nevertheless, he decided to try his best. He began work in June 1934 with the reluctant backing of the controlling body of the motor industry – the *Reichsverband der Deutsche Automobilindustrie* (the R.D.A.).

The backing of other manufacturers was so poor, however, that Porsche's first three prototypes were built in his own garage. Indeed, many manufacturers openly admitted their opposition to the engineer's efforts, notably Opel which was then producing Germany's cheapest 'real' car.

Porsche initially believed that the engine had to be a two-stroke unit to meet the price target, but the first prototype, completed in October 1936, had a low-compression, air-cooled, flat-four, four-stroke engine of 985cc.

Above: Prototype VW3 and VW30, 1936–7

Vast mileages were covered over the next two months in testing the first three prototypes. Many problems were encountered such as torsion bars breaking and engines having short lives. But Hitler was apparently satisfied and in February 1937 told the R.D.A. that the project must have full backing.

Three months later, the *Gesellschaft für Vorbereitung des Deutschen Volkswagens GmbH* (the association for the manufacture of the German people's car) was founded. It was state-backed to the tune of 480,000 Deutschmarks.

A batch of 30 prototypes was built and exhaustively tested, mostly by military drivers. Meanwhile, Porsche twice visited the U.S.A. to study modern mass-production methods.

Hitler made the next move and laid the foundation stone at the factory at Fallersleben, near Hanover, in May 1938. Volkswagenwerk GmbH was registered to produce the cars in October 1938 and Hitler decreed that a town should be built especially for the workers. It was known as Kraft durch Freude Stadt. The name was chosen after the Strength through Joy movement which Hitler used to promote the project.

Hitler announced that the new car would be called the KdF-wagen, much to Porsche's dismay, and that it was to be financed by advance-purchase payments and available through a stamp-saving scheme run by a central agency. Over 350,000 accounts were opened before the outbreak of World War II.

Production started in April 1939, but only 210 KdF-wagens were built before the factory turned its attentions to the war effort. And despite Hitler's odd choice of its name, the car had already become known as the Beetle.

The plant was devastated by bombing and eventually passed to British military control at the end of the war. The British renamed KdF Stadt as Wolfsburg in May 1945 and began a rebuilding programme. Both the plant and the Beetle were offered to other countries – but none showed an interest.

Possibly the only person to recognize the Beetle's potential was Major Ivan Hirst, the British officer in charge. Under his command, production resumed in August 1945, and 1,785 Volkswagens were built by the end of the year, all for the services. The next year saw a vast expansion and more than 10,000 were made, mostly with 1131cc engines.

Above: 1947 export-specification Beetle

The company was handed back to Germany in January 1948 and Hirst appointed Heinrich Nordhoff as general manager.

Nordhoff, a banker's son who had worked for Opel and B.M.W. and was well-versed in American mass-production methods, was a firm believer in exporting, and by 1948 about a quarter of all Beetles went abroad. Nordhoff broke new ground the following year when two cars were exported to the United States – the first of several million.

Porsche had been released from internment by this time and was engaged as an engineering consultant. He received royalties on every Beetle made and the rewards were great enough for him to carry on and build the famous sports cars which bear his name.

The American market quickly expanded, and within a decade half of the cars made were sold there.

July 1949 saw the introduction of a better-equipped export Beetle and the Karmann four-seater cabriolet was introduced at the same time. This latter model went on until early 1979, during which time about 330,000 were built. The Beetle's mechanicals were also used for the March 1950 Transporter van.

Hitler's stamp scheme had left Nordhoff with an expensive legacy from the pre-war years. Many investors asked for discounts and claims cases were heard in courts for many years, some as late as the 1960s.

Partial discounts were eventually given on more than 120,000 cars.

During the 1950s, several overseas VW offshoots were set up including Volkswagen do Brasil, Volkswagen Australia, Volkswagen France and Volkswagen America.

In 1954, the Germans introduced a larger 1192cc engine and continued to improve the Beetle both cosmetically and mechanically. And one year later VW took its relationship with coachbuilder Karmann further by asking it to build the Karmann Ghia Type 1, a sporty-looking coupé.

There was some confusion over who actually owned Volkswagen – national or local government – so the company was reorganized as Volkswagenwerk GmbH and shares were offered to the public. They bought 60 per cent with the rest going to national and local government.

The 1500 saloon complemented the Beetle in 1961 and its 1493cc flat-four

Top right: 1960 U.K.-specification Beetle
Centre right: Rallying Type 3 411 saloon
Right: 1965 1600cc Variant saloon

The Beetle changed remarkably little during its long production life. Most numerous was the 1200, built from 1960 to 1978 and featuring a 1192cc version of the familiar overhead-valve flat-four engine.

engine was used in the Karmann-Ghia coupé.

Production of Volkswagens reached five million by December 1961 and it subsequently never fell below one million a year. In 1971 the figure topped no less than two million. During the 1960s other options were offered such as the Variant estate, the TL fastback and the unitary-construction 411 saloon and estate of 1969. But the Beetle still ruled the roost. From 1965, Volkswagen was also building certain Audi models since taking over Auto-Union from Daimler-Benz.

Nordhoff died in April 1969, shortly before he had planned to retire, and his successor Kurt Lotz almost immediately began to face problems. Doubts were growing about the Beetle's future and Volkswagen had been overtaken as Europe's most prolific car-maker by Fiat.

Volkswagen took over N.S.U. in 1969 and amalgamated it with Audi to form N.S.U. Auto Union AG. The N.S.U. K70 prototype, using a derivative of the Wankel-engined RO80, was launched as the Volkswagen K70 in 1971.

It was a break with tradition, being the first front-engined, water-cooled Volkswagen. But it did little to impress the public and never sold in great numbers.

However, Volkswagen had reason to celebrate in February 1972 when a total of 15,007,034 Beetles had been built, surpassing the Ford Model T's production record (the last German-built Beetle was a cabriolet made in April 1979. The 20

Below: Water-cooled 1972 K70 L
Centre: 1972 411 LE saloon
Bottom: Type 1 Karmann Ghia, c. 1972

Above: 1968 1300cc Beetle Cabriolet
Below: 1969/70 Type 3 estate car

Above: The 411 version of the Type 3 chassis
Below: Type 3 fastback c. 1969/70

millionth Beetle left the production line in Mexico in May 1981).

But the company could not afford to become complacent because Opel overtook it as Germany's leading manufacturer in 1971. As popular and durable as the Beetle was, it needed a replacement.

The first new-generation Volkswagen was the front-wheel-drive Passat, a derivative of the Audi 80, and it came in 1973. The firm was in danger of folding in 1974 but was mainly saved by the Giugiaro-styled Golf and Scirocco – both featured front-wheel drive and used the same running gear.

Top left: 1973 two-door Passat
Far right: Four-door 1973 Type 4 saloon
Right: 1974 Giugiaro-designed Scirocco

Below: The original Golf was introduced in 1974. In its most basic form it featured a 1093cc overhead-camshaft engine and soon became one of the most popular small hatchbacks in the world. U.S.-built Golfs were given the name Rabbit, along with slightly different trim and lights.

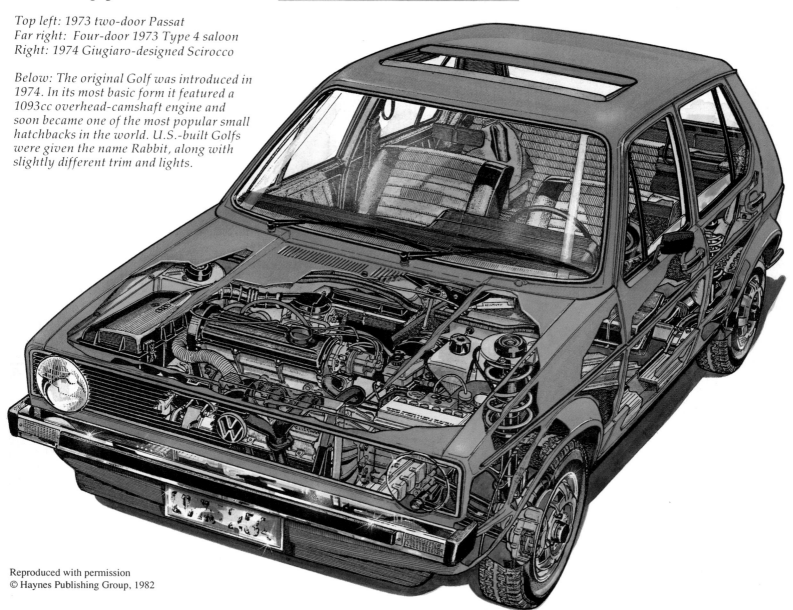

The smaller Polo hatchback came in 1975 and then its 'three-box' derivative the Derby. The Jetta – a three-box Golf – followed in 1979.

The Americans soon took to the Golf – they know it as the Rabbit – and a production plant was opened at New Stanton, Pennsylvania.

Diesel Golfs and Passats were introduced to the range and Volkswagen did much for its image with the 110bhp fuel-injected Golf GTi which had been introduced in 1976.

Above: 1975 Polo hatchback
Above right: 1978/9 Scirocco GLi sports coupé
Right: 1979/80 Jetta, the Mk 1 Golf with a boot

Below: The Mk 1 Golf GTI was available in the U.K. from 1979, but initially only in left-hand-drive form. With a 1600cc fuel-injected engine developing 110bhp, the car was capable of around 183km/h (114mph) and quickly became a true trend-setter.

The 35 millionth Volkswagen rolled off the production line in June 1979 – a German-built Golf.

Volkswagen branched out and agreed for Passats and Polos to be built under licence by SEAT of Spain in 1953. And in 1982, Volkswagen signed an agreement with the Chinese government to have the Santana – a notchback version of the Passat – built at the Shanghai Motor Works. The Santana was also built under licence by Nissan in Japan.

Right: 1982 Polo Classic GL saloon
Below right: Restyled Scirocco for 1982
Below: Polo C three-door hatchback
Bottom: Limited-edition 1982 Scirocco Scala

Below: 1981 Volkswagen Auto 2000 development vehicle. Designed for maximum efficiency, it has a lightweight body, a drag coefficient of 0.25 and is designed to be powered by either a supercharged 1050cc petrol engine or a 1191cc diesel.

Above: 1981 Volkswagen Santana GX four-door saloon

Despite financial losses in the face of increasing competition, Volkswagen continued introducing new models with a sporting bias. They included the fleet-footed 16-valve Scirocco which could comfortably top 209km/h (130mph). The 16-valve engine became available in the GTi by mid-1985, making the car the definitive hatchback by which all the others were judged. And the rallying-inspired Golf Syncro, introduced in 1988, elevated roadholding levels further with permanent four-wheel drive.

In 1989 VW replace the Scirocco with

Below: 1983 Passat five-door hatchback

Below: The Mk 2 Jetta inherited the general front-end appearance of the mechanically similar Mk 2 Golf. Specifications ranged from the 150km/h (93mph) 1272cc C up to the 1.8-litre 112bhp fuel-injected unit used in the 1986 Jetta GT. A 16-valve engine followed in 1988.

another front-wheel-drive 2+2-seater coupé, the Corrado. This is offered with the Golf's 1.8-litre 16-valve four-cylinder engine, or an eight-valve 1.8-litre unit with supercharging. The latter makes 136bhp, taking the Corrado onto territory which in the 1980s had belonged to Porsches – a far cry from the humble Beetle.

Below: 1988 Polo Ranger hatchback

Above: 1984 MK 2 Golf GL
Below: 1988/89 4wd Golf Syncro

Above: 1050cc Polo C saloon of 1985
Below: 1990 Passat GT 16V saloon

Above: 1990 Corrado 16V sports coupé
Below: Catalyst-equipped Polo for 1990

Above: 1990 five-door Golf GL
Bottom right: 1990 Golf GTI Convertible

Above: Rallye Golf G60 of 1990
Below: 1990-specification Scirocco GTII

The Polo was updated in 1990 with a face-lift, but was replaced with a truly new model in 1994. By this time, Seat was building all Polos. Despite the car's relative lack of flair compared with its other European super-mini rivals, it continued to sell well to those who prized the VW badge and the build quality and reliability that went with it. It was praised as having real 'big car feel' and performance became more competitive with the arrival of the 16-valve engine.

A joint venture with Ford provided a people carrier for the Volkswagen range. The Sharan had more kudos than the Ford-badged Galaxy, but the two vehicles were identical apart from the different badging and trim packages.

The Passat was completely updated in 1988, with new aerodynamic styling and continued, with a few minor face-lifts, until it was replaced again in 1996. The 1996 car was completely new. It had more appealing, less dowdy styling than its predecessor, as well as a whole new range of engines, including a rather unusual V5.

The Jetta disappeared with the Mk2 Golf and was replaced by the Vento. Unlike its

Left: Volkswagen's new Beetle. In the mid-1990s Volkswagen decided to create a modern-day Beetle. At first it was just a concept car, but the designers persisted and it started to look as though it would reach production. It used the Volkswagen Golf platform and engines. That means a front-mounted engine and front-wheel-drive

Below: The Volkswagen Sharan was the result of a collaboration with Ford. There were essentially three versions of the same car: the Sharan, the Ford Galaxy and the Seat Alhambra. By collaborating in this way, both Ford and the Volswagen group managed to keep development costs to a minimum when entering the MPV market

Above: Mk3 Golf GTi was bigger and slower than its predecessor

Below: The Vento also came with the VR6 engine

predecessor, the Vento was more of a car in its own right and less of a Golf with a boot. Unfortunately, like the Jetta, the Vento wasn't a huge sales success but remained in the VW range.

In 1996, Volkswagen Group was the fourth largest car manufacturer in the world and the biggest in Europe behind the General Motors Group, the Ford empire and the Japanese giants, Toyota having built a total of 3,537,016 vehicles at all its manufacturing plants around the world, of which approximately 2.5 million were Volkswagen-badged. With its empire growing all the time, the company looked set to begin moving up the rankings.

Left: Unlike previous Volkswagen Golfs, the Mk3 model was available in estate form

Below: The Mk3 Passat was launched in 1997

Volkswagen's fine cars during the 1980s gave the company such an image boost that it seemed nothing could stop it. The Golf had become a legend in its own time and continued to sell well. A new Mk3 version was launched in 1991. This time, the GTi was no longer the top of the range. The new king of the Golfs was the VR6 which was a 170bhp version of Volkswagen's new narrow-angle V6. The same 2.8-litre engine was also fitted to the Corrado. The GTi remained as popular as ever, and comfortably outsold the VR6. It seemed that people were now buying for the GTi badge rather than ultimate performance. The turbodiesel model wasn't short of performance either, with a top speed of over 110mph (177km/h).

VW's worldwide approach saw huge numbers of cars being produced. In 1993, there were more than a million Golfs built in VW's factories in Germany, Belgium, Yugoslavia, Mexico and South Africa. The group's 1991 total of 3.3 million vehicles was a 56 per cent increase over figures from the previous 10 years. A 4-million total was estimated for the turn of the century.

Above: The Polo saloon

Below: Polo five-door hatchback

Above: Mk3 Golf Cabriolet

Below: The Golf VR6 was faster than the GTi

VW/SEAT

To bring the Volkswagen story fully up to date, however, it is necessary to turn to the cosmopolitan mixture of Italian styling, German engineering and Spanish manufacturing expertise that has resulted in the current SEAT range of vehicles.

For over 30 years SEAT had been building Fiat cars under licence in Spain (as well as Volkswagens themselves, of course). In 1980 Fiat terminated this arrangement, forcing SEAT either to close or to develop its own product. The company chose the latter and, in only four years, developed the Ibiza hatchback.

So impressed was Volkswagen with this success that in 1986 it acquired 75 per cent of SEAT from the Spanish government and, during 1990, assumed full control – with a commitment to developing a new model range, new manufacturing facilities and a research establishment.

Top right: Three-door Ibiza 1.5 GLX
Right: Marbella 850 similar to Fiat Panda
Below: 1960 SEAT 600

Right: 1.2-litre Malaga saloon
Below: 1990 Terra Vista light commercial

Above: Ibiza SXi

Below: 1990 Limited-edition Marbella 'Red'

Soon SEAT was building all of Volkswagen's Polos and had some new models of its own. The new Ibiza, first shown at the Barcelona Salon in 1993, was the first example of how Volkswagen was going to improve the Spanish company's product range. Ultra-modern styling, fine build quality and a range of Volkswagen engines gave SEAT a car that attracted a welcome market of new buyers who'd never even heard of the company before. Later in the 1990s, the company added a GTi to the range with the 8-valve VW Golf GTi engine. It was swiftly followed by the more powerful 16-valve engine and a special-edition model called the Cupra, to celebrate the car's Championship win in Group A rallying in 1996. A saloon version, the Cordoba was launched a year later.

SEAT's medium-sized offering was the Toledo four-door hatchback, which also used Volkswagen and Audi power units. Strangely, and despite being entirely owned by Volkswagen, SEAT continued to build the Marbella, the company's version of the Fiat Panda that it had built since 1982. At the other end of the range, SEAT stuck its badge on the VW/Ford MPV, and called it the Alhambra.

Below: 1997 SEAT Toledo SE

Right: SEAT Cordoba 1.4

A new Volkswagen-based small car came in 1997. The Arosa was a three-door super-mini with Volkswagen Polo engine. Designed to compete with Ford's Ka, the Arosa was the first SEAT-badged car to be built at Volkswagen's Wolfsburg factory.

SEAT had built themselves a $2 billion

Top: Base-model Ibiza with 1.0-litre engine
Below: 1997 SEAT Arosa
Bottom: SEAT Alhambra

Above: The SEAT range in 1997. Every model was Volkswagen-based

Right: The SEAT Ibiza Cupra Sport was a special edition to celebrate the car's 1996 victory in Group A of the World Rally Championship

new factory at Martorell, near Barcelona, and its daily production potential of 1200 Ibizas was meant to help SEAT achieve annual rates of over 800,000 cars, 75 per cent of them for export.

Unfortunately 1992 and 1993 were not good years and Volkswagen had to provide emergency aid of over £900 million to keep SEAT afloat. In 1994, to make up for further losses, SEAT was forced to sell its Pamplona plant for $160 million and its commercial operations for $65 million.

Volvo

Sweden
1927 to date

The company was founded by Assar Gabrielsson and Gustav Larson, allegedly during a meal consisting of crayfish, in 1924. Their first car, the 1944cc Jakob, was in production by 1927.

Born in 1891, Gabrielsson had studied economics, and was sales manager for the Swedish bearings company SKF, at the time he joined up with Larson. The latter was four years older, and had worked for automotive company White and Poppe in Coventry, England, from 1911 to 1913, before joining SKF in 1917. In 1920 he left and was working as technical manager for AB Galco when he was reunited with Gabrielsson.

The scheme was to build a vehicle more suited to the Scandinavian climate than were U.S. imports, utilizing high-quality Swedish steel and bought-in components. Gabrielsson financed the completion of ten prototypes, with bodies styled by Swedish artist Helmer Mas-Olle. Marine engineers Pentaverken built and supplied the engines, and SKF was sufficiently impressed to fund the production run of the first thousand cars, built at Lundby, near Gothenburg, from 1927. SKF also allowed the partners to use one of the company's patented names: AB Volvo, which derives from the Latin 'I roll', with its obvious connotations of bearings in action.

The company had planned to build 500 cabriolets and 500 saloons but, in the event, only 205 of the steel-bodied open cars were produced, compared with 721 of the closed fabric-bodied PV4 models. In 1929 a three-litre straight-six was

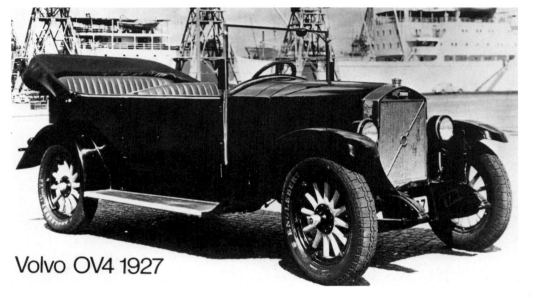

Volvo OV4 1927

Left: Debutante Volvo, the OV4 of 1927
Above: PV651s were built from 1929–1934

Below: Launched in January 1960, the P1800 sports coupé was powered by a 115bhp four-cylinder engine. Initial production was carried out in Great Britain; bodies were made at the Pressed Steel plant at Linwood, and the cars were assembled by Jensen. An estate-car derivative, the P1800ES, continued to be made until 1973.

Above: Volvo's 2-litre 240 Saloon

Above: 1990 workhorse: the 240 Estate

Above: The popular Volvo 340

Above: The spacious and economical 740

Below: 16-valve turbo 740 Estate

Above: Mid-range saloon, the 440 of 1989

Above: The 480ES with a 1721cc engine

Left: Facelifted 760 Estate of 1990
Above: Most luxurious was the 760 Saloon

Above: Volvo S70, 1997

Below: The 960 replacement, the S90

As Volvo started the 1990s, much speculation surrounded it regarding a possible deal with Renault. The deal was to take advantage of economies of scale and maximize the benefits of joint activities in purchasing, with a target of raising the number of shared parts suppliers, and therefore shared components, in order to reduce product costs. The planned link would have put the Renault-Volvo group as the third largest manufacturer in Europe with a 12.3 per cent market share. In the event, the link-up never took place.

Profits were fluctuating in the early nineties with a $120 million profit in 1991 and a $520 million loss in 1992. This was in spite of an increase in sales in 1992 which had come about thanks to the launch of the 850.

The 850 was a big departure for Volvo. Unlike its previous larger cars, the 850 was front-wheel-drive and used an all-new five-cylinder engine. Top of the range was the 850 T5 with a turbocharged 2.3-litre engine. Performance was astounding, and surprised many drivers. The car still had Volvo's tradi-

Above: Volvo V90 estate

Below: 1997 Volvo S40

tional angular styling, albeit slightly updated, but had the performance of a real sports car. Volvo entered the T5 estate in the British Touring Car Championship where it competed very successfully against much sportier-looking cars.

The losses were turned around in 1995, helped partly when Sweden, along with Finland and Austria, joined the European Union. Within the first six months following this event, Volvo's sales were up by 14 per cent in a market which had increased by just 1.2 per cent; in Japan, where overall sales increased by 5.5 per cent, Volvo sold 25 per cent more cars, and in Europe as a whole, where total sales were up only 1.4 per cent, Volvo sales increased by 11 per cent. Volvo executives attributed the success to the company's return to concentrating on Europe, after 30 years of spreading itself too widely and too thinly across the world.

By the late 1990s, Volvo had dropped the three-figure model designations and extended its range. The biggest shock was a Volvo with curves. The S40/V40 range was the result of a joint venture with Mitsubishi. The styling of the car was much more up to date than its predecessor, the 440, and it was hoped to help sales in south-east Asian markets.

The 850, which had done so much for

Volvo by adding a degree of excitement to the company's previously dull image, was replaced in 1996. The new car, designated S70 for the saloon and V70 for the estate version, also brought new innovation to the company with the four-wheel-drive system fitted to certain models.

Another big surprise was the launch of new convertible and coupé models. Called the C70, the new coupé followed in the foot-steps of its spiritual predecessor, the P1800 coupé, by appearing as the Saint's stylish wheels in a Hollywood film remake of the original series.

Above: 1997 Volvo V40

Below: 1997 Volvo S70

Above: The estate version of the S70, the V70

Below: The curvaceous C70 Coupé

White

U.S.A.
1900–1918

Rollin H. White was the son of Thomas H. White, whose White Manufacturing Co. of Cleveland, Ohio, produced a number of articles from sewing machines to roller skates. Rollin built his first steam-powered car, a simple machine with a floor-mounted single-cylinder engine, in 1900. This proved popular, with just under 200 sold in 1901, and two years later a two-cylinder model arrived.

Right: 1906 White Steamer

Below: Early steam-powered Whites were built on an armoured wooden frame, using a front-mounted engine with a condenser in the conventional radiator position. By 1905 a two-speed rear axle was standard.

By 1906 production was running at 1,500 a year. The steam cars were expensive, but pulled well and were noted for reliability. They performed respectably in the Glidden Tours, and specials, like the underslung-frame Whistling Billy of Webb Jay, recorded a speed of 74.04mph (119.15km/h) over a mile. Roosevelt even drove one while in office at the White House.

By 1911 the steamers had given way to petrol-engined models, White having bought the Waltham Manufacturing company in order to do so. Both cars and commercials were built by the company, the latter from 1901.

In 1914 Rollin left White to set up on his own, going on to build the Rollin car during the early 1920s, and the company was reformed as the White Motor Co. During the war years car production declined, to the point where, after 1918, they were made to special order only.

The company then concentrated entirely on commercial vehicles. White was taken over briefly by Studebaker in the early 1930s, then went independent again to build large numbers of military vehicles during World War II. During the 1950s it acquired Sterling, Autocar, Reo and Diamond T, only to sell off most of its holdings during financial problems in the 1970s. White finally went bankrupt in 1980 and was sold to a variety of buyers, including Volvo.

Above: 1905 steam-powered limousine

Below: 2.4-litre Rollin-bodied White

Above: This 1911 car had a petrol engine

Below: 'Town car' on White 158 chassis

Willys

U.S.A.
1907–1963

When John North Willys bought the financially troubled Standard Wheel Company in 1907, he rapidly upgraded production from single- and twin-cylinder runabouts to four-cylinder models and to sixes after 1909. That year, the name Overland appeared and, from 1910, the Willys name was dropped. After 1908, all production was centred on Toledo, Ohio.

By 1914, Overland was a best-selling make, and the following year was second only to Ford in sales. Overland models were supplemented after 1914 by sleeve-valve cars under the Willys-Knight name. A V8 Overland arrived in 1917, but after 1919 only sidevalve fours were available until 1925, when sixes again appeared in both Overland and Willys-Knight ranges.

Peak sales were achieved in 1929, but the Depression caused a sales slump. The four-cylinder models were dropped in 1931, and the Willys-Knight sleeve-valve models died out a year later. From 1933 to 1936, the company was in receivership, and its only product was the low-cost Model 77, marketed as a Willys until 1939, when the Overland name was revived.

The military Jeep, built in huge numbers after 1941, used the engine developed for the 1941 American saloons. Though wartime Jeep production was shared with Ford, Willys had sole rights after 1945 and developed a whole range of civilian variants, the descendants of which are still in production. Jeeps alone were made until 1952, when the Aero saloons were introduced. A year later, the company was bought by Kaiser, but the Aero models continued until 1957. Thereafter, U.S. production was only of Jeeps, but some cars were made under the Willys-Overland name in Brazil until 1967. Elsewhere, the Willys name died out in 1963 when the company's name was changed to the Kaiser-Jeep Corporation.

Right: 1955 Bermuda two-door hardtop

Above: 1920 Willys Overland

Below: 1929 Willys-Knight Great Six

Above: 1968 Jeep Jeepster Commando

Above left: 1961 Jeep Utility Wagon

The 1926 Willys-Overland Whippet was a successful model with a 2.2-litre sidevalve four-cylinder engine.

Winton

U.S.A. 1897–1924

Alexander Winton was a bicycle maker who first experimented with cars in 1897. Of Scottish birth, he founded the Winton Motor Carriage Co. in Cleveland, Ohio, that year, producing his first vehicle for sale, a two-seater, single-cylinder buggy, in 1898. Early owners included the Packard brothers, who set up their own motor manufacturing business with two former Winton employees.

By the turn of the century Winton was the largest American petrol-driven car producer and Alexander Winton had also begun to take part in competition. His first try was an unsuccessful attempt in the first Gordon Bennett Cup event with a single-cylinder vehicle of 3.8 litres.

A new factory was purchased in 1902, and a new two-cylinder model launched. The following year Winton tried again in racing, with two Bullet cars, an 8.5-litre

The 17B Touring of 1911 was the product of the Winton decision to go for the luxury car market exclusively.

four-cylinder vehicle and a four-litre eight-cylinder version, which were driven by Percy Owen and by Winton himself. These were entered in the Gordon Bennett Cup race, but neither completed the event. Both cars, however, went on to small successes in sprint racing.

Four-cylinder-engined cars were offered commercially from 1904, but four years later Winton turned exclusively to luxury sixes, selling a total of 1,200 cars in 1909. By 1915 less-expensive vehicles were offered, forming the basis of Winton's range up to 1920, during which time few changes were implemented.

A change of direction came in 1912 when Winton began making marine diesel engines and stationary machines through the newly formed Winton Gas Engine Manufacturing Co. By 1923 car production had declined considerably and Winton's shareholders chose to concentrate on the diesel-engine side of the business, which eventually became part of General Motors Cleveland Division in 1930. The final Winton car was built in 1924.

Opposite top: One of the first – an 1899 model
Above: The 1903 Winton Bullet racing car
Below: A 1920 Winton Six Model 24 French Limousine

Wolseley

Great Britain
1896–1975

The first Wolseley was a single-cylinder, two-horsepower three-wheeler, made by the company's General Manager, Herbert Austin, in 1896. The first four-wheeled Wolseley appeared in 1899, a 3½-horsepower model. In 1901 tiller steering gave way to a wheel, and the single-cylinder car (now 5hp) was joined by a 2.6-litre 10hp model plus a special-order four-cylinder, five-speed racing machine. The following year a 5.2-litre model was introduced, also with four cylinders.

The famous racing Wolseley Beetles, with flat four-cylinder 11.9hp engines, were highly successful during 1904 and 1905, in which year Austin left Wolseley to form his own company.

J. D. Siddeley designed a 3.3-litre, four-cylinder Wolseley-Siddeley, 1906 versions featuring overhead inlet valves.

Above: 1904 Wolseley 24hp Wagonette with a distinctive wraparound radiator and chain drive

Below: The Wolseley 16/20 became a popular model in the years just prior to World War I. This is a 1911 example, with open bodywork. Dual ignition and air pressure fuel feed were features of 1913 16/20 models.

A wide range of models was produced until 1910, by which time Siddeley had left to join the Deasy company. Wolseleys continued to be built, and by the start of World War I, two bevel-drive six-cylinder models, of 24/30 and 30/40hp, were on offer.

After the war, during which the company had built Hispano-Suiza aircraft engines, Wolseley produced overhead-camshaft-engined models, as well as a sidevalve six-cylinder car of 3.9-litres capacity, made until 1927.

Wolseleys were built in 7, 10 (later, 11/22) and 15hp form during the 1920s, the 15hp model being replaced by a sidevalve 16/35 in 1925. Later Wolseley models were all to feature overhead-camshaft or overhead-valve engines.

Sir William Morris (Lord Nuffield) acquired the bankrupt Wolseley company

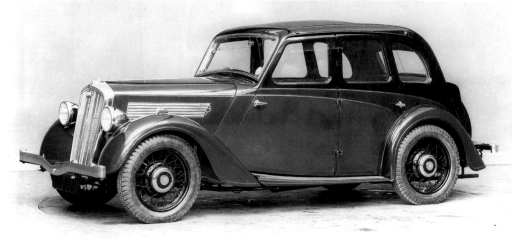

Top: 1910 50hp Limousine
Above: 1923 10hp Doctor's Coupé
Right: 1935 Wolseley 10 saloon
Below: 1937 18hp Wolseley in wartime

in 1927, and one of the interesting cars to emerge under the new management was the 1929 21/60, a hydraulically braked six-cylinder model which closely resembled the Morris Isis.

In 1930 Wolseley introduced the famous six-cylinder 1300cc Hornet, a fast, comfortable small saloon, based on the Morris Minor. Sports and special-bodied versions proved popular.

Larger models of the early 1930s included the 16hp Viper (two litres capacity), and an eight-cylinder version of the 21/60.

The following years saw the introduction of synchromesh and a new 9hp model (1934), and pre-selector gearboxes (1935).

From 1933 all Wolseleys featured an illuminated badge in the centre of the upper part of the radiator grille. This unique identification light was to be fitted to all subsequent Wolseleys.

The Wolseley Wasp replaced the Nine, the Hornet engine was enlarged from 1.3 to 1.4 litres, and a 1600cc 14hp model was introduced in 1935, the engine powering the 80mph (128km/h) Hornet Special.

By mid-1936 (following rationalization after Wolseley was sold to Morris Motors in 1935) all Wolseley engines were overhead-valve units, fitted to up-market versions of equivalent Morris models.

The pre-World War II Wolseley Ten was powered by Morris's 10hp, 1.1-litre M-Series engine, but retained a separate chassis. A 1½-litre, 12hp four-cylinder model was also available, as well as a wide range of six-cylinder models between 14 and 25hp. The 18hp Wolseley was used as fast police transport.

Early post-war Wolseleys included the well-equipped overhead-valve Eight, with similar bodywork to the Morris Eight Series E, and the Ten. A luxurious 2½-litre Twenty-Five was built for a year from 1947. However, two new overhead-camshaft-engined designs, also based on Morris models, emerged for 1949; the smaller of the two being the four-cylinder 4/60, the larger, the six-cylinder 2.2-litre 6/80.

Top: 1939 Wolseley 10 saloon, 1140cc
Above: 1946 Wolseley 8 saloon

Below: The Wolseley Hornet of 1930 was a modestly priced small car, with a 1.3-litre, six-cylinder overhead camshaft engine. Few makers of the time could match the flexibility and power in so small a car.

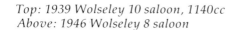

The 4/44 was introduced in 1953, powered by the M.G. Y-type's 1250cc overhead-valve engine. The new model had coil-spring-and-wishbone front suspension and integral-construction bodywork, to be shared with M.G.'s ZA Magnette from 1954.

By 1952 Austin and Morris had merged to form B.M.C., and the group's 1489cc B-Series engine was employed from 1956, in the Wolseley 15/50. B.M.C.'s C-Series six-cylinder engine, of 2.6 litres capacity, was fitted to the new 6/90 in 1955. This model shared its body styling with the Riley Pathfinder of the same era.

The Wolseley 1500 was introduced in 1957, using the 1489cc B-Series engine, and the Morris Minor floorpan and front-suspension/steering design.

The Farina-styled 15/60 saloon was announced for 1959 and, in line with the rest of B.M.C.'s family of Farinas, was updated and fitted with a 1622cc version of the B-Series engine in 1962.

Top: 1952 Wolseley 6/80
Centre left: 1953 Wolseley 4/44
Centre right: 1956 6/90 Police Car
Right: 998cc Hornet, 1962

The larger, extremely well-equipped Farina-styled Wolseleys were the 6/99 of 1959, and the 6/110 of 1962.

The Wolseley Hornet, introduced for 1962, was a luxurious variant of the Mini, and featured an extended luggage boot. B.M.C.'s 1100 model was also given an opulent character in the Wolseley version, which was built from 1965, and replaced in 1967 by the 1300.

In the same year the front-wheel-drive, overhead-valve 18/85 was introduced, based on the large and comfortable Austin 1800.

In 1972 an overhead-camshaft, 2.2-litre, six-cylinder version of the same car – the Wolseley Six – was launched.

In early 1975, the wedge-shaped Wolseley 2200 was introduced, also with the overhead-camshaft six-cylinder engine. This was to be the very last Wolseley model, since it was renamed Princess by British Leyland from October 1975.

Above: Badge engineered 1969 Wolseley 1300 Mk II saloon
Right: 1966 Wolseley 6/110 Mk II with a 2.9-litre engine
Far right: 2.2 litre Wolseley Six, 1974/5
Bottom: The Wolseley 2200, renamed Princess from October 1975, continued in production until 1982.

Index